A Fair Deal on Talent – Fostering Just Migration Governance

Bertelsmann Stiftung (ed.)

A Fair Deal on Talent – Fostering Just Migration Governance

Lessons from Around the Globe
Reinhard Mohn Prize 2015

Verlag BertelsmannStiftung

Bibliographic information published by the Deutsche Nationalbibliothek

The Deutsche Nationalbibliothek lists this publication in the
Deutsche Nationalbibliografie; detailed bibliographic data
is available on the Internet at http://dnb.d-nb.de.

© 2015 Verlag Bertelsmann Stiftung, Gütersloh
Responsible: Matthias M. Mayer
Copy editor: Barbara Serfozo
Production editor: Christiane Raffel
Cover design: Nicole Meyerholz
Cover photos: Veit Mette
Typesetting and Printing: Hans Kock Buch- und Offsetdruck GmbH, Bielefeld
ISBN 978-3-86793-659-0

www.bertelsmann-stiftung.org/publications

Contents

Fostering a Triple Win through Fair Migration Governance 9
Jörg Dräger, Aart De Geus

I. Key Challenges and Opportunities 11

The Benefits of the Migration of Talents: Evidence and Prospects 13
Jean-Pierre Garson

Labor Migration: Achieving a Fairer Deal for Origin Countries 25
Georges Lemaître

II. Fair Migration Governance – An Overview 33

Making Labor Migration Fair: Approaches in Selected OECD States,
Origin Countries and International Organizations 35
Andreas Heimer, Claudia Münch

Reaching a Fair Deal on Talent: Emigration, Circulation and Human Capital
in Countries of Origin 105
Kate Hooper, Madeleine Sumption

III. Mobility and Fairness – Case Studies 133

Perspectives from Destination Countries 133

Lessons from Germany 135
Khushwant Singh

Lessons from Sweden 145
Bernd Parusel

Contents

Lessons from Norway 153
Espen Thorud

Lessons from Denmark 161
Maria Nørby

Lessons from Canada 169
Triadafilos Triadafilopoulos

Lessons from New Zealand 177
Ramasamy Kone

Perspectives from Regions of Origin 183

Lessons from Poland 185
Paweł Kaczmarczyk

Lessons from Eastern Europe 197
Martina Lubyova

Lessons from MENA 205
Jad Chaaban

Lessons from Africa 211
Jonathan Crush

Lessons from Asia 223
Nilim Baruah

Lessons from Latin America 231
Jean-Baptiste Meyer

The Role of International Organizations and NGOs 239

The Role of the European Union in the Fair Management of Migration 241
Florian Trauner

Migration "is" Development: The World Bank's Efforts to Facilitate Labor Mobility 251
Manjula M. Luthria, Casey Alexander Weston

Approaches in Promoting Ethical Recruitment and Fair Migration 257
Lara White, Clara Pascual de Vargas

Development-Oriented Labor Migration Programs and the Role
of Non-Governmental Organizations: Examples from the German Centre
for International Migration and Development (CIM) 271
Lotte Nordhus

The Fair Management of Migration in OECD Countries and the Role of NGOs 279
Grace Annan, Onyekachi Wambu

IV. The Way Forward: Fostering Fairness in Migration Policy 295

Global Skill Partnerships: A Proposal for Technical Training in a Mobile World 297
Michael A. Clemens

Fairness and Development in the Global Governance of Migration 305
Gregory A. Maniatis

Policy Recommendations for Fair Migration Governance 315
Najim Azahaf, Ulrich Kober, Matthias M. Mayer

The Authors 325

Fostering a Triple Win through Fair Migration Governance

If well managed, migration can generate mutual benefits for migrants, destination countries and origin countries. Well-managed migration involves benefits for migrants, as they improve their standard of living, expand their personal skill set and achieve upward social mobility. For destination countries, it can bring innovation, alleviate demographic pressures, generate fiscal benefits and foster cultural diversity. For origin countries, it can bring benefits associated with remittances, knowledge transfers, investments and the cultivation of business relations.

In reality, however, migration-policy failures frequently lead to suboptimal or even negative outcomes. Migrants are often treated unfairly, unable to find employment commensurate with their qualifications or exploited by traffickers or corrupt employers. Poorly managed migration in destination countries can result in wage dumping and a neglected domestic labor force, both of which can subsequently foster social tensions and populist right-wing movements that feed on societal division. In origin countries, the external recruitment of workers may – unnder certain conditions – slow development opportunities and reduce the supply of skilled workers (brain drain).

In 2013, approximately 232 million people worldwide lived in a country other than their native one. Realizing the full potential of migration involves nothing short of a paradigm shift toward the fair management of migration. This is the theme of the Bertelsmann Stiftung's Reinhard Mohn Prize 2015. Already in 2006, Kofi Annan, the former U.N. secretary-general and recipient of the Reinhard Mohn Prize 2013, demanded more fairness in migration policies, saying: "More and more people understand that governments can cooperate to create triple wins – for migrants, for their countries of origin and for the societies that receive them." We need to uphold this triple win as a normative principle for migration policies that are universally fair.

Increasing migration rates around the world make this goal more urgent than ever. Development and urbanization pressures in developing societies are driving migration flows from these countries to many OECD countries currently facing dramatic demographic changes. According to U.N. estimates, by 2050, Europe's working-age population will shrink by 96 million. At the same time, Africa's working-age population will grow by 910 million and Asia's by 517 million. Migration pressures on OECD countries – in particular from African countries –

are therefore destined to grow. In parallel, international competition for labor will intensify. In the medium term, countries that have traditionally been the source of migration, such as China, will begin recruiting workers from abroad. Desired workers in this context include highly skilled professionals as well as persons with medium-level qualifications, particularly in the health care sector.

A further challenge for migration policymaking is posed by increasing refugee flows resulting from political crises, for instance, in the Middle East and Africa. Whereas neighboring countries in particular must deal with a large influx of refugees, many European countries are struggling to deal with growing numbers of refugees. Similarly, there are increasing numbers of people seeking to escape massive poverty and economic insecurity worldwide.

Implementing policies that can achieve a triple win is a challenging endeavor that gives rise to a number of questions. These include: Is the concept of a triple win merely "a fancy European idea" or a reflection of the way things do or should work? What are the respective roles of the market and the state in managing migration? To what extent can and should migration flows be controlled at all? How can we achieve both economic success and social cohesion? Can there be a "social market economy" for migration? What is the best system to manage migration in a fair way?

The present volume addresses these questions by discussing different aspects of fair migration management, examples of good practices from around the world and possible ways forward.

It has the following structure: Chapter I examines the main challenges and opportunities associated with fair migration. Chapter II presents a number of examples of good practices in fair migration management. Chapter III explores the perspectives of and approaches pursued by selected destination countries and regions of origin, as well as the role of international organizations and NGOs in fair migration management. Chapter IV examines how fairness in migration policy can be made fairer and provides policy recommendations for doing so.

The Bertelsmann Stiftung would like to thank all of the authors for their excellent contributions. In particular, we would like to highlight the commitment of the OECD's International Migration Division, which co-organized, together with the Bertelsmann Stiftung, a workshop of international experts that laid the foundation for the present volume. As a complex phenomenon with many intertwined dimensions, migration requires a holistic approach. We hope that the ideas presented here will help find and develop answers to current migration and integration challenges and inspire policymakers – to quote Kofi Annan again – "to create triple wins for migrants, for their countries of origin und for the societies that receive them."

Dr. Jörg Dräger
Member of the
Bertelsmann Stiftung
Executive Board

Aart De Geus
Chairman and CEO,
Bertelsmann Stiftung
Executive Board

I. Key Challenges and Opportunities

The Benefits of the Migration of Talents: Evidence and Prospects

Jean-Pierre Garson

Introduction

"In the fall of 1743, a fourteen-year old boy entered Berlin at the Rosenthaler Tor. [...] We do not know whether he was wearing shoes. [...] The boy, later famous throughout Europe as the philosopher Moses Mendelssohn, was frail and sickly, small for his age. Early years of poverty had left him with [...] a badly humped back" (Elon 2002).

The above quotation shows the extent to which it was risky in Prussia in the mid-18th century to discount the contribution of future talent, even if it appeared insignificant at first glance. A century later in France, the saying "Happy as God in France" testified to the gratitude of immigrants to a host country where they had arrived after having overcome myriad obstacles. How many of these immigrants and their descendants eventually contributed in significant ways to their adopted countries? Even today, it is not always easy for a host country either to identify and nurture talent locally or to attract foreigners from abroad, and it is sometimes even more difficult to retain talented immigrants.

This paper is organized as follows: I briefly review the main aspects of talent recruitment in developed countries and conclude that for the moment, the issue of a "fair deal" (defined as an equitable distribution of the benefits of migration between receiving countries, sending countries and migrants themselves) is not high on receiving countries' political agendas. We then present policy options that could help receiving countries make better use of their immigrants' skills in both the short and long term, and could additionally harness immigrants' talents to foster development within sending countries. Finally, a short note on definitions: In the absence of a measurable definition of "talent," I use the terms "qualified workers" to refer to those with a high-level vocational or tertiary qualification, and "highly qualified workers" to refer to individuals such as scientists, senior researchers and other exceptionally qualified professionals.

The Benefits of the Migration of Talents: Evidence and Prospects

Policies to recruit immigrant workers in OECD countries focus on the qualified without seeking to ensure a "fair deal" relative to migrants' countries of origin

Policies are designed to attract and retain qualified immigrants...

A portion of the current migration flows of qualified workers takes place between countries belonging to a framework, such as the European Economic Area (EEA), that enables the free movement of persons (Desiderio 2012). To a lesser extent, such migration also takes place in other regions, such as the Commonwealth of Independent States (CIS) (Chudinovskikh 2012), and in the context of free-trade or bilateral agreements between two or more partner countries, such as the North American Free Trade Agreement (NAFTA) between Canada, Mexico and the United States. Special programs also apply to skilled non-EU migrants; these include the EU Blue Card, Austria's Red-White-Red Card or Germany's Green Card (established between 2000 and 2005, mainly to recruit computer scientists from India), as well as labor-shortage lists in countries such as France and the United Kingdom. Moreover, employers can also recruit immigrant workers according to their labor-market needs, provided that they first obtain authorization from the receiving country's labor-market authorities (labor-market test). OECD settlement countries (Australia, Canada, New Zealand and the United States) have sought to attract qualified immigrant workers through measures such as special visas or point systems, with a particular focus on foreign investors, high-level scientists and researchers (Chaloff and Lemaître 2009; OECD 2010).

These increasingly selective policies pay little heed to the interests of origin countries, which are confronted with large numbers of qualified emigrants moving to developed countries (Kaczmarczyk 2012; Lubyova 2012; Salt 2012). Moreover, many origin countries would prefer instead to reduce their surplus of low-skilled workers.

...and competition is increasingly intense among developed countries...

Economic globalization has been accompanied by an increasing openness of trade in goods and services, as well as an increase in capital movements. In this context, recent immigrants to OECD countries are on average more highly educated than the average level within receiving countries' labor forces; moreover, the share of women among the highly qualified is increasing (Dumont, Martin and Spielvogel 2007). To succeed in attracting talent, high-level wages have to be complemented by good working conditions and other non-salary incentives, such as housing conditions, good education opportunities for recruited immigrants' children, and high living standards (Goos, Manning and Salomons 2010; OECD 2008b; Kuptsch and Pang 2006; Liebig 2005). It is very hard for developing countries to compete with benefits of this kind offered by developed countries. The former thus face a difficult task in containing the outflow of their own qualified workers, as well as in encouraging those already settled abroad to return to their home country.

...even to attract international students, a source of future talent.

Many developed countries have increased their annual intake of international students. In most cases, the calculation is that the best and brightest will succeed in obtaining a diploma and a qualification fully recognized in the country, excellent language skills (Chiswick and Miller 2014), and good knowledge of the functioning of the labor market and the society at large. Language skills are a prerequisite for many occupations and professions, and indeed some English- and French-speaking countries benefit from having potential qualified laborforce reserves abroad in areas with the same mother tongue (Chaloff and Lemaître 2009).

This strategy, which proposes to match immigrant workers' qualifications to local labor-market needs, rests on the hypothesis that international students trained in the host country will stay following the completion of their studies rather than migrate to another developed country or return to their country of origin or that of their parents. The current trend in some OECD countries toward a high increase in the annual inflow of international students indicates that these countries assume international talent mobility will not increase in the medium term, and/or that employers will try to retain the talented persons they recruit. It is consequently likely that international-student retention rates will increase in some OECD countries (Australia, Canada, France, the United Kingdom and the United States). It is not clear how origin countries can benefit from such a situation, especially if the primary and secondary education of these students is funded by origin countries (OECD/MAE 2012).

Mobility among qualified workers is high between developed countries as well...

Countries that are fully open to international trade experience two opposing migration patterns: On the one hand, an outflow of qualified residents takes place along with the export of goods, services and direct investments abroad, while on the other, these countries design policies with the aim of increasing the inflow of qualified immigrant workers who are expected to alleviate labor shortages in some sectors and occupations. Even an apparent loss of skilled workers, as in the first case, should not inevitably be interpreted as a net negative. Germany, for example, as the leading global exporter, could not maintain its trade surplus in the medium term without the support of qualified German technicians, experts and managers working abroad in Germany's main export areas. Thus, at least for a developed country, having a share of qualified native-born workers working abroad is not per se an issue of brain drain hindering economic development. However, the overall assessment of net migration must be made with reference to a country's capacity either to train a sufficient number of workers to respond to labor-market needs (which can take time) or, alternatively, to quickly increase recruitment of immigrant workers with needed skills (which can also be difficult). Again, in this race for talent, origin countries are typically at a strong disadvantage worldwide in recruiting qualified immigrant workers. Inequality of human-capital resources is increasing, and the countries most affected are those that have the greatest share of their qualified workers working and living abroad (Dumont, Spielvogel and Wiedmaier 2010).

The Benefits of the Migration of Talents: Evidence and Prospects

...yet the political debate in many receiving countries is focused on the global impact of international migration on the labor market, public finances and social transfers.

The increase in immigration flows in many OECD countries during the two past decades has raised concerns about the overall impact of immigration on the labor market, housing, health expenditures and public finances. Some economists have tried to measure the effects of migration on the salary of natives, on native worker displacement and on increases in inequality, especially when immigrants and natives act as close substitutes (Borjas 2004; Kerr and Kerr 2011). Other researchers have focused on the increase in the social cost of immigration (housing, health and education expenditures) or the attractiveness of social-protection systems in the destination countries (welfare magnet). The economic crisis and the increase in the unemployment rate of immigrants and their children have had an impact on public opinion, at least among that share of the population not convinced of the merits of an increased reliance on immigrant workers. Clearly, the issue of a "fair deal" is not yet high on the agenda of the destination countries.

Migration of talent: How can benefits to migrants themselves and to their countries of origin be increased?

The benefits of migration of talent are not always what immigrants themselves expected...

Economic analyses that focus on brain-drain or brain-gain issues show that the emigration of talent from developing to developed countries can benefit the migrants themselves in terms of human capital, but also those left behind, and even the origin countries more broadly. The authors of these studies explain that thanks to emigration, those left behind invest more in education and vocational training in hopes that they in turn might emigrate in the near future. The authors conclude that, on average, the level of human capital rises in emigration countries much more than if there were no ability to emigrate (Mountford 1997; Batista, Lacuesta and Vicente 2007). In addition, migrants have the opportunity to enhance their vocational training and professional experience in their destination countries; if they do return, these new skills benefit their country of origin. Finally, migrant remittances contribute to improved living conditions (income, education and health) for family members in addition to providing hard currency to their countries of origin (Boeri and Brücker 2012).

...and the beneficial effects of migration for countries of origin should be qualified...

Developing countries that are facing a continuous increase in their population's fertility rate and that do not or cannot carry out efficient and continuous family-planning policies will not benefit from an increase in their human capital due to the structural effects of this "demographic time bomb." Remittances are often regarded as an opportunity for origin countries; however, these remittances belong to emigrants and not to their respective origin countries.

In many origin countries, remittances are used in part for family members' current consumption expenditures. Another portion is devoted to financing children's educations, often with the intention of giving these young people a chance to emigrate and obtain a better job and social status abroad than that held by their parents or other members of the family left behind. If we generalize about this first-generation migrant behavior, the reproduction of migrant talent will be financed by the primary providers of remittances as they send earnings home to other members of their family (OECD 2005).

For the moment, there is no evidence of a "fair deal" on the migration of talent, especially if we consider origin countries faced with a looming crisis in their health care workforce (OECD 2008a) and the loss of skilled personnel in the education sector. Migration of qualified workers in these two sectors primarily benefits destination countries and, to a lesser extent, the emigrants themselves, as their qualifications are not always fully recognized in the destination countries (see below). New policy options are needed in order to increase benefits from the emigration of talented individuals, but these should be primarily oriented toward the economic development of less-developed emigration countries as well as toward migrants and their family members, rather than focusing on the nature and the magnitude of migration flows.

...however, new opportunities are emerging that will allow migration to foster development within origin countries.

Because employment and investment opportunities are lacking in their home countries, many qualified migrants do not expect to return. Nor do they expect to contribute to their native country's economic development. Encouraging and supporting origin countries in their development of policies reducing obstacles to skilled migrants' return migration would provide a positive contribution to a "fairer deal" (OECD 2009). Such policy options might include good economic-governance measures, an increase in investment opportunities at local and regional levels, and measures improving confidence in financial and administrative institutions. These are areas where cooperation between origin and receiving countries can be strengthened in order to give emigrants sufficient incentives to migrate back to their home countries and, especially in the case of talented individuals, to better contribute to the economic development of their country of origin (Kaczmarczyk 2013; Mereuta 2013).

In this regard, it is useful to distinguish between policies that could be put in place in the short term and those that necessitate structural changes, the effects of which would be evident only in the medium or long term. The aim of all such policies is to move toward a "fairer deal" among the main stakeholders: enterprises (both in destination and origin countries), immigrants living in destination countries (including members of diaspora communities), and origin countries. Other partners, such as civil society groups (including migrant associations involved in economic development), in both origin and receiving countries (Ould Aoudia 2012) can also be usefully included in this deal.

Policy measures that could be carried out or strengthened in the short term

Developed countries are often looking for more qualified workers, even as their labor markets contain many skilled immigrants who are overqualified for their current jobs (Dumont and Monso 2007; Quentini 2011). Native-born workers are also subject to this problem of overqualification, but immigrants are relatively more affected by this displacement. Recognizing immigrants' qualifications would be a first step toward a "fairer deal." In addition, bridging education and vocational training programs (as is already in place in countries such as Sweden) would also represent progress, as would any other measure that increases the portability of immigrants' human capital (Friedberg 2000; Niknami and Schröder 2012). Similarly, it could be useful to accelerate recruitment of international students and to help them realize their potential by better recognizing their qualifications and degrees, thus helping to avoid untapped skills (OECD 2012b).

Moving toward a "fairer deal" does not imply that brain drain should be the only issue to be taken into account. It simply seems more realistic and efficient to expand the current approach to immigrant workers, irrespective of their qualification level. For example, governments' discourse about the economic contribution of migration would benefit from being more balanced. Discourses that distinguish between "good" qualified migrants and "unwanted" low-skilled migrants may offend and ultimately repel talented migrants who believe that their low-skilled countrymen also contribute to the economic growth and international trade of destination countries (Hatzigeorgiou 2010). Another example of such complementarity links native-born and immigrant workers. A recent study carried out in the United States demonstrated the need to analyze the effects of immigration on all destination-country groups through different channels and at different regional levels (Cortés and Tessada 2011). According to the authors, an increase in low-skilled immigration into a region leads to an increase in the labor supply of highly skilled native women. This contrasts with theories that highly skilled women do not choose demanding careers because they place a higher value on staying home with their children.

Another example relates to the immigrant job-search measures (job-seeker visa), sometimes irrespective of migrants' qualification levels, recently implemented in European countries including Sweden (OECD 2011b), Germany and Austria. Under these policies, migrants who are able to find a job before the expiration of a limited period of time can obtain a residence permit that is renewable as long as they remain employed. These new measures demonstrate that labor-market adjustment is acceptable as long as the country's legal pay and working-conditions rules are respected. Indeed, Sweden's job-search measures resulted in an increase in middle- and low-skilled labor immigration. In Germany, a previous policy to recruit qualified migrants was deemed comparatively unsuccessful, mainly because it was too cautious and too burdensome at the administrative level. However, the liberalization of these policies in 2012 (in part to add a job-search incentive), especially for the highly qualified, has resulted in an increase in immigrants in mainly middle-skilled jobs (OECD 2013a). It is too soon to draw lessons from these trends without taking into account the effects of the business cycle; however, they may indicate that the ostensibly urgent need for highly qualified workers is in fact less important than imagined, and that employers might in fact prefer to hire skilled and highly skilled workers who are already in Germany. Finally, recruiting more middle-skilled labor abroad may have had additional benefits through a kind of "added effect" regarding overqualified resident workers both in Germany and Sweden.

Medium- and long-term policy measures should focus more on development than on migration.

Migrants can clearly support development in their country of origin, but they cannot initiate it (Luo and Wang 2001; Ould Aoudia 2012; OECD/MAE 2012). Migrants not only provide their home country with remittances and other forms of financial transfers; they can also serve as channels for invisible transfers of modernity, social and political changes, and learning processes at the family, community and citizenship level. Here again, it is crucial to increase the portability of returning migrants' human capital so as to increase the return on experience acquired abroad and foster development in their home countries (OECD/MAE 2012).

Origin countries themselves have an important role to play in strengthening relationships between local institutions, local workers, immigrants and immigrant associations. They could also design new measures to create investment opportunities, such as the "creative state" measures taken in countries such as Morocco and Mexico (Iskander 2010), to mobilize immigrants' savings and orient them toward local development projects without requiring migrants or members of the diaspora to return permanently. In this context, the former president of the France-based Migration and Development association, which provides considerable support for rural projects in Morocco, has proposed the following redefinition of the so-called pull and push factors: "Pull factors are those that contribute to identifying investment opportunities in origin countries, and push factors are those that help identifying candidates among internal and international migrants who are ready to invest in the territorial development" (Ould Aoudia 2012; Iskander 2010).

The extension of decentralized cooperation is another policy option that could help increase the benefits of emigration, provided that public authorities can mobilize the support of migrants and other partners (including enterprises) in destination countries (e.g., associations promoting economic development in migrants' origin countries, working in cooperation with migrants). A large number of projects funded or otherwise supported through this model have been and are being carried out, including infrastructure works, care centers, rural tourism facilities, and more (Ould Aoudia 2012).

Encouraging the transfer of skills and experiences through the mobilization of diaspora members is another challenge. Some origin countries, especially in Asia (Luo and Wang 2001; Rosenzweig 2007), have been supportive of diaspora communities. Nevertheless, migrants and larger diaspora communities have come to be increasingly connected to their countries of origin (Diminescu and Pasquier 2010). In addition, thanks to the work done by the OECD and others, migrant and diaspora profiles (Dumont, Spielvogel und Widmaier 2010) are coming to be better understood. This may in turn facilitate opportunities to harness migrants' (and diaspora) skills in order to foster home-country development. Policy options are currently under review (OECD/AfD 2012).

Efficiently mobilizing migrants and diaspora communities is a long-term process, however. One of the main obstacles is the time required for the integration of migrants in the receiving country, which may be considerable. Integration status may affect migrants' opinions regarding possible contributions to development in their home country; and, indeed, many prove unwilling to contribute in this regard. Any active policy to facilitate and support the integration of immigrants and their children (OECD 2010) in the destination country, including through naturalization (Liebig and Von Haaren 2011; Steinhardt 2011) and the recognition of qualifications (see above), would represent a structural approach toward a "fairer deal" (Ould Aoudia 2012; OECD/MAE 2012).

With time, policy options targeting diaspora communities may increase benefits accruing to origin countries (Kapur 2010). Here, it is once again development rather than migration per se that is at stake, and many young and qualified actors, including entrepreneurs, are engaging in initiatives that help developing countries benefit from technology transfers, scientific and technical education, vocational programs and other such goods. These participative initiatives and other forms of partnerships may increase the prospect of a "fairer deal" associated with labor migration. Clearly, this participative strategy is different from a tax, such as that proposed (but never implemented) in the 1970s (Bhagwati and Delafar 1973) on the income earned by skilled migrants, an issue still discussed in the brain-drain/brain-gain debate. Adopting such a tax would not only hamper the freedom of mobility (Dumitru 2012), but would also give money to sending countries without any guarantee that it would be used for economic-development purposes or to create jobs for those left behind.

In my view, the structural approach described above also excludes policies designed to increase circular migration (Constant, Nottmeyer and Zimmermann 2012) that do not per se fit either within the perspective of origin countries' economic development or within destination countries' policies aimed at better regulating and managing migration flows. Indeed, circular migration is a concept mainly aimed at limiting immigrant workers' duration of stay and the costs of their integration into destination countries. In addition, opening destination countries' labor markets to more temporary migration would increase emigration incentives for potential migrants who in fact had no previous intention to move. Moreover, the nature of the demand-driven aspect of labor migration (temporary or permanent) cannot be decreed by the government, but stems from employers making decisions under the oversight of public authorities (OECD 2009).

Conclusion

For the moment, the migration of talent primarily benefits destination countries (mainly employers) and qualified immigrants themselves. New developments in the management of labor migration are doing little to change this. If a "fairer deal" on talent is to be achieved, an approach is needed that focuses on origin countries' economic development more than on migration per se. Mobilizing migrants to participate in development efforts in their country of origin offers opportunities to all primary actors: migrants themselves, employers in destination countries and origin countries, origin countries and other partners interested in helping origin countries increase their benefits from migration. The policy options presented in this paper illustrate the fact that central stakeholders have to modify their agendas both in terms of migration and development. The current deal is not "fair" for all actors, but it could be made "fairer" if the whole range of migrant qualifications were to be taken into account, and if origin countries were to reduce obstacles preventing return migration and the mobilization of diaspora communities behind development efforts.

References

Batista, Catia, Aitor Lacuesta and Pedro C. Vicente. "Brain Drain or Brain Gain? Micro Evidence from an African Success Story." *IZA Discussion Papers 3035*. Bonn: IZA, 2007.

Bhagwati, Jagdish, and William Delafar. "The Brain Drain and Income Taxation." *World Development* (1) 2: 94–101, 1973.

Bobeva, Daniela, and Jean-Pierre Garson. "Overview of Bilateral Agreements and Other Forms of Labor Recruitment." *Migration for Employment. Bilateral Agreements at a Crossroads*, edited by OECD. Paris: OECD Publishing, 2004: 11–29. doi: http://dx.doi.org/10.1787/9789264108684-en.

Boeri, Tito, and Herbert Brücker (eds.). *Brain Drain and Brain Gain*. Oxford: Oxford University Press, 2012.

Borjas, George J. "Immigration in High-skill Labor Markets: the Impact of Foreign Students on the Earnings of Doctorates." *Working paper*. Boston: Harvard University, 2004.

Chaloff, Jonathan, and Georges Lemaître. "Managing Highly Skilled Labor Migration: a Comparative Analysis of Migration Policies and Challenges in OECD Countries." *OECD Social, Employment and Migration Working Papers 79*. Paris: OECD Publishing, 2009.

Chiswick, Barry, and Paul Miller. "International Migration and the Economics of International Migration." *Handbook of the Economics of International Migration 1A*, edited by Barry Chiswick and Paul Miller. North Holland: Elsevier, 2014: 4–27.

Chudinovskikh, Olga. "Migration and Bilateral Agreements in the Commonwealth of Independent States." *Free Movement of Workers and Labor Market Adjustment: Recent Experiences from OECD Countries and the European Union*, edited by OECD. Paris: OECD Publishing, 2012: 251–276.

Constant, Amelie F., Olga Nottmeyer and Klaus F. Zimmermann. "The Economics of Circular Migration." *IZA Discussion Papers 6940*. Bonn: IZA, 2012.

Cortés, Patricia, and José Tessada. "Low-Skilled Immigration and the Labor Supply of Highly Skilled Women." *American Economic Journal: Applied Economics* (3) 3: 88–123, 2011.

Desiderio, Maria Vincenza. "Free Labour Mobility Areas Across OECD Countries: an Overview." *Free Movement of Workers and Labour Market Adjustment: Recent Experiences from OECD Countries and the European Union*, edited by OECD. Paris: OECD Publishing, 2012: 35–104.

Diminescu, Dana, and Dominique Pasquier (eds.). *Les migrants connectés. TIC, Mobilités et migrations*. Paris: La Découverte, 2010.

Dumitru, Speranta. "Skilled Migration: Who Should Pay for What? A Critique of the Bhagwati Tax." *Diversities* (14) 1: 9–23, 2012.

Dumont, Jean-Christophe, and Olivier Monso. "Matching Educational Background and Employment: A Challenge for Immigrants in Host Countries." *International Migration Outlook 2007*, edited by OECD. Paris: OECD Publishing, 2007: 131–159.

Dumont, Jean-Christophe, John Martin and Gilles Spielvogel. "Women on the Move: the Neglected Dimension of the Brain Drain." *IZA Discussion Papers* No. 2920, 2007.

Dumont, Jean-Christophe, Gilles Spielvogel and Sarah Widmaier. "International Migrants in Developed, Emerging and Developing Countries: An Extended Profile." *Social, Employment and Migration Working Papers, No. 114*. Paris: OECD Publishing, 2010.

Elon, Amos. *The Pity of it All: A History of Jews in Germany, 1743–1933*. New York: Metropolitan Books/Henry Holt and Company, 2002.

Friedberg, Rachel. "You Can't Take It With You? Immigrant Assimilation and the Portability of Human Capital." *Journal of Labor Economics* (18) 2: 221–251, 2000.

Goos, Maarten, Alan Manning and Anna Salomons. "Explaining Job Polarisation in Europe: The Roles of Technologies, Globalisation and Institutions." *LSE, CEP Discussion Papers No 1026*. London: Centre for Economic Performance, 2010.

Hatzigeorgiou, Andreas. "The Contribution of Migrants in Enhancing Foreign Trade." *Open for Business: Migrant Entrepreneurship in OECD Countries*, edited by OECD. Paris: OECD Publishing, 2010: 273–279.

Iskander, Natasha. *Creative State. Forty Years of Migration and Development Policy in Morocco and Mexico*. Ithaca: Cornell University Press, 2010.

Kaczmarczyk, Pawel. "Labour market impact of post-accession migration from Poland." *Free Movement of Workers and Labour Market Adjustment: Recent Experiences from OECD Countries and the European Union*, edited by OECD. Paris: OECD Publishing, 2012: 173–194.

Kaczmarczyk, Pawel. "Matching the Skills of Return Migrants to Labour Market Needs in Poland." *Coping with Emigration in Baltic and East European Countries*, edited by OECD. Paris: OECD Publishing, 2013: 111–126.

Kapur, Devesh. *Diaspora, Development and Democracy: The Domestic Impact of International Migration in India*. Princeton: Princeton University Press, 2010.

Kerr, Sari Pekkala, and William R. Kerr. "Economic Impact of Immigration: A Survey." *NBER Working Paper No. 16736*. Cambridge, MA: NBER, 2011. doi: 10.3386/w16736.

Kuptsch, Christiane, and Eng Fong Pang (eds.). *Competing for Global Talent*. Geneva: International Institute for Labour Studies, 2006.

Liebig, Thomas. *A New Phenomenon: The International Competition for Highly Skilled Migrants and its Consequences for Germany*. Bern: Haupt Verlag, 2005.

Liebig, Thomas, and Friederike Von Haaren. "Citizenship and the Socio-economic Integration of Immigrants and their Children. An Overview across European Union and OECD Countries." *Naturalisation: A Passport for the Better Integration of Immigrants?*, edited by OECD. Paris: OECD Publishing, 2011: 23–64.

Lubyova, Martina. "Changing Demographic, Educational and Migration Patterns in New EU Member Countries." *Free Movement of Workers and Labour Market Adjustment: Recent Experiences from OECD Countries and the European Union*, edited by OECD. Paris: OECD Publishing, 2012: 235–248.

Luo, Yu-Ling, and Wei-Jen Wang. *High-Skill Migration and Chinese Taipei's Industrial Development*. Paris: OECD Publishing, 2001.

Mereuta, Cristina. "Mobilising Migrants' Skills and Resources in Romania." *Coping with Emigration in Baltic and East European Countries*, edited by OECD. Paris: OECD Publishing, 2013: 127–141.

Millar, Jane, and John Salt. "Portfolios of Mobility: the Movement of Expertise in Transnational Corporations in Two Sectors – Aerospace and Extractive Industries." *Global Networks* (8) 1: 25–50, 2008.

Mountford, Andrew. "Can a Brain Drain be Good for Growth in the Source Economy?" *Journal of Development Economics* 53: 287–303, 1997.

Niknami, Susan, and Lena Schröder. *Using Bridging Courses to Make Better Use of Migrants' Skills*. Stockholm: SOFI, 2012.

OECD (Organization for Economic Co-operation and Development). *International Mobility of the Highly Skilled*. Paris: OECD Publishing, 2001.

OECD. *Migration, Remittances and Development*. Paris: OECD Publishing, 2005.

OECD. *The Looming Crisis in the Health Workforce. How Can OECD Countries Respond?* Paris: OECD Publishing, 2008a.

OECD. *The Global Competition for Talent. Mobility of the Highly Skilled*. Paris: OECD Publishing, 2008b.

OECD. *International Migration Outlook*. Paris: OECD Publishing, 2009.

OECD. *Equal Opportunities? The Labour Market Integration of the Children of Immigrants*. Paris: OECD Publishing, 2010.

OECD. *Naturalisation: A Passport for the Better Integration of Immigrants?* Paris: OECD Publishing, 2011a.

OECD. *Recruiting Immigrants Workers: Sweden*. Paris: OECD Publishing, 2011b.

OECD. *Free Movement of Workers and Labour Market Adjustment. Recent Experiences from OECD Countries and the European Union*. Paris: OECD Publishing, 2012a.

OECD. *Untapped Skills. Realising the Potential of Immigrant Students*. Paris: OECD Publishing, 2012b.

OECD. *Recruiting Immigrant Workers: Germany*. Paris: OECD Publishing, 2013a.

OECD. *Coping with Emigration in Baltic and East European Countries*. Paris: OECD Publishing, 2013b.

OECD/AfD (Agence française de développement). *Connecting with Emigrants. A Global Profile of Diasporas*. Paris: OECD Publishing, 2012.

OECD/MAE (Ministère français des Affaires étrangères). *Harnessing the Skills of Migrants and Diasporas to Foster Development: Policy Options*. OECD and French Ministry of Foreign Affairs, 2012.

Ould Aoudia, Jacques. "La migration, une pratique sociale d'une infinie diversité sur laquelle les politiques publiques peinent à intervenir." Paris: unpublished manuscript, 2012.

Plaza, Sonia, and Dilip Ratha (eds.). *Diaspora for Development in Africa*. Washington, D.C.: The World Bank, 2011.

Quentini, Glenda. "Over-Qualified or Under-Skilled: A Review of Existing Literature." *OECD Social, Employment and Migration Working Papers No. 121*. Paris: OECD Publishing, 2011.

Rosenzweig, Mark. "Higher Education and International Migration in Asia: Brain Circulation." *Working Paper.* New Haven, CT: Yale University, 2007.

Salt, John. "The United Kingdom Experience of Post-Enlargement Worker Inflows from New EU Member Countries." *Free Movement of Workers and Labour Market Adjustment: Recent Experiences from OECD Countries and the European Union.* Paris: OECD Publishing, 2012: 117–132.

Steinhardt, Max Friedrich. "The Impact of Naturalisation on Immigrant Labour Market Integration in Germany and Switzerland." *Naturalisation: A Passport for the Better Integration of Immigrants?*, edited by OECD. Paris: OECD Publishing, 2011: 146–151.

Labor Migration: Achieving a Fairer Deal for Origin Countries

Georges Lemaître

Measures to ensure a fairer deal for origin countries

It is generally believed that benefits can accrue to origin countries when skilled nationals who have migrated abroad return to their countries of origin, bringing with them the knowledge, skills, entrepreneurial know-how and income they have acquired in destination countries. However, one should not hold illusions with regard to the likelihood of such returns – unless, of course, the issue is only temporary migration, where a return has always been intended. Although returns following a successful migration do occur in cases of permanent migration, they tend to make up a minority of such circumstances, especially if migrants move to destination countries with their families. Data from Australia and Canada suggest that as many as one-fourth to one-third of permanent labor migrants to those countries do eventually leave. That said, research has shown that most such departures take place in the early years following arrival, which does not suggest a positive migration experience. In the following, we will nevertheless assume that cases in which highly skilled migrants return to their country of origin are generally beneficial for the origin country, even if it is uncertain that this is always the case in practice.

Destination countries and employers in need of highly skilled workers often have little interest in seeing skilled immigrant workers who have been recruited from abroad, trained and employed for some time in the destination country leave their jobs and return home. Nevertheless, in the interests of fairness, one could argue that destination-country policies should at the very least be neutral with regard to returns and should not create disincentives to such decisions. Rather, the judgment should be left to the immigrant alone.

This contribution provides an overview of some policy measures that could be implemented to ensure a fairer deal for origin countries on labor migration. It considers a number of disincentives to return migration that could be eliminated, but it also looks at other types of revenue-neutral measures. Finally, it considers more proactive policies that would involve expenditure outlays and involve collaboration with origin countries.

Flexible residence permits

One disincentive to return migration is the loss of residence rights if the migrant returns to the origin country for longer than a short, specified period of time. Returns to the origin country are more likely if immigrants retain the right to come back to the destination country after a certain period of time spent abroad. The surest way of guaranteeing this right is clearly for the immigrant worker to become a citizen of the destination country, and in many EU countries, the conditions for the acquisition of citizenship by immigrants have indeed been relaxed in recent decades (OECD 2011a). But in those cases where the origin or destination countries do not allow dual nationality or the immigrant wishes to retain the nationality of his or her origin country, flexible residence permits allowing temporary returns of a certain maximum length without the need to reapply for entry could usefully be implemented.

Portability of pension contributions and benefits

A second disincentive concerns the non-portability of pension contributions and/or benefits (see Holzmann and Koettl 2012 for a general overview). A migrant worker will clearly be less likely to return if the pension contributions he or she has made cannot be withdrawn following a definitive return to the origin country or cannot be received abroad upon retirement. Switzerland, for example, allows immigrants who have contributed to the pension system for at least a year to withdraw the contributions they and their employers have made if they leave Switzerland definitively with their spouses and children under 25 years of age (OFM 2010). Note that the value of the reimbursed contributions ought to take into account any increases in the cost of living that have taken place since the contributions were made; otherwise the immigrant's contributions will effectively be devalued upon reimbursement.

Facilitating temporary migration

Rather than the elimination of a disincentive per se, a third desirable measure involves the facilitation of temporary movements, which are arguably of more benefit to origin countries. Because the movements are temporary and overstay is less likely for highly skilled migrants, there is room to loosen constraints with respect to this type of migration, allowing more flexibility than currently exists with regard to eligible occupations and minimum salary levels. The impact on domestic jobs, especially those for which proficiency in the native language is important, is not likely to be very high, especially in countries whose native language is spoken to only a limited extent outside national borders.

Making the most of permit fees

Most applications for work-related immigration permits involve fees for the recruiting enterprise, which are generally charged to cover the cost of processing the application (OECD 2011b). The fees charged by national governments are generally comparatively low (often less than $700), so there is some room for increasing them in order to fulfill objectives other than those of covering administrative costs.

Fees are increasingly being regarded as an appropriate means by which to regulate the scale and type of movements. We will not go into detail here on the rationale for this or describe specifically how this could be done in practice; instead, we will focus on possible uses for the funds generated through immigration fees. In the United States, immigration fees are sometimes earmarked to fund training programs for domestic workers in the occupations for which recruitment is being carried out (for example, in the case of the United States H-1B visa). Another possible use might be to create a development fund tasked with financing specific aid-related projects in origin countries. However, this practice may not generate a substantial amount of funds. For example, if 10,000 work or residence permits were to be issued, each with a €5,000 fee, this would generate €50 million for development purposes. This is not a large sum in comparison with the development-aid budgets in countries such as France and Germany. In addition, as work- or residence-permit fees were increased, the wages paid to immigrants by employers would need to be verified to ensure that the cost of the fees was not being recouped from recruited immigrants following entry.

Adapting international student tuition fees for development objectives

Another possible measure would involve using the tuition fees charged to international students for development purposes. Currently, countries such as France and Germany charge low tuition fees for international students, making university attendance in these countries possible for students from comparatively low-income backgrounds. It should be noted that both countries currently count the imputed tuition fees for students from developing countries as development aid (technical assistance) to the origin countries, even if the students remain in the country of study (or, for that matter, move to another developed country) after the completion of their studies.

Many international students in European countries currently come from non-EU OECD countries, while others are from comparatively high-income backgrounds in emerging economies or even less-developed countries. A more development-oriented approach might involve charging non-EU international students tuition fees and using the funds generated from students with high-income backgrounds to fund scholarships for those from less-advantaged situations or countries. If current expenditures for international students were maintained, then the reallocation of funds generated by charging tuition fees to students from high-income backgrounds to needy students in the form of scholarships would result in an increase in international-student enrollment from developing countries (see below). Such a measure was in fact implemented by Sweden in recent years, when its introduction of tuition fees for international students was accompanied by an increase in scholarship funding for needy international students.

Not all international students remain in the destination country once they finish their studies. Estimates suggest that between 15 and 35 percent of international students, depending on the country of destination, stay on in the country of study for reasons of work, marriage or asylum (OECD 2010). It is worth noting that since these figures are measured as a proportion of all international students, including those who do not complete their studies, the figures for those who complete their studies may be higher. Those staying for reasons of work must generally find employment within a specified period in order to stay on.

Most international students from non-EU countries appear to leave, presumably to return to their countries of origin and contribute to its economic and social development. The funding of study for students from needy countries can thus be expected to bring benefits to these countries that would not have occurred otherwise.

Beyond neutrality

The measures described above are predicated on the assumption that labor migration will generally continue to be demand-driven in EU countries. As noted above, under these conditions, governments have limited ability to intervene directly; however, opportunities for indirect actions do exist, for example, by removing disincentives to migrants' returns, by facilitating movements considered to yield positive effects for origin countries, and by earmarking or redirecting existing or generated funds to support development objectives more efficiently. Note that the measures described thus far have not involved any funding out of general taxes. In the difficult budget environment currently faced by many countries, the use of general tax revenue can be a difficult option; hence the focus on revenue-neutral measures that yield positive benefits for origin countries and for which direct costs cannot be invoked as an impediment to implementation.

The extent to which more proactive measures by governments are possible will depend on employers' ability and willingness to recruit from abroad in order to satisfy their skill needs. There is evidence from Sweden that multinationals and ethnic businesses are the primary drivers of recruitment from abroad, and that very few small or medium-sized enterprises look beyond national borders for employees (Employment Service Sweden 2012). The implication here is that some means of assisting such employers in recruiting from abroad may be necessary, provided that candidates with the necessary skills and language proficiency can be found.

One additional issue of concern is whether employers in EU countries in general are recruiting at a level sufficient to support growth. A number of studies suggest that only a minority of employers intend to go abroad to satisfy skill needs (Lemaître 2014). If this is so, one possible scenario for the future might be a fall in the size of the workforce, a reduction in social security contributions accompanied by an increase in the size of the retired population, and a move or outsourcing of production facilities abroad. In other words, there may be negative externalities associated with depending only on employer demand for immigrant workers.

Decisions made by individual employers to ensure the continued profitability of their firms may result in negative outcomes for society as a whole.

In both cases, the question is whether governments should act to increase the pool of immigrants who employers are willing to recruit or to facilitate their recruitment. The universe of measures that can practically be taken will naturally be constrained by budget considerations, but let us examine a number of possibilities. All of them presuppose that education and training expenditures will be required in order to "produce" candidates who employers would be interested in hiring. None are programs automatically requiring participants to return to their country of origin; indeed, the decision to migrate or not, or to return or not, is left to the individual. It is true that programs stipulating temporary stays could be designed and implemented, and a potential immigrant candidate pool would very likely exist. However, it is assumed here that destination countries' needs are or will be for permanent migrants, and that expenditures on migration programs only make sense if at least some candidates migrate and stay on for good. Conversely, the accrual of benefits by origin countries requires that not all program beneficiaries migrate permanently. In practice, immigrants' own decisions have generated both outcomes.

Increasing international student enrollment from developing countries

Measures that further increase the number of international students from developing countries – over and above the possible increase associated with the revenue-neutral reallocation of tuition fees cited above – represent one clear avenue for such government action. However, when the size of the domestic youth cohort declines, as is the case in some countries, the government can offset this without increasing education spending by recruiting more students from abroad. Note that study in the host-country language would be necessary if graduating students were to have any chance of being recruited by anybody other than multinational corporations that function internally using international languages.

Financing education abroad

More advantageous to the origin country, however, as well as cheaper for the destination country, would be the organization and funding of study abroad, with instruction in the language of the destination country, and focusing on the skills required in the destination country's labor market. This would create an enlarged pool of potential migrants in origin countries. Some of these students would likely be recruited to the destination country and would thus migrate following the completion of their studies, but some would also remain in their countries of origin. This type of program would also involve transfers of knowledge and technology to the origin country, and in some cases could lead to improvements in the quality and nature of the education provided.

It is beyond the scope of this note to address the organization and funding of such education in detail. However, it would require collaboration between employers and education providers in both origin and destination countries in order to ensure that graduating students have the skills valued and required by employers (including language skills) in both countries (OECD 2008).

This type of program would likely have to involve close partnerships with only a limited number of origin countries owing to the need to concentrate efforts. This in itself would involve difficult choices, as some countries would consequently be "favored" for funding and immigration over others, a situation at variance with traditional "equal-treatment-for-all" policies. Many countries have policies that, in practice, favor persons from certain origin countries, but these policies do not usually entail funding slated for origin countries.

Although some such initiatives have been attempted in the past, they have generally been small in scale, often no more than pilot programs, and have not generally involved post-secondary-level studies. Future needs may instead require large-scale programs capable of generating significant numbers of migrants. In addition, the feasibility of such programs would require strong employer buy-in and perhaps funding, as well. Employer interest will depend on how serious skill shortages become and on whether employers widely perceive the training and recruitment of immigrants to be a possible solution. Certainly, the situation does not appear to have reached that point yet.

Conclusion

Labor-migration policies have rarely been designed with the interests of origin countries in mind. Rather, the labor-market needs of destination countries have been paramount and have dictated the form and nature of labor-migration regulations and work permits. Origin countries have often seen the emigration of their highly educated citizens as a drain on their educational resources and development potential, and have at times lobbied for remuneration in return for the benefits that destination countries have gained from migrants' skills. Although the debate on this issue has receded somewhat due to the realization that origin countries can also benefit from migration (though remittances, technology transfers, investments), the issue of fairness remains in the background.

This note describes a number of measures that could contribute to the development of a more equitable migration system. Most of the measures described are revenue-neutral, not only because current budgetary situations in many destination countries are difficult, but also because such measures can be regarded as low-hanging fruit that can be harvested with little effort or controversy, and that could nonetheless produce benefits for origin countries.

More significant efforts will depend on how serious labor shortages become. Moreover, a hurdle exists in the fact that employers appear to be willing to recruit from abroad only if they can find there the competencies they need, paramount among which are language skills in the case of highly skilled jobs. Expanding the pool of potential migrants in origin countries may involve significant budgetary outlays, which will be a "sellable" policy only if there is employer and societal buy-in, something that is not an obvious scenario in present-day EU countries. The benefits for origin countries would flow from the fact that organizing appropriate education programs abroad would necessarily involve transfers of knowledge and technology as well as financing, and from the fact that not all students benefiting from such programs would ultimately leave their countries of origin. Moreover, a proportion of those who did migrate to destination countries would not stay there permanently. Although it is difficult to quantify the costs and benefits associated with such a system, the record of labor migration of the highly skilled in the recent past suggests that there are potentially gains for all sides.

References

Employment Service Sweden. *Arbetsförmedlingens Återrapportering – Strategi för ökade informationsinsatser om arbetskraftsinvandring från tredjeland. Bilaga, 2012-10-15.* Stockholm: Arbetsförmedlingen, 2012.

Holzmann, Robert, and Johannes Koettl. "Portability of Pension, Health, and other Social Benefits: Facts, Concepts, and Issues." *CESifo Working Paper No. 4002.* Munich: CESifo, 2012.

Lemaître, Georges. "Migration in Europe – an overview of results from the 2008 immigrant module with implications for labor migration." *Matching Economic Migration with Labour Market Needs*, edited by OECD/European Union. Paris: OECD Publishing, 2014: 349–379.

OECD (Organization for Economic Co-operation and Development). *The Looming Crisis in the Health Workforce.* Paris: OECD Publishing, 2008.

OECD. *International Migration Outlook.* Paris: OECD Publishing, 2010.

OECD. *Naturalisation: A Passport for the Better Integration of Immigrants?* Paris: OECD Publishing, 2011a.

OECD. *Recruiting Immigrant Workers: Sweden.* Paris: OECD Publishing, 2011b.

OFM (Office federal des migrations). *Assurances sociales: séjour en Suisse et départ, Informations à l'attention des ressortissants étrangers.* Bern: OFM, 2010.

II. Fair Migration Governance – An Overview

Making Labor Migration Fair: Approaches in Selected OECD States, Origin Countries and International Organizations

Andreas Heimer, Claudia Münch

1 International study background

As a result of the demographically driven decline in the labor force and the growing importance of human capital as a contributor to economic strength, a gap of about 4 million skilled workers will emerge in the German labor market by 2035 (Prognos 2012). In the federal government's skilled-labor strategy, immigration is one of the primary paths for maintaining the skills base over the long term. Since other developed countries are in a similar situation, an international competition for highly skilled labor is emerging.

In addition to the national interest in obtaining as many as possible of the sought-after skilled workers for the domestic labor market, there is also a responsibility from the global perspective to shape immigration so that all participants can benefit from it, including destination countries, countries of origin and the skilled workers themselves. This is thus about the realization of a triple win. This potential-oriented view of migration has been promoted particularly by the Global Commission on International Migration, founded by Kofi Annan.

In its final report, published in 2005, the Commission called for a strengthening of migration's positive impact on economic activity and development: "The role that migrants play in promoting development and poverty reduction in countries of origin, as well as the contribution they make toward the prosperity of destination countries, should be recognized and reinforced. International migration should become an integral part of national, regional and global strategies for economic growth, in both the developing and the developed world" (Global Commission on International Migration 2005: 4).

The triple-win approach stands for structuring the international migration system for skilled workers in a responsible and fair way. Responsible and fair means:
- that a global perspective is taken into account in dealing with skilled-labor migration (normative),
- that through this global perspective, the specific interests of migrants, destination countries and origin countries in the migration process become clearer (awareness-building),

Making Labor Migration Fair

- that by taking these interests into account as migration unfolds, parallel, balanced and lasting benefits for migrants, destination countries and origin countries can be achieved (balanced and forward-looking), and
- that labor migration can be regulated in a fair and transparent way, and structured based on competences and needs (intentional and successful).

The triple-win approach can be demonstrated through success in the three levels of observation – countries of origin, destination countries and the individual – which are depicted in Figure 1:

Figure 1: Triple win

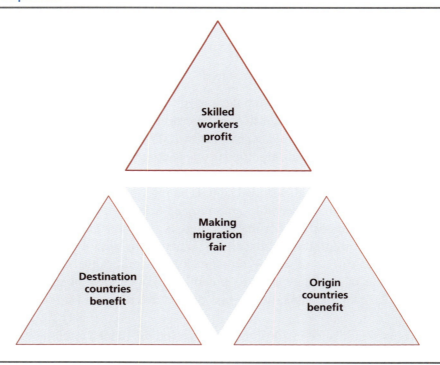

Source: Prognos AG

The design of a fairer migration system should encompass not just the immigration process in its narrow sense, from one country to another, but rather the entire migration cycle. This begins with selection of the origin countries in which skilled workers are recruited, covers the recruitment and integration process in the destination countries, and includes aspects such as the diaspora's reconnection with the home country and the temporary or permanent homeward or further migration.

How specifically is it possible to shape skilled-labor migration so that the interests of all parties are satisfied, and so that benefits in the sense of a triple win are produced? The Bertelsmann Stiftung has addressed this societally and economically significant question in an inter-

International study background

Figure 2: Migration cycle: Origin country – Destination country – Origin country

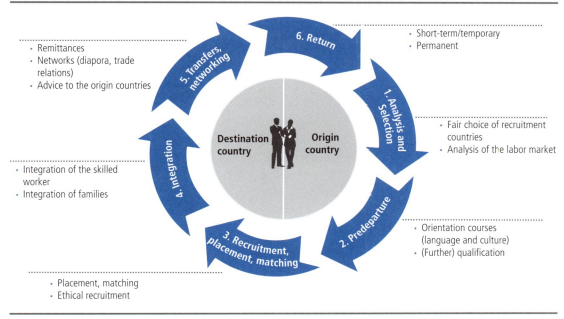

Source: Prognos AG

national study carried out in conjunction with Prognos AG. To this end, 10 OECD countries facing similar demographic and economic challenges were selected. Against the backdrop of these countries' current migration and migration-policy environments, various initiatives, projects and programs that contribute to the fair and goal-oriented management of international skilled-labor migration were examined. In addition to programs in traditional migrant-destination countries, such as Canada, New Zealand and the United States, activities in Denmark, Germany, France, the Netherlands, Sweden, Switzerland and the United Kingdom were examined. The perspective of migrant-origin countries was also taken into account. For these countries, a fair labor-migration system offers the opportunity to use the return flows of money and know-how to achieve their own development goals. Finally, the activities of international organizations as thought leaders and promoters of the triple-win idea were included in the research.

The results of the research were presented to an expert commission convened by the Bertelsmann Stiftung in June 2014. A key finding was that the ideal form of a triple-win-approach – that is, one that takes all three involved parties into account and includes the entire migration cycle – is very rare in practice. However, it became clear at the same time that fair skilled-labor migration is to some extent already attainable through innovative approaches that succeed in realizing individual aspects of the triple win at different points in the migration cycle.

In a second phase, the study was deepened through on-site visits in selected countries (Canada, Germany, the Netherlands, the Philippines, Sweden and the United States). Inter-

Figure 3: Countries included in this study

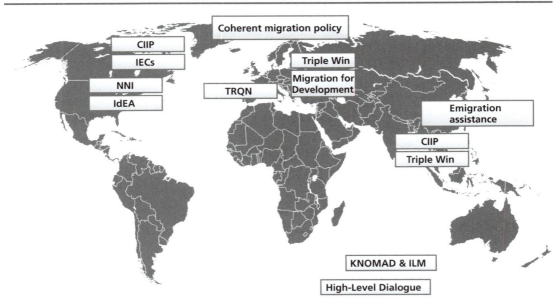

Source: Prognos AG

views with program directors and actors from the political, academic and civil society spheres enabled – in the sense of 360-degree feedback – a comprehensive view of local activities.

The following examples provide illustrations of fair skilled-labor-migration approaches:

- Sweden is a county that has comprehensively and coherently shaped the conditions for labor migration, and has in this respect systematically taken aspects of fairness into account (in the sense of a "whole-of-government" approach).
- Canada, with its concept of Immigrant Employment Councils (IECs) and the Canadian Integration and Immigration Program (CIIP), offers successful examples of the effective labor-market integration of skilled immigrant labor.
- The International diaspora Engagement Alliance (IdEA) in the United States, the Temporary Return of Qualified Nationals (TRQN) program in the Netherlands, and the Centre for International Migration and Development (CIM) in Germany offer striking demonstrations of how skilled workers living abroad can productively utilize their know-how and financial resources in their home countries.
- The Philippines, for years a sending country for skilled labor, has supported the emigration process with a variety of specialized agencies in order that it may benefit from overseas workers' remittances, among other reasons.
- The Gesellschaft für Internationale Zusammenarbeit's (GIZ) Triple Win nurses project in Germany, along with global skills partnerships such as those tested by Nurses Now International in the United States, are examples of bilateral cooperation between migrant-desti-

nation and migrant-origin countries that take the interests of both sides fittingly into account.
- As globally active actors, international organizations seek to anchor principles of fairness more deeply within global migration-policy structures. The United Nations' High-Level Dialogue, the resultant Global Forum on Migration and Development, the Global Knowledge Partnership on Migration and Development (KNOWMAD), and the World Bank's International Labor Mobility (ILM) program are good examples of the creation and exchange of knowledge on structuring migration so as to achieve a triple win.

Figure 4: Components of a fair skilled-labor migration system

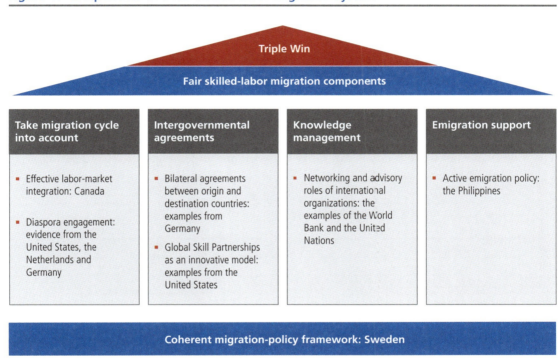

Source: Prognos AG

These approaches are described in the following chapters. First, the migration and migration-policy background in the 10 OECD countries examined is presented. Innovative activities pursued by political, economic and civil society actors that contribute in a goal-oriented way to the fair management of international skilled-labor migration will be presented in text boxes. Chapter 2 shifts the perspective to the activities of selected countries of origin as they deal with migration. Chapter 3 describes the role of international organizations in the promotion of fair skilled-labor migration. Finally, a conclusion summarizes the results of the international research.

2 Aspects of fair labor migration in 10 OECD countries

The following chapter outlines migration policies in 10 selected OECD countries facing demographic and economic challenges similar to those in Germany. In the course of this review, aspects that support fair skilled-labor migration will emerge.

The country chapters will be preceded by demographic and migration-policy indicators: population figures and birthrates; old-age dependency ratios; foreign-born population shares and main origin countries; the share of employment-related immigration and the share that takes place in the context of free movements of labor; and employment and unemployment rates.[1] These overviews will additionally contain two summary indexes drawn from the Bertelsman Stiftung's Sustainable Governance Indicators (SGI):

- The SGI Labor Market Index assesses how countries succeed in reducing unemployment and achieve labor mobility sufficient to balance supply and demand in the labor market.
- The SGI Integration Index assesses the strength of integration within each country on the basis of equitable access for migrants and natives to labor markets and education, as well as opportunities for family reunification, political participation among migrant groups, access to permanent residency rights and effective protection against discrimination.

The index values in these sections can range between one and a maximum of 10 points.

2.1 Denmark – Improving the welcoming process

Birthrate	1.76 (2011)
Population	5.6 million (2013)
Dependency ratio[2] 2010 vs. 2030	28.2 vs. 40.3
Share of foreign-born population	8.2 % (2012)
Main countries of origin	Poland (9 %), Romania (9 %), Germany (5 %) (2012)
Share of employment-related immigration (without accompanying family)	13.5 % (2012)
Immigration in the context of free movements	57.7 % (2012)
Employment rate, immigrants vs. native Danes	63.4 % vs. 78.8 % (2012)
Unemployment rate, immigrants vs. native Danes	14.7 % vs. 6.8 % (2012)
Sustainable Governance Indicators (SGI) – Labor Market Index	7.3
SGI – Integration Index	6.2

Sources: Birthrate: OECD 2014a; population: World Bank 2014; dependency ratio: United Nations 2013; share of foreign-born population, main countries of origin, employment-related immigration, immigration in context of freedom of movement: OECD 2014b; employment rates, unemployment rates: OECD 2014c; SGI – Labor Market Index and SGI – Integration Index: Bertelsmann Stiftung 2014

---

1 With regard to the share of employment-related immigration, it should be noted that due to international agreements such as that on the freedom of movement between EU member states, many migrants who in fact immigrate on economic or familial grounds are captured in the "free movements" category.
2 The dependency ratio is the ratio of the population aged over 64 to the working population between 20 and 64 years of age.

Context of labor migration

Less than 10 percent of Denmark's population was born outside the country. Employment-related immigration from non-EU or non-European Economic Area (EEA) countries as a share of total immigration is 13.5 percent and therefore higher than in most of the European countries considered here. However, assessed on the basis of the employment and unemployment rates, labor-market integration is not optimal, as the unemployment rate among native Danes is significantly lower than that among immigrants. In addition, the employment rate among native Danes in 2012 was more than 10 percent higher than that for immigrants.

Denmark's current immigration policy focuses on a liberalization for qualified skilled workers and their families. Thus, for immigration to Denmark from countries outside the European Union (EU), the EEA or the Nordic countries (Finland, Iceland, Norway, Sweden), a residence/work permit is required. The issuance of this permit depends to a significant degree on academic qualification levels, even for students and doctoral candidates. This system is governed by a variety of legal regulations and programs, the most recent example of which is an April 2014 draft law that pursues four objectives in particular:

- Making it easier for Danish employers to recruit internationally;
- Attracting and retaining international students in Denmark;
- Guaranteeing that foreign-born and native Danish employees are accorded equivalent income and working conditions; and
- Improving the "welcoming process" for foreign workers and their families.

The improvement of the welcoming process is currently being furthered through two programs. Work in Denmark, a state institution addressing the issue of international labor recruitment, launched the successful Spouse Program in 2012, providing immigrant workers' spouses with access to the Danish labor market. The six-month program offers information on the labor market, job-interview preparation and internship placements.

The International Citizen Centers represent another approach intended to facilitate foreign skilled workers' start in Denmark. Operating in Denmark's four largest cities, they combine the services of the various government offices relevant to newcomers. This includes services providing support in bureaucratic matters, personalized assistance with job searches or language courses, and the provision of information on living and working conditions in Denmark, school issues and child care.

Skilled-labor immigration is governed primarily though the Greencard scheme, which enables highly qualified workers to stay in Denmark in order to seek employment, but also grants residence permits though a point-based system under which at least 100 points in the areas of education, language skills, work experience, adaptability and age must be attained. In addition, proof of medical insurance and financial resources sufficient for the first year must be demonstrated.

In order to attain a sufficient number of points, applicants must have at least the equivalent of a Danish bachelor's degree. Additional points can be obtained for attendance at high-ranking universities (according to the current QS world rankings[3]), as well as for being younger than 40 years old. Periods of study or work in other EU or EEA countries, as well as Switzerland, will also be taken as an indicator of adaptability and rewarded with additional points. The Greencard scheme thus aims at the selection of academically highly qualified and young applicants who have already acquired work or study experience within a European context.

In addition to immigration through the Greencard scheme, Denmark has a "Positive List" of occupations in which there is an officially recognized labor shortage; a candidate with a job offer in one of these occupations receives expedited access to the Danish labor market. Currently, engineers and individuals working in the medical or health care fields are among those being sought, and a large number of academic professions are also included on the list. The Pay Limit Scheme offers an additional opportunity for immigration; this program makes it comparatively easy for skilled foreign workers with a well-remunerated offer of work to immigrate, as long as annual gross income is above DKK 375,000.

Additionally, the Corporate Scheme offers international companies with offices in Denmark the ability to send employees to the country to work. Participants receive a firm-specific residence permit that allows them to move back and forth between Denmark and the other country. Under the Greencard, Pay Limit and Corporate schemes, as well under the Positive List program, qualified applicants can be accompanied by members of their close family.

Current developments

In the process of liberalizing access for skilled labor, restrictive regulations have also been introduced in recent years. The tightening of Danish immigration legislation is primarily attributable to the electoral success of the right-wing populist Danish People's Party. As a part of this trend, the minimum length of stay before receiving a permanent residence permit has been increased from four to five years. For family reunification, the minimum age for both partners was fixed in 2012 at 24 years. These regulations are primarily related to long-term stays and family reunification; however, they will affect the country's appeal with regard to skilled-labor immigration.

---

[3] See QS Top Universities Rankings: www.topuniversities.com/university-rankings/world-university-rankings/2014#sorting=rank+region=+country=+faculty=+stars=false+search=.

2.2 Germany – Migration- and development-policy pioneer projects

Birthrate	1.36 (2011)
Population	80.6 million (2013)
Dependency ratio 2010 vs. 2030	34.4 vs. 52.1
Share of foreign-born population	13.3 % (2012)
Main countries of origin	Poland (18 %), Romania (12 %), Bulgaria (6 %), Hungary (6 %) (2012)
Share of employment-related immigration (without accompanying family)	5.5 % (2012)
Immigration in the context of free movements	75.8 % (2012)
Employment rate, immigrants vs. native Germans	69.4 % vs. 79.8 % (2012)
Unemployment rate, immigrants vs. native Germans	8.7 % vs. 4.9 % (2012)
SGI – Labor Market Index	7.8
SGI – Integration Index	7.3

Sources: Birthrate: OECD 2014a; population: World Bank 2014; dependency ratio: United Nations 2013; share of foreign-born population, main countries of origin, employment-related immigration, immigration in context of freedom of movement: OECD 2014b; employment rates, unemployment rates: OECD 2014c; SGI – Labor Market Index and SGI – Integration Index: Bertelsmann Stiftung 2014

Context of labor migration

According to a recent report by the Organization for Economic Co-operation and Development (OECD 2014d), Germany has become one of the world's top destination countries for immigrants: In 2012, with approximately 400,000 permanent migrants, it was the most popular destination country after the United States. Overall, about 13 percent of Germany's more than 80 million residents were born elsewhere. In 2012, about 6 percent of immigration from third countries took place for the purposes of labor migration, while family reunification accounted for nearly 14 percent. The "free movements" category accounted for about three-quarters of immigration. The noticeably higher unemployment rate among immigrants as compared to the native population makes it clear that further action is necessary with regard to labor-market integration.

A number of programs and directives govern immigration to Germany today. The principle of free movement for workers applies to EU citizens. The migration of highly qualified third-country workers has been regulated in Germany since 2012 under the EU Blue Card Directive, which member states are required to transpose into their own law. Germany has opted for a particularly liberal and generous implementation (for more on this, see Section 4.6).

Minimum salaries enabling the granting of a residence permit under the Blue Card program were set at a comparatively low level (in 2014, an annual salary of €47,600, although special minimum-income regulations exist for occupational groups with a clear shortage of labor). Moreover, the priority-review instrument was waived, and family members were given unrestricted access to the labor market. After 33 months of residence in Germany (or another EU country), or after 21 months with sufficient German-language knowledge, migrants can apply for a permanent residence permit. Two years after its introduction, Germany has issued more than 16,000 Blue Cards, making it the European leader in this regard. To increase these figures further, experts see a particular need to increase awareness of the Blue Card program abroad.

In addition, the federal government has introduced a new six-month residence permit specifically enabling qualified skilled workers to engage in a job search (§ 18c of the Residence Act). In this regard, it has departed from the central migration-policy principle of allowing no immigration without an employment contract.

Current developments

Immigration has been a controversial and much-discussed theme in Germany at least since the 1990s. At this time, as well as in the early years of the new millennium, migration was typically regarded with a critical eye. High levels of immigration inflow at the beginning of the 1990s, the difficult economic situation in Germany, the 2001 PISA study results that exposed the difficulties faced by students with an immigrant background, and the widespread fear of Islamist terrorism following the 9/11 attacks were all dominant features of discourse on the issue. Germany blocked migrants from Central and Eastern Europe from entering its labor market longer than almost any other country.

During the 2000s, however, other aspects came to the fore. The sustained economic upswing beginning in 2007 led in some areas to what is already a notable shortage of skilled workers. In addition, the challenges presented by Germany's particularly extreme incipient demographic shift were becoming increasingly evident. In both the political and economic spheres, it was recognized that these challenges would have to be met with a decisive opening of the country to foreign skilled labor, among other approaches.

The "Make it in Germany" skilled-labor portal, a part of the skilled-labor offensive mounted by the Federal Ministry for Economic Affairs and Energy, the Federal Ministry of Labor and Social Affairs, and the Federal Employment Agency, offers an example of this rethinking. With this portal, a skilled professional abroad interested in emigration can gain information about work opportunities in Germany; moreover, the site is intended to strengthen the "culture of welcome" within Germany itself.

The International Placement Services (ZAV) program, run jointly by the Federal Employment Agency (BA) and the Gesellschaft für Internationale Zusammenarbeit (GIZ), delivers a high level of innovation with regard to development-oriented migration. Its efforts have included a pilot project to promote the legal mobility of highly qualified Tunisian engineers, as well as the "Triple Win" nurses project.

"Triple Win" nurses – Sustainable recruitment of nurses from four countries

The "Triple Win" nurses project is jointly implemented by the Federal Employment Agency's (BA) International Placement Services (ZAV) and the Gesellschaft für Internationale Zusammenarbeit (GIZ). Participating countries include Serbia, Bosnia-Herzegovina, and the Philippines. A further placement agreement has been struck with Tunisia.

The program's starting point was the idea of reducing the unmet demand for skilled nursing-care workers through the placement of qualified nurses from abroad. At the same time, this approach can reduce the surplus of skilled nursing labor in participating partner countries, while making possible employment that fits these skilled individuals' qualifications. The project's target group is thus trained nursing professionals with a basic knowledge of the German language.

The project starts with the selection of partner countries. The selection criterion, in addition to compliance with the World Health Organization's (WHO) code of practice on the recruitment of health care personnel (see Section 4.6), is a current oversupply of nurses. In a second step, all necessary agreements between the BA and the appropriate partner agency in the foreign country are concluded. These include the nurses' obligation to obtain recognition of their training qualifications within the first year of their employment in Germany. On this basis, they receive a temporary residence and work permit. If the recognition process is not successful, the residence permit is not renewed.

As a part of the implementation process, ZAV uses selection interviews to check candidates' personal, professional and linguistic qualifications. GIZ provides support for the process throughout, carrying out the technical preparation for the work in Germany as well as integration support following arrival. It also addresses nurses' language skills; by the time of their departure for Germany, they must have reached at least the B1 level.

Figure 5: The Triple Win nurses project

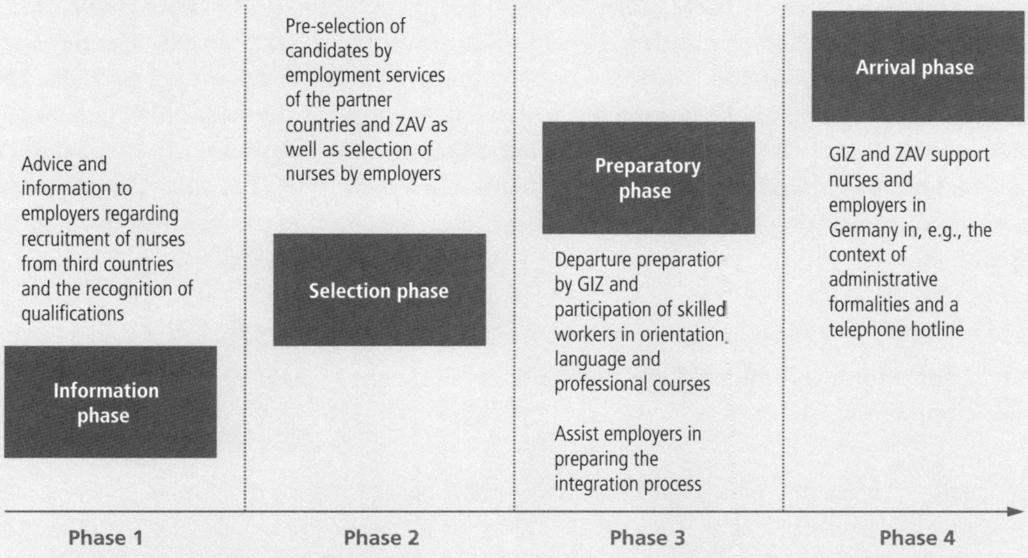

Phase 1	Phase 2	Phase 3	Phase 4
Information phase	**Selection phase**	**Preparatory phase**	**Arrival phase**
Advice and information to employers regarding recruitment of nurses from third countries and the recognition of qualifications	Pre-selection of candidates by employment services of the partner countries and ZAV as well as selection of nurses by employers	Departure preparation by GIZ and participation of skilled workers in orientation, language and professional courses. Assist employers in preparing the integration process	GIZ and ZAV support nurses and employers in Germany in, e.g., the context of administrative formalities and a telephone hotline

Source: Prognos AG

Health-sector workers interested in the program are provided with information on the conditions of participation and the selection and placement procedures. There is no cost to participating individuals. Employers in Germany with whom the nurses are placed pay €3,700 per skilled employee.

> In the 2011–2012 pilot phase with Bosnia-Herzegovina, around 75 nurses were successfully placed. In the project phase, from 2013 to the end of 2014, the number of placements was about 650 as compared to an originally planned 2,000. While the demand on the part of nurses in the countries of origin has been significantly above the targeted level, employers in Germany remain hesitant. This is due in part to the economic situation in Southern and Eastern Europe as well as to the consequent migration of skilled personnel from these states. Moreover, some uncertainty is evident among German employers regarding the differences in nursing training between the countries of origin and Germany.
>
> Interviews with participants from the Philippines, Bosnia and Serbia shed light on the difficulty of labor-market environments in the countries of origin, where high rates of unemployment and low pay are common. Nurses interested in the program want to improve their career and personal prospects. Those nurses who have already been placed report very positive experiences in Germany and want to stay here for the long term.
>
> The project is highly innovative within the area of development-oriented migration, as it seeks to take the interests of the destination country, the country of origin and skilled labor into account. The project's duration has been extended for an additional two years, until 2016.

With regard to development-policy work, the activities of the Centre for International Migration and Development (CIM) to promote the engagement of migrants living in Germany are well worth highlighting. Diaspora communities send funds to relatives or friends, invest in their home countries or become involved in development projects. Most importantly, they speak both languages and are familiar with the particularities of countries of origin as well as destination countries. Diasporas are consequently important civil society actors that can contribute to the realization of a triple win. The Migration for Development program represents a successful example of their integration into development cooperation.

> **The Centre for International Migration and Development's (CIM) Migration for Development program**
>
> Migrants can make substantial contributions to the development of their countries of origin on the basis of their knowledge and experiences. The Centre for International Migration and Development's (CIM) Migration for Development program promotes the multifaceted engagement of migrants under the framework of three subprojects.
>
> In the Returning Experts Program, CIM supports foreign professionals who – after study, a course of training or at least two years of professional employment in German or another OECD country – want to use their knowledge for the development of their countries of origin. This support includes the following elements:

- Individual counseling regarding return and career planning
- Information on the origin country's labor market
- Job-placement services
- Continuing support in re-entering a career within the target country
- Provision of local contacts, particularly development organizations

Furthermore, depending on the returning skilled workers' qualifications and the development-policy relevance of their intended activity, CIM provides financial grants toward travel and transportation costs, the establishment of a workplace and (for a limited time) the recipient's income. This funding is provided by the Federal Ministry for Economic Cooperation and Development (BMZ).

The *Business Ideas for Development* subproject is aimed at migrants who want to start their own independent business in their home country, with the subsequent aim of promoting the local economy and triggering innovation. CIM supports the founding process through counseling and networking, thus helping with the establishment of a new company in the country of origin.

Finally, the *Promoting the Development Activities of Migrant Organizations* subproject is directed toward people who are not returning to their country of origin, but who nevertheless want to commit to its economic and societal development and therefore become involved in a migrant organization. To this end, CIM offers partial financial support of up to 50 percent of a planned project's entire cost, up to a maximum of €50,000. In addition to the financial support, CIM facilitates projects by assisting with organization members' further qualification and provides consulting services regarding planning, implementing and sustainably integrating projects within local structures.

2.3 France – No margin for fairness

Birthrate	2.0 (2011)
Population	66.0 million (2013)
Dependency ratio 2010 vs. 2030	28.6 vs. 43.4
Share of foreign-born population	11.6 % (2011)
Main countries of origin	Algeria (15 %), Morocco (12 %), Tunisia (7 %) (2012)
Share of employment-related immigration (without accompanying family)	12.1 % (2012)
Immigration in the context of free movements	36.9 % (2012)
Employment rate, immigrant vs. native French	60.7 % vs. 73.5 % (2012)
Unemployment rate, immigrant vs. native French	16.0 % vs. 9.2 % (2012)
SGI – Labor Market Index	5.3
SGI – Integration Index	6.4

Sources: Birthrate: OECD 2014a; population: World Bank 2014; dependency ratio: United Nations 2013; share of foreign-born population, main countries of origin, employment-related immigration, immigration in context of freedom of movement: OECD 2014b; employment rates, unemployment rates: OECD 2014c; SGI – Labor Market Index and SGI – Integration Index: Bertelsmann Stiftung 2014

Making Labor Migration Fair

Context of labor migration

While even long after World War II, the vast majority of migrants to France came from within Europe, more than two-thirds today come from Algeria, Morocco and Tunisia, the former French colonies or protectorates in North Africa.

Until the middle of the 1970s, labor migration dominated immigration to France. Since the end of all recruitment programs for foreign workers, family reunification has become the predominant form of immigration (2012: around 38%), although with a slightly declining share since 2007 thanks to the Hortefeux law. Among other measures, this measure provides for language tests and preparatory courses in countries of origin and requires families to sign a so-called integration contract. In addition, the tenure of president Nicolas Sarkozy (2007–2012) was characterized by the consistent deportation of irregular migrants, mass expulsions of Roma and the burqa ban.

As a consequence of the anemic economic growth of recent years, the rate of unemployment among the general French population has risen to new levels. On the whole, immigrants are affected more strongly by unemployment than are natives, as they face particular hurdles to labor-market integration, such as the legal exclusion of non-EU immigrants from many public-sector occupations. This poses a significant problem for long-term integration and ensures that migrants' economic potential cannot be fully exploited. Furthermore, the long-term integration of immigrants is undermined by the restrictive conditions placed on family reunification.

Current developments

Following the mid-2012 assumption of power of President François Hollande's new government, a mild easing of the restrictive migration and integration policies has been evident. Hollande himself speaks of a cautious change in course. Given the country's persistently weak economic performance, he has affirmed the need to reduce labor migration; however, at the same time, the minimum stay to qualify for naturalization was reduced from 10 to five years. In addition, a permanent employment contract is no longer a condition for naturalization. Moreover, discussion of granting local voting rights to non-EU immigrants who have lived in France for at least five years has gained momentum. However, since the French constitution would have to be amended to accomplish this, no voting-rights changes are expected in the short term.

The TEAM project (Professionnaliser les Services Publics de l'Emploi des pays TEAM: Tunisie, Égypte, Algérie, Maroc, Mauritanie) is intended to help mitigate long-term shortages of skilled workers in certain occupations. To this end, placement structures are erected in the employment services of the countries of origin, with the goal of giving young skilled workers occupational experience in France that can then be used later in the home country. Another objective is to strengthen employment agencies in North Africa in order to forestall illegal labor migration. Capacity-building is accomplished through training programs and modules focusing on international job placement as well as through support in the construction of international-recruitment websites, for example.

The approach is currently being tested with two pilot projects in Tunisia and Morocco. The French employment agency, Pôle emploi, as well as the French Office for Immigration and Integration (Office française de l'immigration et de l'intégration, OFII), are responsible for the program, and the Belgian employment agency is also involved. The project partner in North Africa is the ANAPEC employment agency in Morocco. However, for political reasons (high levels of unemployment), the project has thus far been publicized only within the community of subject-area experts.

2.4 United Kingdom – Facilitating remittances and a culture of evaluation

Birthrate	1.97 (2011)
Population	64.1 million (2013)
Dependency ratio 2010 vs. 2030	27.8 vs. 39.3
Share of foreign-born population	11.9 % (2012)
Main countries of origin	China (11 %), India (9 %), Poland (8 %) (2012)
Share of employment-related immigration (without accompanying family)	38.8 % (2012)
Immigration in the context of free movements	25.5 % (2012)
Employment rate, immigrants vs. native British	71.3 % vs. 75.4 % (2012)
Unemployment rate, immigrants vs. native British	9.1 % vs. 7.9 % (2012)
SGI – Labor Market Index	6.4
SGI – Integration Index	7.5

Sources: Birthrate: OECD 2014a; population: World Bank 2014; dependency ratio: United Nations 2013; share of foreign-born population, main countries of origin, employment-related immigration, immigration in context of freedom of movement: OECD 2014b; employment rates, unemployment rates: OECD 2014c; SGI – Labor Market Index and SGI – Integration Index: Bertelsmann Stiftung 2014

Context of labor migration

About 7.9 million immigrants (2013) live in the United Kingdom today. This figure has increased by nearly 3 million since the year 2000. For many years, the most significant country of origin has been India.

Until the 1990s, the majority of immigrants entered the country on the basis of family reunification. Since the mid-1990s, the targeted recruitment of qualified labor has become a focus of migration policy. Since that time, labor migration from third countries has become the most significant form of immigration, accounting for nearly 40 percent (2012) of the whole. Because EU citizens are counted separately under the "free movements" category, it can be assumed that this figure is in fact even higher.

The high number of immigrants has regularly led to contentious debates within the British public. To support their arguments, immigration opponents point to migrants' incomplete integration and lack of identification with the United Kingdom as well as to competition for jobs and housing. The dispute culminated at the beginning of this century in riots that had the additional effect of harming the reputations of leading public figures of British multiculturalism.

Between 2008 and 2010, the Labour government introduced a point-based system for the regulation of immigration from countries outside the European Union and the European Free Trade Association (EFTA). This system consists of five "tiers." In Tier 1 are highly qualified workers, such as entrepreneurs, investors and "exceptional talents." Skilled workers with a job offer from a British employer are categorized in Tier 2. This group also includes workers in occupations included on a list of those deemed to be suffering labor shortages, workers for jobs for which no British citizen could be found and, finally, workers wanting to work at a UK location of a foreign-based company. The currently suspended Tier 3 is intended to apply to low-skilled workers who can fill temporary shortages in the UK labor market.

Tier 4 applies to students, while Tier 5 includes temporary workers and "youth mobility" (e.g., those seeking au pair jobs or work-and-travel experiences). In addition, a ceiling on net immigration was imposed in 2010; under this measure, inward migration is to be limited to 100,000 persons per year through 2015 – a goal experts say is highly unlikely to be achieved due to the lack of control over immigration by EU citizens.

A unique feature of migration policy in the United Kingdom is the Migration Advisory Committee (MAC), convened by the British Home Office in 2007 to serve as a scholarly advisory commission. Its goal is to provide evidence-based, independent and nonbinding migration-policy advice to the government. The Commission's recommendations are also available to the general public, and interested parties can access its work at any time. The amount of justification provided by the government when it elects not to follow the Commission's recommendations is correspondingly high. The MAC also produces the above-noted list of occupations experiencing labor shortages.

The United Kingdom has also taken a lead with regard to facilitating the transfer of remittances, which often account for a considerable share of economic activity in countries of origin. The Send Money Home website, created in 2005 by the Department for International Development (DFID), was intended to make transfer options more transparent while promoting competition among the funds-transfer service providers, with the ultimate aims of reducing transaction costs for the transfers and improving service providers' reliability. This has been successful. Since the website's introduction, the cost of transfer fees in the countries covered by the initiative have fallen by an average of 5.6 percent, and even by 20 percent in the case of India. The site is today financed primarily by advertising, partner links and private investment. In addition, it receives some government subsidies. The Send Money Home model has already been adopted in many other countries (e.g., France: envoidargent.org, Germany: geldtransfair.de, Australia and New Zealand: sendmoneypacific.org).

Current developments

The persistently high levels of immigration remain a controversial issue in the United Kingdom. According to the current British Social Attitudes Survey, 47 percent of British citizens hold the opinion that immigration is harmful to the economy. Moreover, 56 percent want a notable reduction in immigration. The euroskeptic U.K. Independence Party (UKIP) was able to attract 29 percent of the vote in the last European ballot, emerging as the election's clear winner.

In an autumn 2014 speech, Prime Minister Cameron announced plans to reduce social benefits for immigrants and called for a policy that would also require EU migrants to demonstrate an employment relationship prior to immigration in addition to only rendering them eligible to receive social benefits after four years of employment. Furthermore, he called for a strengthening of measures against illegal migration.

2.5 Canada – Avoiding brain waste

Birthrate	1.61 (2011)
Population	35.2 million (2013)
Dependency ratio 2010 vs. 2030	22.5 vs. 41.3
Share of foreign-born population	19.8 % (2012)
Main countries of origin	China (13 %), Philippines (13 %), India (11 %) (2012)
Share of employment-related immigration (without accompanying family)	26.5 % (2012)
Immigration in the context of free movements	–
Employment rate, immigrants vs. native Canadians	73.2 % vs. 77.4 % (2012)
Unemployment rate, immigrants vs. native Canadians	8.5 % vs. 7.0 % (2012)
SGI – Labor Market Index	7.2
SGI – Integration Index	8.2

Sources: Birthrate: OECD 2014a; population: World Bank 2014; dependency ratio: United Nations 2013; share of foreign-born population, main countries of origin, employment-related immigration, immigration in context of freedom of movement: OECD 2014b; employment rates, unemployment rates: OECD 2014c; SGI – Labor Market Index and SGI – Integration Index: Bertelsmann Stiftung 2014

Context of labor migration

As a traditional country of immigration, Canada has well over 100 years of experience with migration and integration policy. In 2012, nearly 20 percent of Canada's population had been born outside the country. Immigrants originate primarily from European countries and, in the last 10 years, increasingly from Asian states. Although family reunification previously played a significant role, the focus of Canadian migration policy today lies on the immigration of skilled workers.

Although the country gains nearly 1 percent of its population annually through immigration, changes in the population's composition have begun to influence economic dynamics in Canada as well. As early as 2004, a study by the Canadian Policy Research Networks explored the implications of a potential skills shortage. Furthermore, the Canadian Chamber of Commerce confirmed in a 2012 report that a lack of skilled labor in specific industries and occupations had become a serious risk factor for the Canadian economy.

Labor migration in Canada is managed through a number of programs. The Federal Skilled Worker Program (FSWP), based on a point system introduced in 1967, manages permanent labor immigration at the federal level. In addition to a minimum number of points in the categories of education, work experience, language skills, age and flexibility, applicants must fulfill one of these three conditions: 1) have at least one year of experience in a skilled trade or technical activity or in a management position included on an official listing of required occupations; 2) have a work offer; or 3) have status as a graduate of a Canadian doctorate program. The FSWP covers 81 percent of economic immigration and 46 percent of total immigration to Canada.

Challenges with regard to labor-market integration and the ongoing aging of the population resulted in a reform of the point system in January 2013. Stronger weight is now given to mastering one of the country's two languages, English or French; to the required professional qualification; and to the immigrant's having a comparatively low age. In this way, Canada has sought to take a stronger demographic perspective in its immigration management. Previous work experience outside Canada is now given less weight, as well.

Another new feature in the immigration system is the Federal Skilled Trades Program (FSTP), which has facilitated skilled workers' immigration to Canada since 2013. This program is limited to occupational groups specified on a list of currently desired professional categories.

Figure 6: The Canadian immigration system

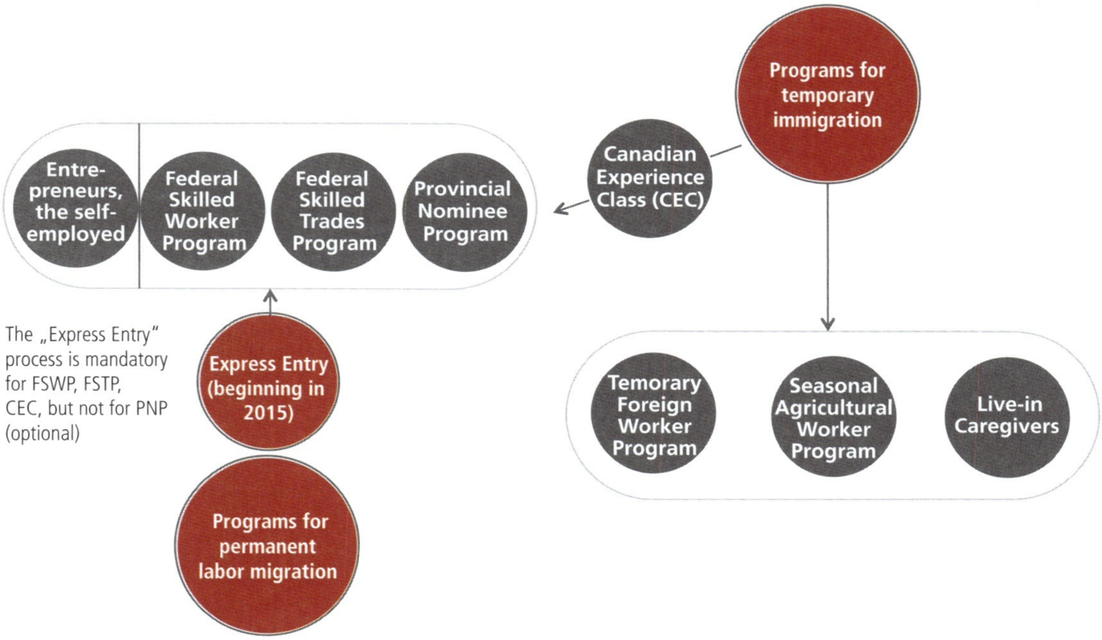

Source: Prognos AG

Alongside the programs for permanent immigration, temporary immigration is regulated primarily by the Temporary Foreign Worker Program (TFWP). Originally conceived as a means of filling skills shortage mostly within the petroleum industry, the program was expanded in January 2002 to include the hotel and hospitality industry, restaurant work, construction and manufacturing.

The so-called Live-in Caregiver Program was established in 1992. The goal here is to meet the demand for skilled workers to provide care and nursing services for children, the elderly or disabled people. The program also offers qualified persons the ability to apply for permanent-resident status in Canada after a certain time as a temporary skilled worker. Until recently, the work itself had to take place in the homes of the people or children requiring care. However, since the end of November 2014, two alternative paths in addition to the Caregiver Program (the Caring for Children pathway and the Caring for People with High Medical Needs pathway) have been implemented; these dispense with the live-in requirement, but nevertheless offer an applicant the possibility of attaining a permanent residence permit.

Under the Seasonal Agricultural Worker Program (SAWP), Canadian agricultural employers have for almost 50 years had the ability to recruit workers for a period of up to eight months. The program's partner countries are Mexico, Anguilla, Antigua and Barbuda, Barbados, the Dominican Republic, Grenada, Jamaica, Montserrat, St. Kitts-Nevis, St. Lucia, St. Vincent and the Grenadines, and Trinidad and Tobago.

A further aspect of Canadian immigration policy concerns naturalization. Here, too, far-reaching changes have been introduced since 2006, increasing requirements for the national citizenship and language tests, among other shifts. This has been accompanied by a two-stage configuration of the immigration process, in which immigrants initially arrive in Canada on a temporary basis and can apply for a permanent residence status at a later date.

The integration of immigrants into the labor market in Canada takes place relatively successfully. Indicators in this regard include an unemployment rate that is only slightly higher for immigrants than for native-born Canadians and an employment rate that is only slightly lower. Nevertheless, challenges are evident even in such a time-tested destination country as this. Despite the targeted selection of economically exploitable skills, migrants have on average significantly lower incomes and disproportionately often pursue activities that are below their skill level. Several innovative approaches have been developed in Canada seeking to improve the process of matching skilled immigrant workers and employers, thus preventing brain waste. The Canadian Immigrant Employment Councils (IECs) and the Canadian Immigrant Integration Program (CIIP), both described in detail below, set the standard in this regard.

Canadian Immigrant Integration Program (CIIP)

The CIIP was initiated in 2007 by the government's Department of Citizenship and Immigration Canada as a two-year pilot project and subsequently funded through 2014. Implementation is carried out by the Association of Canadian Community Colleges, an association of 130 publicly funded colleges and institutes.

The project's goal is to provide foreign skilled workers with information before their entry into Canada and to use individual counseling to develop a personal road map for successful integration, enabling them to find jobs suitable to their skills and experience.

Participants must be in the process of applying for a Canadian visa and be a citizen of one of the 25 countries in which the program is currently offered. As a rule, applicants will be directly invited to participate through the visa process itself.

The program consists of three modules:
- In a one-day orientation workshop, participants are given information about Canada's working culture and labor-market prospects, among other issues, along with tips enabling them to speed up the job-search process before their departure.
- The personalized counseling also results in the creation of individualized plans for the emigrating skilled workers, instructing them in what steps they must take both before and after their arrival in Canada. If possible, direct contract with employers is established, bringing the integration process underway even before departure.
- An Internet portal offers online help, workshops and mentoring programs as well as occupation-specific presentations. The portal also offers the ability to establish direct contact with Canadian employers.

Offices have been opened in China, the United Kingdom, India and the Philippines, which in turn offer the program in a total of 25 countries. More than 30,000 people have registered for the CIIP since 2007, and more than 25,000 have already successfully completed the program.

Figure 7: Canadian Immigrant Integration Program (CIIP)

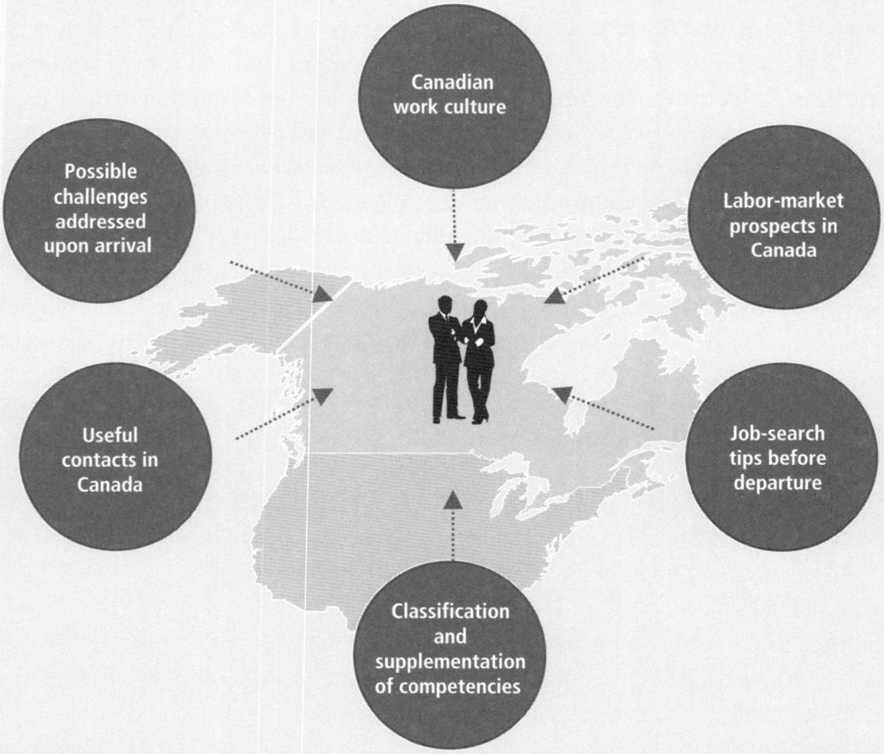

- Canadian work culture
- Labor-market prospects in Canada
- Job-search tips before departure
- Classification and supplementation of competencies
- Useful contacts in Canada
- Possible challenges addressed upon arrival

Source: Prognos AG

An evaluation has demonstrated the program's ongoing success. Nearly all participants find it very useful; 66 percent recommend making it mandatory for all labor migrants; three out of four state that it supported them in their hunt for a suitable job; and a follow-up survey showed that half of the CIIP graduates found employment within three months, the majority of them in a position suitable to their professional skills. Interviews with participants from the Philippines confirmed the positive impact. The program provides more certainty regarding the decision to emigrate and gives participants comprehensive information about the process ahead.

The CIIP is a pioneering and innovative program. In contrast to many other immigrant-support services, it provides not just preparatory services, but also builds a connection between preparation in the home country and the local Canadian support system from the very start. As one participant in the program said, "Canada was the only one who came to our country and is welcoming us. For me, it is very important to feel welcomed."

In 2014, the CIIP was awarded the IPAC/Deloitte Public Sector Leadership Award. A further three-year extension is probable; negotiations on this topic were opened in July 2014.

Immigrant Employment Councils (IECs)

The goal of the IECs is to bring local-level stakeholders from the business sector, politics and society together to improve the matching of skilled immigrants and Canadian employers. These bodies can thus be regarded as a catalyst insofar as they support the implementation of other organizations' programs (e.g., placement and mentoring programs) and function as network coordinators and information interfaces.

IECs exist in many of Canada's cities and provinces, including Fredericton and Moncton, Halifax, the Waterloo region, London, North Bay, Montreal, Niagara, Ottawa, Toronto, Calgary, British Columbia, Edmonton und Auckland. They do not follow a uniform model ("No two IECs are alike"), but are rather designed with an eye to local political and economic conditions. They can take the form of an independent body or be established inside an existing organization (e.g., a foundation or local agency).

The Assisting Local Leaders with Immigrant Employment Strategies (ALLIES) program, a Maytree Foundation initiative launched in 2007 to support the establishment of further IECs, is helpful in propagating this model. However, the Councils' success story begins with the Toronto Region Immigrant Employment Council (TRIEC), which was founded in 2003 by the Maytree Foundation and the Toronto City Summit Alliance. This project was triggered by an imbalance in the regional labor market: While the region was suffering from a lack of skilled workers in many areas, many highly qualified migrants were at the same time having difficulty finding employment suitable to their skills. Using this problem as a starting point, TRIEC's goal is to make the public and particularly employers aware of the phenomenon and to create an environment and programs making it possible to utilize migrants' know-how.

Making Labor Migration Fair

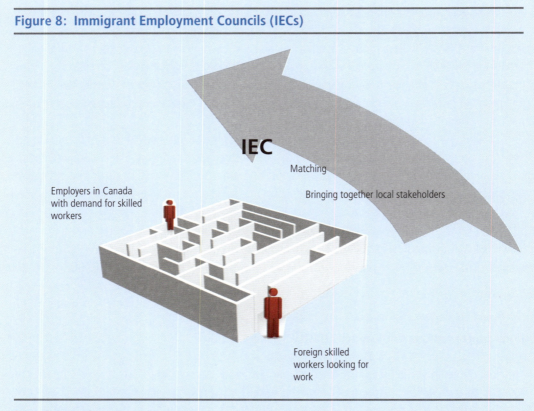

Figure 8: Immigrant Employment Councils (IECs)

Source: Prognos AG

All relevant actors in the Toronto region's labor market are brought together under the TRIEC umbrella, including employers, local authorities, training institutions and civil society representatives. Various mechanisms have been created that initially enable successful contact between employers and the skilled workers and, as a second step, facilitate the integration of the skilled workers in the labor market. In recent years, TRIEC has launched a number of different initiatives:
- In the mentoring program, skilled migrants are brought together with experienced workers from the Toronto region's labor market. During the program phase, the mentors share their knowledge, experiences and networks with the skilled immigrant workers.
- The Career Bridge Program enables migrants to participate in a paid internship of four to 12 months. A large range of internships in various areas, such as human resources, IT and marketing, are offered. Two-thirds of the interns have a masters' degree.
- The Immigrant Success Award annually honors TRIEC-associated persons or organizations that have successfully implemented innovative measures in the recruitment, employment or advancement of skilled migrants.
- TRIEC acts through numerous campaigns to raise awareness of the issue of immigration among the general public and specifically among employers.

> The project has grown steadily since its start. The mentoring program alone has successfully supported more than 7,000 skilled immigrant workers between 2004 and 2012. Around 70 percent of the participants find work in their target area within six months. Professionals who have participated in the mentoring program can attain a significant increase in their income.
>
> Funding for TRIEC is secured through a large network of policy actors from the political and business spheres.

Current developments

Extensive changes to the Canadian immigration system, intended to orient inward migration flows more strongly toward market demands, came into force in 2015. Since January, the former Expression of Interest (EOI) process has been operating in reconfigured form as the Express Entry procedure. The specific needs of the Canadian labor market are given a priority here, with the new program striving for a more targeted, employer-based and above all faster selection of the most suitable candidates, irrespective of the order of immigration applications.

An Express Entry status in combination with a valid job offer or a nomination under the Provincial Nominee Program (PNP) is now intended to expedite the application process for a permanent residence permit. A processing time of under six months is sought for qualified Express Entry candidates, who subsequently carry out their immigration under the framework of one of the existing programs (FSWP, FSTP, PNP and Canadian Experience Class, CEC). The Express Entry process is mandatory before entering the FSWP, the FSTP or the CEC. Suitable candidates are initially placed in a pool and compared with their fellow applicants. The best fits (e.g., those with capabilities that are in particular demand) may then seek a permanent residence permit. Specific job offers from employers lead to priority treatment within this selection process.

2.6 New Zealand – Incorporation of the diaspora and support for newcomers

Birthrate	2.06 (2011)
Population	4.5 million (2013)
Dependency ratio 2010 vs. 2030	22 vs. 36.6
Share of foreign-born population	24.1 % (2012)
Main countries of origin	United Kingdom (14 %), India (14 %), China (12 %) (2012)
Share of employment-related immigration (without accompanying family)	23.6 % (2012)
Immigration in the context of free movements	8.4 % (2012)
Employment rate, immigrants vs. native New Zealanders	76.1 % vs. 79.5 % (2012)
Unemployment rate, immigrants vs. native New Zealanders	7.6 % vs. 7.0 % (2012)
SGI – Labor Market Index	6.5
SGI – Integration Index	8.4

Sources: Birthrate: OECD 2014a; population: World Bank 2014; dependency ratio: United Nations 2013; share of foreign-born population, main countries of origin, employment-related immigration, immigration in context of freedom of movement: OECD 2014b; employment rates, unemployment rates: OECD 2014c; SGI – Labor Market Index and SGI – Integration Index Bertelsmann Stiftung 2014

Context of labor migration

New Zealand annually gains around 45,000 residents through immigration. At the same time, however, many young New Zealanders leave to live and work abroad. An estimated three-quarters of the New Zealand diaspora lives in neighboring Australia. Workers are for this reason needed throughout the country in the services sector (particularly in tourism), in the export-oriented agriculture and forestry sector, and in the food industry.

Nearly one-quarter of New Zealand's 4.5 million residents were born elsewhere. This is a comparatively high share and demonstrates the importance of migration to the country. Labor immigration in particular plays a vital role, accounting for 24 percent of immigration to New Zealand.

Indications of successful labor-market integration policy for migrants include the comparable unemployment and employment rates among immigrants and native New Zealanders.

The implementation of the Immigration Amendment Act in 1991 introduced a point system for the selection of migrants seeking permanent immigration. Under this system, foreign workers who want to work permanently in New Zealand must attain a minimum number of points assigned in categories such as age, skills, English-language knowledge, previous (study or work) stays in New Zealand, and employability.

With the advent of the 1990s, the allocation of points began to be handled more restrictively. Since that time, the government has used the New Zealand Residence Programme (NZRP) to set targets with regard to how many permanent-immigration slots will be provided on the basis of needed skills and international humanitarian obligations. In addition, with the implementation of the Citizenship Amendment Act in 2005, eligibility for citizenship was granted only after five years, instead of three years, as previously.

By contrast, opportunities for temporary labor migration have been expanded. In addition to the development of the Working Holiday Visa, the Silver Fern Visa was introduced in 2010, enabling young skilled migrants to obtain a temporary work permit. In addition, numerous other opportunities to obtain temporary work in New Zealand are currently in place (including the Essential Skills Work Visa, the Study to Work Visa, the Work Exchange Stream and the Free Trade Agreement Special Work Categories, among others). In this regard, New Zealand's approach is to let temporary work permission lead to permanent labor migration.

The government's 2004 introduction of the Settlement Support New Zealand (SSNZ) program, operated in conjunction with migrant organizations, created a means of providing immigrants with better local-level support and facilitating the integration process. Activities focus on the long-term integration of migrants with skills needed by New Zealand's economy. To this end, offices serving as contact points were opened around the country. A central aspect of the SSNZ's work is the preparation of information for newcomers and employers: Handouts and Internet sites provide information on the residency-establishment process, while providing guidance and regionally focused information on issues such as (further) education and employment opportunities, contact points for job searches, opportunities for improving English-language capabilities, medical care and housing searches.

Due to the persistent shortage of labor in New Zealand's two major export industries, horticulture and viticulture, the Recognised Seasonal Employers Scheme (RSE) was put in place in 2007, under which seasonal laborers can work in New Zealand for a period of seven to nine months. The program is open to all Pacific Forum countries as well as to countries from which New Zealand employers had recruited before the program's start (e.g., Indonesia, Thailand and Malaysia).

Program elements provide workers with everyday knowledge about New Zealand's economic and social aspects, and offer additional information on literacy, creating small businesses and health and nutrition. Since 2011, New Zealand has also promoted technical cooperation with participating Pacific Island states through the initiative, with measures including training programs, workshops and delegations of public officeholders to New Zealand. Plans for individual country projects have been created that set thematic priorities for development cooperation in the context of the Strengthening Pacific Partnerships Initiative (SPPI). In addition to the island nations and the New Zealand government ministries, SPPI partners include the World Bank, the New Zealand Horticulture Industry Training Organization (ITO) and the New Zealand Council of Trade Unions.

Against the backdrop of the country's high emigration rates, the "Kiwi Expat Association Incorporated (Kea) – New Zealand's Global Network" was founded in 2001. Kea's goal is to strengthen bonds between New Zealanders and their homeland through the creation of a emigrant network and the development of contacts between emigrants and actors in New Zealand, thus facilitating investment by members of the diaspora and the return of skilled workers. The network currently counts more than 100,000 members and is publicly funded.

Current developments

New Zealand wants to expand its appeal as a country of destination in order to contend successfully in the international competition for skilled workers.

In addition to the creation of additional (bilateral) temporary labor programs – for example, in the context of free-trade agreements with China, Hong Kong and Thailand – the focus has above all been on the continued development of the immigration system and of better mechanisms for the regulation of immigration.

In 2014, the OECD issued several recommendations for the New Zealand immigration system and for the management of labor migration in New Zealand. Given the large number of temporary-work-visa categories, a merging of categories was suggested in order to make immigrants' visa-application process more transparent. In addition, with regard to the management of temporary labor migration, further improvements in the information on job vacancies and job seekers are needed.

2.7 The Netherlands – Civil society approaches to migrant integration

Birthrate	1.76 (2011)
Population	16.8 million (2013)
Dependency ratio 2010 vs. 2030	25.3 vs. 45.4
Share of foreign-born population	11.5 % (2012)
Main countries of origin	Poland (16 %), Germany (8 %), China (4 %), Bulgaria (4 %), UK (4 %), Spain (4 %) (2012)
Share of employment-related immigration (without accompanying family)	8.8 % (2012)
Immigration in the context of free movements	65.6 % (2012)
Employment rate, immigrant vs. native Dutch	66.6 % vs. 79.7 % (2012)
Unemployment rate, immigrant vs. native Dutch	10.6 % vs. 4.5 % (2012)
SGI – Labor Market Index	7.6
SGI – Integration Index	7.3

Sources: Birthrate: OECD 2014a; population: World Bank 2014; dependency ratio: United Nations 2013; share of foreign-born population, main countries of origin, employment-related immigration, immigration in context of freedom of movement: OECD 2014b; employment rates, unemployment rates: OECD 2014c; SGI – Labor Market Index and SGI – Integration Index: Bertelsmann Stiftung 2014

Context of labor migration

About 11.5 percent of the Netherlands' 16.7 million current residents were born in another country. In 2012, pure labor migration from third countries accounted for approximately 9 percent of total immigration. Family reunification, in turn, constituted 20 percent of immigration. The 10.6 percent unemployment rate among immigrants (2012) is significantly higher than that among the native Dutch, at 4.5 percent, indicating challenges with regard to labor-market integration.

The Netherlands' current immigration policy is focused almost exclusively on high-skilled individuals, while immigration for those with low or medium skills is difficult. The guidelines governing this issue are contained in the Highly Skilled Migrant Scheme and the EU Blue Card Directive. Both programs have the same goal: to recruit highly skilled workers from states outside the European Union. However, they differ in certain respects.

The Highly Skilled Migrant Scheme has enabled Dutch employers to recruit highly skilled foreign workers since 2004. In order to obtain a work permit, individuals over the age of 30 who are interested in immigration must show an annual income of at least €52,643. For immigrants under 30 years of age, the minimum salary is €38,466; for foreigners who have just completed a course of study in the Netherlands, this floor is €27,566. Applications for a work and residence permit must be accompanied by a work contract that states the amount of salary to be earned. Participation in the program does not require a college degree. In addition, immigrants can bring their families, who are also allowed to engage in work activities in the Netherlands. This applies to married or unmarried partners as well as to minor children.

Since 2011, the EU Blue Card Directive has also been focused on highly skilled workers who fulfill certain conditions. Applicants must show an employment contract valid for at least one year as well as annual income of at least €61,000 and a college degree. After a five-year period of residence in the Netherlands, immigrants under either the EU Blue Card Directive or the Highly Skilled Migrant Scheme gain a right to permanent of residence within the European Union. Because requirements are looser in the Highly Skilled Migrant Scheme, the EU Blue Card Directive is rarely utilized in the Netherlands.

International companies that want to invest in the Netherlands are provided with support from the Netherlands Foreign Investment Agency, which provides counseling particularly on issues related to labor migration. In addition, the Foreign Investors Scheme offers investors who want to invest more than €1.25 million in Dutch companies, stocks or mutual funds the ability to apply for a residence permit. However, there has been little demand for this program to date due to elaborate screening procedures aimed at preventing money-laundering activities.

International students who have graduated in the Netherlands" receive a one-year residence permit for the purposes of a job search. In 2013, low retention rates prompted the Dutch Social and Economic Council (SER) to create the "Make it in the Netherlands" strategic plan, with the aim of persuading more international students to remain in the Netherlands. In addition, since 2009, graduates from the top 200 universities in the world (according to the current QS world ranking) can obtain a one-year residence permit for the purposes of a job search.

Current developments

For many years, the Netherlands cultivated a very liberal understanding of migration, placing a high value on tolerance toward other cultures and religions. The first noticeable changes in migration policy came in the 1990s. From this point forward, the focus was placed on immigrants' integration into the labor market and society, as a large share of migrants lived in perpetually poor socioeconomic living conditions. At the end of the 1990s, the Netherlands was the first country to introduce mandatory language courses. The 9/11 terror attacks portended a significant turning point in the country's conception of migration policy. Right-wing parties – particularly those of the subsequently murdered politician Pim Fortuyn and, in recent years, of Geert Wilders, which have opposed immigration above all from culturally Muslim areas – received a swell of support and have ensured that immigration remains a controversial issue through the present day.

In the meantime, a new fundamental consensus seems to have emerged that differs from the previously held concept of multiculturalism. The integration of immigrants into mainstream society is considered a top priority, with learning the Dutch language and recognizing certain fundamental majority-society values being viewed as the most important goals.

Nevertheless, there are promising approaches in the Netherlands coming from civil society, many of which bolster the notion of a fairly designed labor-migration system. The Hague Process on Refugees and Migration (THP) is one such example. This independent non-profit organization based in The Hague is supported by a global network of individuals, institutions and public and civil society organizations. The THP's core goal is to stimulate an exchange of knowledge between stakeholders in the area of immigration. In 2002, the organization received formal recognition from Kofi Annan and the United Nations General Assembly in the context of the Declaration of The Hague on the Future of Refugee and Migration Policy.

Making Labor Migration Fair

As a part of its Strategic Plan 2010–2015, the THP is seeking to forge partnerships between cities and local business communities with the aim of improving migrants' integration processes. An initial pilot project has been begun in Rotterdam; here, the THP, the Port of Rotterdam, the city of Rotterdam and Erasmus University are developing business-city partnerships with the goal of improving migrants' labor-market integration and thus countering labor shortages in certain sectors (e.g., in IT, health care and transportation). The project is financed in part by the Dutch Ministry of Foreign Affairs.

Another example is offered by the Temporary Return of Qualified Nationals (TRQN) program, created by the International Organization for Migration Netherlands, which is intended to help migrants living in the Netherlands employ their knowledge productively in their countries of origin.

Temporary Return of Qualified Nationals (TRQN)

The TRQN program started in 2002 as an initiative sponsored and funded by the Dutch Ministry of Foreign Affairs and is operationally run by the International Organization for Migration Netherlands (IOM). The program seeks to build bridges between skilled immigrant workers and their home countries. To this end, migrants are given support to cover living expenses when they return to their countries of origin for a limited time in order to employ their knowledge in capacity-building within government and non-government institutions.

Figure 9: Temporary Return of Qualified Nationals (TRQN)

Target countries of TRQN III:
- Afghanistan
- Armenia
- Cape Verde
- Georgia
- Ghana
- Iraq
- Morocco
- Somalia
- Sudan

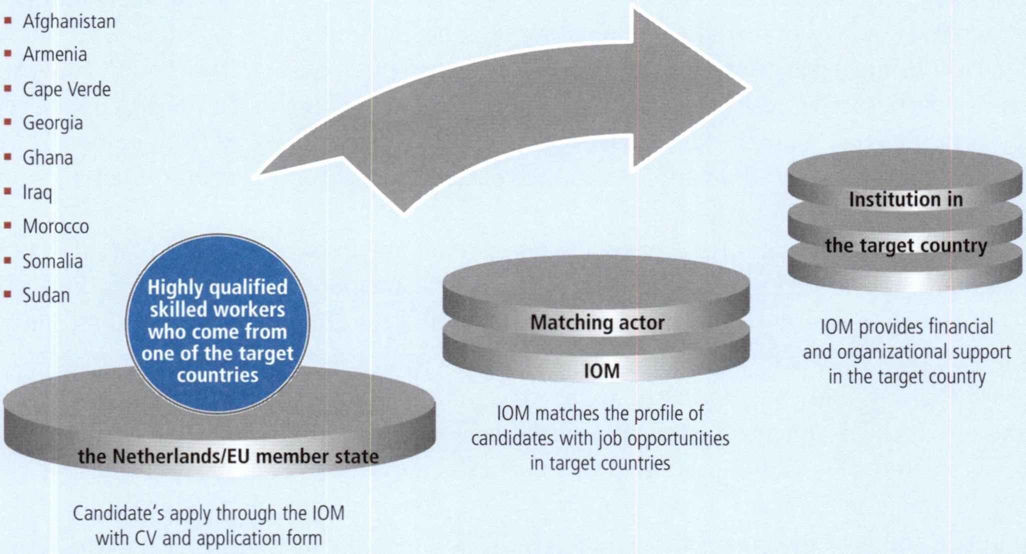

Highly qualified skilled workers who come from one of the target countries
the Netherlands/EU member state
Candidate's apply through the IOM with CV and application form

Matching actor
IOM
IOM matches the profile of candidates with job opportunities in target countries

Institution in the target country
IOM provides financial and organizational support in the target country

Source: Prognos AG

Following a limited pilot phase with Afghanistan as a partner country between 2002 and 2005, TRQN is currently being carried out in a third program phrase (2012–2015). Current target countries are Afghanistan, Armenia, Cape Verde, Georgia, Ghana, Iraq, Morocco, Somalia and Sudan.

The program has a demand-driven design. First, the needs of the partner country are examined, and the skilled workers (generally with at least a bachelor's degree) are deployed on the basis of demand and according to their own professional experience.

The current phase of the program aims at 400 placements, with each participant provided with €1,500 per month for rent and living costs, as well as €100 for mobility costs. In the previous program phases, a total of 530 skilled workers were placed.

An evaluation of the pilot phase by the University of Maastricht indicated success in the target country through successful knowledge transfer, capacity-building and the effective utilization of the diaspora members resident in the Netherlands. As an additional outcome, the report noted that the self-esteem of participants as well as their career prospects in the Netherlands were improved. In interviews with project participants, they confirmed their high level of motivation to pass on their knowledge and experience, in this way contributing to the development and stability of their home country (migrants of change). However, the program is also assessed realistically: Despite the positive impact in the partner countries, the actual influence on capacity-building is limited due to the small number of participants. A continuation of the evaluation is desirable, as there is currently a lack of impact-related data on the three program phases.

2.8 Sweden – Consistent mobility policy

Birthrate	1.90 (2011)
Population	9.6 million (2013)
Dependency ratio 2010 vs. 2030	31.2 vs. 40.8
Share of foreign-born population	15.5 % (2012)
Main countries of origin	Syria (6 %), Afghanistan (6 %), Somalia (5 %), Poland (5 %) (2012)
Share of employment-related immigration (without accompanying family)	5.3 % (2012)
Immigration in the context of free movements	32.3 % (2012)
Employment rate, immigrants vs. native Swedes	67.9 % vs. 85.9 % (2012)
Unemployment rate, immigrants vs. native Swedes	16.1 % vs. 6.5 % (2012)
SGI – Labor Market Index	6.9
SGI – Integration Index	6.4

Sources: Birthrate: OECD 2014a; population: World Bank 2014; dependency ratio: United Nations 2013; share of foreign-born population, main countries of origin, employment-related immigration, immigration in context of freedom of movement: OECD 2014b; employment rates, unemployment rates: OECD 2014c; SGI – Labor Market Index and SGI – Integration Index: Bertelsmann Stiftung 2014

Making Labor Migration Fair

Context of labor migration

With a share of about 16 percent of the population born outside the country as of 2012, Sweden ranked in the middle of the states considered here. Migrants' most common countries of origin today are Syria, Afghanistan, Somalia and Poland.

The Migrant Integration Policy Index (MIPEX), an instrument for the comparative evaluation of integration policy in the 27 EU member states, Norway, Switzerland, Canada and the United States, gives its top place to Sweden's integration policies. Of the 31 countries surveyed, Sweden – with 83 out of a possible 100 points – was ranked first in the overall evaluation (the EU average was just 52 points). Indeed, the country scored above average in all areas, but particularly well in the areas of labor-market mobility (first place, 100 points), education (first place, 77 points), access to citizenship (second place, 79 points), long-term residence permits (third place, 78 points) and anti-discrimination (third place, 88 points).

However, Sweden too faces challenges with regard to labor-market integration. In 2012, for example, the employment rate for immigrants was significantly under the average for native-born Swedes. Immigrants' unemployment rate, at around 16 percent, was above the average.

Since the turn of the millennium, positive economic growth and the associated rising need for skilled workers have ensured that discussions about immigration have focused increasingly on the issue's economic aspects. In particular, the Swedish business community has pointed to the difficulty in filling vacancies in numerous sectors. According to studies carried out by the Public Employment Service, the Swedish Migration Board and Statistics Sweden, shortages of skilled workers exist in 63 occupational groups.

This trend affects highly skilled professional categories, such as doctors, psychologists, teachers and nurses, as well as occupations in which comparatively lower skill levels are needed. For this reason, at the end of 2008, a reform of the immigration law was launched under the auspices of the Ministry of Justice that was supported by all political parties, the social partners and associations. The outcome of this process has been an example of policy creating a broadly coherent migration-policy framework, which has in turn received considerable international attention.

Sweden's mobility-promoting migration policy

Over the course of the last decade, Sweden's migration policy was reformed with a strong demand orientation so as to facilitate employers' ability to recruit skilled foreign workers. At the same time, a legal framework was created that takes account of the central aspects of fairness underlying the triple win. Thus, equality of working conditions for skilled native-born and immigrant workers is a core condition for immigration. If this is fulfilled, immigrants receive broad-ranging residence and working rights at an early stage. It is essential in this regard that the legal status thus achieved is retained even in the case of migration to a third country or a temporary return to the country of origin. In this regard, the Swedish model supports individual mobility decisions in the sense of circular migration.

As a September 2010 fact sheet from the Swedish Ministry of Justice additionally notes: "Circular migration can be understood as back-and-forth mobility which can promote development in both countries of origin and destination, as well as benefit migrants themselves." Significant here is that the circularity is not mandated by legislation or other programs, but is rather driven by the skilled workers' own mobility needs and opportunities.

In practice, the Swedish Migration Board checks for the existence of a binding job offer from a Swedish employer that conforms to the working conditions of comparable native-born workers. The unions are also involved in this process. If the board makes a positive assessment, an initially temporary two-year residence and work permit can be granted, which will be automatically extended for two years and ultimately made permanent if employment is continued. In the case of temporary job loss, this legal status will be maintained for three to six months to cover a job-search phase. The Swedish Migration Board is also obliged to check that promised working conditions are complied with and to disclose any abuses. Additional features of the regulations include the following:

- The possibility of dual citizenship
- A facilitation of foreign remittance transfers
- An avoidance of double taxation, and
- The portability of social-security benefits.

The reform process was initiated by the center-right government's migration minister, Tobias Billström, who in 2006 and 2009 convened two commissions tasked with developing the reform. This successfully produced a cross-party and cross-departmental understanding of how migration policy should be structured and implemented on all administrative levels. The unions' approval of a demand-oriented migration policy enabled the above-noted principle of equality of treatment for skilled domestic and foreign workers as well as the joint oversight by the Migration Board and the unions themselves.

Since that time, the Swedish Migration Board has undergone a service-oriented organizational reform with the aim of speeding up the review and approval process. The Public Employment Service developed a transition mechanism enabling asylum applicants to switch tracks to the labor-migrant immigration procedures. The inclusion of the development-assistance ministry took place within the context of the Policy Coherence for Development (PCD) program, a mechanism instituted in 2008 for reviewing all proposed legislation on the basis of their development-policy implications.

For this reason, the reform can be regarded as a politically coordinated overall strategy that comprises a variety of different legislative vehicles and that spreads its philosophy through various levels of the country's administration. This positive overall assessment is shared by all political parties, the social partners and associations. This makes it likely that the policy will be continued without interruption by the government newly elected in September 2014.

However, opportunities for further optimization are being discussed, such as a more comprehensive oversight of cases of abuse related to the failure to provide equal working conditions and the appropriate sanctions for employers. Moreover, there is still not enough reliable data to enable statements to be made about the skills groups and sectors benefiting from the legislation. However, the IT, health care and nursing sectors as well as other areas requiring lower skill levels, such as the food and agriculture industries, are mentioned with particular frequency.

> Overall, immigration amounts to about 12,000 to 15,000 labor migrants annually, thus remaining behind expectations. There is no current data on actual return- and further-migration rates. Nevertheless, Sweden's immigration-law reform is internationally regarded as a coherent and proactive migration policy that has created the necessary conditions for fair migration among skilled workers. In addition, the strict demand orientation, coupled with the observance of equal-treatment principles, is attracting attention because it ensures suitable employment for skilled immigrant workers.

Current developments

For decades, Sweden was held up as a model of successful immigration and integration policy. A relatively open immigration policy, social benefits that were generous by international standards, as well as integration offerings such as free language courses seemed to ensure the policy's success. It was therefore a shock for many Swedes in 2013 when serious unrest erupted in the poorer suburbs of major cities, with young migrants being the primary participants – images that people in Europe previously associated only with French and English suburbs. The unrest threw a spotlight on the weak point of Sweden's integration policy: the high rate of unemployment among young immigrants.

As they have become more significant, these problems have also had an effect on immigration-policy debates. Voices seeking to reinstate tighter limits on immigration are multiplying. The Sweden Democrats, a party characterized by distinct anti-immigrant rhetoric, among other features, has become the third-strongest party in the country.

2.9 Switzerland – Balancing migration and development policy

Birthrate	1.52 (2011)
Population	8.1 million (2013)
Dependency ratio 2010 vs. 2030	27.2 vs. 38.1
Share of foreign-born population	27.9 % (2012)
Main countries of origin	Germany (19 %), Portugal (13 %), Italy (9 %) (2012)
Share of employment-related immigration (without accompanying family)	1.7 % (2012)
Immigration in the context of free movements	77.0 % (2012)
Employment rate, immigrants vs. native Swiss	78.0 % vs. 85.8 % (2012)
Unemployment rate, immigrants vs. native Swiss	7.1 % vs. 3.1 % (2012)
SGI – Labor Market Index	8.5
SGI – Integration Index	7.0

Sources: Birthrate: OECD 2014a; population: World Bank 2014; dependency ratio: United Nations 2013; share of foreign-born population, main countries of origin, employment-related immigration, immigration in context of freedom of movement: OECD 2014b; employment rates, unemployment rates: OECD 2014c; SGI – Labor Market Index and SGI – Integration Index: Bertelsmann Stiftung 2014

Context of labor migration

Switzerland's non-native population is composed mainly of nationals of European Union or European Free Trade Agreement countries. Additional immigrants originate mainly from other European countries. In 2012, the country's foreign-born population accounted for more than a quarter of the whole, the largest such share among the 10 countries presented here. In 2012, Germans were the largest immigrant group. The West Balkan diaspora is also comparatively large, as a consequence of the wars in the former Yugoslavia.

With regard to labor-market conditions for immigrants, the unemployment rate in Switzerland is comparatively low overall, and employment rates are accordingly high. Yet here, too, a pattern can be seen in which native-born Swiss are less often unemployed than are immigrants.

In the course of the strong postwar economic upswing, the recruitment of skilled foreign workers was promoted in a targeted way, and immigration rose to a previously unprecedented extent. This growth has continued through the present day. However, immigration policy has been influenced with growing frequency by xenophobic voices in recent decades, rendering it increasingly restrictive. At the end of the 20th century, a dual admissions system was introduced that privileged immigration from EU and EFTA countries and limited migration from other countries primarily to the highly skilled and for family reunification.

Despite an overall restrictive immigration policy, the Federal Council improved the coherence of Switzerland's foreign-policy approach to migration in 2011. The aim is to coordinate development-policy activities with measures for the international management of legal migration. The following serve as guiding principles:
- Holistic approach: Recognize migration as a global phenomenon
- Partnership-based approach: Intensify cooperation with origin, transit and destination countries
- Whole-of-government approach: Ensure a coherent use of domestic- and foreign-policy instruments as well as close interdepartmental coordination

Backed by a report on the issue of international cooperation on migration, responsibilities on this issue were bundled and backed by a binding political mandate. Since that time, interdepartmental cooperation has taken place through the plenum of the Interdepartmental Working Group for Migration, the Committee for International Migration Cooperation and the various working groups for regions, federal states and individual issues of focus.

Current developments

In recent years, two popular referendums that concerned Swiss migration policy caused significant international stirs. At the end of 2011, an initiative "For the Deportation of Criminal Foreigners" was adopted, followed in February 2014 by an initiative "Against Mass Immigration." The latter instructed the legislature to limit immigration by setting annual caps and quotas on the basis of Switzerland's overall economic interests. Implementation may fundamentally limit future opportunities for the recruitment of foreign workers. The initiative also calls for changing bilateral agreements between Switzerland and the European Union that entail the freedom of movement for persons. The ultimate strength of the limitations resulting from the initiative remains unclear, as implementation is still pending.

2.10 USA – Public-private partnerships and domestic diaspora support

Birthrate	1.89 (2011)
Population	316.1 million (2013)
Dependency ratio 2010 vs. 2030	21.8 vs. 36.8
Share of foreign-born population	13.0 % (2012)
Main countries of origin	Mexico (14 %), China (8 %), India (6 %), Philippines (6 %) (2012)
Share of employment-related immigration (without accompanying family)	6.4 % (2012)
Immigration in the context of free movements	–
Employment rate, immigrants vs. native-born Americans	71.3 % vs. 72.4 % (2012)
Unemployment rate, immigrants vs. native-born Americans	8.1 % vs. 8.3 % (2012)
SGI – Labor Market Index	5.7
SGI – Integration Index	7.6

Sources: Birthrate: OECD 2014a; population: World Bank 2014; dependency ratio: United Nations 2013; share of foreign-born population, main countries of origin, employment-related immigration, immigration in context of freedom of movement: OECD 2014b; employment rates, unemployment rates: OECD 2014c; SGI – Labor Market Index and SGI – Integration Index: Bertelsmann Stiftung 2014

Context of labor migration

The United States is the most important destination country for immigration worldwide. In 2012, about 41 million immigrants lived there. The dominant form of immigration is family reunification. With a share of more than 70 percent, this form of immigration has a significantly higher importance in the United States than in other OECD countries. Employment-related immigration, by contrast, plays a rather subsidiary role. In 2012, nearly 30 percent of the immigrants living in the United States came from Mexico. In addition, China and India are important countries of origin. The significance of European immigration has fallen since the 1960s.

With regard to labor-market integration, the immigrant and native-born populations receive largely equal treatment. Thus, immigrants with official U.S. resident status have unrestricted access to the labor market. In contrast to the other countries examined here, the employment rates of immigrants and native-born Americans are approximately the same. However, immigrants are more often employed in the service sector, in construction and in manufacturing, and less often as managers or professionals.

The U.S. immigration system is today considered to be rigid and inefficient. For skilled workers who want to enter the country on the basis of employment-related immigration, one way to permanent-resident status is the residence permit for highly skilled and unskilled workers, which is divided into various categories with temporary and permanent durations.

Generally, a concrete offer from an employer is required. The processes by which visas are granted are quite lengthy.

Legal migration in the United States is subject to caps that have been unchanged since the middle of the 1990s and that include specific limits for permanent labor migration as well as for family-based immigration, for example. Quotas for employment-related immigration opportunities are thus very limited and largely fail to cover the U.S. economy's demand for skilled workers. Thus, the annual quota for the H1-B visa for highly skilled workers (good for three years, with an option for an additional three-year extension), which is very popular among businesses, is generally exhausted after only a few weeks.

As with all employment-related visas, long delays are difficult to reconcile with the needs of employers. The North American Free Trade Agreement (NAFTA) enables skilled workers exclusively from Canada and Mexico to take up employment arranged before arrival, which represents a flexible alternative to the rigid and lengthy general visa regime.

Nurses Now International is a project that originated out of U.S.-Mexico cooperation and that took advantage of NAFTA's visa-easing features. The project's aim was to use Mexican nurses to meet the need for bilingual nursing personnel in the United States.

Nurses Now International (NNI)

NNI was founded and funded in the United States by MexConex, a group of U.S. and Mexican companies led by Blue Equity LLC. The core idea was to meet the outstanding need in the United States particularly for bilingual health care professionals through the recruitment, training and subsequent placement of Mexican nurses in Texas hospitals. Despite broad popularity among the participants and the U.S. hospitals, the program ran into financial constraints due to a lack of cofinancing by hospitals or the U.S. health care system, and it was ultimately discontinued because profit levels for the private funders (Blue Equity) were too low. Nevertheless, the high level of satisfaction on the part of the nurses and the employers makes NII a good-practice example with regard to the design of migration practices.

The program took advantage of the geographical proximity of the two countries as well as the potential for cooperation represented by the growth of the Latin American population in the United States. The target group was skilled Mexican nurses with some career experience and a basic knowledge of English. They were admitted in a three-step training program in order to engage in the technical preparation for the NCLEX exam, a requirement for legal employment in U.S. hospitals, while still in Mexico.

Language instruction and basic and advanced medical training took place in Mexico. An intensive training program to prepare for the certification process followed in the United States. Overall, this process lasted three years and was funded in the United States from the second stage on by NNI and Blue Equity. Only the first stage required payment by participants, for a total of $37 per month.

Placement in U.S. hospitals followed the completion of the training program. This assignment was limited to three years, with a possible extension of an additional two years, and was based on the TN visa, a temporary work permit made possible under the NAFTA agreement. At the end of the program, the hospitals could make their own contracts with the nurses.

Figure 10: Nurses Now International (NNI)

Source: Prognos AG

During the course of the program's three-year existence, 40 skilled workers were successfully placed in the United States, according to the program manager. Despite this small number, the program is well regarded. In addition to its contribution to meeting the U.S. need for (particularly bilingual) skilled workers, it bolstered the nurses' long-term career prospects in Mexico, supported capacity-building and knowledge transfer, and strengthened Mexico's training and advanced-education programs by providing training in the country of origin. Moreover, experts point out that the United States benefited from clear cost advantages, as it is many times more expensive to train nurses in the United States.

The main advantage for nurses and their families lay in the much higher wages available in the United States. Moreover, the nurses' domestic and foreign career prospects improved following completion of the program. The nurses themselves cite the significantly higher esteem given to the profession in the United States as a great benefit to them. However, they add that contact with their home country was extremely important, so typically envisaged a return migration.

NNI was awarded the seal of the Alliance for Ethical International Recruitment Practices. The program is consistent with the concept of global skill partnerships, although it does not use this term itself.

The 9/11 terror attacks have in recent years led to a link between immigration policy and internal-security issues. Numerous laws tightening border controls and facilitating the deportation and detention of immigrants have been enacted in the years since. In this context, the issue of illegal immigration has again played an increasingly prominent role on the political agenda. A growing demand for labor and the low caps on legal immigration continue to encourage illegal immigration. One of the biggest challenges in the United States is the integration of what is estimated to be more than 11 million illegal immigrants.

Current developments

The legal-immigration system in the United States no longer meets the economy's requirements. This increasingly demands a rethinking of immigration policy. The U.S. Bureau of Labor Statistics forecasts a shortage of about 10 million skilled workers by 2020 in the industrial sector alone. Although numerous attempts at piecemeal reform of the rigid and inefficient immigration system have been made, no comprehensive reform at the national level has yet succeeded. In particular, the rising demand for labor has conflicted with the growing security concerns and the low quotas for temporary and permanent residence permits.

However, recent developments could lead to a turnaround. In the 2012 elections, the great number of Americans with an immigrant background who were also eligible to vote helped rekindle debate on the reform of immigration law. The result was a new legal initiative that was passed by the U.S. Senate in 2013 and is currently in front of the House of Representatives. Key themes of the initiative, in addition to the general revision of the current immigration system (e.g., the expansion of legal-immigration opportunities), include internal security – in particular, the tightening of border controls – and the legalization of illegal immigrants.

Although, at the overall political level, aspects of fairness regarding labor migration are associated most strongly with the protection of the domestic population, a number of business-sector and civil society measures in the United States are promoting the concept of fair labor migration from the perspective of migrants and countries of origin. An example of this is the work of the International diaspora Engagement Alliance (IdEA).

International diaspora Engagement Alliance (IdEA)

The non-profit organization IdEA was established by then-U.S. Secretary of State Hillary Clinton at the Global Diaspora Forum in May 2011. It is managed as a public-private partnership between the U.S. State Department, the United States Agency for International Development (USAID) and the Calvert Foundation (which provides direct organizational management).

The task of the IdEA network is to facilitate initiatives by U.S.-resident diaspora communities to provide economic and social support to their various home countries. The network is broad and addresses the areas of investment and entrepreneurship, innovation, and volunteerism and philanthropy. A current focus supports the creation of small businesses through crowdfunding; entrepreneurs are given the opportunity to present their business ideas and seek funds at "marketplace events." In addition to financial support, diaspora-community individuals or institutions can use their knowledge

> online to support entrepreneurs in the implementation of their business idea. A mentoring program for this purpose has been running for more than a year and a half. In addition, the network carries out diaspora-networking measures, such as the annual Global Diaspora Forum.
>
> Internal reviews attest that the IdEA network contributes, on the one hand, to the networking of diaspora communities in the United States and strengthens their identities. On the other hand, it successfully mediates between support needs in countries of origin and diaspora members' abilities to contribute. The networking and information transparency, the idea of "entrepreneurship instead of welfare" in countries of origin, and the crowdfunding-based financing are regarded as important factors in this success.
>
> The importance of diasporas for countries of origin is made clear in the case of Macedonia, for example. More than 500,000 people from Macedonia live abroad, with remittances' share in GDP over the last 10 years falling by between 13 and 21 percent. The United Macedonian Diaspora (UMD), a member of the IdEA network, advocates for Macedonia's relations with other states and sees itself as a link between emigrant Macedonians and their home country. Membership in IdEA offers the opportunity to network with other organizations and learn from their work: "IdEA is a great mechanism to learn about others who do similar work."
>
> IdEA's funding is secure through September 2015. The organization currently has two staff positions covering all substantive and organizational tasks. Because of the very positive response, this low level of staffing represents a limiting factor for the network's further development. The organization is thus considering a strategic shift in the direction of a substantive or regional focus for future activities.

3 Origin countries' migration strategies

The recruitment of foreign workers risks undermining development potential within countries of origin by reducing their base of skilled workers. At the same time, workers living abroad can represent an important economic resource for origin countries insofar as they can benefit from remittances or knowledge and technology transfers.

The following chapter switches perspective to describe origin countries' efforts to develop targeted migration policies. In this regard, the Philippines offers an outstanding example in international comparison. However, countries such as Mauritius, Thailand, Mexico and Honduras also seek to mobilize the resources of their skilled expatriate workers for their national benefit.

3.1 Emigration policies in the Philippines

In the 1970s, the Philippines experienced a strong wave of emigration as a result of stagnant economic growth, an increasing population and a simultaneously rising need for skilled workers abroad. The government of then-President Ferdinand Marcos responded to this situation in 1974 with a program promoting work abroad. The program was originally aimed at Filipinos' temporary emigration. In the years since, the number of permanent emigrants has overtaken the number of those living only temporarily abroad. In 2011, around 10.5 million Filipinos were working overseas, or more than 11 percent of the country's entire population. Around 50 percent of today's emigrants are skilled workers with a university degree. The United States and Canada are among the most popular destination countries.

Due to the low level of foreign investment and the decline in development aid, the Philippines is today reliant on the emigration of the country's workers. Their remittances in 2013 amounted to around $25 million and are an important factor in the country's economy. In recent years, this has represented about 10 percent of the Philippines' GDP and thus contribute more to growth than do domestic economic sectors. The remittances enable migrants' families to meet living expenses and invest in the education of their children. One in four households in the Philippines receives international remittances.

The Philippine government supports people in every phase of the migration process (recruitment, emigration, overseas employment, reintegration upon return). The Philippine Overseas Employment Administration (POEA) is responsible for this processes and additionally licenses, regulates and oversees private recruitment agencies in order to protect labor migrants from excessively high placement fees.

While the POEA assists with all preparations before departure, the Overseas Workers' Welfare Administration (OWWA) is responsible for migrants who are already abroad. The OWWA helps with job placement and remittances, and it provides further-education and career-advancement offerings.

The Philippine government's Technical Education and Skills Development Agency (TESDA) is responsible for vocational education and training. The vocational-education and certification systems developed by TESDA not only serve the domestic labor market, but are also consciously oriented toward labor markets overseas in order to facilitate emigration. In 2007, TESDA created the Language Skills Institute, which offers language and culture courses for popular destination countries. Participation can be financed through government grants.

The rights of skilled workers living abroad are also protected by the Migrant Workers and Overseas Filipinos Act, adopted in 1995, which defines legal and social standards for employment abroad. In essence, the labor migration law has the following goals:
- Enabling workers to be posted in safe destination countries
- Supporting emigrants with legal matters
- Preventing illegal recruitment activities
- Supporting Filipino migrants in the protection of their rights and freedoms, and
- Providing migrants with the resources necessary for successful emigration.

In addition, the government seeks to protect the rights of skilled emigrant workers through bilateral, multilateral and international agreements. To this end, it is a member of the U.N. International Convention on the Protection of the Rights of All Migrant Workers and Members of Their Families, among other agreements. In March 2013, the Philippines concluded an agreement with Germany governing the recruitment of 500 Filipino nurses. The agreement, which also covers the triple-win project described in the previous chapter, aims to ensure that the Filipino health care workers' qualifications will be recognized in Germany, and that they can be employed on an equal basis with German nurses. To this end, they receive a work permit and a temporary, renewable residence permit.

The Philippine government has received international praise for its active support of emigration. Nevertheless, experts note difficulties in implementing the legal regulations. In addition to the unmonitored recruitment of workers, illegal migration channels represent a challenge for the Philippine government. In addition, there is the risk that migrants will fall into debt as a result of illegal or too-high placement fees. Despite the Philippine government's efforts to protect the rights of Filipinos abroad, the country's labor migrants often fall victim to exploitation, violence and discrimination. About a third of labor migrants are women, who often work in unregulated employment environments. Unskilled labor, in particular, should thus be better protected in the future.

In addition, experts see a middle- to long-term risk of brain drain in the one-sided policies focusing on skilled-worker emigration. As the number of permanent emigrants now exceeds the number of temporary migrants, strategies must be developed to provide incentives for the return of skilled workers and to facilitate their reintegration. The ability of Filipino migrants to acquire dual citizenship and participate in national elections represents one step already taken in this direction, and it should help strengthen ties to the home country.

The Business Advisory Council of the Asia-Pacific Economic Cooperation (APEC) has also developed a draft model (the "Earn, Learn and Return" Model) for strengthening legal migration channels and promoting the return of migrants to their home countries. Under this model, uniform and sector-specific standards for recruitment and the certification of qualifications and workers' postings are intended to render the migration process more transparent and effective. In addition, migrants would have access to social protections in all APEC member states and have the opportunity to travel regularly to their home country. Service fees would no longer be paid by the migrants themselves, but instead by their employers. The draft model also envisions inexpensive remittance, communication and travel opportunities.

While acknowledging the Philippine strategy, it must be noted that the systematic promotion of emigration cannot replace investment in the country's social and economic infrastructure.

3.2 Promoting mobility in Mauritius

Migration in Mauritius is similarly characterized by labor-related emigration. A large wave of migration took place in the 1980s due to a weak economy, but economic fluctuations and the related high rates of employment have encouraged emigration in recent times, too. Currently, about 14 percent of Mauritius's population lives abroad, with a large share resident in France, the United Kingdom and Canada, among other destinations. The emigration of the highly skilled is a particular problem for Mauritius, with about 41 percent of the country's highly skilled population living in OECD countries as of 2010.

In 2005, the government responded to these difficulties with an ambitious reform program. Working closely with the International Organization for Migration (IOM), it developed a concept for circular migration based on the following principles:

- Mauritian citizens should have the opportunity to be employed outside the country, acquire new skills, save money and then return to the country in order to engage in business there.
- Remittances to Mauritius should be stimulated.
- Moreover, the Mauritian diaspora's knowledge should be mobilized in support of the country's economic development.

The initiative has resulted in migration programs with Canada and France that are above all intended to produce remittances and knowledge transfers, and are generally focused on low- and medium-skilled Mauritians. The effects of the financial crisis meant that the program started rather slowly, particularly with France. However, by 2012, around 300 Mauritian migrants were already employed in Canada under the program.

Evaluations of the reform show an increase in remittances as well as opportunities to promote the creation of businesses in Mauritius. About 80 skilled workers have been given support in returning to the country.

3.3 Thailand's Reverse Brain Drain Project

In 1997, Thailand's National Science and Technology Development Agency (NSTDA) launched the Reverse Brain Drain (RBD) Project. This is aimed at highly skilled members of the Thai diaspora and supports them in the creation of scientific networks and projects for knowledge and technology transfer. Initially, it facilitated the temporary return of highly skilled Thais from abroad by creating work opportunities in the public and private sectors. The implementation of lectures, seminars and workshops led by highly skilled Thais living abroad represents another form of knowledge transfer. In addition, the program offers highly skilled members of the diaspora financial incentives for a permanent return.

Today, an increasing number of cooperation projects have been established that no longer focus specifically on the return of diaspora members. Thus, the program offers financial support for innovative projects that harness the experience of Thai diaspora-community members. Opportunities for collaboration between highly skilled Thais living in and outside the country are offered through the implementation of joint research programs, for example.

Since 1997, 35 projects have been implemented and completed, and numerous patents have been filed. Eight people have been motivated to return permanently to Thailand, and more than 100 guest visits have been supported. In addition, several international conferences have been held.

3.4 The Mexican government's support of the Mexican diaspora community

In 2003, the Mexican government founded the Institute for Mexicans Abroad (IME), which supports the Mexican diaspora, especially in the United States and Canada. The organization is led by the Consejo Nacional, a coalition of 11 Mexican ministries, as well as an advisory board consisting of 156 people from the Mexican diaspora.

The IME's goals are to strengthen links between members of the Mexican diaspora and their homeland and to improve their lives in the countries where they currently reside. Specifically, the project ranges from campaigns encouraging Mexicans abroad to buy houses in their country of origin, to the organization of events on the issue of migration, to measures that enable diaspora members to vote in Mexico.

3.5 Establishment of a science network in Honduras

Migration and the diaspora's role are also important issues in Honduras. Particularly in the 1990s and the 2000s, there was a large number of emigrants from Honduras, mostly in the direction of the United States and often as illegal immigrants. About 10 percent of Honduras' citizens now live outside their country and make a significant contribution to the Honduran economy through their remittances. In 2008, these remittances accounted for more than a fifth of total GDP; this share is now about 17 percent (2011).

Highly skilled Hondurans, in particular, see better development opportunities abroad. In 2008, the Honduras Global network was created with the aim of mobilizing the diaspora and their resources for the country's development. The formation of the Honduras Global Foundation followed in 2011. Honduras Global is characterized by a close collaboration between representatives of the private sector and scientific community, and is supported by a variety of actors, including GIZ in Germany and the Honduran government. The network carries out a variety of campaigns, falling generally under three main objectives in the following fields of activity:

- Promotion of science, innovation and business: organization of conferences and seminars, support of international projects, initiation of mentoring entrepreneurship programs
- Knowledge transfer and development of the national human capital: summer-school offerings, placement of interns and the promotion of scientific networks
- Improvement of Honduras' image at the national level: public relations, international networks, round tables.

The network's success is reflected by the rising number of members, among other indications. In addition, the organization has successfully carried out seminars and conferences, and has placed interns. Moreover, network members have founded research institutions in Honduras, including a research and innovation center.

4 International organizations as drivers of fair labor migration

Creating fair systems for skilled-labor migration is a global challenge. For this reason, multilateral cooperation is of great importance. International organizations – such as the United Nations (UN), the IOM, the International Labour Organization (ILO), the World Bank and the

WHO – are important actors with regard to advancing the debate on fair migration structures and in advising governments on testing innovative approaches. The following section addresses the contribution and activities of international organizations in promoting fair labor migration.

4.1 The United Nations as a sponsor of the triple win

The relationship between migration and development has been a much-discussed issue for decades. However, the concept of the triple win is relatively new. The United Nations, in particular, has served to point the way in this regard: In October 2006, the General Assembly of the United Nations organized the High-Level Dialogue on International Migration and Development under the rubric "Making Migration Work." The basis for the dialogue was an agenda for a global migration and development policy drafted by the General Secretariat. This addressed the following:
- The protection of all migrants' human rights
- A reduction in the costs arising from labor migration
- Protection from exploitation
- Assistance for migrants who are unable to return to their home country
- Improvements in the public perception of migrants
- The integration of migration issues into development policy
- The optimization of the available data, and
- The expansion of dialogue and cooperation on the issue of migration.

Intensive engagement with this agenda led to a comprehensive statement in which the member states committed to closer cooperation on migration policy, among other items.

Another outcome was the creation of the Global Forum on Migration and Development, an annual meeting of U.N. member-state and civil society representatives held since 2007. The Global Forum serves as an informal platform for exchanges between the political, civil society and practitioner communities, with the goal of developing practical concepts for migration policy and of encouraging cooperation between states on this basis. In the eight years of its existence, the Global Forum has become an established institution that helps shape the international migration- and development-policy agenda.

In 2014, under the Swedish chairmanship, the development-policy dimension of international migration served as a particular focus of the group's work. The goal was to develop models for a coherent migration policy that did not regard economic and social developments as separate, but rather treated them as related phenomena. Work activities focused on the recognition of qualifications and the effective matching of skilled workers with demand in destination countries, as well as on the promotion of diaspora engagement in trade, investment and knowledge transfer activities, along with social development, health care and education in origin counties. Recommendations on these issues were presented to the U.N. secretary-general.

4.2 ILO defends the human-rights perspective

As a specialized U.N. agency, the International Labour Organization (ILO) protects human and labor rights, in particular, and verifies compliance with international labor standards. To this end, it develops binding agreements (conventions) as well as recommendations for member states. A unique feature of the ILO is its tripartite structure, as its committees contain government, employer and labor-organization representatives from all member states. With regard to the international migration of labor, the ILO is concerned with the relationship between migration and economic development, the balance between the interests of and benefits received by origin and destination countries, and ensuring that immigrant and native workers receive social protections and equal treatment.[4] In this context, it explicitly speaks of a triple win. It regards the generation and transfer of knowledge, technological exchange, social rejuvenation and economic development through remittances as key indicators of success in a well-designed labor-migration system.

The organization has been implementing its ILO Plan of Action for Migrant Workers since 2004 with the support of all 181 member states. The plan references skilled-labor migration through a call for more rapid recognition of educational qualifications and for the support of technology transfers between destination and origin countries. The plan's implementation is carried out by the Labour Migration Branch (MIGRANT). In addition, the ILO Multilateral Framework on Labour Migration includes rights-based guidelines and principles for a fairly designed labor-migration system.

The ILO's human-rights-based approach is an important point of reference for the work of other international activities, including the High-Level Dialogue on Migration and Development and the GFMD. The Global Migration Group, a coordinating committee of 16 U.N. organizations, the World Bank and the WHO that was chaired by the ILO in 2014, also makes reference to the ILO Plan of Action and the Multilateral Framework. Despite this generally high esteem, studies by the Maastricht Graduate School of Government indicate that the level of efficiency within the ILO with regard to legal standards and implementation structures is too low. In order to receive an appropriate level of attention, the school recommends that the ILO pursue targeted message-dissemination campaigns, and that its implementation structures be furnished with greater resources.

4.3 World Bank promotes free labor-market access

Another thought leader regarding the triple-win approach is the World Bank. At its core, it addresses the issues of poverty prevention and economic development. In this regard, the free movement of labor as a production factor, or free access to labor markets analogous to free world trade, plays an important role. In many country studies, the World Bank addresses issues of labor supply and demand, the creation of value through labor migration, the accessibil-

---

4   Basic standards on these topics include conventions No. 97, the Migration for Employment Convention (1945, revised 1952, 49 ratifications), and No. 143, Migrant Workers (1975, 23 ratifications).

ity of labor markets for unskilled labor and skilled workers, and the amount and importance of remittances. To this end, it has developed approaches for the good management of international labor migration. In its publications, the organization notes that labor migration "has appeal on both sides – receiving countries are able to have services performed in sectors where it is becoming increasingly difficult to attract native workers and sending countries are able to use the safety valve of overseas employment for workers for whom their own domestic environments are unable to provide enough economic opportunities – resulting in greater socio-economic stability, remittances, and even skill enhancements" (Luthria 2011: 2).

The International Labor Mobility Program (ILM) at the Center for Mediterranean Integration (CMI) in Marseille serves as an operational focus for the World Bank in the area of labor migration. This initiative provides evidence-based policy advice with the aim of better shaping labor migration in the Middle East and North Africa (MENA) region. The program links questions of mobility to social security, health care and education, while bridging the perspectives of the sending and receiving countries. As its core pillars of activity, the program carries out data-driven analyses, helps shape international processes of dialogue between public and private actors, and provides advice to individual countries.

The links with other divisions of the World Bank dealing with issues such as health care and labor markets, as well the ongoing networking with the ILO, the WHO and the Global Forum on Migration and Development, testifies to the high impact of the work, which is now slated to be extended to other regional World Bank centers, as well (Central and East Asia, Pacific). The ILM's function as a catalyst was clearly shown with the April 2014 presentation of the global-skill-partnership idea in Germany, Sweden and France. This offers an innovative concept by which developing countries' skilled-worker potentials and industrialized countries' needs can be simultaneously addressed. In such a partnership, the financial contributions of employers in the destination country help fund sending-country training courses for workers who will later go abroad. Global skill partnerships are implemented as bilateral public-private partnerships. Very ambitious in detail, they embody the concept of the triple win (Clemens 2014). The groundwork for the first pilot projects with German participation (GIZ) is being laid in Morocco.

A second focal point for the World Bank in the area of migration and development is the Global Knowledge Partnership on Migration and Development (KNOMAD) program. This is located within the World Bank's Development Prospects Group and is planned to run from 2013 to 2018. Like ILM, through with less of an operational orientation, KNOMAD has the goal of improving evidence-based policy advice. To this end, more than 50 well-known international experts are brought together in numerous working groups. The results of KNOMAD's work will be published in the form of data and full studies. KNOMAD works closely with the Global Forum on Migration and Development and the Global Migration Group. It is financed through a fund created by the World Bank to which a number of states contribute, with Switzerland, Germany and Sweden being among the largest donors.

As a complement to the ILO's rights-based approach, the World Bank has developed a strong economic argument that issues of economic development and poverty prevention should be handled in conjunction with one another. This line of reasoning is based on data and has produced outcomes ranging from dialogue processes to specific, country-focused advice and concepts.

4.4 IOM reinforces the ethical and humanitarian perspective on migration

With its 156 member states, the IOM has been among the most important organizations advocating on humanitarian grounds for a regulated and fair international-migration system since its founding in 1951. It promotes international exchange on this topic, in part through the focus of the International Dialogue on Migration, a global summit. In addition, the IOM provides its member countries with in-depth advice and training on the issue of migration management, with a particular light cast on the rights and responsibilities of migrants as well as on gender and health issues. A key area of work for the IOM is the consideration of ethical standards in the recruitment of foreign labor and skilled workers.

Activities in support of ethical recruiting will be implemented through the International Recruitment Integrity System (IRIS), which today remains under development. IRIS is a cooperative venture between governments, employers and recruiters who are jointly advocating for an ethical recruiting system, and who have consequently combined forces under the Public-Private Alliance for Fair and Ethical Recruitment. A voluntary accreditation approach on the basis of ethical principles is being developed; this would entail, for example, relinquishing placement fees for those seeking work and would bar the retention of personal documents, such as a passport. Moreover, a portal providing information on all accredited recruiters is intended to increase transparency for job seekers. The group also offers assistance to victims of illegal or unethical job-placement practices though a complaint mechanism.

4.5 WHO creates oversight criteria for health-sector recruitment

The WHO also addresses the issue of the fair recruitment of skilled workers. Against the backdrop of rising migration among health care professionals, the WHO Global Code of Practice on the International Recruitment of Health Personnel was adopted in May 2010 at the 63rd World Health Assembly. The WHO code is intended to ensure that the migration of skilled health care workers does not have a negative impact on health care in the countries of origin.

The code contains fundamental principles regarding bilateral and international cooperation (for instance, the promotion of circular migration among health personnel), recruiting practices and the protection of migrants' rights (e.g., with regard to working conditions). Under the terms of the code, recruitment from countries with a "critical shortage" of health care personnel should be avoided. Additional recommendations concern the provision of technical and financial support to upgrade health care systems and the promotion of training and advanced-education programs for health professionals.

The more than 190 signatories to the code have voluntarily agreed to comply with the agreed-upon recruitment principles and to transpose these into national law. Many countries (including Germany and the United Kingdom), when engaging in the recruitment of health care personnel, take into consideration the WHO-produced list of 57 countries that show a "critical shortage" of health-sector workers. In Germany, skilled workers from these countries can be recruited or placed only by the Federal Employment Agency (§§ 38 and 39 of the Employment Regulation).

However, critics and even the WHO itself advocate an open approach to the list: It offers guiding principles for the selection of countries targeted by recruitment, but it should not be regarded as an exhaustive resource with regard to the selection of countries, they say. This caution is based on methodological grounds; the process of defining a so-called critical shortage through the use of a boundary value for the supply of skilled medical personnel has not been scientifically substantiated, and the data on which the current calculations of health-personnel supply are based are in part outdated. The WHO thus recommends that countries engaging in international recruitment perform comprehensive analysis of potential countries of origin and their health care systems in order to assess the current state of affairs.

4.6 EU concept for greater migration-policy coherence

At the pan-European level, too, the issue of migration is gaining increasing significance. In 2005, the European Council adopted the Global Approach to Migration and Mobility (GAMM). In 2011, a further development of this approach was expressed in a communication on the harmonization of migration policy on the basis of stronger partnerships with countries of origin. The approach combines migration- and development-policy goals and seeks to better utilize the opportunities provided by well-managed migration. It is an important step toward a coherent and comprehensive migration policy, something which – despite the treaties of Amsterdam, Nice and Lisbon – currently exists only with regard to asylum policy and external-border security.

The goals of the approach as a whole include the improvement of legal migration and mobility, the prevention of irregular migration and human trafficking, support for the international protection of refugees, and a better management of migration and mobility in the service of economic development. In order to meet the growing need for skilled workers within the EU, the European Commission will seek to simplify visa policies (e.g., for students, researchers and family members) and to secure portability for social-insurance and pension benefits.

One of the key migration-policy management instruments contained in the GAMM is the concept of EU mobility partnerships. These agreements provide a flexible framework for practical, project-based collaborations between the EU and third countries. Thus far, mobility partnerships have been concluded with Tunisia, Morocco, Moldova, Cape Verde, Georgia, Armenia and Azerbaijan. Negotiations on a partnership agreement have been opened with Jordan. The mobility partnerships established thus far differ in their focus as well as in the number of participating member states. For example, five EU states participate in the partnership with Cape Verde, which encompasses 30 projects, while 14 member states are part of the agreement with Moldova, which contains more than 60 projects.

Proponents of the program see the mobility partnerships as an opportunity to draw closer to a triple win insofar as migrants are provided with legal migration channels, countries of origin are supported from a development-policy point of view, and the EU countries gain access to skilled workers. However, criticisms have been offered from several perspectives. First, some argue that the criteria for the selection of partner countries are not comprehensive enough, and that the partnerships aim primarily at preventing irregular migration and employment while neglecting the relationship between migration and development. Second, critics also note that the goals of the partnerships as established are not clearly defined, and that previously ongoing activities have simply been renamed as "mobility partnerships" (Angenendt 2012).

The Blue Card is an important tool that has made Europe more attractive as a destination continent for migration. Having secured this permit, non-EU foreigners and their families can enter an EU member state, live and work there, and travel to other EU countries. While there, they have the same rights as EU-country nationals with regard to working conditions, social security, pension benefits and the recognition of educational qualifications. Those applying for a Blue Card must have an employment contract or a binding job offer with a salary that is at least 1.5 times the average annual income (or 1.2 times in fields with skills shortages) in proposed country of residence as well as relevant educational qualifications.

Member states are responsible for determining the specific conditions under which Blue Cards are awarded. Thus, they can decide on precise minimum-income limits, on how many people should be granted Blue Cards, and on how long they should be valid (normally between one and four years). After the passage of a year and a half, Blue Card holders have the ability to move to another member state, though only under the conditions established by that country. As a pan-European recruitment instrument, the program and its various national transpositions have received varying assessments by experts. In Germany, the EU directive on the issue was implemented on 1 August 2012. Since that time, the Blue Card has become the main residence permit used for expert academic personnel from non-EU countries (see Section 2.2).

5 Conclusions for the creation of a fair labor-migration system

As a conclusion of this study, seven points can be identified that support the creation of a fair labor-migration system:

Figure 11: Elements of a fairly designed labor-migration system

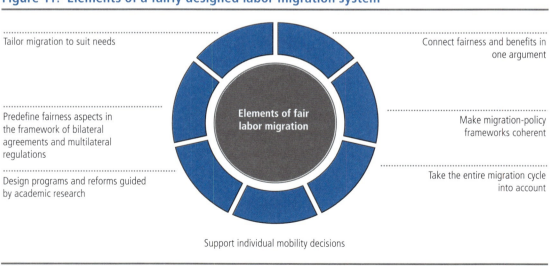

Source: Prognos AG

Link fairness and benefits in a single rationale

A fair labor-migration system takes into account the interests of migrating workers as well as those of origin and destination countries. This triple-win idea is gaining an increasing profile in international migration-policy discussions. It makes clear the fact that migration can be an ideal means of triggering development at the individual and national levels in both origin and destination countries.

At the national level, this positive conception of migration can serve as the foundation for a broad-ranging information strategy that increases societal acceptance for employment-related immigration and promotes recognition of cultural diversity as a societal asset. Canada and New Zealand provide excellent examples in this regard. However, in order to meet this standard, no displacement can take place on the labor market, and employment standards cannot be lowered. These requirements make for a convincing argument.

Ensure the coherency of migration-policy frameworks

The immigration of skilled workers has an impact not only on the labor market, but also on numerous other areas of life and politics, in the destination country as well as in the country of origin. If migration policy is applied using a whole-of-government approach, as in the Swedish model, it can succeed in incorporating all relevant stakeholders from the policy, economic and societal spheres, thus enabling coordination of the various areas of policy influence. In this way, a greater degree of coherence can be achieved in the design of national, European and international migration policies.

Take the full migration cycle into account

A consideration of the entire migration cycle is also necessary for a coherent design of migration policy. This begins with the analysis and careful selection of countries of origin for potential skilled immigrants. Examples from Germany show how this can be done: The GIZ and ZAV projects (Triple Win, for nurses, and the promotion of legal mobility for highly qualified Tunisian workers) initially analyze labor-market environments in potential partner countries and subsequently make a conscious decision with the goal of easing labor-market conditions in the sending countries while avoiding negative effects associated with skilled-labor recruitment.

The migration cycle continues with the recruitment, preparation and integration of the skilled workers into the destination country's labor market and society. Studies show that successful activities can begin before the actual immigration. In this regard, it is important that integration efforts also involve the partners and families of the skilled foreign workers in order to increase the likelihood of a long-term stay in the destination country. The Canadian Immigrant Integration Program and the Spouse Program of Denmark each offer interesting models in this area.

A number of positive examples show how migrants' contact with their country of origin can successfully be strengthened during their period of residence in the destination country, enabling them to serve an intermediary role between the two countries. Opportunities for skilled foreign workers to return temporarily to their countries of origin intensify the transfer of knowledge. The CIM's Migration for Development program in Germany, the TRQN in the Netherlands and IdEA in the United States are all good models demonstrating that diaspora communities are important civil society actors that can contribute to the realization of a triple win. If migrants ultimately want to return permanently to their countries of origin, programs such as the CIM's Returning Experts provide them with support in their job searches and in reintegrating in their homeland.

Initiatives emulating the United Kingdom's Send Money Home model additionally make an important contribution with regard to keeping the transaction costs for remittances as low as possible.

Support individual mobility decisions

Individual mobility decisions can be supported in such a way that skilled immigrant workers can be awarded permanent residency and work rights at an early stage and retain these rights even should they later choose to move to a third country or back to their country of origin. Such a policy would entail, for example, the portability of earned social-security benefits, the avoidance of double taxation and the suspension of caps on allowed periods of absence after which residency status is withdrawn, and it would permit dual citizenship and temporary returns to countries of origin. As Sweden's experience has shown, offerings of this kind increase migrants' interest in returning permanently or temporarily to their homes to contribute to local economic and social development.

In addition, immigration laws can be designed so that refugees' labor-market potential can be utilized in their host countries in the interests of all concerned. Here, too, Sweden's reform program has played a pioneering role.

Design migration systems in a needs-based manner

As has been established in recent years in Sweden and Germany, a demand-driven migration policy facilitates the matching of labor supply and demand, and prevents skills from being wasted. The business community is thus simultaneously an important target group and a partner for migration-policy activities. Companies can furthermore provide support in communicating the economic added value of a flexible and liberal migration policy.

Strategies for securing skilled labor may also see skills-related components be integrated into the immigration system. This may take the form of a point system or of programs allowing qualified workers to conduct a job search in the destination country.

Integrate aspects of fairness into bilateral agreements and multilateral regulations

Bilateral agreements can offer opportunities for coordination between the participating countries in such a way as to prevent unfair employment conditions or illegal migration and to realize synergies between migration and development policies. In these bilateral agreements, it is important that origin and destination countries establish which industries and sectors can safely be targeted by specific cooperative undertakings without producing negative effects associated with the loss of knowledge and skills. This has been implemented in the GIZ and ZAV projects, for example.

Multilateral regulations and internationally applicable standards are additional reference points in implementing the triple win. Examples include the WHO code for the international recruitment of health care personnel as well as the IOM's proposal to construct an accreditation approach on the basis of ethical principles.

Ensure that programs and reforms are informed by research

If the successes and failures of implemented reforms and innovative pilot projects are to produce useful lessons, data-driven evaluations are ultimately necessary. The United Kingdom's independent MAC expert commission offers a positive example here, as it oversees evaluation programs and develops evidence-based recommendations for fair migration management.

Literature/Links for RMP Country Case Studies

General

Angenendt, Steffen. *Triple-Win Migration – Challenges and Opportunities*. Framework Paper for the Migration Strategy Group on Global Competitiveness. Stuttgart/Berlin: Robert Bosch Stiftung/German Marshall Fund, 2014.

Bertelsmann Stiftung. Sustainable Governance Indicators. 2014. www.sgi-network.org/2014/.

Deutsche Gesellschaft für Internationale Zusammenarbeit (GIZ). *Fachkräftemigration aus der Sicht von Partnerländern. Wege zu einer entwicklungsorientierten Migrationspolitik*. Bonn and Eschborn: Federal Ministry for Economic Cooperation and Development, 2013.

Expert Council/Expert Advice on Migration and Integration (Sachverständigenrat deutscher Stiftungen für Integration und Migration, SVR). *Triple-Win oder Nullsummenspiel? Chancen, Grenzen und Zukunftsperspektiven für Programme zirkulärer Migration im deutschen Kontext*. Berlin: SVR, 2011.

Global Commission on International Migration. *Migration in an Interconnected World: New Directions for Action*. 2005. www.queensu.ca/samp/migrationresources/reports/gcim-complete-report-2005.pdf.

Huddleston, Thomas, and Jan Niessen. *Index Integration und Migration III – Migrant Integration Policy Index*. Brussels: MIPEX, 2011. www.mipex.eu/sites/default/files/downloads/mipex_iii_de.pdf.

International Centre for Migration Policy Development (ICMPD) and the European Centre for Development Policy Management (ECDPM). *Migration and Development Policies and Practices. A Mapping Study of Eleven European Countries and the European Commission.* Geneva: Swiss Agency for Development and Cooperation, 2013.

OECD (Organization for Economic Co-operation and Development). *Society at a Glance 2014: OECD Social Indicators.* Paris: OECD, 2014a. http://dx.doi.org/10.1787/soc_glance-2014-en.

OECD. *International Migration Outlook 2014.* Paris: OECD, 2014b. http://dx.doi.org/10.1787/migr_outlook-2014-en.

OECD. *OECD Factbook 2014: Economic, Environmental and Social Statistics.* Paris: OECD, 2014c. http://dx.doi.org/10.1787/factbook-2014-en.

OECD. *International Migration Outlook 2013.* Paris: OECD, 2013a. http://dx.doi.org/10.1787/migr_outlook-2013-en.

OECD. *OECD Factbook 2013: Economic, Environmental and Social Statistics.* Paris: OECD, 2013b. http://dx.doi.org/10.1787/factbook-2013-en.

Prognos AG. *Arbeitslandschaft 2035.* Munich: Vereinigung der Bayerischen Wirtschaft e.V., 2012.

United Nations, Department of Economic and Social Affairs (UN DESA), Population Division. *World Population Prospects: The 2012 Revision.* New York: UN DESA, 2013.

Link

World Bank. Country Information 2014. http://data.worldbank.org/.

Denmark

European Commission. *Mapping and Analysing Bottleneck Vacancies in EU Labour Markets – Overview report Final.* Brussels: EC, 2014.

Hedetoft, Ulf. *Denmark: Integrating Immigrants into a Homogeneous Welfare State.* Copenhagen: MPI, 2006. www.migrationpolicy.org/article/denmark-integrating-immigrants-homogeneous-welfare-state.

Hinte, Holger, Ulf Rinne and Klaus F. Zimmermann. "Ein Punktesystem zur bedarfsorientierten Steuerung der Zuwanderung nach Deutschland." *IZA Research Reports* No. 35. Bonn: IZA, 2011. www.iza.org/files/report35.pdf.

Liebig, Thomas. "The Labour Market Integration of Immigrants in Denmark." *OECD Social, Employment and Migration Working Papers* 50. Paris: OECD, 2007. www.oecd.org/social/soc/38195773.pdf.

OECD (Organization for Economic Co-operation and Development). *Developing Highly Skilled Workers: Review of Denmark.* Paris: OECD, 2004. www.oecd.org/sti/ind/34458043.pdf.

Rambøll Management Consulting. "'Bottleneck Vacancies in Denmark,' Country fiche – Overview report: Mapping and Analysing Bottleneck Vacancies in EU Labour Markets – Denmark." Brussels: EC, 2014.

WHO (World Health Organization). *Healthy Ageing in Denmark.* Copenhagen: WHO, 2012. www.euro.who.int/__data/assets/pdf_file/0004/161797/Denmark-Healthy-Aging-Strategy-Final-July-2012.pdf.

Links

Bertelsmann Stiftung. "What is the Ratio of Foreign-born to Native Tertiary Attainment?" Sustainable Governance Indicators. Gütersloh: Bertelsmann Stiftung, 2014. www.sgi-network.org/2014/Policy_Performance/Social_Policies/Integration/FB-N_Tertiary_Attainment. International Citizen Service. http://icitizen.dk/.

MIPEX 2014. www.mipex.eu/denmark.

The Danish Immigration Service. "New rules for family reunification." *Newtodenmark.dk,* May 11, 2012. www.nyidanmark.dk/en-us/news/news/danish_immigration_service/2012/maj/new_rules_for_family_reunification.htm.

The Danish Immigration Service and the Danish Agency for Labour Market and Recruitment. www.nyidanmark.dk/en-US/.

Work in Denmark. www.workindenmark.dk/en/Find_information/Information_for_employers/Step-by-step/Residency_Integration/Spouse.

Germany

Bax, Daniel. "Von wegen Armutsmigration." *Die Tageszeitung,* December 28, 2013. www.taz.de/!130016/.

CIM (Centre for International Migration and Development). *Migration und Entwicklung. Das Potenzial Rückkehrender Fachkräfte.* www.bamf.de/SharedDocs/MILo-DB/DE/Rueckkehrfoerderung/Rueckkehrberatung/AllgInformationen/i-cim-rueckkehrende-fachkraefte-download.pdf?__blob=publicationFile.

Federal Employment Agency (Bundesagentur für Arbeit Zentrale Auslands- und Fachvermittlung, ZAV). *Gekommen um zu bleiben. Berichte und Thesen zur qualifizierten Zuwanderung nach Deutschland.* Bonn: ZAV, 2013.

Federal Employment Agency. *Der Arbeitsmarkt in Deutschland – Fachkräfteengpassanalyse Dezember 2013.* Nuremberg: ZAV, 2013.

Federal Employment Agency and Deutsche Gesellschaft für Internationale Zusammenarbeit (GIZ). *Triple Win Pflegekräfte. Nachhaltig ausgerichtete Gewinnung von Pflegekräften – Unser Ansatz.* Brochure.

Federal Ministry of the Interior. "64.539 Asylerstanträge im Jahr 2012." Press release. January 15, 2013. www.bmi.bund.de/SharedDocs/Pressemitteilungen/DE/2013/01/asylzahlen_2012.html.

Federal Ministry of the Interior. "Das neue Staatsangehörigkeitsrecht." Berlin: Federal Press Office, 1999.

Klingholz, Reiner. "Anleitung zum Wenigersein." *Frankfurter Allgemeine Zeitung,* May 6, 2014. www.faz.net/aktuell/feuilleton/debatten/demografischer-wandel-anleitung-zum-wenigersein-12926171-p2.html.

"Länderprofil Deutschland." *focus Migration* Nr. 1, May 2007. www.bpb.de/gesellschaft/migration/laenderprofile/57537/deutschland.

Lobig, Caro. "Zahlen gegen Vorurteile." *Süddeutsche Zeitung*, November 8, 2013. www.sueddeutsche.de/politik/deutsche-asylpolitik-zahlen-gegen-vorurteile-1.1799703.

OECD (Organization for Economic Co-operation and Development). *Is Migration Really Increasing? Migration Policy Debates*. Paris: OECD, 2014d.

Links

CIM (Centre for Migration). "Migranten als Brückenbauer." www.cimonline.de/de/2262.asp.

Foreign Ministry. "Was ist die Blaue Karte EU/EU Blue Card?" Catalog of Questions. www.auswaertiges-amt.de/DE/Infoservice/FAQ/ArbeitLebenDeutschland/02a-Blue%20Card%20EU.html?nn=383016.

Federal Office for Migration and Refugees. "Fragen und Antworten zur Blauen Karte EU." 2014. www.bamf.de/DE/Infothek/FragenAntworten/BlaueKarteEU/blaue-karte-eu-node.html.

GiZ (Gesellschaft für Internationale Zusammenarbeit). "Pilotvorhaben zur Förderung der legalen Mobilität von hochqualifizierten Fachkräften aus Tunesien." www.giz.de/de/downloads/giz2012-de-legale-mobilitaet-fachkraefte-tunesien.pdf.

GiZ. "Wenn alle gewinnen." www.giz.de/de/mit_der_giz_arbeiten/11666.html.

GiZ. "Förderung der legalen Mobilität hochqualifizierter tunesischer Fachkräfte." www.giz.de/de/weltweit/19727.html.

Infoportal "Make it in Germany". www.make-it-in-germany.com/.

France

Bouchet-Petersen, Jonathan. "Hollande veut limiter l'immigration légale." *Libération*, March 16, 2012. www.liberation.fr/politiques/2012/03/16/hollande-veut-limiter-l-immigration-legale_803524.

Engler, Marcus. "Frankreich: Einwanderungsgesetz erschwert Familiennachzug." *Migration & Bevölkerung*, October 24, 2007. www.migration-info.de/artikel/2007-10-24/frankreich-einwanderungsgesetz-erschwert-familiennachzug.

"Frankreich: Neustart in der Einwanderungspolitik." *Newsletter Migration & Bevölkerung*, November 11, 2012. www.bpb.de/gesellschaft/migration/newsletter/144245/neustart-in-der-einwanderungspolitik.

Knupp, Marcus. "Arbeitsmarkt in Frankreich steht unter Spannung". *Germany Trade & Invest*, March 7, 2014. www.gtai.de/GTAI/Navigation/DE/Trade/maerkte,did=972800.html?view=renderPdf.

"Länderprofil Frankreich." *focus Migration* Nr. 2, Mai 2012. www.bpb.de/gesellschaft/migration/laenderprofile/135107/frankreich.

Link

Bertelsmann Stiftung. "How effectively do policies support the integration of migrants into society?" Sustainable Governance Indicators. Gütersloh: Bertelsmann Stiftung, 2014. www.sgi-network.org/2014/Policy_Performance/Social_Policies/Integration/Integration_Policy.

Canada

Berlin Institute for Population and Development. *Nach Punkten vorn – Was Deutschland von der Zuwanderungs- und Integrationspolitik Kanadas lernen kann.* Berlin: Berlin Institute, 2012. www.berlin-institut.org/fileadmin/user_upload/Nach_Punkten_vorn/Kanada_final.pdf.

Bloemraad, Irene. *Understanding "Canadian Exceptionalism" in Immigration and Pluralism Policy.* Washington, D.C.: MPI, 2012. www.migrationpolicy.org/research/TCM-canadian-exceptionalism.

Canadian Chamber of Commerce (CcoC). *Canada's Skills Crisis: What We Heard. A Canadian Chamber of Commerce report on cross-country consultations in 2012.* Ottawa: CCoC, 2012. www.chamber.ca/advocacy/issues/skills-and-immigration/.

"Canadian Multiculturalism – The More the Merrier." *The Economist,* January 18, 2014. www.economist.com/news/americas/21594328-debates-over-immigration-are-often-toxic-not-canada-more-merrier.

Carrillo, Luis Manuel Muñoz. *Seasonal Agricultural Workers Program Mexico – Canada: Costs and Benefits.* www.gwu.edu/~ibi/minerva/Spring2011/Luis_Munoz.pdf.

Galarneau, Diane, and René Morissette. "Immigrant's Education and Required Job Skills." *Perspectives on Labour and Income* (9) 12 2008. Statistics Canada – Catalogue no. 75-001-X. www.statcan.gc.ca/pub/75-001-x/2008112/pdf/10766-eng.pdf.

Government of Canada. "Improving Canada's Caregiver Program – Government of Canada Announces Reforms to End the Live-in Requirement, Reduce Family Separation and Provide More Options to Caregivers in Canada.", October 31, 2014. http://news.gc.ca/web/article-en.do?nid=898729.

IOM (International Organization for Migration). "Migration and Development: Achieving Policy Coherence. Examples of working-level policies and practices from Albania, Canada, Guatemala, Italy, the Netherlands, South Africa, Sri Lanka, the UK and elsewhere." *IOM Migration Research* (34) 2008. http://publications.iom.int/bookstore/free/MRS_34.pdf.

IOM. Mission Guatemala. *Seasonal Agricultural Workers Program – Guatemala – Canada.* Guatemala City: IOM, 2008. www.iom.int/jahia/webdav/site/myjahiasite/shared/shared/mainsite/activities/countries/docs/guatemalan_seasonal_workers_summary08.pdf.

Keung, Nicholas. "Canadian Dream Dims for Immigrants." *Hamilton Spectator,* March 3, 2014. www.thespec.com/news-story/4393286-canadian-dream-dims-for-immigrants/.

Macdonald, Alistair. "Canada Seeks Immigrants Who Fit Better." *The Wall Street Journal,* August 31, 2013. http://online.wsj.com/news/articles/SB10001424127887323980604579030964060914466.

McMullin, Julie Ann, and Martin Cooke. *Labour Force Ageing and Skill Shortages in Canada and Ontario*. Work Network Project W-092. Canadian Policy Research Networks Inc. Ottawa: CPRN, 2004. www.cprn.org/documents/31517_en.pdf.

Schmidtke, Oliver. "Einwanderungsland Kanada – ein Vorbild für Deutschland?" *Aus Politik und Zeitgeschichte (APUZ)* 44: 25–30, 2009. www.bpb.de/apuz/31674/einwanderungsland-kanada-ein-vorbild-fuer-deutschland?p=all.

Schmidtke, Oliver. *Der Wert der Vielfalt – Kanadas Immigrations- und Integrationsregime*. New York: Rosa Luxemburg Stiftung, 2012. www.rosalux-nyc.org/wp-content/files_mf/schmidtke_wert_der_vielfalt.pdf.

Winter, Elke. *Becoming Canadian – Making Sense of Recent Changes to Citizenship Rules*. IRPP Study 44. Montreal: Institute for Research on Public Policy, 2014. http://irpp.org/wp-content/uploads/assets/research/diversity-immigration-and-integration/becoming-canadian/Winter-No44.pdf.

Links

ALLIES 2014, Toronto: http://alliescanada.ca/resources/toolkits/establishing-an-immigrant-employment-council/introduction/.

Bertelsmann Stiftung. Sustainable Governance Indicators. Gütersloh:Bertelsmann Stiftung, 2014. www.sgi-network.org/2014/.

Canadian Immigrant Integration Program 2014. www.newcomersuccess.ca/.

Destination Canada. Ottawa 2008–2014. www.destinationkanada.ca/auswandern/.

EOS Immigration 2012. www.eos-immigration.ca/de/neuigkeiten/allgemein/einwanderung-nach-kanada-die-kanadische-regierung-ueberarbeitet-einwanderungsvorschriften/.

Government of Canada. "Amendments to the Immigration and Refugee Protection Regulations to Support Mandatory Electronic Applications for Prescribed Applications under the Express Entry system." April 22, 2014. www.cic.gc.ca/english/department/acts-regulations/forward-regulatory-plan/irpr-eoi.asp.

Government of Canada. "Backgrounder – Expression of Interest (EOI): Preparing for Success in 2015". October 28, 2013. www.cic.gc.ca/english/department/media/backgrounders/2013/2013-10-28b.asp?_ga=1.265996559.1267250839.1399275389.

Goverment of Canada. "Notice – Change to Offers of Arranged Employment in the Federal Skilled Worker Program." March 8, 2013. www.cic.gc.ca/english/department/media/notices/2013-03-08.asp.

Government of Canada. "Offering 'Express Entry' to Qualified Economic Immigrants." April 8, 2014. http://news.gc.ca/web/article-en.do?nid=836509.

Goverment of Canada. www.canada.ca/en/.

Goverment of Canada. www.esdc.gc.ca/eng/home.shtml.

Library of Congress. Washington, D.C.: www.loc.gov/law/help/points-based-immigration/canada.php.

Migration Policy Institute. Washington, DC 2001–2014: www.migrationpolicy.org/article/canadas-immigration-policy-focus-human-capital; www.migrationpolicy.org/research/building-new-skills-immigration-and-workforce-development-canada.

MIPEX 2014. www.mipex.eu/countries; www.mipex.eu/canada.

New Zealand

Bedford, Charlotte Elisabeth. *Picking Winners? New Zealand's Recognised Seasonal Employer (RSE) Policy and its Impacts on Employers, Pacific Workers and their Island-based Communities*. Adelaide: University of Adelaide, 2013.

Colmar Brunton. *The Kea Every Kiwi Counts Survey 2013*. Kea New Zealand. Presentation. 2013. www.keanewzealand.com/ekc.

Controller and Auditor-General. *Immigration New Zealand: Supporting New Migrants to Settle and Work*. Wellington: Government of New Zealand, 2013. www.oag.govt.nz/2013/new-migrants/2013/new-migrants/docs/oag-new-migrants.pdf.

Controller and Auditor-General. "Auditor-General's Overview." www.oag.govt.nz/2013/new-migrants.

Department of Labour. *Working across the ditch: New Zealanders working in Australia*. Wellington: Government of New Zealand, 2010. www.dol.govt.nz/publications/research/ditch/working-across-the-ditch.pdf.

Department of Labour. *Auckland Regional Settlement Strategy 2009–2014*. Wellington: Government of New Zealand, 2010.

Department of Labour. *Settlement National Action Plan*. Wellington: Government of New Zealand, 2007. www.immigration.govt.nz/NR/rdonlyres/5A045541-0E5F-4B37-A2F4-0D0A80ABF2D6/0/ActionPlan.PDF.

Department of Labour. *Our Future Together. New Zealand Settlement Strategy*. Wellington: Government of New Zealand, 2007. www.immigration.govt.nz/NR/rdonlyres/F2D460BA-8A84-4073-8A12-84C2BE0B1BB8/0/Strategy.pdf.

Department of Labour. *The New Zealand Settlement Strategy Outline. A Future Together. Settlement National Action Plan*. Wellington: Government of New Zealand, 2004. www.immigration.govt.nz/NR/rdonlyres/E869C333-69C1-4983-862B-288C9C493839/0/NZImmigrationSettlementStrategyOutline.pdf.

Elliot, Susan. *Supporting Refugees and Migrants*. Report for the Tindall Foundation and ASB Community Trust. Wellington: Government of New Zealand, 2007.

Gibson, John, and David McKenzie. *Development through Seasonal Worker Programs. The Case of New Zealand's RSE Program*. The World Bank. *Policy Research Working Paper 6762* 2014.

Gibson, John, and David McKenzie. "The Development Impact of New Zealand's RSE Seasonal Worker Policy". Powerpoint Presentation. Hamilton: University of Waikato, 2010.

Immigration New Zealand. "Recognised Seasonal Employer (RSE) Work Category." 2014. www.immigration.govt.nz/migrant/stream/work/hortandvit/rse/.

ILO (International Labour Organization). *Labour Migration and Development: ILO Moving Forward*. Background paper for discussion at the ILO Tripartite Technical Meeting on Labour Migration. Geneva, November 4–8, 2013.

ILO. "Labour Migration – The Challenge." 2014. www.ilo.org/suva/areas-of-work/labour-migration/lang--en/index.htm.

ILO. "The Recognized Seasonal Employers Scheme (RSE), New Zealand." 2014. www.ilo.org/dyn/migpractice/migmain.showPractice?p_lang=en&p_practice_id=48.

LIRC (Labour and Immigration Research Centre). *Medium-Long Term Employment Outlook – Looking ahead to 2020.* Wellington: LIRC, 2012. www.dol.govt.nz/publications/research/medium-long-term-employment-outlook/medium-long-term-employment-outlook.pdf.

LIRC. *Points of Difference – Does the Skilled Migrant Category Points System Predict Wages?* Wellington: LIRC, 2012. www.dol.govt.nz/publications/research/points-of-difference/points-of-difference.pdf.

MBIE (Ministry of Business, Innovation and Employment). *Migration Trends and Outlook 2012/2013.* Wellington: MBIE, 2013. www.dol.govt.nz/publications/research/migration-trends-1213/MigrationTrend-and-Outlook-12-13.pdf; www.dol.govt.nz/publications/research/migration-trends-1213/index.asp.

MBIE. *The Labour Market and Settlement Outcomes of Migrant Partners in New Zealand.* Wellington: MBIE, 2013. www.dol.govt.nz/publications/research/labour-market-settlement-outcomes-migrant-partners-nz/settlement-outcomes-migrant-partners-nz.pdf.

MBIE. *The rise of temporary migration in New Zealand and its impact on the labour market.* Wellington: MBIE, 2013. www.dol.govt.nz/publications/research/rise-temp-migration-nz-impact-labour-market-2013/rise-of-temporary-migration-in-NZ-and-its-Impact-on-the-Labour-Market2013.pdf.

MBIE. *Migration Trends Key Indicators Report.* Wellington: MBIE, 2014. www.dol.govt.nz/research/migration/monthly-migration-trends/index.asp.

MBIE. *Immigration Survey Monitoring Programme (ISMP). Migrant Survey Indicators.* Wellington: MBIE, 2014. www.dol.govt.nz/research/migration/ismp/ismpindicators.asp.

MBIE. *Longitudinal Immigration Survey: New Zealand (LisNZ). Fast Facts.* Wellington: MBIE, 2014. www.dol.govt.nz/research/migration/lisnz/fastfacts.asp.

MBIE. "Recognised Seasonal Employer (RSE) Policy." Wellington: MBIE, 2014. www.dol.govt.nz/initiatives/strategy/rse/.

MFAT (Ministry of Foreign Affairs and Trade). *Annual Report 2012/2013.* Wellington: MFAT, 2013. http://mfat.govt.nz/downloads/media-and-publications/annual-report/MFAT%20Annual%20Report%20201213.pdf.

Moore, David, and Bastiaan van der Scheer. *Kea Evaluation: Final Report.* Wellington: Ministry of Economic Development, 2009. www.med.govt.nz/about-us/publications/publications-by-topic/evaluation-of-government-programmes/kea-report.pdf.

Nunns, Heather, Mathea Roorda, Charlotte Bedford and Richard Bedford. *Mid-term evaluation of the Strengthening Pacific Partnerships Project.* Wellington: Government of New Zealand, 2013.

OECD (Organization for Economic Co-operation and Development). *Migration Policy Debates – Is migration really increasing?* Paris: OECD, 2014. www.oecd.org/berlin/Is-migration-really-increasing.pdf.

OECD. *Society at a Glance 2014 Highlights: New Zealand OECD Social Indicators.* Paris: OECD, 2014. www.oecd.org/newzealand/OECD-SocietyAtaGlance2014-Highlights-NewZealand.pdf.

OECD. *Recruiting Immigrant Workers: New Zealand 2014.* Paris: OECD, 2014.

Papademetriou, Demetrios G., and Madeleine Sumption. *Eight Policies to Boost the Economic Contribution of Employment-Based Immigration.* Washington, D.C.: MPI, 2011. www.migrationpolicy.org/research/boosting-economic-contribution-employment-based-immigration.

Poot, Jacques. *Trans-Tasman Migration, Transnationalism and Economic Development in Australia.* Motu Economic and Public Policy Research. *Motu Working Paper 09-05.* May 2009. http://motu-www.motu.org.nz/wpapers/09_05.pdf.

Ramasamy, Sankar. *Reflections on New Zealand's Recognised Seasonal Employer (RSE) Policy.* GFMD thematic workshop, June 13–15, 2011. Marseilles 2011.

Ramasamy, Sankar, Vasantha Krishnan, Richard Bedford and Charlotte Bedford. "The Recognised Seasonal Employer Policy: Seeking the elusive triple wins for development through international migration." *Pacific Economic Bulletin* (23) 3: 171–186, 2008.

Wickramasekara, Piyasiri. "Circular Migration: A Triple Win or a Dead End?". *Global Union Research Network Discussion Papers.* No. 15. Geneva: ILO, March 2011.

Links

Immigration New Zealand. www.ssnz.govt.nz.
Kea New Zealand 2014. www.keanewzealand.com/.
MBIE (Ministry of Business, Innovation and Employment). "Settlement." www.dol.govt.nz/research/migration/settlement.asp.

The Netherlands

IOM (International Organization for Migration). *Temporary Return of Qualified Nationals (TRQN) Project. Making a Contribution to the Reconstruction and Development of Afghanistan, Bosnia-Herzegovina, Kosovo, Montenegro, Serbia, Sierra Leone and Sudan.* www.slcu.nl/images/IOM.pdf.

IOM The Netherlands. *Temporary Return of Qualified Nationals (TRQN III) Infosheet.* 2014. www.iom-nederland.nl/en/component/docman/cat_view/11-migratie-en-ontwikkeling?orderby=dmdate_published&ascdesc=DESC.

Kuschminder, Katie, and Melissa Siegel. "Temporary Return Programmes." Maastricht University. Presentation 2014. www.migrantservicecentres.org/userfile/Melissa%20Siegel.pdf.

"Länderprofil Niederlande." *focus Migration* No. 11, November 2007. www.bpb.de/gesellschaft/migration/laenderprofile/57748/niederlande.

OECD (Organization for Economic Co-operation and Development). *OECD Wirtschaftsausblick Ausgabe 2013/2.* Paris: OECD, 2013.

Social and Economic Council of the Netherlands. *Make it in the Netherlands!* Advisory Report 2013. www.ser.nl/~/media/db_deeladviezen/2010_2019/2013/make-it-in-the-netherlands/make-it-in-the-netherlands-actieplan-en.ashx.

Stabenow, Michael. "Schwerer Dämpfer für Europafeind Wilders." *Frankfurter Allgemeine Zeitung,* May 23, 2014. www.faz.net/aktuell/politik/europawahl/niederlande-schwerer-daempfer-fuer-europafeind-wilders-12954317.html.

The Hague Process on Refugees and Migration. "Expert Consultation for Business and Cities." http://thehagueprocess.org/wordpress/wp-content/uploads/2013/01/Introductory-document-Expert-Consultations.pdf.

The Hague Process on Refugees and Migration. "Global Hearing on Refugees and Migration." Report on the meetings on June 4–5, 2012 in The Hague.

Van der Wilk-Carlton, Kathleen. *Enabling Dual Careers in the Global Workplace*. Permits Foundation 2001–2014. Presentation on April 4, 2014. www.permitsfoundation.com/wp-content/uploads/Permits-intro-web-version-April-14.pdf.

Links

Permits Foundation. *Den Haag 2001–2014*. www.permitsfoundation.com.

The Hague Process on Refugees and Migration. http://thehagueprocess.org.

Sweden

Cerna, Lucie. "Changes in Swedish Labour Immigration Policy: A Slight Revolution?" The Stockholm University Linnaeus Center for Integration Studies (SULCIS), *Working Paper* 2009: 10.

European Commission. *Country Factsheet: Sweden 2012. European Migration Network*. http://ec.europa.eu/dgs/home-affairs/what-we-do/networks/european_migration_network/reports/docs/country-factsheets/sweden-emn-ountry-factheet_en.pdf.

Expert Council/Expert Advice on Migration and Integration (Sachverständigenrat deutscher Stiftungen für Integration und Migration, SVR). *Zirkuläre Migration: Rechtliche Grundlagen auf dem Prüfstand*. Berlin: SVR, 2011.

Migrationsverket. *Temporary and Circular Migration: Empirical Evidence, Current Policy Practice and Future Options in EU Member States*. Stockholm: Migrationsverket, 2010. http://ec.europa.eu/dgs/home-affairs/what-we-do/networks/european_migration_network/reports/docs/emn-studies/circular-migration/26a._sweden_national_report_circular_migration_final_version_9dec2010_en.pdf.

MOJ (Ministry of Justice). *Migration policy. Fact Sheet*. Stockholm: MoJ, 2014. www.government.se/content/1/c6/24/55/96/1acc82b1.pdf.

MOJ. *Sweden's Committee for Circular Migration and Development*. Stockholm: MoJ, 2010. www.government.se/content/1/c6/15/61/06/aab20cd9.pdf.

MOJ. *New Rules for Labour Immigration*. Stockholm: MoJ, 2008. www.osce.org/eea/36344?download=true.

Neuding, Paulina. "How to Explain the Swedish Riots." *The Weekly Standard,* June 10, 2013. www.weeklystandard.com/articles/how-explain-swedish-riots_732055.html.

Quirico, Monica. "Labour Migration Governance in Contemporary Europe. The Case of Sweden." *FIERI Working papers*. Turin, April 2012.

"Sweden's migration policy." *The World Bulletin,* October 2, 2013. www.worldbulletin.net/?aType=haber&ArticleID=119595.

Literature/Links for RMP Country Case Studies

Links

Bertelsmann Stiftung. "How effectively do policies support the integration of migrants into society?" Sustainable Governance Indicators. Gütersloh: Bertelsmann Stiftung, 2014. www.sgi-network.org/2014/Policy_Performance/Social_Policies/Integration/Integration_Policy.
MIPEX 2014. www.mipex.eu/sweden.

Switzerland

"Asylgesetz klar angenommen." *Schweizer Radio und Fernsehen,* June 9, 2013. www.srf.ch/news/schweiz/abstimmungen/abstimmungen/asylgesetz/asylgesetz-klar-angenommen.
Eidgenössisches Departement für auswärtige Angelegenheiten (EDA). *Bericht über die internationale Migrationszusammenarbeit.* Bern: EDA, 2011. www.eda.admin.ch/dam/eda/de/documents/topics/bericht-internationale-migrationszusammenarbeit_de.pdf.
"Länderprofil Schweiz." *focus Migration* No. 4, October 2012. www.bpb.de/gesellschaft/migration/laenderprofile/139678/schweiz.
Liebscher, Stephan. "Schweizer Volksentscheid: Einwanderungsbeschränkung mit hauchdünner Mehrheit beschlossen." *Migration & Bevölkerung. Das Online-Portal zur Migrationsgesellschaft,* February 27, 2014. www.migration-info.de/artikel/2014-02-27/schweizer-volksentscheid-einwanderungsbeschraenkung-hauchduenner-mehrheit.
"Referendum: Große Mehrheit der Schweizer für verschärftes Asylgesetz." *Spiegel Online,* June 9, 2013. www.spiegel.de/politik/ausland/schweiz-grosse-mehrheit-fuer-verschaerftes-asylgesetz-a-904650.html.
Schweizerische Eidgenossenschaft. *Bericht des Bundesrates über die Aktivitäten der Schweizerischen Migrationsaussenpolitik 2011–2012.* June 18, 2013. www.ejpd.admin.ch/dam/data/bfm/internationales/internat-zusarbeit/ber-br-migpol-2011-2012-d.pdf.
"Sommaruga in Kroatien: Gespräche zur Personenfreizügigkeit." *news.ch,* April 8, 2014. www.news.ch/Sommaruga+in+Kroatien+Gespraeche+zur+Personenfreizuegigkeit/622410/detail.htm.

Links

Federal Office for Migration and Refugees (Bundesamt für Migration, BFM). "Teilrevision des Bundesgesetzes über die Ausländerinnen und Ausländer (Ausländergesetz, AuG)." Berlin: BFM, 2013. www.bfm.admin.ch/bfm/de/home/aktuell/gesetzgebung/teilrev_aug_integration.html.
MIPEX 2014. www.mipex.eu/switzerland.

United Kingdom

"David Cameron's immigration speech: full text." *The Spectator,* November 28, 2014. http://blogs.spectator.co.uk/coffeehouse/2014/11/david-camerons-immigration-speech-full-text/.

Government UK. "Migration Advisory Committee." Agencies and other public bodies. www.gov.uk/government/organisations/migration-advisory-committee.

Hummitzsch, Thomas. "Großbritannien: Streit um Einwanderung." *Migration & Bevölkerung. Das Online-Portal zur Migrationsgesellschaft,* February 27, 2014. www.migration-info.de/artikel/2014-02-27/grossbritannien-streit.

ILO (International Labour Organization). "Send Money Home." Good practices database – Labour migration policies and programmes. Geneva: ILO, 2014. www.ilo.org/dyn/migpractice/migmain.showPractice?p_lang=en&p_practice_id=31.

Institute for Public Policy Research. *A Fair Deal on Migration for the UK.* London: IPPR, 2014. www.ippr.org/assets/media/images/media/files/publication/2014/03/Fair-deal-on-migration_Mar2013_11970.pdf.

"Länderprofil Vereinigtes Königreich." *focus Migration.* No. 12, December 2007. http://focus-migration.hwwi.de/typo3_upload/groups/3/focus_Migration_Publikationen/Laenderprofile/LP_12_Vereinigt_Koenigreich.pdf.

National Centre for Social Research (NatCen Social Research). *British Social Attitudes 2013: Attitudes to immigration.* London: NatCen Social Research, 2013. www.natcen.ac.uk/media/205573/immigration-bsa31.pdf.

PBI, NOP World and DFID. *Sending Money Home? A Survey of Remittance Products and Services in the United Kingdom.* London: DFID, 2005. www.eldis.org/vfile/upload/1/document/0708/DOC17981.pdf.

Rebeggiani, Fatma. "Vereinigtes Königreich: Debatte um Zuwanderung von Rumänen und Bulgaren." *Migration & Bevölkerung. Das Online-Portal zur Migrationsgesellschaft,* February 25, 2013. www.migration-info.de/artikel/2013-02-25/vereinigtes-koenigreich-debatte-um-zuwanderung-rumaenen-und-bulgaren.

"Rechtspopulisten ganz oben." *Deutschlandfunk,* May 26, 2014. www.deutschlandfunk.de/europawahlen-in-grossbritannien-rechtspopulisten-ganz-oben.2024.e.html?dram:article_id=287420.

Salt, John, and Janet Dobson. "Cutting Net Migration to the Tens of Thousands: What Exactly Does that Mean?" *Migration Research Unit Discussion Paper.* London: UCL Department of Geography, 2013. www.ucl.ac.uk/news/news-articles/1113/Salt_Dobson_291013.pdf.

Spengler, Jochen. "Cameron will Sozialleistungen kürzen." *Deutschlandfunk,* November 28, 2014. www.deutschlandfunk.de/einwanderungspolitik-cameron-will-sozialleistungen-kuerzen.1766.de.html?dram:article_id=304639.

Link

Bertelsmann Stiftung. "How effectively do policies support the integration of migrants into society?" Sustainable Governance Indicators. Gütersloh: Bertelsmann Stiftung, 2014. www.sgi-network.org/2014/Policy_Performance/Social_Policies/Integration/Integration_Policy.

USA

Dyer, John. "Einwanderungsgesetz spaltet US-Politik." *Neues Deutschland*, June 29, 2013. www.neues-deutschland.de/artikel/825941.einwanderungsgesetz-spaltet-us-politik.html.

Federal Agency for Civic Education. "Länderprofil Vereinigte Staaten von Amerika." *focus Migration* No. 4, October 2012. www.bpb.de/gesellschaft/migration/laenderprofile/143975/vereinigte-staaten-von-amerika.

Giovagnoli, Mary. *Overhauling Immigration Law: A Brief History and Basic Principles of Reform*. Washington, D.C.: Immigration Policy Center, 2013. www.immigrationpolicy.org/perspectives/overhauling-immigration-law-brief-history-and-basic-principles-reform.

Jacoby, Tamar. *The Employer Perspective: The Role of the Private Sector in the U.S. Immigration Debate*. Migration Strategy Group on Global Competitiveness. Berlin/Stuttgart: GMFUS/Robert Bosch Stiftung, 2014. http://gmfus.wpengine.netdna-cdn.com/wp-content/uploads/2014/04/MSG-policy_brief_Jacoby-US-Employer-Perspective-FINAL.pdf.

Nurses Now International. *Skills y Programa Intensivo de Capacitación*. Presentation 2011.

Links

Bertelsmann Stiftung. "How effectively do policies support the integration of migrants into society?" Sustainable Governance Indicators. Gütersloh: Bertelsmann Stiftung, 2014. www.sgi-network.org/2014/Policy_Performance/Social_Policies/Integration/Integration_Policy.

IdEA (International diaspora Engagement Alliance). 2014. http://diasporaalliance.org/.

Nurses Now International 2012. www.nursesnowinternational.com/page.php?men=16&con=13.

Literature/Links Countries of Origin

Honduras

Hirsch, Sarah. "Migration and Remittances – the Case of Honduras." *Rural 21*. March 2010. www.lai.fu-berlin.de/disziplinen/oekonomie/mitarbeiter_innen/Sarah_Hirsch/R21_Migration_and_remittances_Honduras_0310_01-1.pdf.

Reichman, Daniel. *Honduras: The Perils of Remittance Dependence and Clandestine Migration*. Washington, D.C.: MPI, 2013. www.migrationpolicy.org/article/honduras-perils-remittance-dependence-and-clandestine-migration.

Links

Deutsche Gesellschaft für Internationale Zusammenarbeit (GIZ). www.giz.de/de/weltweit/13813.html.

Honduras Global. www.hondurasglobal.us/.

Mauritius

For the Promotion of Economic Migration. "Partnership Agreements between France and Mauritius Regard to the Circular Migration of Professionals." January 19, 2011. www.immigration-professionnelle.gouv.fr/en/latest-news/news/signing-of-two-partnership-agreements-between-the-ofii-director-general-and-the-nef-president-with.

International Organization for Migration (IOM). "Mauritius." 2011/2014. www.iom.int/cms/en/sites/iom/home/where-we-work/africa-and-the-middle-east/southern-africa/mauritius.default.html?displayTab=latest-news.

Jatha, Jennifer. "La France disposée à accueillir 850 Mauriciens par an." *Le Mauricien*, January 19, 2011. www.immigration-professionnelle.gouv.fr/sites/default/files/fckupload/Le_Mauricien_19_01_11_Migration_circulaire_convention_de_partenariat.pdf.

Kokil, Anil K. *Circular Migration as a Development Tool – The Mauritian Approach*. Presentation June 13–15, 2011. http://cmimarseille.org/cmiarchive/_src/SELM3_wk2/SELM3_wk2_Session2_Kokil.pdf.

Nayeck, Joyker. "Circular Migration – The Case for Mauritius." Presentation for International Conference on Diaspora for Development, July 13–14, 2009, World Bank, Washington. http://siteresources.worldbank.org/INTPROSPECTS/Resources/334934-1110315015165/Nayeck.pdf.

OECD/UN DESA (Organisation for Economic Co-operation and Development/United Nations Department of Economic and Social Affairs). *World Migration in Figures*. Paris/New York: OECD/UN DESA, 2013. www.oecd.org/els/mig/World-Migration-in-Figures.pdf.

Siegel, Melissa, and Vivianne van der Vorst. *Evaluation of the "Blue Birds" Circular Migration Pilot in The Netherlands*. Maastricht: Maastricht University, 2012. www.government.nl/documents-and-publications/reports/2013/01/23/evaluation-of-the-blue-birds-circular-migration-pilot-in-the-netherlands.html.

Wickramasekara, Piyasiri. *Circular and temporary migration regimes and their implications for family*. QScience Proceedings 2013, Family, Migration & Dignity Special Issue. 2013. www.qscience.com/doi/pdf/10.5339/qproc.2013.fmd.1.

Links

Global Forum on Migration & Development 2014. www.gfmd.org/pfp/ppd/1645; www.gfmd.org/pfp/ppd/16.

"Migration and Development – The Mauritian Perspective". www.iom.int/jahia/webdav/shared/shared/mainsite/microsites/IDM/workshops/return_migration_development_070708/speech_seewoorthun.pdf.

Mexico

International Labour Organization (ILO). "Institute for Mexicans Abroad (IME)." 2014. www.ilo.org/dyn/migpractice/migmain.showPractice?p_lang=en&p_practice_id=34.

Link

Institute for Mexicans Abroad: www.ime.gob.mx/.

Philippines

Business Advisory Council APEC. "Earn, Learn, Return – A Draft report on the 'Earn, Learn, Return' Model: A New framework for Managing the movement of Workers in the APEC Region to Address Business Needs." http://hrd.apec.org/images/3/3c/ELR.pdf.

Newland, Kathleen, and Dovelyn Rannveig Agunias. *Learning by Doing: Experiences of Circular Migration*. Washington, D.C.: MPI, 2013.

Rieder, Lila Patricia. "Pflegekräfteimport als Erfolgsmodell? 500 philippinische Krankenpflegekräfte für Deutschland." *südostasien* 3/2013. www.asienhaus.de/fileadmin/uploads/soai/Zeitschrift_SOA/2013/2013-3/SOA_2013-03_Rieder_Pflegekraefteimport-Philippinen.pdf.

Links

Bangko Sentral ng Pilipinas. "Overseas Filipinos' (OF) Remittances." 2014. www.bsp.gov.ph/statistics/keystat/ofw.htm.

German Federal Agency for Civic Education. "Auswanderung und Auswanderungspolitik." 2014. www.bpb.de/gesellschaft/migration/laenderprofile/178398/auswanderungspolitik.

Migration Policy Institute. "The Philippines Culture of Migration." 2006. www.migrationpolicy.org/article/philippines-culture-migration.

Overseas Workers Welfare Administration (OWWA). www.owwa.gov.ph.

Philippine Overseas Employment Administration (POEA). www.poea.gov.ph.

Technical Education and Skills Development Authority (TESDA). www.tesda.gov.ph.

Thailand

International Labour Organization (ILO). "The Reverse Brain Drain Project, Thailand." 2014. www.ilo.org/dyn/migpractice/migmain.showPractice?p_lang=en&p_practice_id=43.

Meyer, Jean-Baptiste, and Mercy Brown. *Scientific Diasporas: A New Approach to the Brain Drain*. Presentation prepared for World Conference on Science, UNESCO-ICSU, Budapest 1999. www.unesco.org/most/meyer.htm.

Links

Ministry of Science, Technology and Environment – National Science and Technology Development Agency. "The Reverse Brain Drain Project." Presentation (see References). www.ilo.org/dyn/migpractice/migmain.showPractice?p_lang=en&p_practice_id=43.

Reverse Brain Drain Project (RBD). http://rbd.nstda.or.th/rbdweb/about_rbd/index.php; http://rbd.nstda.or.th/index.php.

International organizations

Angenendt, Steffen. *Migration, Mobilität und Entwicklung. EU-Mobilitätspartnerschaften als Instrument der Entwicklungszusammenarbeit*. Berlin, SWP, 2012.

Angenendt, Steffen, Michael Clemens and Meiko Merda. "Der WHO-Verhaltenskodex. Eine gute Grundlage für die Rekrutierung von Gesundheitsfachkräften?" *SWP-Aktuell* 25. 2014.

Clemens, Michael A. "Global Skills Partnerships. A Proposal for Technical Training in a Mobile World." *CGD Policy Paper 040*. May 2014.

European Commission. *Mitteilung der Kommission an das europäische Parlament, den Rat, den europäischen Wirtschafts- und Sozialausschuss und den Ausschuss der Regionen. Gesamtansatz für Migration und Mobilität*. Brussels: EC, 2011.

Expert Council/Expert Advice on Migration and Integration. "Deutschland ist Europas absoluter Spitzenreiter bei der Blue Card." Berlin: SVR, 2014. www.svr-migration.de/presse/presse-svr/deutschland-europas-spitzenreiter/.

ILO (International Labour Organization). *ILO Multilateral Framework on Labour Migration. Non-binding principles and guidelines for a rights-based approach to labour migration*. Geneva: ILO, 2006. www.ilo.org/dyn/migpractice/docs/28/multilat_fwk_en.pdf.

International Labour Conference. *Resolution Concerning a Fair Deal for Migrant Workers in a Global Economy*. Geneva: ILO, 2004. www.ilo.org/wcmsp5/groups/public/---ed_protect/---protrav/---migrant/documents/genericdocument/wcms_178658.pdf.

International Labour Office. *Implementation of the ILO Plan of Action for Migrant Workers*. Geneva: ILO, 2008. www.ilo.org/wcmsp5/groups/public/---ed_norm/---relconf/documents/meetingdocument/wcms_090601.pdf.

International Labour Office. *Towards a Fair Deal for Migrant Workers in the Global Economy*. Geneva: ILO, 2004.

Kuptsch, Christiane, and Eng Fong Pang (eds.). *Competing for Global Talent*. Geneva: ILO, 2006.

Luthria, Manjula. "Labor Mobility for the Poor: Is it Really Possible?" Washington, D.C.: World Bank, 2011.

Links

Center for Mediterranean Integration (CMI). http://beta.cmimarseille.org.
MIGRANT. www.ilo.org/migrant/lang--en/index.htm.
International Recruitment Integrity System (IRIS). http://iris.iom.int/about-iris.
Global Forum on Migration and Development (GFMD). www.gfmd.org/process.
Global Knowledge Partnership on Migration and Development (KNOMAD). www.knomad.org.

List of institutions contacted

Australia
Australian Government, Department of Employment
University of Adelaide
Canada
Assisting Local Leaders with Immigrant Employment Strategies (ALLIES), a Maytree Idea
Canadian Immigrant Integration Program (CIIP)
Maytree Foundation
Mission of Canada to the European Union*
Toronto Region Immigrant Employment Council (TRIEC)
Denmark
Danish Agency for Labour Retention and International Recruitment
Workindenmark
France
Pôle emploi, Direction Affaires et Relations Internationales
Ministry of Foreign Affairs, Migration and Development
Germany
Federal Employment Agency
Centre for International Migration and Development (CIM)
Entwicklungsgesellschaft für berufliche Bildung mbH (ebb)
Gesellschaft für Internationale Zusammenarbeit (GIZ)
Institute for Employment Research (IAB), Working Group Migration and Integration
Institute for European Healthcare and Social Economy Sectors (IEGUS)
terres des hommes
Placement Services (ZAV)
New Zealand
Kea New Zealand
Ministry of Business, Innovation and Employment, Settlement Unit
OECD New Zealand
University of Waikato, National Institute of Demographic and Economic Analysis
Norway
Norwegian Ministry of Children, Equality and Social Inclusion, Department of Integration
Sweden
Ministry of Justice, Division for Migration and Asylum Policy
Swedish Board of Migration
Swedish Public Employment Service
The Swedish Confederation for Professional Employees (TCO)
Switzerland
State Secretary for Migration SEM
Development and Cooperation (DEZA), Section Global Programme Migration and Development
Federal Commission on Migration (EKM)*
Université de Neuchatel, Institut de géographie

Making Labor Migration Fair

The Netherlands
International Organization for Migration (IOM) The Netherlands
Maastricht Centre for Citizenship, Migration and Development
Ministry of Justice, Migration Policy
WRR – Scientific Council for Government Policy
Permits Foundation
Society Impact
The Hague Process on Refugees and Migration (THP)
University of Amsterdam, Faculty of Social and Behavioural Sciences, Transnational Configurations, Conflict and Governance
United Kingdom
Comic Relief
Department for International Development (DFID), Emerging Policy, Innovation and Capability (EPIC)
University College London, Department of Geography, Migration Research Unit
University of Sussex, Department of Geography, School of Global Studies
University of Oxford, Centre on Migration, Policy and Society (COMPAS)
USA
Center for Global Development*
Georgetown University, Institute for the Study of International Migration*
German Marshall Fund Berlin
International diaspora Engagement Alliance (IdEA)
Nurses Now International (NNI)
International organizations
International Organization for Migration (IOM), Labour Migration and Human Development Department of Migration Management
World Bank, Marseilles Office: Center for Mediterranean Integration, International Labor Mobility Program (ILM)
Global Knowledge Partnership on Migration and Development (KNOMAD), World Bank
* Email correspondence

List of on-site visits (countries and institutions)

Canada
Assisting Local Leaders with Immigrant Employment Strategies (ALLIES), a Maytree Idea
Canadian Immigrant Integration Program (CIIP)
Maytree Foundation
Mission of Canada to the European Union
Toronto Region Immigrant Employment Council (TRIEC)
Germany
Gesellschaft für Internationale Zusammenarbeit (GIZ), Centre for International Migration and Development (CIM), Placement Services (ZAV)
Krankenhaus Nordwest, Frankfurt am Main

List of on-site visits (countries and institutions)

Philippines
Canadian Immigrant Integration Program Philippines Regional Office
Department of Labor and Employment, Fair Migration Practice (POEA)
Deutsche Gesellschaft für Internationale Zusammenarbeit Manila Office; Berlitz language school Manila
German-Philippine Chamber of Commerce and Industry
Migration Policy Institute Manila Office
Peter Döhle Schifffahrt, Ausbildungszentrum Manila
The Philippines' Technical Education Skills and Development Authority (TESDA)

Sweden
Caritas, Migration Department
Ministry of Justice, Division for Migration and Asylum Policy
Stockholm University, Swedish Institute for Social Research (SOFI)
Swedish Board of Migration
Swedish Public Employment Service

The Netherlands
International Organization for Migration (IOM) The Netherlands
Ministry of Foreign Affairs, Cluster Migration and Development
Ministry of Justice, Migration Policy
Ministry of Employment and Social Affairs, Social Dialogue and Labour Migration; Integration and Society
Permits Foundation
The Hague Process on Refugees and Migration (THP)
University of Amsterdam, Faculty of Social and Behavioural Sciences, Transnational Configurations, Conflict and Governance

USA
Center for Global Development
Georgetown University, Institute for the Study of International Migration
International diaspora Engagement Alliance (IdEA); Calvert Foundation
Migration Policy Institute
New York University College of Nursing
Nurses Now International
US Department of Homeland Security, Immigration Policy Office
US Department of Labor

International organizations
World Bank, Marseilles Office: Center for Mediterranean Integration, International Labor Mobility Program (ILM)
Global Knowledge Partnership on Migration and Development (KNOMAD), World Bank

Reaching a Fair Deal on Talent: Emigration, Circulation and Human Capital in Countries of Origin

Kate Hooper, Madeleine Sumption

Introduction

Skilled migration produces widely acknowledged economic benefits both for destination countries and migrants themselves, but many policymakers and analysts remain concerned about the impact of skilled emigration on countries of origin. In particular, the risk that "brain drain" will deplete human-capital stocks and undermine prospects for economic development is commonly cited. In recent years, however, the research debate on migration has shifted to emphasize the potential benefits for origin countries. The most easily quantified benefit is associated with migrants' remittances, which far outstrip the volume of formal development aid and provide income directly to households in developing and emerging economies. But beyond this purely financial assistance, the skills, experience and networks developed by migrants overseas also provide opportunities for innovation and economic growth in sending countries. In particular, emigration is thought to help open up new markets for trade and investment, while the circulation of skilled workers between origin and destination countries offers opportunities to transfer new knowledge, technology and business practices back to migrants' home countries (For details on how diaspora members have contributed to institutional change in their countries of heritage, see Kuznetsov 2013).

A few origin countries actively facilitate skilled emigration for reasons that range from a lack of job opportunities at home to the desire to encourage remittances or open up the trade and investment links facilitated by migration (de Haas and Vezzoli 2011: 21–22). The Philippines, for example, is now well known for its concerted push to encourage emigration among middle-skilled workers. Several countries have also sought to increase the export of professional services and improve emigration opportunities for their high-skilled workers, in part through trade and investment agreements with destination countries. Examples include the EU-Canada Comprehensive Economic and Trade Agreement (CETA), the EU-Korea free-trade agreement and U.S. trade agreements negotiated with Chile, Singapore and Australia.

The research debate on these questions is far from closed. Quantifying the benefits of skilled emigration is difficult. Some analysts – and even more governments within countries of origin – remain skeptical that the benefits could ever outweigh the costs. Nonetheless, the idea that migrants, origin countries and destination countries should all be able to profit from migration is compelling. This idea of mutual benefit to all parties is often termed the "triple win," a phrase popularized by former U.N. Secretary-General Kofi Annan in 2006.

In practice, a clear road map to the creation of such benefits has been elusive. No single policy or set of policies can conclusively achieve the goal of balancing migration's benefits more equitably. This has instead left policymakers to rely on a host of smaller policies and initiatives that tackle specific pieces of the puzzle. Many of the projects in question are highly specialized, small in scale or difficult to evaluate rigorously. They are also scattered across policy fields, including education and training, international development, migration, trade and foreign affairs. As a result, the actors driving these initiatives – including the governments origin and destination countries, educational institutions of various kinds, non-profit organizations and the private sector – have varied widely, bringing different motivations and interests to the table.

This chapter provides an overview of existing policy measures and initiatives in this field, focusing on projects that develop skills and human capital. The discussion covers four stages in the migration cycle: (1) developing skills in countries of origin before departure; (2) applying those skills productively at a migrant's destination; (3) reintegrating returnees into the labor market in their origin country; and (4) enabling diaspora members who never permanently return to contribute to the skills base in their countries of origin or heritage. The lines between these categories are of course blurred, and some fall into more than one category.

In many cases, evaluating the benefits of a policy or program is difficult due to data limitations or the lack of control groups against which to compare beneficiaries. As a result, this report does not attempt to identify which projects represent the best investments or have had the greatest impact. Instead, it seeks to explain and categorize the types of interventions that exist and to provide some initial observations regarding their advantages and limitations.

Training in origin countries

Education and training systems in countries of origin are first and foremost designed to build skills within the domestic labor force. With some exceptions in countries with very high emigration rates and within certain occupations, the vast majority of people trained in their home country will not emigrate abroad. But training in countries of origin also affects workers' options for working overseas. Most international migrants to high-income destinations complete their formal education and training in their countries of origin – indeed, this rate is between 50 and 70 percent in most OECD countries, according to a recent analysis (OECD 2014). Consequently, origin and destination countries alike have an interest in the quality, content, cost and financing mechanisms associated with the training that takes place before people migrate as well as in the ease with which both formally and non-formally acquired skills can be transferred across borders.

The relationship between training and emigration abroad is complex and politically sensitive. Workers who hope to move abroad have an incentive to seek out education that meets international standards – for example, programs that meet regulatory requirements or employers' expectations in major destination countries. Facilitating emigration could thus be a by-product of training workers to meet standards similar to those of major destination countries, whether or not this is an explicit goal. Policymakers in countries that experience significant emigration thus often fear the costs of losing workers they have paid to educate and worry that training workers to meet international standards will encourage them to leave.

On the other hand, skilled emigration is unlikely to be an entirely zero-sum game. Some studies have found that the prospect of moving abroad raises the value of vocational skills and thus encourages people to invest in training they would not otherwise have completed (for a discussion of this, see Katseli, Lucas and Xenogiani 2006). While some of the people who seek training for this reason successfully migrate, others remain at home – for example, because they fail to find work abroad or simply because the additional training was an investment in an option they decided not to exercise.

At the same time, skills that position people to work abroad can also help raise standards at home. For example, health professionals with occupational English proficiency may find work abroad more easily; but, even at home, English gives them access to the international research literature, allowing them to improve domestic standards of care by keeping abreast of new developments in their field (Rietig and Squires forthcoming). Similarly, several developing countries have sought to import education and training models from higher-income nations because these are seen as a useful tools for raising the quality of education overall.

The cost of training looms large in this debate. It is often considerably cheaper to train a migrant in his or her country of origin than in the destination country; indeed, one study estimates that it is five to eight times cheaper to train a nurse in parts of North Africa than in Western Europe, for example (Clemens 2014: 1). However, origin countries naturally also have significantly fewer resources available to finance training. This has created particular interest in programs that either encourage migrants trained in their home country to serve a given period there before moving abroad or else transfer the burden of financing from origin countries to destination-country employers, governments or even migrants themselves (the greatest beneficiaries of migration).

This section reviews a spectrum of initiatives and policies designed to boost the supply of internationally transferrable skills, whether for individuals expected to migrate or those likely to stay at home.

Adapting training to other countries' standards

Internationally oriented education and training opportunities have been developed in several countries, though their purpose and the role that migration plays in them varies widely. Some are designed primarily to improve the quality of education in origin countries, while others aim more directly to facilitate the emigration or circulation of migrants. In practice, directly transposing one country's training system to another is extremely difficult and, in any case, some level of local customization is likely to be desirable. At least in theory, however, initiatives of this kind hold out the promise of lowering barriers to skilled employment abroad.

The Philippines' Technical Education Skills and Development Authority (TESDA) is a commonly cited and relatively large-scale example. TESDA administers a certification and training system that aims to serve both the domestic and international labor markets in return for relatively low enrollment fees. The certifications are used within the Philippines' domestic labor market and are not designed solely for prospective migrants. In email correspondence with the authors, Matthew Lisiecki (co-author of "Creating Valuable Skills") explained, however, that over the years, these certifications have gained recognition outside the Philippines, and several have been drawn up with the assistance of industry representatives from destination countries, such as Canada, Germany and Australia. TESDA's vocational-education and training program and its competency-assessment and certification program were themselves certified by the International Organization for Standardization (ISO) in 2012 (TESDA 2012).

An alternative to adapting domestic institutions is to bring in foreign providers. However, creating high-quality educational institutions and qualifications from scratch is a difficult, long-term project. In the short and medium term, therefore, several developing countries have turned to foreign education providers or accreditors to meet this need – both by encouraging foreign providers to set up local branches or accredit local qualification programs and by funding scholarships for their nationals to study abroad.

India's Ministry of Overseas Indian Affairs (MOIA), for example, is running a project with the International Organization for Migration (IOM) that offers vocational training and skills development to potential international migrants from the eight northeastern states of India. Following an initial pilot program between 2011 and 2013 and a preliminary labor-market assessment in six European countries, City & Guilds and Edexcel, two private UK-based qualifications-awarding organizations, developed the courses in partnership with existing academic institutions and vocational-training centers, focusing on health care (nursing assistants and geriatric care), education (teaching English), and hospitality (ILO 2011). The initiative aimed to build aspiring migrants' skills for these in-demand sectors of the labor market and will be rolled out nationally (SFG 2012: 20).

At the university level, foreign providers have become a common fixture in emerging economies. Over the past two decades, some of the world's major universities have set up international campuses, including some in countries of origin for international migration – particularly student migration – such as China (for an overview, see Lawton and Katsomitros 2012, and Lane 2011: 7). One long-standing example is the University of Nottingham, whose campuses in Ningbo (China) and Semenyih (Malaysia) deliver University of Nottingham degrees with English as the language of instruction. Nottingham's Ningbo campus was the first foreign provider authorized by China's Ministry of Education to confer its own qualifications; typically, foreign institutions in China must provide a transnational education in conjunction with a local higher-education institute (McNamara, Knight and Fernandez-Chung 2013). Moreover, it is almost entirely funded through students' fees (QAA 2012: 3). In 2012, there were approximately 34,000 students enrolled at Nottingham's U.K. campus, another 4,400 at its Malaysian campus, and 5,300 at its Chinese campus (University of Nottingham 2013). A 2012 evaluation of Nottingham's Chinese campus, where more than 90 percent of current students are from mainland China, Hong Kong, Macau or Taiwan, found that 65 percent of its graduates went on to study at U.K., U.S. or Canadian universities, and that 35 percent of its graduates went on to find employment in China or overseas (QAA 2012).

Interestingly, international qualifications of this kind do not necessarily eliminate problems of qualifications recognition when graduates move into the workforce, largely because it is difficult to create a single qualification that will be recognized in more than one country. In particular, similar course content does not lead to automatic professional licensing. Because University of Nottingham campuses issue identical degrees, there is limited flexibility in adjusting curricula to meet the (sometimes conflicting) demands of U.K. and Malaysian licensing bodies. Some programs are now recognized by both authorities; others are automatically recognized by just one licensing body (requiring additional credential-recognition processes in the other); and, in some cases, constrained by degree requirements, programs do not lead to automatic licensing in either country (QAA 2010: 4–6).

Other initiatives designed to bring in foreign education providers have been developed with the support of destination countries themselves. The Australian government, for example, has run various development-oriented initiatives in the Pacific region that provide full Australian qualifications to local students. Two case studies that have received detailed evaluations, the Australia-Pacific Technical College (APTC) and the Kiribati Australia Nursing Initiative (KANI), demonstrate some of the challenges associated with exporting qualifications to other countries in a cost-effective manner.

The APTC trains skilled students (who already have post-secondary qualifications and/or experience) in subjects such as construction, electrical work, engineering and plumbing, and "tops up" their existing skills with Australian qualifications (Clemens, Graham and Howes 2014). The APTC operates as an independent college in the Pacific region and delivers its education entirely on-site with Australian instructors. KANI, on the other hand, funds students to travel to Queensland, Australia, and receive their education from existing Australian educational institutions. It is also unusual in that it trains those who have left school rather than those with existing post-secondary education (e.g., awarding Australian nursing diplomas and certificates up to a bachelor's of nursing).

In theory, both programs were designed to facilitate migration to Australia. But while the caliber of the APTC education has been praised by employers and graduates alike (Alampi et al. 2013: 32; APTC 2013), very few students (fewer than 3%) have in fact migrated to Australia or New Zealand (Clemens, Graham and Howes 2014: 1). By contrast, the majority of KANI graduates remained in Australia or New Zealand, working in full- or part-time roles (40%), looking for work (22%) or continuing their studies in Australia (18%). Only 20 percent returned home, according to an evaluation of the project (Shaw, Edwards and Rimon 2013: 8–9). In addition to strong demand for nurses in Australia, one likely reason for this outcome is that, by bringing students to Australia, KANI was able to help them acquire local networks and employer contacts. In addition, APTC's courses, which were initially modeled on Australian curricula for occupations on Australia's Skilled Occupations List (SOL), were not updated to keep pace with changes to the SOL or to the work-experience and skills requirements of the Australian points system. This meant that opportunities for graduates to qualify for visas to migrate to Australia were limited (Alampi et al. 2013: 29–39). One study suggests this also reflects a lack of political commitment in the Pacific region and Australia to the APTC's original goal of encouraging skills mobility (Clemens, Graham and Howes 2014: 20–23).

Both models have proved to be extremely expensive, delivering qualifications at Australian prices and thus requiring extensive funding by the Australian government. The APTC spends around AUD 53,000 on each student; this is the equivalent of taking the course in Australia and between five and 10 times more expensive than equivalent Fijian programs (Alampi et al. 2013: 32). KANI annually spends nearly AUD 50,000 on each bachelor's of nursing student and nearly AUD 80,000 on its graduate diploma of nursing students, with each student's full qualification costing nearly a quarter of a million AUD (Shaw, Edwards and Rimon 2013: 10). As a result, some analysts have argued that upgrading local institutions to deliver Australian (or Australian-standard) qualifications through the use of local instructors would be more cost-effective, while simultaneously providing greater benefits for local communities by improving overall educational capacities (Alampi et al. 2013: 22–23).

> **Private qualifications with global recognition**
>
> In some fields with particularly global labor markets, employers and professional associations have developed international standards and qualifications for mobile professionals largely without government intervention. Several of these certifications have been specifically designed to facilitate movement across borders, making them of particular interest to learners and policymakers with an interest in international migration.
>
> Some certifications are offered by professional associations that want to facilitate mobility within the profession and standardize training, while simultaneously establishing themselves as a global brand. One example is the Association of Chartered Certified Accountants (ACCA), whose certificates are widely recognized by private-sector employers and regulatory bodies in countries around the world. As of February 2014, this includes the 28 EU member states, Canada and some countries in Asia, Africa and the Caribbean – but not the United States. Another example is the American Concrete Institute (ACI), which has chapters throughout the world that sponsor ACI certification programs for workers in the concrete construction industry (ACI 2014). In both cases, candidates seeking certification must pay to join the association as well as for relevant study materials and examination fees.
>
> In some industries, such as information and communication technology (ICT), private companies may also offer certifications that demonstrate candidates' proficiency in certain areas or specialties. The market leaders for ICT certifications are Cisco Systems, Microsoft and Oracle, whose certifications are focused on the use of their own software. Cisco's Networking Academy program features 10,000 academies in 165 countries and more than 1 million students worldwide (CISCO 2014). Cisco additionally partners with educational institutions, NGOs and community centers to help students prepare for entry-level ICT jobs by providing online-curricula-based training, virtual-learning tools, teacher training and instructions, and professional-development opportunities for instructors. Similarly, education institutions worldwide can pay to become a Microsoft IT academy, giving them permission to use Microsoft's curricula and resources to train IT students. In the 2012–2013 academic year, Microsoft issued over 1 million certificates (Microsoft 2014). Oracle offers online courses and certifications

(for a fee) that help bring developers and administrators to a level of proficiency in its platforms and products, such as Java.

Several German auto and auto-components manufacturers, including Siemens and Volkswagen, have also developed their own qualifications and have worked with local colleges across the world to make them available to students, often in areas where German companies have invested and want to hire personnel with qualifications trusted by employers. Efforts to export German vocational qualifications have also been supported by Germany's central education department and its overseas chambers of commerce and industry (AHKs).

Opportunities for study and work abroad

Developing countries cannot create world-class education and training institutions for their citizens overnight. However, they can help students access these opportunities overseas. Several countries of origin have promoted study abroad as a strategy to boost their own skills base, requiring graduates to return home to work for a set period as a condition of their scholarship. Exchange programs and overseas work-placement initiatives have also been developed to give workers professional experience abroad – in some cases as a purely temporary training initiative, and in others as a first step toward longer-term migration.

Scholarships for study abroad

Large numbers of international students study at universities in high-income OECD countries, and a majority does not stay on after graduation. This makes international study a substantial source of skills for countries of origin. Some destination countries contribute to this education by funding scholarships that may require students to return home after their studies rather than staying on to enter the destination-country labor force. The OECD allows countries to include scholarships, grants and estimated imputed student costs as part of their official development assistance (ODA) totals (OECD, DCD/DAD 2010).

Many origin countries also fund study abroad, and some of the programs – such as those in Brazil and Saudi Arabia – are quite large. These programs send students or young professionals to acquire additional education or expertise at a level not readily available in their home country.

Brazil's Science Without Borders program, for example, sponsors Brazilians wishing to study abroad at a foreign institution in the fields of science, technology, engineering or mathematics. Its goal is to promote technological advances in Brazil through international exchange and knowledge transfer (CSF 2014). As of 25 June 2014, the program had awarded 83,200 of its 101,000 planned scholarships, and it is supposed to be renewed for a second phase in 2015, with the aim of providing an additional 100,000 scholarships (ICEF 2014). Students must either return home for a certain period after graduation or repay their scholarships if they stay overseas. The scholarships typically fund foreign study for between six months and one year. As a result, students generally do not complete their studies abroad, creating an additional incentive to return to Brazil to finish their degrees. The return requirement is also reinforced in major student destinations, such as the United States, Australia, Canada and the United Kingdom, through visa policies that restrict scholarship recipients' pathways to temporary or permanent migration after graduation.

Professional experience abroad

For many occupations, formal education is not the most important way to build skills; professional experience is equally or more important. Both prospective long-term migrants and workers who plan to return to their countries of origin can therefore benefit from professional expertise and networks gained abroad, especially if their experience brings them into contact with new technologies or practices that have been underexploited at home. This type of tacit knowledge transfer can be valuable across the skills spectrum and in a range of industries, from agriculture to high-tech (cf. Iskander and Low 2011: 51–52).

Some programs promoting professional experience overseas are driven by origin countries. The Japanese government launched its Global Action for Careers and Employability (Global ACE) program in 2013, with an initial goal of sponsoring around 400 students to go overseas for at least three months to gain temporary work experience or language training (Pie News 2013). Participants are provided with a career-development consultant who helps them develop skills-building goals for their time abroad. Pursuing a different strategy, Mexico supported the creation of a special professional work visa as a part of the North American Free Trade Agreement (NAFTA), which allows Mexican and Canadian nationals to work in the United States on a temporary basis.

Destination countries have been the driving force behind several other programs facilitating migrants' acquisition of professional experience abroad. In a handful of cases, destination countries have deliberately encouraged return migration to developing countries by providing strictly temporary visas that do not allow holders to switch to other visas or apply for permanent residence. However, the assumption that requiring professionals to leave the country after a certain period of time is a good way to maximize overall contributions to countries of origin is controversial, since it limits individuals' opportunities for development and ignores other ways they can contribute (as described in the next section). Nonetheless, the United States trains large numbers of students and professionals on the basis of its J-1 visa, which requires many individuals to return to their home countries. If participants in this "exchange visitor" program are funded either by their origin country or the U.S. government, are deemed to have specialized knowledge and skills deemed necessary for the development of their home country, or have received graduate medical training, they are required to return to their home country for at least two years once their visa expires and cannot apply for other U.S. employment- or family-based visas during that time, though they may apply for other visas, such as the F-1 student visa (USDS BECA 2014). At the low-skilled level, both New Zealand and more recently Australia operate strictly temporary seasonal-worker programs for Pacific Island nationals to work in the agricultural sector. These programs were deliberately designed to facilitate remittances without requiring the host countries to accept new permanent residents with low skill levels, although skills transfers to origin countries have also been touted as potential benefits of the programs (NZ-MFAT 2010).

Beyond providing visas to facilitate temporary work experience, destination countries may also directly provide work placements to foreign nationals. One example is a pilot project for engineers in Tunisia run by Germany's Federal Foreign Office (AA) in conjunction with ZAV, the international-placement services arm of Germany's Federal Employment Agency. The project, which ran from 2012 to 2013, provided 100 unemployed Tunisian engineers with five months of language and intercultural training in Tunis and Germany, subsequently providing participants with scholarships for six-month work placements at German companies (GIZ 2012a). At the end of the project, 65 participants had acquired jobs working either in Germany or at German companies in Tunisia (ibid.). This program has similarities with programs that train and recruit foreign caregivers or nurses for positions overseas, such as the Philippines-Japan agreement that allows Filipino nurses and caregivers to move to Japan (see the section "Training, retraining and placement services") and Germany's pilot program to train Vietnamese nurses to become geriatric nurses in Germany (GIZ 2012b).

Tailoring skills and experience within destination countries

Despite the strong economic and institutional forces that fuel large-scale global migration among the highly skilled, the skills and experience that migrants take across borders are often underexploited. Genuine differences in education and experience gained in different countries, coupled with employers' lack of familiarity with foreign credentials, can mean that workers make limited use of their training after they migrate. This phenomenon is exacerbated by language barriers, migrants' lack of knowledge of job opportunities and recruiting norms, and licensing systems that require those trained abroad to reapply for the right to practice their profession after they move.

For policymakers concerned with ensuring that migration's impact on skills development is "fair," and that international migration does not inadvertently deplete skills in which migrants and sending countries have invested, this presents a considerable challenge. Barriers to transferring skills across borders are thought to reduce opportunities for the circulation of skilled professionals who might be beneficial to both origin and destination countries; they also jeopardize migrants' ability to integrate successfully within the destination country. This "brain waste" also represents a cost to destination countries' economies, which do not reap the benefits of their immigrants' human capital (cf. Sumption 2013 and Hawthorne 2013).

Several promising models have been developed in recent years to improve recognition of migrants' qualifications (ibid.). Some are designed primarily to encourage integration on the part of migrants becoming long-term residents of destination counties, while others are intended to facilitate emigration or boost trade and investment opportunities for countries of origin. A common feature of all these programs is that they go beyond merely theoretical or classroom-based training, instead taking an active approach to connecting immigrants with jobs, contacts and local work-experience opportunities – a crucial part of the qualifications-recognition puzzle. While a full review is beyond the scope of this chapter, this section reviews some key initiatives.

International cooperation on recognizing qualifications

Seeking to reduce the barriers to mobility and integration often created by professional regulation, governments and professional associations in several countries have negotiated mutual recognition agreements (MRAs). These agreements set out rules for licensing practitioners who move between signatory countries. Their goal is to reduce or even eliminate the need for case-by-case assessments when applicants have been trained in systems conferring essentially comparable skills and knowledge. If meaningful gaps in education and training do exist, agreements may give applicants credit for their home-country qualifications but require a certain amount of additional testing, training or work experience. Others provide temporary or limited registrations that allow migrants to perform work for which they are qualified while avoiding tasks for which they are not qualified (Sumption, Papademetriou and Flamm 2013).

Reaching mutual recognition agreements is difficult, and relatively few successful agreements have been negotiated. (The mutual recognition of qualifications among European Union member states has been a large and notable exception.) Recently, Quebec and France negotiated and implemented a series of recognition agreements in more than 80 regulated occupations, making it a relatively rare case of a wide-ranging MRA between countries that are not part of a single market. In each occupation, agreements define requirements for professionals moving between the two countries and, in some – though not all – cases, considerably reduce the amount of retraining required. Some of the agreements, such as that for nursing, provide for short orientation courses designed to fill any skills gaps quickly and at relatively low cost. Like most mutual recognition agreements, this initiative governs movement between two countries with relatively similar levels of economic development; however, discussions are currently underway to assess the potential for additional agreements with Francophone countries in North Africa – a move that, if successful, would represent a significant step toward the extension of mutual-recognition frameworks to developing countries.

When gaps in education and training are large enough to make mutual recognition difficult, it may nonetheless be possible to reduce the cost of taking licensing exams by making them more widely available. In particular, offering professional examinations in origin countries can help migrants acquire qualifications more quickly, speeding up their integration into regulated professions upon arrival. This strategy has been explored by several professional associations in Canada (Prince St-Amand 2014), for example, as well as by the United States' Commission on Graduates of Foreign Nursing Schools (CGFNS 2014).

Training, retraining and placement services for those trained abroad

Migrants often require additional knowledge, training or language skills before they can practice their professions overseas. In regulated occupations, they may need a host-country license or certification. But navigating licensing systems can be difficult, and migrants with small gaps in their knowledge do not always have good options for filling those gaps without repeating years of training. As a result, governments, non-profit organizations and private-sector employers in several countries have designed and supported specialized programs to help migrants acquire necessary local qualifications or knowledge. Some of these programs operate wholly within destination countries, while others involve cooperation across borders, in part to take advantage of the lower costs associated with origin-country training and to facilitate faster integration by beginning the process before departure.

A good example of intensive retraining is that provided by Nurses Now International (NNI), a private company that offered a credentialing program between 2009 and 2012 for Mexican nurses moving for long-term staffing placements at U.S. hospitals (Squires and Beltrán-Sánchez 2013: 30–35). Participants took three months of English classes with a focus on nursing, 10 weeks of classes with U.S. nurses, and a six-week supervised work placement in a U.S. hospital to practice and develop their skills. Graduates of the program generally passed the U.S. nurse licensing examination (NCLEX-RN) within four months, with first-time pass rates equivalent to those of U.S. nurses (by contrast, usually only around 25 percent of candidates from El Salvador, Guatemala, Honduras and Mexico pass on the first time) (ibid.: 28). Participants received a stipend to encourage their completion of the program; this and the general costs of training 80 nurses a year were covered by a venture capital firm and other investors. Despite the success of the training and its business model, at least initially, NNI was affected by the economic downturn of 2008 and the subsequent collapse in U.S. demand for internationally educated nurses. Coupled with bureaucratic delays (such as in obtaining educational transcripts from candidates' nursing programs in Mexico or the slow evaluation of credentials in the United States), this prevented NNI from becoming a self-sustaining, profit-generating business within three years, as initially predicted; several investors pulled out, prompting NNI's eventual closure in 2012. That said, the model retains considerable potential for other efforts to provide high-quality training (perhaps on a non-profit basis, instead).

In the Philippines, as discussed above, TESDA has also developed programs that help migrants acquire credentials for overseas markets. In 2011, it developed the Preparatory Japanese Language Training Program to prepare Filipino caregivers and nurses to work in Japan. Under the Japan-Philippine Economic Partnership Agreement (JPEPA) of 2006, Japan matches up to 200 certified nurses and 300 certified caregivers with Japanese hospitals per year, allowing them to work for up to three years as nurses' aides – an occupation below their level of training, but which is better remunerated than the work of fully licensed nurses in the Philippines (Yagi et al. 2014) – before taking government-sponsored qualification examinations to practice as nurses (Sun 2012). Passing these examinations also makes Filipino nurses and caregivers eligible for renewable residence permits (Amante 2007). However, because candidates struggled with language requirements, pass rates on the Japanese-language test were low, resulting in a poor return on investment for the Japanese government and participating hospitals (Yagi et al. 2014). In response, TESDA introduced a Japanese-language program, funded by the Japanese government, that offers six months of compulsory pre-departure language instruction in addition to the six months of post-arrival language and skills training initially called for in JPEPA. Critics have called for further measures to provide Japanese-language instruction in the Philippines to help boost Filipino pass rates (ibid.).

Numerous other initiatives worldwide have aimed at improving recognition of migrants' foreign qualifications. For example, Mexico's Institute for Mexicans Abroad (IME) and Colombia's National Service of Learning have both established adult-education initiatives in destination countries to help their nationals integrate more effectively (for details, see Délano 2010 and CMRECNU 2008). Other credentialing initiatives are driven by non-profit organizations seeking to support immigrants' integration within destination countries. These include vocation-specific training and language-instruction programs designed to help candidates prepare for licensing exams and find work in their field. A retraining project for immigrant doctors and nurses in Portugal run by the Calouste Gulbenkian Foundation is one such example. Other credentialing initiatives include guidance and job counseling for foreign professionals, such as programs that connect immigrants with mentors in their target occupations as well as facilitating internship and other work-experience opportunities. Examples of this include the Czech non-profit META program, which provides occupation-specific language instruction and counseling, and the Canadian organization Assisting Local Leaders with Immigrant Employment Strategies (ALLIES), which runs mentoring and work-experience projects.

Taken together, the initiatives demonstrate the wide range of actors who have supported and funded retraining and credential-recognition programs, including origin governments, destination governments, non-profits and the private sector. In practice, financing regimes depend on the goals of the project. While employer-sponsored credentialing initiatives are by no means the norm, and governments and non-profits currently provide most of the funding, initiatives such as the NNI point toward a model for retraining and credential-recognition that could potentially be employer-funded and ultimately financially self-sustaining.

Facilitating return and reintegrating returnees

Facilitating return migration and ensuring that those who do return reintegrate successfully is the most direct strategy by which origin countries can benefit from their emigrants' skills. Some migrants may be willing to return in theory but need a "nudge" to overcome the immediate barriers to doing so, such as the difficulties in finding work, connecting with local contacts in their fields, and moving their families from one country to another. Various initiatives have been developed to assist with this process. These projects typically target those with the highest skill levels, including scientists and entrepreneurs, and are often driven by origin-country governments, though in some cases they are led by development agencies or non-profit organizations.

A second target group for return-migration initiatives is made up of people who are returning without specific job opportunities previously arranged. This includes migrants whose visas have expired, who can no longer find work in their destination country, or who want to return for family or other personal reasons. These return migrants can find it difficult to reintegrate, particularly after a prolonged absence. A recent study of Mexican migrants returning from the United States, for example, found that only 28 percent of employed returnees were using skills acquired in the United States in their current work in Mexico, and that only 4 percent had received help from government programs upon their return (MATT 2013: 47–51). In other words, returnees' skills may be wasted, and origin countries may fail to benefit from them as a consequence. Several initiatives have been developed to address this problem, including efforts connecting return migrants with job opportunities within their origin countries, providing support for entrepreneurial ventures, and helping returning workers have their foreign-acquired skills recognized at home.

However, facilitating return migrants' contributions within their home countries appears to be a weak area within the field of migration and skills development. While several voluntary-return programs have been developed to target rejected asylum seekers and migrants whose visas have expired, only a few initiatives have focused on reintegrating economic migrants returning of their own accord. One possible reason for this is that sending countries, which are in theory better placed than destination countries to facilitate such programs, often lack the infrastructure or resources to implement them and may not view reintegrating returnees as a priority in economies that already provide limited opportunities for citizens who have stayed at home.

Policies to facilitate return

A 2011 global survey on countries' emigration policies found that, of the top 25 sending countries, 15 had targeted policies in place to try and encourage their citizens to return home (UN DESA 2013). Attracting overseas talent back home is of course easier for some countries than others. The most "desirable" returnees are the highly skilled professionals and entrepreneurs who also have good options within their destination countries and who will only move if they have compelling career opportunities back home. Not surprisingly, migrants are far more likely to return home to a country with a stable political, economic and social climate and with a level of development similar to that of the destination country (OECD 2009: 163–164). Access to venture capital, research infrastructure and educated workforces are also frequently cited preconditions for attracting successful emigrants back to their home countries (Saxenian 2005). While not all countries currently provide these conditions, rapid growth and foreign investment in many developing countries – most obviously in Asia, but more recently in Africa, as well – should make attracting emigrants and diaspora members back to their countries of origin a realistic aspiration for a growing range of emigration countries.

Many sending countries have policies such as tax breaks in place with the aim of encouraging their overseas nationals to return. Examples include Ecuador, which offers return migrants the ability to repatriate their personal belongings without paying any tariffs, and Malaysia (through its Returning Expert Program), which offers a similar deal along with a flat tax rate of 15 percent and permanent-resident status for participants' spouses and children. Considerably fewer operate programs that actively target and recruit their highly skilled emigrants to practice specialist professions in their country of origin. A first set of initiatives in this regard targets highly skilled professionals to match them directly with jobs in their origin country or provide them with resources to facilitate their return. For example, Taiwan's National Science Council and Ministry of Education both recruit Taiwanese academics living overseas to return to Taiwanese universities on a temporary or permanent basis (O'Neill 2003). China also runs a number of programs that seek to attract overseas academics back to their origin country to "serve the nation" on a temporary or permanent basis (Zweig, Fung and Han 2008).

Programs facilitating return have also been developed in destination countries. While many of the initiatives based in destination countries provide limited post-return assistance and are primarily aimed at securing the return of unsuccessful asylum seekers or other unauthorized migrants, some have been more substantively designed with development goals in mind. For example, the German government's Centre for International Migration and Development (CIM) has run a program for returning experts since 1980 that helps place and reintegrate foreign nationals with professional qualifications obtained in Germany who wish to contribute to development goals in their countries of origin (CIM 2011). It is funded by the German Federal Ministry for Economic Cooperation and Development (BMZ). The CIM advertises jobs to these foreign nationals and puts them in touch with companies offering suitable positions, sometimes carrying out the initial screening of candidates for these firms. In some discretionary cases (those deemed to benefit development in the region), the CIM also provides financial support, offering subsidies for relocating and setting up a new workplace and supplementing candidates' salaries for up to two years. Between 2004 and January 2011, the program had assisted more than 10,000 returning experts (ibid.).

Korea's Happy Return program is another example, matching low- or middle-skilled foreign workers whose visas are expiring with Korean companies in their countries of origin. In theory, this encourages temporary migrants to leave Korea while contributing to their reintegration at home. It offers free pre-departure business-skills workshops and advice on transferring benefits, and it runs job fairs with Korean companies in countries of origin (SK MEL 2014). However, employment rates upon return have been rather low; of the 2,000 returnees who attended job fairs in 2012, only around 400 found employment (ILO 2014). This may be partly attributable to an amendment to Korea's Employment Permit System that year that allowed workers to return to their home countries for three months before returning to Korea on a renewed work permit; as a result, some participants may not have actively sought jobs in their home country, but instead simply waited for the three-month period to expire.

A second common program type targets overseas business entrepreneurs, for example, by connecting them with private-sector jobs or offering them space and funding to pursue business ventures. Taiwan and China's technology hubs or "science parks" are well-known examples of this latter strategy. Both of these governments established special economic zones in which highly skilled returnees and foreign experts can set up business ventures in the science and technology sectors. China's Zhongguancun Science Park (based in Beijing; often referred to as China's "Silicon Valley") has set up liaison offices in places such as Silicon Valley and London with the aim of attracting talent from overseas, and it has close ties with overseas academic and professional associations. Zhongguancun additionally offers financial incentives to its returnees, such as low-cost housing, reduced tariffs on equipment, subsidies and simplified procedures for investment and trade (Xie et al. 2011).

Another example is the French government's Program for the Creation of Innovative Companies in the Mediterranean (PACEIM), a partnership between France's Institut de Recherche pour le Développement (IRD) and ministries in Algeria, Tunisia, Morocco and Lebanon. The initiative sponsors North Africans with French graduate degrees in science and technology in starting businesses in their countries of origin. Candidates with technology- or research-based business ideas apply through a competitive process to receive up to €35,000 in start-up capital along with an individualized mentoring plan and logistical or technical support to help them with business development and implementation. The initial support is provided in France, with further assistance provided in countries of origin, over a total period of 15 months. While some participants plan to remain French residents in the long term, others have used the program to re-establish themselves permanently in their country of origin (IRD 2014a). France provides 80 percent of the funding, while origin governments provide the remaining 20 percent. Though still in its early stages, the project aims to provide opportunities for highly qualified emigrants to use their skills at home, to create businesses with the potential to provide jobs for highly educated graduates from North African institutions, and to help develop more competitive tech sectors in these origin countries (IRD 2014b).

Policies helping migrants use their skills upon return

Return migrants may struggle to find work in their home country's labor market that fits their foreign-acquired skills and expertise. This may reflect the origin country's poor recognition of foreign qualifications and experience or result from a mismatch between migrants' foreign-acquired skills and expertise and the origin country's labor-market needs. Targeted employment services, such as job-matching, (re)training and credential-recognition initiatives, are designed to mitigate some of these challenges.

Initiatives based in destination countries can provide information and financial assistance and have the advantage of reaching individuals early in the process of returning home. However, those based in countries of origin may be better placed to provide ongoing, longer-term support for returning migrants as they reintegrate. Colombia's Plan Retorno (Return Home Plan) program, for example, has established special offices for return migrants in some of the departments that experience the highest levels of international migration, such as Antioquia and the Bogotá capital district. These centers provide migrants with counseling services, information on training and apprenticeship opportunities through the National Learning Service (SENA), assistance with finding jobs and details on financial support available for starting businesses (CMRE 2014).

Similarly, Mexico's Ministry of the Interior launched the Somos Mexicanos (We Are Mexicans) program in March 2014 to assist returnees with the return process, in part by providing referrals to job opportunities and educational programs (PdMR 2014). This builds on earlier work by non-profits, such as Mexicans and Americans Thinking Together (MATT). A MATT-commissioned study found that many returnees to Mexico struggled to utilize their U.S.-acquired credentials and received very little support in the course of their return and reintegration. MATT's Yo Soy México (I Am Mexico) initiative tries to fill this gap by providing returnees with information on available social programs and support networks, and by linking them with job opportunities in the private sector through the organization's online portal. It also works with the private sector and government officials on broader challenges facing returnees, such as negative perceptions of migrants' alleged criminality (arising from unauthorized crossings of the U.S.-Mexico border) and a lack of financial literacy that can discourage investment or entrepreneurship (Hazan 2014).

Finally, support for returning migrants can come through mainstream institutions, such as public-employment services. In Albania, for example, an Instrument for Pre-Accession (IPA) project funded by the European Union and implemented by the International Labour Organization (ILO), which was scheduled to run through August 2014, provides reintegration services for returning migrants as part of a broader series of labor-market reforms in Albania. By March 2014, the initiative had established employment offices in five locations and had provided specialized training for its staff to advise returning migrant workers with foreign-acquired skills. As of the time of writing, the project was designing a skills-certification initiative targeted at returning migrant workers, with the aim of facilitating their reintegration into the Albanian labor market.

Diaspora engagement

Even if migrants choose to settle permanently overseas, they and their descendants are not necessarily "lost" to the origin country. In an age of swift global communication and deepening economic ties between countries, diaspora communities can maintain strong ties with their country of heritage and contribute to its development in a number of ways without physically returning. The economic impact of diaspora remittances is well documented. But the diaspora can also be a resource producing human-capital development and economic growth in origin countries by providing access to skills, experience and overseas networks (Kuznetsov 2013).

After years of criticizing emigrants for abandoning their countries of origin, many countries now celebrate their diaspora communities and attempt to benefit from their skills and resources (Gamlen 2006: 6–7). Numerous origin countries and diaspora members have set up initiatives to facilitate diaspora contributions, often with assistance from host countries' foreign-affairs or development agencies. These projects vary widely. Some focus on building networks of diaspora members with the aim of encouraging contact with their origin-country peers and attracting donations or investments for philanthropic or business purposes. Others require a more hands-on contribution, with diaspora members delivering support in-person, either by delivering specialist knowledge in a particular field or by offering more general capacity-building services, such as managerial experience (MSA 2012). The variety of initiatives pursued also reflects the composition of a country's skilled diaspora community, which may encompass entrepreneurs, academics and other talented professionals, all with discrete contributions to offer (Agunias and Newland 2012; Aikins and White 2011; Kuznetsov 2013; Newland 2010).

Networking and mentoring

A preliminary stage in efforts to engage the diaspora community is that of outreach: identifying diaspora members and their skill sets, assessing their needs and setting up networks to encourage them to contribute their expertise to their country of origin. One model is the academic network, which targets diaspora researchers and has been a popular tool for organizations seeking to facilitate the transfer of knowledge and skills between origin and destination countries. Some of the best-known efforts to set up diaspora networks have been in Colombia, whose first network for diaspora scientists was established in 1991 (Agunias and Newland 2012: 174). Australia has also been active in this field, with a network receiving both public and private funding designed to encourage emigrants to make business connections and consider returning home (ibid.: 135). This initiative, called Advance Australia, offers repatriation information and has an online forum for posting job opportunities. It also runs industry-specific forums and networking events that aim to make business connections between Australians and others who might consider themselves "Friends of Australia." As of 2011, this network had more than 24,000 members in 80 countries (Aikins and White 2011: 166–168).

Some networks envision a more active role for their diaspora members, encouraging them to provide individualized mentoring to local entrepreneurs. GlobalScot, for example, draws upon a network of diaspora businessmen and entrepreneurs to provide mentoring services for individuals and businesses based in Scotland. It was founded in 2001 by Scottish Enterprise, a Scottish government agency, as an exclusive invitation-only network. Members must hold senior positions in business and are personally welcomed by Scotland's first minister. It runs networking events, but it also organizes mentoring activities for entrepreneurs based in Scotland. GlobalScot helps Scottish entrepreneurs and fledgling entrepreneurs at schools and universities identify business opportunities in Scotland. It also provides some support for the entrepreneurial process, for instance, in the negotiation of business deals, the acquisition of financial backing and the design of business plans (Agunias and Newland 2012: 137–138). As of 2011, GlobalScot had around 650 members and had apparently generated GBP 30 million in revenue for Scottish enterprises (Aikins and White 2011: 168–172).

Networking initiatives are hard to evaluate. The desired outcomes (such as fostering business connections and sharing knowledge) are intangible and difficult to measure or attribute to specific activities. Nonetheless, they can be a relatively inexpensive tool to encourage contributions from diaspora members, such as mentoring or business and research collaborations, even if evidence regarding their impact is largely anecdotal.

Support for diaspora entrepreneurs

Encouraging diaspora entrepreneurship has been the goal of several development-focused initiatives. These projects have taken varying approaches, including support for diaspora members hoping to return on a temporary or permanent basis as well as for nationals who have never left their home country. Several projects draw on the expertise of diaspora members to provide short-term entrepreneurial advice. This type of mentorship and tailored business advice is designed to build capacity among diaspora communities and in countries of origin, leading to new businesses and wealth creation in origin countries.

An example of an organization that provided intensive support for entrepreneurs can be seen in the IntEnt Foundation, which operated in the Netherlands from 1996 to 2013 and helped diaspora entrepreneurs set up businesses in Morocco, Turkey, Suriname, Ghana, Ethiopia, Curacao and Afghanistan. The program consisted of several stages in which participants were selected and then given assistance in establishing small or medium-sized enterprises (SMEs). The foundation ran a series of promotional and selection processes designed to pick participants, including entrepreneurship tests and formal interviews. The orientation phase included group training focused on developing business plans, market research and data collection and was accompanied by individual counseling. Candidates then received external evaluation and assistance in acquiring third-party support and start-up capital (Molenaar 2009: 18). According to former IntEnt CEO Klaas Molenaar, the "vast majority" of participants also used their own funds or loans from relatives to finance their businesses (ibid.: 31). By 2009, more than 10,000 fledgling migrant entrepreneurs had contacted IntEnt for assistance, and around 350 businesses had been launched, over 90 percent of which were still running after three years (Agunias and Newland 2012: 143; Molenaar 2009: 13–15).

The International diaspora Engagement Alliance (IdEA), another example of an initiative designed to encourage diaspora entrepreneurship, conducts business-plan competitions for diaspora members with ideas for businesses in their countries of heritage (IdEA 2014). Managed by the U.S. Department of State, USAID and the Calvert Foundation, with partners from both the private and non-profit sectors, IdEA has run competitions for U.S.-based African, Caribbean and Latin American diaspora entrepreneurs. The first, in Africa, was run by USAID as a pilot project between 2009 and 2010. USAID's evaluation of this first business-plan competition identified some significant challenges; for instance, none of the 12 businesses evaluated achieved their business goals, and only four of the businesses appeared to be sustainable in the short term (USAID 2011: 5–7). The report called for greater USAID involvement in selecting, designing, implementing and monitoring the project, and for technical advisers to help contestants with the areas of financing and operations. The second iteration of the African competition offered larger grants, placed a greater emphasis on technical assistance (including technical mentors to provide assistance, with funding for this task handled separately) and aimed to produce clearer business plans, goals and milestones (ADM 2014).

Temporary return for local capacity-building

A range of initiatives draws on highly skilled diaspora-community members to provide mentoring or training for capacity-building purposes by temporarily returning to their origin countries for a number of weeks or months. These projects often additionally aim to foster deeper links between diaspora members and their countries of heritage. Indeed, anecdotal evidence from some projects suggests that some diaspora members have chosen to relocate to the country permanently following their temporary placement. For example, the Liberia Scott Fellows Program – a program in which select temporary returnees serve in high-level government consultant roles in President Ellen Johnson Sirleaf's cabinet – reports that, between 2007 and 2011–2012, all Liberian fellows (and five non-Liberian fellows) had opted to remain in Liberia (JSI 2014).

One notable example of temporary return for diaspora members was provided by the African Foundation for Development (AFFORD), which offered African entrepreneurs living in the United Kingdom the opportunity to return temporarily to offer support for small and medium-sized enterprises (SMEs) in Sierra Leone and Ghana. This program, called Support Entrepreneurs and Enterprise Development in Africa (SEEDA), was part of the Diaspora Volunteering Initiative (DVI), a three-year program funded by the U.K. government's Department for International Development (DFID). It sent a total of 150 volunteers, usually in groups of 15 to 25 people, to provide bookkeeping and business-planning training for new and existing businesses, usually for two to three weeks at a time. SEEDA provided support to more than 800 businesses. It also established a business-support development agency in Sierra Leone with an accompanying national business-planning competition, which has provided more than $200,000 in investment for SMEs in Sierra Leone. Some of the volunteers subsequently invested in SMEs in Ghana or Sierra Leone, or even chose to relocate permanently back to their country of heritage.

Temporary-return programs have some natural limitations. Social norms in the country of origin may reduce the opportunities available for certain diaspora members – particularly female and younger members of the diaspora entering male-dominated business or political environments (HIPS 2014). Participants in some countries, such as Nigeria and Somalia, have highlighted security as a key concern (MSA 2012: 4). Perhaps the most common criticism is the high cost of travel and living expenses for returning experts. Some projects, including AFFORD, have sought to mitigate these cost by asking volunteers to cover a proportion of their own expenses. Even with these contributions, the costs make it difficult to expand temporary-return projects to a significantly larger scale. In a discussion with the authors on 3 April 2014, AFFORD director Onekachi Wambu explained that proponents recognize that evaluations of the projects' effectiveness depend strongly on their ability to bring longer-term benefits, for instance, by encouraging future investment and support for diaspora and non-diaspora entrepreneurship.

Conclusion

As demand for skills increases worldwide, all countries have an interest in developing human capital and ensuring that it is put to good use. Countries of emigration have historically been concerned about losing their best minds to destinations overseas and, with them, the opportunity to raise productivity and living standards at home. After all, the vast majority of a country's skills base comes from its permanent population. But an interconnected global economy in which migration plays an integral part also provides wide-ranging opportunities for these countries to improve their access to skills in less traditional ways. Under the right conditions, mobile workers – including emigrants who return home permanently, workers who circulate between origin and destination countries, and diaspora members who offer their expertise without returning for the long term – can make meaningful contributions. This prospect has generated new interest in projects and policies that facilitate these potential benefits.

This report has described a varied spectrum of initiatives designed to support the development of internationally portable skills, each of which were created for different reasons and driven by different actors. Despite this diversity, some common themes and challenges emerge.

Developing internationally transferrable skills

Skills transferability is at the heart of most of the initiatives, from programs designed to develop internationally recognized qualifications in countries of emigration to those that enable the foreign-trained to apply their skills within destination countries, help returnees do the same back home or encourage diaspora members to share their knowledge and connections. If skills are depleted as people move across borders, the economic benefits of skilled migration and its potential to connect origin countries with the global knowledge economy could be considerably reduced.

Despite numerous promising examples of projects in this field, the genuine portability of skills remains a distant aspiration. In large part, this is attributable to the sheer difficulty of the task. Curricula and standards in some fields may be converging, particularly in the most globalized fields, such as IT or architecture. Moreover, students have an ever-expanding range of choices and growing purchasing power in an international market for qualifications. But local differences in the skills individuals actually learn are inevitable. Training itself, as well as the ways in which it is applied, continues to respond to local norms and institutions. Even without these differences, merely creating processes for the formal certification of foreign qualifications would not be enough in itself. Internationally mobile professionals may also require local work experience, language instruction and mentoring. As a result, education and training alone are not always valuable if they are disconnected from the labor market or do little to channel participants into jobs upon completion.

Several of the training-based initiatives designed to bridge migrants' skills gaps explicitly recognize this issue, focusing as a consequence on work experience and on-the-job training rather than on classroom instruction alone. Others seek to foster local knowledge, such as through mentoring. These more intensive programs can be costly and time-consuming to provide, however. As a result, despite significant investments by non-profit organizations and the governments of some countries (such as the United States and Canada), barriers to the transfer of skills persist.

It is also worth noting that while many models exist to support skills development for migrants or would-be migrants who are already (often highly) qualified, fewer programs seek to build vocational skills from scratch by targeting school-leavers. Most have sought the "low-hanging fruit" of already-educated workers whose competences can be brushed up more quickly and at lower cost, leaving fewer options for would-be migrants with fewer existing credentials.

Enabling returning migrants to put their foreign-acquired skills to use at home is equally difficult. These individuals do not face language barriers and have the benefit of local knowledge and cultural familiarity, but this does not mean they will find opportunities to use new skills. Local employers may not be familiar with formal qualifications acquired abroad, especially if these new skills are not associated with a global brand. Perhaps more importantly, returnees can find it hard to demonstrate the value of their foreign work experience. They may also find that their origin countries' labor markets offer few job opportunities in the industries that employed them abroad. At the same time, origin-country governments' limited capacities, as well as often-limited ecosystems of civil society organizations, may make it difficult to provide intensive support in the specific location where returnees are seeking employment. Incorporating returnees into labor markets that already struggle to employ growing populations of domestic workers has not always been viewed as a high political priority.

Initiatives responding to this problem include relocation support, information services and job-placement programs; some origin countries have developed targeted strategies to entice people home and directly into jobs – particularly the "most desirable" returnees in fields such as science and business. At the middle-skilled levels, however, programs offering intensive support comparable to that available in some destination countries are less extensive. Many of the programs that do exist target entrepreneurs, leaving fewer options for the majority of migrants who are seeking regular employment.

Supporting effective interventions

Another common theme is the challenge of sustainability and scale. The initiatives highlighted in this chapter have been driven by different actors, each of which face different challenges with regard to implementing effective programs reaching meaningful numbers of participants.

At one end of the spectrum, private-sector or fee-based models are appealing because they are financially self-sustaining and thus do not rely on external funders. Some of the most interesting innovations in broadening access to internationally recognized or accredited qualifications have come from independent actors, such as universities, professional associations and private companies. Examples include private qualifications issued by organizations such as the ACCA or Siemens, or the foreign campuses of universities, such as the university of Nottingham. These initiatives have been successful in part because they exploit market demand, including that of fee-paying students.

Similarly, employers have often been willing to meet the costs of training prospective migrant employees when demand for workers is high. Projects funded by employers are particularly alluring for policymakers interested in the equitable development of human capital since they are financed by the "users" of skills and are more likely to be focused on real labor-market needs. These initiatives nonetheless remain vulnerable to shifts in economic conditions. The U.S.-Mexico nurse-training initiative, for example, flourished during the boom but collapsed with the global recession and the growth in the United States' supply of domestically trained nurses.

On the other hand, many of the initiatives described are financed by philanthropic sources or through government funding streams from host countries' development agencies or international institutions. These include small, non-profit-run projects that have flourished in the United States and Canada as well as projects like the Gulbenkian Foundation's health-workforce training projects in Portugal. Compared to private-sector initiatives, these projects have more flexibility to provide intensive, tailored training. They can also provide excellent laboratories for experimentation, especially if evaluation is built into the project design. But many close or lose funding after just a few years, raising the question as to whether lessons from the project are ultimately lost.

Governments have played an important role in directly developing several of the initiatives this report has described, even beyond simply providing funds. Public-sector organizations may not be as well-placed as private companies to respond to ground-level market demand or to provide carefully tailored services to heterogeneous populations, but they offer the advantage of size. Governments can rely on existing mainstream institutions and bureaucracies to deliver services on a substantial scale, such as through public-employment services, as was the case with the Albanian skills-recognition initiative. TESDA in the Philippines has also been able to rely on a public-sector model to reach thousands of students.

Finally, governments can take a broader role in facilitating the work of independent or private-sector organizations. For example, they can collaborate on initiatives that require regulatory approval of some kind. They also control broader policy levers that may affect individuals' ability or willingness to circulate between countries, such as the right to dual citizenship and the portability of social-security benefits.

There is no perfect formula for making migration "fair" for origin countries seeking to develop their access to human capital. Reasonable analysts may disagree on which of the projects this report has discussed truly meet this definition and on which have had the most significant impact. Evaluation remains a weak link, leaving real uncertainty about where to invest. At the same time, creating initiatives at a scale large enough to genuinely shift the costs and benefits of skilled migration presents formidable difficulties. Nonetheless, the range of programs that have been developed and the diversity of actors that have supported them suggest that with enough political will, persistence and commitment to evaluation, ample opportunities exist to move closer to a "fair deal" on talent.

References

ACI (American Concrete Institute). Technical Documents. Farmington Hills, MI: ACI, 2014. www.concrete.org/Publications/TechnicalDocuments.aspx.

ADM (African Diaspora Marketplace). "About the African Diaspora Marketplace 2014." 2014. www.diasporamarketplace.org/about-african-diaspora-marketplace.

Agunias, Dovelyn Rannveig, and Kathleen Newland. *Developing a Road Map for Engaging Diasporas in Development: A Handbook for Policymakers and Practitioners in Home and Host Countries*. Washington, D.C.: Migration Policy Institute, 2012.

References

Aikins, Kingsley, and Nicola White. *Global Diaspora Strategies Toolkit.* Dublin: Diaspora Matters, 2011.

Alampi, Amanda, Jillian N. Anderson, Grisel Caicedo, Cosmo Fujiyama, Yady Ibarra, Matthew A. Lisiecki, Heidi McAnnally-Linz, Mercedes Pepper, Natalie Relich, Andreina Seijas, Maria Claudia Sarta Herrera, Fiona Wanqing He, Casey Weston and Ali K. Wimer. *Creating Valuable Skills: A New Framework for Migration as Development.* New York: World Bank, NYU and Capstone, 2013. https://wagner.nyu.edu/files/faculty/publications/Creating-Valuable-Skills-A-New-Framework-for-Migration-as-Development-Policy-May-2013-SecureJune23.pdf.

Amante, Maragtas S.V. "Labor Dimension of the Japan-Philippine Economic Partnership Agreement (JPEPA)." *Institute of Developing Economics Visiting Research Fellow Monograph Series* No. 429: 24–28, 2007. www.ide.go.jp/English/Publish/Download/Vrf/pdf/429.pdf.

Annan, Kofi. "How We Envy the World Cup." UN speech held on June 30, 2006. www.un.org/sport2005/newsroom/worldcup.html.

APTC (Australia-Pacific Technical College). *Graduate Student Tracer Survey Report.* Nadi, Fiji: APTC, 2013. www.aptc.edu.au/images/Publications/Student_TracerSurvey_Report_Web_Version_020414.pdf

Bhaskar, T.L.S. (Head of Skills Development Initiatives at the Indian Centre for Migration). Correspondence with author, February 25, 2014 and April 22, 2014.

CGFNS International (Commission on Graduates of Foreign Nursing Schools). Certification Program 2014. www.cgfns.org/services/certification-program/.

CIM (Centre for International Migration and Development). "Returning Experts Programme." Berlin: GIZ/German Federal Employment Agency, 2011. www.cimonline.de/documents/CIM-Flyer-prf-en.pdf.

CISCO. CISCO Networking Academy, 2014. www.cisco.com/web/learning/netacad/index.html?academyID=6345.

Clemens, Michael A. "Global Skills Partnerships: A Proposal for Technical Training in a Mobile World." *CGD Policy Paper 40.* Washington, D.C.: Center for Global Development, 2014.

Clemens, Michael, Colum Graham and Stephen Howes. "Skill Development and Regional Mobility: Lessons from the Australia-Pacific Technical College." *Working Paper 370,* June 2014. Washington, D.C.: Center for Global Development, 2014. www.cgdev.org/publication/skill-development-and-regional-mobility-lessons-australia-pacific-technical-college.

CMRE (Cancillería Ministerio de Relaciones Exteriores). Return Home Plan 2014. www.cancilleria.gov.co/footer/join-us/work/plan.

CMRECNU (Cancillería Ministerio de Relaciones Exteriores and Colombia Nos Une). "SENA tendrá sede en Valencia, España, para formar a colombianos immigrantes." News release. Redes Colombia, June 12, 2008. www.redescolombia.org/content/SENA-tendr%C3%A1-sede-en-Valencia,-Espa%C3%B1a,-para-formar-a-colombianos-inmigrantes.

CSF (Ciências Sem Fronteiras/Science without Borders). "Goals 2014." 2014. www.cienciasemfronteiras.gov.br/web/csf-eng/goals.

Délano, Alexandra."Immigrant Integration vs. Transnational Ties? The Role of the Sending State." *Social Research* (77) 1: 237–268, 2010.

Gamlen, Alan. "Diaspora Engagement Policies: What are They, and What Kinds of States Use Them?" *Working Paper No. 32*. Oxford: University of Oxford, Centre on Migration, Policy and Society, 2006.

GIZ (Deutsche Gesellschaft für Internationale Zusammenarbeit). "Promotion of Legal Mobility of Highly-Qualified Tunisian Experts." Project duration 2012–2014. 2012a. www.giz.de/en/worldwide/19727.html.

GIZ. "Training nurses from Viet Nam to become geriatric nurses in Germany." Project duration 2012–2016. 2012b. www.giz.de/en/worldwide/18715.html.

de Haas, Hein, and Simona Vezzoli. "Leaving Matters: The Nature, Evolution and Effects of Emigration Policies." *University of Oxford International Migration Institute Working Paper 34*. Oxford: Oxford University Press, 2011.

Hawthorne, Lesleyanne. "Recognizing Foreign Qualifications: Emerging Global Trends." Washington, D.C.: Migration Policy Institute, 2013.

Hazan, Miryam. Interview with Miryam Hazan, research director at MATT, April 25, 2014.

HIPS (Heritage Institute for Policy Studies). "Diaspora Return to Somalia – Perceptions and Implications." Policy Brief, June 2014. www.heritageinstitute.org/wp-content/uploads/2014/06/HIPS_Policy_Brief_007-2014_ENGLISH.pdf.

ICEF (International Consultants for Education and Fairs). "Brazil Extends Science Without Borders with 100,000 New Scholarships." Bonn: ICEF Monitor, 2014. http://monitor.icef.com/2014/07/brazil-extends-science-without-borders-with-100000-new-scholarships/.

IdEA (International diaspora Engagement Alliance). About Us. 2014. http://diasporaalliance.org/about-us/.

ILO (International Labour Organization). "Report: Workshop on Skills Recognition for Migrant Workers." Workshop held on August 4–5, 2011 at Taj Samudra, Colombo, Sri Lanka. Colombo: ILO, 2011. http://apskills.ilo.org/events/workshop-on-skills-recognition-for-migrant-workers-sri-lanka/at_download/file3.

ILO. "Direct Request (CEACR) – adopted 2013, published 103rd ILC session (2014)." NORMLEX – Information System on International Labor Standards, Discrimination (Employment and Occupation) Convention, 1958 (No. 111), Korea. 2014. www.ilo.org/dyn/normlex/en/f?p=NORMLEXPUB:13101:0::NO::P13101_COMMENT_ID:2255873.

IRD (Institut de Recherche pour le Développement). "PACEIM: Lauréat 2012." 2014a. www.ird.fr/les-partenariats/valorisation-et-transfert-de-technologie/accompagner-la-creation-d-entreprises/paceim.

IRD. "PACEIM: Programme d'aide à la création d'entreprises innovantes en Méditerranée." 2014b. www.ird.fr/les-partenariats/valorisation-et-transfert-de-technologie/accompagner-la-creation-d-entreprises/paceim.

Iskander, Natasha, and Nichola Lowe. "The Transformers: Immigration and Tacit Knowledge Development." *NYU Wagner Research Paper No. 2011-01*. New York: NYU, 2011.

JSI (John Snow International). "The Liberia Scott Fellows Program 2014." 2014. www.johnsnow.org/Independent/Docs/liberia-fellows-program.pdf.

Katseli, Louka T., Robert E.B. Lucas and Theodora Xenogiani. "Effects of Migration on Sending Countries: What Do We Know?" *OECD Development Centre Working Paper* No. 250, June 2006. Paris: OECD Publishing, 2006. www.oecd.org/dev/poverty/37053726.pdf.

References

Koehn, Selma. "Behind the Scenes of Vocational Training in China." German Chamber Ticker, June/July 2012. http://china.ahk.de/fileadmin/ahk_china/Dokumente/GC-Ticker/GCT_JuneJuly2012.pdf.

Kuznetsov, Yevgeny (ed.). *How Can Talent Abroad Induce Development at Home? Towards a Pragmatic Diaspora Agenda.* Washington, D.C.: Migration Policy Institute, 2013.

Lane, Jason E. "Global Expansion of International Branch Campuses: Managerial and Leadership Challenges." *New Directions for Higher Education* 155: 5–17, 2011.

Lawton, William, and Alex Katsomitros. *International Branch Campuses: Data and Developments.* London: The Observatory on Borderless Higher Education, 2012. www.obhe.ac.uk/documents/view_details?id=894.

MATT (Mexicans and Americans Thinking Together). "The US/Mexico Cycle: End of an Era. Quantitative Research Study, Preliminary Findings and Insights, December 2013." San Antonio, TX: MATT, 2013. www.matt.org/uploads/2/4/9/3/24932918/returnmigration_top_line_www.pdf.

MATT. Economic Development 2014. www.matt.org/economic-development.html.

McNamara, John, Jane Knight and Rozilini M. Fernandez-Chung. *The Shape of Things to Come. The Evolution of Transnational Education: Data, Definitions, Opportunities and Impact Analysis.* London: British Council, 2013.

Microsoft. Microsoft IT Academy. 2014. www.microsoft.com/education/itacademy/Pages/certification.aspx.

Molenaar, Klaas. *Enterprising Migrants in the Driver's Seat: Dreams Cross Borders and Become Reality.* The Hague: IntEnt Foundation, 2009.

MSA (Management Strategies for Africa). "Research Report: Engaging Nigeria Diaspora and National Volunteers to Develop Civil Society." Accra: MSA, 2012. www.msforafrica.org/completion-of-comic-relief-funded-report-on-engaging-diaspora-and-national-volunteers-to-develop-civil-society/.

Newland, Kathleen (ed.). *Diasporas: New Partners in Global Development Policy.* Washington, D.C.: Migration Policy Institute, 2010.

NZ-MFAT (New Zealand Ministry of Foreign Affairs and Trade, New Zealand Aid Programme). "Seasonal Employment – A Migration Win-Win." *Currents* 23: 16–19, November 2010. www.aid.govt.nz/webfm_send/60.

OECD (Organization for Economic Co-operation and Development). "Migrants' Skills: Use, Mismatch and Labour Market Outcomes. A First Exploration of the Survey of Adult Skills (PIAAC)." Paper presented at EU-OECD Dialogue on International Migration and Mobility: Matching Economic Migration with Labour Market Needs conference, February 24–25, 2014 in Brussels, Belgium. Paris: OECD, 2014.

OECD. *International Migration Outlook 2008.* Paris: OECD Publishing, 2009.

OECD, DCD/DAD (Development Co-operation Directorate/Development Assistance Committee). DAC Statistical Reporting Directives. Paris: OECD, 2010. DCD/DAC(2010)40/REV1. www.oecd.org/dac/stats/38429349.pdf.

O'Neill, Kevin. "Brain Drain and Gain: The Case of Taiwan." Washington, D.C.: Migration Policy Institute, 2003. www.migrationinformation.org/feature/display.cfm?ID=155.

QAA (The Quality Assurance Agency for Higher Education). "UK Collaboration in Malaysia: Institutional Case Studies. University of Nottingham Malaysia Campus." Gloucester: QAA, 2010. www.qaa.ac.uk/InstitutionReports/Reports/Documents/Malaysia_NottinghamCS10.pdf.

QAA. "Review of U.K. transnational education in China: The University of Nottingham Ningbo Campus." Gloucester: QAA, November 2012. www.qaa.ac.uk/InstitutionReports/Reports/Pages/TNE-Nottingham-12.aspx.

PdRM (Presidencia de la Républica México). Programa "Somos Mexicanos." March 30, 2014. www.presidencia.gob.mx/programa-somos-mexicanos/.

Pie News. "Japan's Global ACE gives youth global work experience." August 9, 2013. http://thepienews.com/news/japans-global-ace-gives-youth-global-work-experience/.

Prince St-Amand, Corinne. Presentation at the Intergovernmental Consultations on Migration, Asylum and Refugees (IGC) in Geneva, April 8–9, 2014. Ottawa: Integration at Citizenship and Immigration Canada, 2014.

Rietig, Victoria, and Allison Squires. *Harmonized Regional Nurse Qualifications: Obstacles and Ways Forward*. Washington, D.C.: Migration Policy Institute, forthcoming.

Saxenian, AnnaLee. "From Brain Drain to Brain Circulation: Transnational Communities and Regional Upgrading in India and China." *Studies in Comparative International Development* (40) 2: 1–30, 2005.

SFG (Strategic Foresight Group). "Trends." *Asian Horizons* (3) 11: 18–22, 2012. New York: Rockefeller Foundation, 2012.

Shaw, Lea, Murray Edwards and Akka Rimon. "KANI Independent Review, AidWorks Initiative Number: ING466, Review Report." Sydney: KANI, 2013.

SK MEL (South Korean Ministry of Employment and Labor). Employment Permit System. "Happy Return Program 2014." 2014. www.eps.go.kr/en/supp/supp_02.jsp.

Squires, Allison, and Hiram Beltrán-Sánchez. *Strengthening Health Systems in North and Central America: What Role for Migration?* Washington, D.C.: Migration Policy Institute, 2013.

Sumption, Madeleine. "Tackling Brain Waste: Strategies to Improve the Recognition of Immigrants' Foreign Qualifications." Washington, D.C.: Migration Policy Institute, 2013.

Sumption, Madeleine, Demetrios G. Papademetriou and Sarah Flamm. "Skilled Immigrants in the Global Economy: Prospects for International Cooperation on Recognition of Foreign Qualifications." Washington, D.C.: Migration Policy Institute, 2013.

Sun, Ohno. "Southeast Asian Nurses and Caregiving Workers Transcending the National Boundaries: An Overview of Indonesian and Filipino Workers in Japan and Abroad." *Southeast Asian Studies* (49) 4: 541–569, 2012.

TESDA (Technical Education and Skills Development Authority). "TESDA Receives ISO 9001:2008 Certifikation." February 12, 2012. www.tesda.gov.ph/News/Details/172.

UN DESA (United Nations Department of Economic and Social Affairs, Population Division). *International Migration Policies 2013*. New York: UN DESA, 2013. www.un.org/en/development/desa/population/publications/policy/international-migration-policies-2013.shtml.

University of Nottingham. "Facts and Figures 2013: Britain's Global University in Malaysia." 2013. www.nottingham.edu.my/AboutUs/documents/UNMC-FACTS-AND-FIGURES-AWFORWEB.pdf.

USAID (United States Agency for International Development). *Assessments and Lessons Learned from African Diaspora Marketplace*. Washington, D.C.: USAID, 2011.

USDS BECA (U.S. Department of State, Bureau of Educational and Cultural Affairs). "J-1 Visa Exchange Program: Common Questions for Participants." 2014. http://j1visa.state.gov/participants/common-questions/.

Wambu, Oneykachi. Correspondence with Onyekachi Wambu, Director of AFFORD, April 3, 2014.

Xie, Zhao, Tim K. Mackey, Bryan A. Liang and Lorna Gerlt. "Zhongguancun: Talent for Transformation." *China Daily*, December 22, 2011. http://en.zgc.gov.cn/2011-12/22/content_14308152.htm.

Yagi, Nozomi, Tim K. Mackey, Bryan A. Liang and Lorna Gerlt. "Policy Review: Japan-Philippines Economic Partnership Agreement (JPEPA) – Analysis of a Failed Nurse Migration Policy." *International Journal of Nursing Studies* (51) 2: 243–250, 2014.

Zweig, David, Chung Siu Fung and Donglin Han. "Redefining the Brain Drain: China's 'Diaspora Option.'" *Science, Technology and Society* (13) 1: 3–5, 2008.

III. Mobility and Fairness – Case Studies

Perspectives from Destination Countries

Lessons from Germany

Khushwant Singh

As Germany's population ages and the size of its workforce undergoes a related decline, the immigration of skilled labor is playing an increasingly important labor-market role. As yet, there is no nationwide skills shortage in Germany. However, bottlenecks already exist in some regions and occupations. This is particularly true of health care and nursing work, as well as in certain technical occupations. Shortages will worsen in the health care and the nursing sector, in particular over the next few decades, since demographic factors will likely produce both a drop in the availability of skilled labor and a rise in the demand for long-term care as the population ages. In April 2014, there was a shortage of 117,300 skilled workers in technical occupations. By 2020, it appears that some 700,000 additional skilled workers will be needed merely to replace those who are retiring. Taking into consideration additional needs that have already become apparent, the shortage of skilled workers is likely to amount to 1.4 million people in this area. Moreover, the technical occupations are likely to need about 88,000 more graduates than the German education system is projected to produce (Anger, Koppel and Plünnecke 2014).

The decline in the workforce and the related skills shortages have a direct impact on economic output and social and technological progress. In order to counter this development, the German government is increasingly focusing on the immigration of high-skilled individuals. To this end, it is examining aspects such as the transparency of information about the migration process as well as development-policy issues related to the design of measures aimed at attracting qualified individuals from around the world.

Political background

With an eye to mitigating the effects of ongoing demographic developments, the German government has made securing sufficient supplies of skilled labor a central plank of its policies. The Skilled Labor Strategy (Fachkräftekonzept) adopted in 2011 places a renewed focus on all people capable of work in Germany – particularly mothers, single parents, older people and people with a migrant background – with the aim of supporting their integration into the labor market. However, since even optimal utilization of the domestic potential will not obviate the need for labor-market-oriented immigration of qualified professionals from other countries, the German government has been working since 2012 to attract such people on the global labor market. The Accessing Skilled Labor Abroad and Creating a Culture of Welcome (Ausländisches Arbeitskräftepotenzial erschließen und Willkommenskultur schaffen) working group is co-chaired by the Federal Ministry for Economic Affairs and Energy and the Association of German Chambers of Commerce and Industry. As an element of the German government's demography strategy, the group focuses on increasing qualified-immigrant flows to Germany. It has drawn links between existing measures and designed new ones, such as the establishment of the central "Working and Living in Germany" hotline providing comprehensive advice to international professionals interested in coming to Germany to live and work (BMI 2013). The hotline offers information and advice in German and English on issues such as job searches, working in Germany, careers, the recognition of foreign vocational qualifications, entry residence requirements and German language acquisition.

Attractive legal conditions for qualified immigration

Qualified professionals from around the world are interested not only in career opportunities, but also in the rules and regulations governing their choice of place to live and work. For this reason, the German government adopted the Act to Implement the Blue Card Directive of the European Union (EU), which provides an important step toward enabling qualified immigration through the EU Blue Card residence permit. The EU Blue Card enables graduates and their families from outside the European Union simplified access to the German labor market. In addition, the ability to obtain recognition of vocational qualifications obtained abroad has been improved (BMBF 2014). Further relaxations in the law are focused on foreign-national graduates from German higher-education institutions. After gaining their degrees, graduates now have 18 months in which to find a job appropriate to their qualification in Germany.

Do good things, and tell the world about it: Make it in Germany

Even the best reforms and initiatives will fail if their target groups don't know about them. In order to prevent this, the Federal Ministry for Economic Affairs and Energy, the Federal Ministry of Labour and Social Affairs and the Federal Employment Agency launched the Qualified Professionals Initiative (Fachkräfte-Offensive). Since June 2012, this initiative has supported the government's Skilled Labor Strategy with a campaign to raise awareness of the issue that is addressed to people, businesses and qualified professionals from Germany and around the world. According to a survey conducted at the end of 2013 on behalf of the Federal Ministry of Labour and Social Affairs, 32 percent of all residents in Germany had heard about the Make it in Germany initiative.

As a part of the Qualified Professionals Initiative, the Make it in Germany welcome portal targets qualified professionals from around the world (Singh and Hierl 2013). It spreads the word about the new rules on immigration and the advantages of living and working in Germany, and it aims to send a signal indicating an open and welcoming culture. The intention is to whet foreign professionals' appetite for work in Germany, thus boosting Germany's chances in the global competition to attract top talent. By February 2015, the portal had been visited by nearly 6 million people from around the world and, according to a user survey conducted at the end of 2013, 83 percent of visitors reported an increased desire to emigrate to Germany as a result of visiting the site. At the same time, the portal brings together various information and advisory services, thus making it easier to learn about opportunities to immigrate to Germany and living conditions in the country. This helps people make well-informed decisions with regard to migration and to prepare their moves appropriately.

Keeping the public and businesses on board: Yes, we're open!

In addition to raising awareness among qualified professionals around the world, Germany's skilled labor campaign is also deliberately targeted at members of the general public, municipalities, authorities and businesses. After all, promoting an attractive image of Germany and telling people in other countries about Germany's new rules is one part of the task. Another part involves the creation of an open and welcoming culture in Germany. This requires an unprejudiced, fact-based public debate as well as positive ownership and emphasis of the advantages of immigration.

The "Yes, We're Open! – Willkommen in Deutschland" roadshow is making a contribution toward this end. The exhibition highlights the importance of immigration for Germany as well as the social, economic and cultural contributions made by people with a migrant background (www.yes-we-are-open.info). The exhibition aims to raise awareness of the need for a welcoming culture and to promote openness toward people of different cultural backgrounds. Visitors are given an interesting presentation of information on issues such as the history of immigration, integration, citizenship, the need for qualified professionals from other countries and demographic change. Companies that exemplify a "culture of welcome" and perform well in terms of integrating professionals from abroad are awarded a prize by the Federal Ministry for Economic Affairs and Energy. After all, although the issue of recruiting professionals from outside Germany is still unexplored territory for many small and medium-sized businesses, it is possible to find role models and help others learn from their experiences.

However, a true culture of welcome goes well beyond helpful rules and regulations, transparent administrative and visa procedures, and the world of work. It is reflected in day-to-day life, in visits to authorities, in the search for jobs and housing, and in leisure activities and neighborhood life. If people who have immigrated have a bad time and feel unwelcome, their experiences will soon become known back in their countries of origin. This will, in turn, cause people interested in emigrating to strike Germany off their list of potential destinations. By contrast, positive impressions will help make Germany more popular and increase immigrants' sense of belonging.

Lessons from Germany

Fair migration: A win-win for everyone involved

A recent study on the careers and added value of qualified professionals from around the world for small and medium-sized enterprises in Germany, undertaken on behalf of the Federal Ministry for Economic Affairs and Energy, shows that professionals from abroad are making an important contribution toward ensuring a sufficient supply of skilled labor in Germany (BMWi 2014a). In addition to the specialist skills that help keep German firms competitive, employers also emphasize aspects, such as the additional language and intercultural skills of immigrant professionals. In some cases, professionals from abroad have helped companies access markets in their countries of origin.

An overall picture also requires a look at the impact of the emigration of professionals on their countries of origin. The aim of a responsible policy to secure skilled labor via immigration cannot be to entice qualified workers away from labor markets in countries that badly need them. For this reason, campaigns like the German government's Make it in Germany are managed with great sensitivity. In the field of long-term care, for example, no nurses are targeted through job advertisements in countries that themselves have labor shortages in the health care sector. This approach is in line with the standards of the international World Health Organization code on the recruitment of health personnel (WHO 2010).

However, countries of origin can also benefit from the time their professionals spend abroad. For example, migrants working in Germany can share their experiences and pass on their newly acquired specialist knowledge and methodological expertise to their country of origin. This might take place via cooperation or in the form of a temporary or permanent return to the migrant's country of origin (Gibson and McKenzie 2011; Krobisch 2012). A high level of mobility among qualified professionals can result in closer economic and scientific cooperation and increased technology transfer, as is shown by the example of the Indian information-technology (IT) specialists returning from the United States to Bangalore in India (Chacke 2007). In addition, money transfers from immigrants to their families at home help boost standards of living and support local development (Angenendt 2014). Immigrants also frequently involve themselves to a significant extent in improving economic and social development within their countries of origin, and use the expertise acquired abroad to run charitable projects (CIM/GIZ 2014).

Guiding principles for the German government: Assistance throughout all stages of the migration process

Today, Germany has a varied program of measures in the area of migration. These include the establishment of numerous Internet portals to provide those interested in living and working in Germany with comprehensive information on services designed to help them prepare for their move and to promote a culture of welcome. They also include integration and language courses (e.g., through the German Federal Office for Migration and Refugees) as well as programs that support migrant organizations, aid migrants who want to return to their countries of origin to help accelerate development in their professional sector, and assist those who want to start up their own company (see CIM/GIZ's Triple Win project, support for skilled Tunisian workers and programs supporting Vietnamese long-term caretakers (GIZ 2014a and 2014b)). By offering these services throughout all stages of the migration process (recruitment of qualified professionals, migrants' preparations for the move, migration itself, integration, circular migration, return to the home country), the German government thus keeps the principle of fairness closely in mind. However, there is still scope for raising the profile of these programs internationally. One way this can be done is through pilot projects conducted on behalf of the German government.

Securing qualified professionals fairly: Best-practice pilot projects

As an outward-looking country home to many immigrants, Germany has taken a number of important steps, including setting up the Make it in Germany Internet portal, hosting exhibitions and establishing various business awards designed to address the country's demographic problem. However, these measures alone are not enough to position Germany as an open country with fair rules governing immigration in an international arena. The Federal Ministry for Economic Affairs and Energy has therefore commissioned the Deutsche Gesellschaft für Internationale Zusammenarbeit (GIZ), in cooperation with the International Placement Services (Zentrale Auslands- und Fachvermittlung, ZAV) of the Federal Employment Agency (Bundesagentur für Arbeit, BA) to conduct various projects designed to secure the skilled labor that Germany needs. These include pilot projects in India, Indonesia and Vietnam that are designed to provide qualified professionals interested in migrating to Germany with relevant advice while they are still in their home countries. These projects take heed of important aspects of development policy, such as the potential for brain drain; for example, no health care professionals are targeted, an approach that is in line with the WHO code. The pilot projects are designed in line with the criteria for programs to encourage migration as set out in a study on temporary and circular migration from a development-policy perspective that was conducted by the German Institute for International and Security Affairs (see Angenendt 2014). These criteria include special rules on migration that are based on qualification type.

As an element of these projects, local advisers promote the welcome portal and the new rules on immigration, and provide counseling on issues relating to job-hunting and departure to graduates with technical degrees who are interested in migrating to Germany. The advisers work closely with locally based German institutes, particularly foreign missions. The personal, locally provided advice service reflects an open and welcoming culture in Germany and helps those seeking to migrate make the necessary preparations. It also serves to provide information on the services migrants can use during the different stages of the migration process. The pilot projects in Asia can serve as models for similar service in other regions. The experience gained in targeting and attracting qualified professionals from outside Europe can therefore be processed and built into broader policies before the effects of demographic change become even more noticeable.

Lessons from Germany

Successes and challenges

Having created flexible legal options for immigration to Germany and implemented various measures and initiatives supporting this process, Germany is well on the way to establishing itself as an outward-looking country with a high proportion of immigrants and one that has transparent and fair processes. Although these changes to Germany's immigration law have proven effective, a 2014 study conducted by the Federal Ministry for Economic Affairs and Energy underscored the need to improve practical and administrative enforcement of these regulations in the migration processes of qualified professionals from abroad (BMWi 2014b). There are problems with information gaps among authorities, for example, that lead to inconsistent decision-making. Problems with electronic communication systems also slow the visa process (ibid). Nonetheless, Germany's new immigration regulations and the Make it in Germany welcome portal have been praised by the Organization for Economic Co-operation and Development (OECD), the Expert Council of German Foundations on Integration and Migration (Sachverständigenrat deutscher Stiftungen für Integration und Migration) and the business community. According to the OECD, Germany now offers several migration opportunities for qualified professionals when compared with other European countries (OECD 2013).

The success of the efforts made so far has also become evident in the country's immigration figures. In 2013, net immigration to Germany stood at around 400,000 – the highest level in the past 20 years, making Germany the world's second-largest country for immigration after the United States (IW 2014). What is striking is that the immigrants who have come to Germany over the last 10 years generally have a higher level of education and training than the German population. Some 43 percent of new immigrants have a university degree or technical qualification. Within the working-age population in Germany, this figure is around 25 percent (Brücker 2013).

However, this immigration can largely be traced back to migration within Europe. In 2013, around two-thirds of immigrants came from European countries (Destatis 2013). Labor-market experts do not anticipate that this intra-European immigration will persist at recent rates. According to their forecasts, as soon as the economic situation in the countries most affected by the economic and financial crisis improves sufficiently, a certain proportion of the qualified professionals who have migrated abroad will return to their countries of origin. It is also important to remember that a large number of countries in Europe are facing demographic challenges similar to those in Germany. It is therefore important to target qualified professionals in countries outside of Europe, as well. Given that Germany has to compete for qualified professionals with other countries around the world, the impact of the changes made to immigration law, as well as the initiatives described above, should not be underestimated. Moreover, it will also be important to further develop the EU Blue Card and to promote it more effectively. Germany has already issued this card to more than 16,000 highly qualified professionals since 2012 – a large number compared with that of other European countries (SVR 2014).

Conclusion

In recent years, figures on the immigration of skilled workers to Germany have been promising. The processes involved are becoming more flexible, and the information services and related procedures more transparent. Immigration numbers are rising, and most new immigrants are highly skilled. At the same time, Germany faces several challenges.

The country has to compensate for several disadvantages compared to nations that have traditionally had high immigration levels. Among these disadvantages are language barriers and the fact that, because of Germany's federal structure, different federal states have different rules and regulations on issues such as the recognition of professional qualifications. Prospective immigrants may find this to be puzzling, cumbersome and lacking in transparency. Moreover, there are German citizens who still think Germany should not welcome immigrants and refugees, as the developments in 2014 associated with the PEGIDA demonstrations illustrate. In addition, there are some outside of Germany who believe the country is per se opposed to immigration and mired in red tape. Immigrants still cannot take it for granted that they will encounter a culture of welcome in their personal and professional lives. More product information communicated on public notice boards should routinely be made available in English and other relevant languages. Within the local and federal authorities, intercultural skills need to be systematically developed. Intercultural awareness should be taught in schools, and young people should be made aware of how different economies interact and are interdependent in a globalized world. Companies also have some internal hurdles that must be overcome. For instance, small and medium-sized companies, which often say they suffer from a skills gap, are still quite reluctant to hire qualified professionals from abroad. The aforementioned study commissioned by the Federal Ministry for Economic Affairs and Energy to ascertain the extent to which qualified professionals from abroad are beneficial to companies revealed that more than 80 percent of SMEs that have already recruited qualified professionals from abroad – an admittedly small number to date – would do so again. This demonstrates a high level of satisfaction and suggests that more should be done to encourage SMEs to become interested in internationalizing and diversifying their workforce.

In the interest of maximizing the positive effects of immigration for all involved while also minimizing the risk of negative effects, such as human trafficking, exploitation and wage dumping, it is essential that, in the long term, immigration processes are fair and that society is kept well-informed about and given a voice in the immigration debate. This will only be possible if policymakers and society as a whole take a positive and forward-looking view on immigration that extends beyond the next election campaign.

Finally, it is also important to remember that immigration is about human beings and not only about their intellectual skills or economic usefulness. Immigrants are people, each of whom have their own personal history; are rooted in a specific culture, religion, language and family; and have expectations of their own. Immigration and economic policies that are responsible will do as much as possible to take all this into account, both by offering the support that is needed for immigration processes to be successful and by assessing individual immigrants' skills and needs without relying solely on a rigid interpretation of formal qualifications or references.

The author would like to thank Stefanie Sieloff and Sarah Jeske for their commitment and support in preparing this article.

References

Angenendt, Steffen. *Entwicklungspolitische Perspektiven temporärer und zirkulärer Migration.* Berlin: SWP, 2014. www.swp-berlin.org/fileadmin/contents/products/studien/2014_S13_adt.pdf.

Anger, Christina, Oliver Koppel and Axel Plünnecke. *MINT-Frühjahrsreport 2014. MINT – Gesamtwirtschaftliche Bedeutung und regionale Unterschiede.* Cologne: IW, 2014. www.iwkoeln.de/_storage/asset/167127/storage/master/file/4559183/download/MINT-Fr%C3%BChjahrsbericht.pdf.

BAMF (Federal Office for Migration and Refugees). Integration courses – what are they? www.bamf.de/EN/Willkommen/DeutschLernen/Integrationskurse/integrationskurse-node.html.

BMBF (German Federal Ministry of Education and Research). Anerkennung in Deutschland. 2014. www.anerkennung-in-deutschland.de/html/de/.

BMI (German Federal Ministry of the Interior). Jedes Alter zählt. Demografiestrategie der Bundesregierung. Berlin: BMI, 2013. www.bundesregierung.de/Content/DE/_Anlagen/Demografie/demografiestrategie-langfassung.pdf?__blob=publicationFile&v=2.

BMWi (German Federal Ministry for Economic Affairs and Energy). "Werdegang internationaler Fachkräfte und ihr Mehrwert für KMU." Berlin: BMWi, 2014a. www.bmwi.de/DE/Mediathek/publikationen,did=670296.html.

BMWi. "Wirkungsanalyse des rechtlichen Rahmens für ausländische Fachkräfte." Berlin: BMWi, 2014b. www.bmwi.de/DE/Mediathek/publikationen,did=641160.html.

Brücker, Herbert. *Auswirkungen der Einwanderung auf Arbeitsmarkt und Sozialstaat: Neue Erkenntnisse und Schlussfolgerungen für die Einwanderungspolitik.* Gütersoh: Bertelsmann Stiftung, 2013.

Chacke, Elizabeth. "From Brain Drain to Brain Gain: Reverse Migration to Bangalore and Hyderabad. India's Globalizing High-Tech Cities." *Geo Journal* (68): 131–140, 2007. www.academia.edu/221127/From_Brain_drain_to_brain_gain_Reverse_migration_to_Bangalore_and_Hyderabad_Indias_globalizing_high_tech_cities.

CIM/GIZ (Centre for international Migration and Development/Deutsche Gesellschaft für Internationale Zusammenarbeit). "Migranten als Brückenbauer: Förderung des entwicklungspolitischen Engagements von Migrantenorganisationen." Berlin: CIM, 2014. www.cimonline.de/de/2110.asp.

Destatis (German Federal Statistics Office). "Bevölkerung und Erwerbstätigkeit. Preliminary migration results." Berlin: Destatis, 2013. www.destatis.de/DE/Publikationen/Thematisch/Bevoelkerung/Wanderungen/vorlaeufigeWanderungen5127101137004.pdf?__blob=publicationFile.

Gibson, John, and David McKenzie. *Eight Questions about Brain Drain.* Washington, D.C.: World Bank, 2011. https://openknowledge.worldbank.org/bitstream/handle/10986/3431/WPS5668.pdf?sequence=1.

References

GIZ (Deutsche Gesellschaft für Internationale Zusammenarbeit). GIZ Triple Win Pilotprojekt, "GIZ Förderung der legalen Mobilität hochqualifizierter tunesischer Fachkräfte." 2014a. www.giz.de/de/weltweit/19727.html.

GIZ. "Ausbildung von Arbeitskräften aus Vietnam zu Pflegefachkräften." 2014b. www.giz.de/de/weltweit/18715.html.

IW (Cologne Institute for Economic Research). "Rekordwerte auf Zeit." Cologne: IW, 2014. www.iwkoeln.de/en/infodienste/iw-nachrichten/beitrag/zuwanderung-rekordwerte-auf-zeit-166978.

Krobisch, Verena. "Braindrain is Better than Brain in the Drain." *CIM Paper Series* No. 2, Frankfurt am Main: CIM, 2012. www.cimonline.de/documents/02-cim-paper-series-empirie.pdf.

OECD (Organization for Economic Co-operation and Development). *Recruiting Immigrant Workers: Germany.* Paris: OECD Publishing, 2013. http://dx.doi.org/10.1787/9789264191747-de; www.svr-migration.de/content/wp-content/uploads/2014/04/SVR-Jahresgutachten-2014_Kernbotschaften.pdf.

Rzepka, Gabriele. *A Triple Win for Everyone.* Berlin: GIZ, 2014. www.giz.de/en/downloads/giz2012-en-akzente04-triple-win-pilot-project.pdf.

Singh, Khushwant, and Katharina Hierl. "'Make it in Germany' stärkt Willkommenskultur." *Schlaglichter der Wirtschaftspolitik. Monatsbericht Januar 2013.* Berlin: BMWi, 2013: 17–22. www.bmwi.de/Dateien/BMWi/PDF/Monatsbericht/schlaglichter-der-wirtschaftspolitik-01-2013.

SVR (Sachverständigenrat Deutscher Stiftungen). Homepage 2014. www.svr-migration.de.

WHO (World Health Organization). *The WHO Global Code of Practice on the International Recruitment of Health Personnel.* Geneva: WHO, 2010. www.who.int/hrh/migration/code/code_en.pdf?ua=1.

Lessons from Sweden

Bernd Parusel

Introduction

While the concept of "fairness" is not explicitly a guiding principle of migration policies in Sweden, the country's laws and practices on the issues of immigration and asylum – particularly with regard to aspects such as protection for refugees, equal rights and non-discriminatory access to the welfare system for all residents – in large part make the Swedish approach appear realistic and fair. In recent years, Swedish immigration policies have received considerable attention internationally, not least with regard to the country's openheartedness toward asylum seekers and its generous and flexible system for work-related immigration. Quite recently, the Swedish parliament adopted a range of measures aimed at stimulating voluntary circular migration and making it easier for rejected asylum seekers to stay in the country as labor immigrants. In a number of ways, Sweden deviates from many other European countries and their tough stances on asylum and increasingly selective policies toward immigrant workers.

The objective of this article is to provide an overview of immigration trends, migration policies and policy changes in Sweden in recent years and to highlight a few examples of policies and measures that can be identified as "fair."

The government's guiding principles for immigration policy

In a regularly updated, official fact sheet on migration policy, the Swedish government describes its ambition of maintaining a "sustainable migration policy that safeguards the right to seek asylum and, within the framework of regulated immigration, facilitates mobility across borders, promotes demand-driven labor migration, harnesses and takes into account the effects of migration on development and deepens European and international cooperation." Moreover, the document adds, immigration "helps to revitalize the Swedish society, the labor market and the economy, as immigrants bring new knowledge and experience from their countries of origin" (GOS 2014: 1).

It is true that, since 2010, the xenophobic Sweden Democrats party (Sverigedemokraterna) has managed to increase its presence in the political system to a significant degree, particularly within local administrations and governments, and since the parliamentary elections of September 2014 at the national level, as well. However, they have thus far been prevented from affecting Sweden's immigration policy. The former center-right minority government under Fredrik Reinfeldt (2010–2014) and the succeeding red-green government of Stefan Löfven (in power since September 2014), which also lacks a parliamentary majority, have both relied on broad, cross-party agreements on immigration policies in order to secure parliament's backing for legislation in this domain. The Reinfeldt government negotiated an agreement with the Green Party that even Löfven supported when he became prime minister. The overall orientation of immigration and asylum policies is thus founded on a broad consensus that excludes only the extreme right, guaranteeing relative stability and predictability. Another characteristic feature of Swedish immigration policies is that amendments to the Aliens Act, the primary legal measure governing the entry and stay of foreigners, are usually preceded by (sometimes lengthy) processes of evaluation and consultation. Draft bills originating in government offices are often discussed in advance by parliamentary inquiry committees dealing with specific relevant topics and then sent for comments and suggestions to a wide range of stakeholders, such as government authorities, agencies and civil society interest groups, before being subsequently revised, redrafted and passed on to parliament for approval. Inputs from external stakeholders are not binding for the government or for parliament, but policymakers normally seek to accommodate their opinions to the greatest extent possible.

Recent immigration trends

In quantitative terms, immigration to Sweden has expanded through almost all channels in recent years. While slightly more than 60,000 people were granted a first-time permit to reside in Sweden in 2005, this figure had almost doubled by 2013, when more than 116,000 new residence permits were issued – the highest annual figure in Sweden to date (Migrationsverket 2014: 8).

People who immigrated for reasons of family reunification or other family-related purposes constituted the largest category of immigrants in 2013. Residence permits issued for humanitarian reasons (asylum), as in the case of refugees or persons otherwise in need of protection, represented the second-largest group. Compared to other EU countries, the number of asylum seekers has been disproportionally high in Sweden. In 2013, with more than 54,000 people applying for protection, Sweden ranked third (after Germany and France) in absolute numbers, especially due to the strong increase in the number of people arriving from war-torn Syria. Calculated on a per capita basis, Sweden received the largest share of asylum seekers in Europe (Eurostat 2014). More than half of all asylum applicants (28,000) were granted a residence permit in 2013 (see Table 1). The overall protection rate was roughly 53 percent (Bitoulas 2014: 11).

Persons moving to Sweden from elsewhere within the European Union or European Economic Area (EEA) were the third-largest group, followed by labor immigrants and international students (Migrationsverket 2014: 7).

Table 1: First-time residence permits granted in Sweden, 2012 and 2013

	2012	2013
Family reasons and adoptions	41,156	40,026
Free movement rights (EU/EEA)*	25,501	20,712
Employment reasons	19,936	19,292
Humanitarian reasons/protection**	16,893	28,438
Education reasons	7,092	7,559
Other reasons***	512	560
Total	111,090	116,587

* EU and EEA citizens do not need a residence permit but are supposed to register if planning to reside in Sweden.
** This includes refugees, individuals being resettled and people granted residence permits due to exceptionally distressing circumstances.
*** This includes persons who were found not to be in need of protection but who could not be returned to their country of origin.

Source: Migrationsverket (Swedish Migration Board)

An open approach to labor immigration

While the number of people coming to Sweden for work may seem modest compared to people moving for family reasons or asylum, the country's current framework for admitting workers from third countries has received much attention and admiration, with the OECD describing it as the "the most open labor-migration system among OECD countries" (OECD 2011: 11). In fact, Sweden radically reformed the rules of admission in 2008 by phasing out its previous agency-based labor-market-needs test. Until December 2008, the Swedish employment agency was required to investigate whether domestic or EU workers were available to fill vacant jobs, and employers could only recruit from outside the European Union when this was not the case. Now, companies themselves determine whether they can find suitable candidates within Sweden or the European Union, or whether they want to hire job seekers from non-EU countries. All they have to do before hiring from third countries is publicly advertise open positions in order to make it possible for Swedish residents or EU citizens to apply, and give trade unions an opportunity to assess the proposed working conditions and salaries. Once these conditions have been fulfilled, the Swedish Migration Board then issues a residence and work permit.

Compared to other EU member states, in which selective policies focusing on "talent" or highly skilled workers have in many cases been put into place (EMN 2013), the Swedish system is open to individuals of all skill or qualification levels and any country of origin, and there are no quotas or any other qualitative or quantitative restrictions. Labor immigration thus takes place in the engineering and IT sectors, but also in agriculture, forestry and the catering, cleaning and hotel businesses, among others. A critical feature of the Swedish approach is that all immigrant workers with a residence permit valid for at least one year enjoy access to welfare benefits and health care under the same conditions as Swedish nationals. Moreover, they can be accompanied by close relatives, who are also provided with access to the labor market and welfare services. There is no requirement that foreign workers must be able to support their families financially.

Lessons from Sweden

While employer organizations have embraced the new system from its start, trade unions and left-wing parties have remained skeptical due to fears of wage-dumping and exploitation of foreign workers. These fears have in part turned out to be justified. As the Swedish Trade Union Federation (LO) documented in a recent report, some employers have recruited foreign workers based on false promises, as working conditions and salaries did not always correspond to what companies had promised in job offers. LO also criticized the fact that much employment-related immigration took place in sectors in which no shortage of domestic labor was evident (LiS 2013; Bevelander et al. 2014: 56–73).

Reacting to such criticism, the Swedish Migration Board has iteratively introduced stricter requirements for the recruitment of foreign workers within certain industrial sectors. Since 2012, businesses in the cleaning, hotel and restaurant, service, construction, staffing, commerce, agriculture and forestry, and automobile-repair sectors, as well as all new enterprises, have to prove ex ante that they can actually pay salaries during a new employee's prospective employment period. In 2014, parliament passed an amendment to the Aliens Act enabling the Migration Board to carry out post-arrival checks on employers to verify whether admitted third-country nationals have genuinely begun work and whether businesses are complying with the terms offered. To compensate for these additional checks, trustworthy employers that frequently hire job seekers from third countries can now receive certifications ensuring that the Migration Board will process their applications for residence permits quickly. Electronic applications from workers with a job offer from a certified employer are usually decided upon within five days.

Despite this addition of increased oversight, on the one hand, and the creation of a quick processing system for credible businesses, on the other, the Swedish labor-immigration system remains controversial. From a fairness point of view, it is still problematic that immigrant workers often pay a higher price as a consequence of wage dumping and exploitation than do employers. When, after arriving, labor immigrants do not receive the job they were originally offered, or when an employer violates the terms and conditions of the job offer, the workers risk losing their right to stay in the country if they are unable to find a new job within four months. Negative consequences for abusive employers are much less immediate and less punitive.

International students

For young people coming to Sweden from non-EU countries for university studies, there have been ups and downs in recent years. While Sweden was increasingly popular among international students through 2010, the numbers of such students dropped sharply in 2011, when parliament introduced tuition fees. With the exception of EU citizens and young people coming to Sweden under official exchange programs, students from abroad now have to pay fees ranging from €10,000 to more than €25,000 per academic year, depending on the subject of study. While official scholarships do exist, and students from wealthier countries (such as the United States and China) have continued to arrive, Swedish universities are now no longer attractive to students from comparatively poor African or Asian countries.

However, studying in Sweden does continue to offer certain advantages. Incoming foreign students have full access to the labor market, enabling them to earn some money and acquire working experience while studying. Moreover, they are allowed to transform their study-based residence permit into a work permit if they find a job or start their own business before the study-related permit expires. Since August 2014, students have also been allowed to stay in Sweden for up to six months after graduation in order to look for work.

Immigration status changes

In terms of fairness, a striking and internationally unique feature of the Swedish immigration policy is rejected asylum seekers' ability to change their irregular status and stay in the country as labor immigrants. Within two weeks of receiving a negative decision on their claim, asylum seekers who have been found not to be in need of protection may apply for a residence permit for work purposes. This is in turn issued whenever an asylum seeker has been working for at least four months before rejection, and when the employer will guarantee that the work contract will continue for some time into the future. Neither the type of work nor the job's full- or part-time status matter as long as working conditions are in line with Swedish collective agreements and the monthly salary is at least SEK 13,000.

This status-change option was originally introduced in 2008 and was streamlined further in 2014. Under the old rules, failed asylum seekers had to be employed for at least six months in order to qualify for a status change. Today, four months are sufficient. While many still cannot make use of this measure due to the difficulty in finding a job for newly arrived people, almost 1,400 former asylum seekers managed to change tracks and receive a work permit in 2012, and almost 1,000 did so in 2013. These status changes are seen positively in Sweden, not only because they give rejected applicants who do not want to leave a second chance, but also for more pragmatic reasons: Any rejected asylum applicant who manages to become a legal labor immigrant makes a costly forced-return procedure unnecessary (Parusel 2014: 88). The exact reasons for the somewhat lower number of status changes in 2013 as compared to 2012 are difficult to establish, but this may be related to the smaller number of asylum applicants rejected overall and the increased competition for relatively few jobs.

Circular migration

Finally, when it comes to fairness to migrants and their needs and preferences – particularly with regard to migrants' ability to leave Sweden for certain periods of time, move back to their countries of origin or on to other countries, and eventually return to Sweden – the country's circular-migration policy is worth mentioning. In 2009, the government appointed an independent parliamentary committee to examine the connection between circular migration and development. The final report of the committee, published in 2011, included several proposals, including allowing migrants to take longer periods of absence from Sweden without losing their residency status, providing public support to diaspora groups and their development-related projects in other countries, establishing a website that enables migrants to compare fees charged by services transferring remittances back to their home countries, and improving the coherence of the country's migration and development strategies (SOU 2011). One of the outcomes of the report was a government bill enacted by parliament in 2014 that aims at facilitating circular movement to and from Sweden. Under the terms of the new policy, a permanent residence permit is revoked only after a migrant has been outside Sweden for two years or more, and labor immigrants with temporary residence permits are allowed to spend certain periods of time outside Sweden and still qualify for permanent residence permits seven years after their first entry. In a similar vein, foreign doctoral students are allowed to leave the country for several years while retaining their right to reside in Sweden and ultimately qualify for permanent residence. With these measures, Sweden may have given new impetus to the international policy debate over circular migration and its potential benefits – a debate that had stagnated for many years. The legislature also made it clear that Sweden does not trust "managed" circular-migration policies that, for example, allow labor migrants to stay in the country only for a predetermined period of time. Instead, from the Swedish perspective, the migrants themselves should be able to decide. If they want to leave and come back, they may do so; if they want to stay, that is also an acceptable option.

Conclusion

In sum, it may be concluded that a progressive and pragmatic stance, combined with a positive view of migration and its potential for Swedish society, permeates Swedish immigration policies. Recurring throughout individual measures are a concern for equal treatment, a trust in market-economic values and a grounding in humanism. Thus, it appears largely appropriate to call the policies "fair." Indeed, recent migration trends confirm that Sweden's policies are not only an expression of idealism or wishful thinking, as many migrants are making eager use of the immigration channels the Scandinavian country has opened up for them.

However, some serious concerns remain. The exceptionally high numbers of asylum seekers that arrived in Sweden in 2013 and 2014 revealed severe bottlenecks with regard to the country's integration capacities. While the Swedish Migration Board has so far been able to cope with the tasks of processing the rising number of applications and providing the newly arrived with a roof over their heads – in large part thanks to the government's willingness to channel additional funds into the board's operations, allowing it to employ hundreds of new caseworkers – there is a distinct lack of subsidized housing and jobs. As many refugees are unable to find affordable housing or work, even those with an established right to stay often get stuck in the reception system for asylum seekers and, thus, in passivity. The unemployment rate among third-country nationals was almost 30 percent in 2012, more than three times that of Swedish nationals (EC/EMN 2014: 81).

On the one hand, the high level of unemployment among third-country nationals is not necessarily surprising, given that the number of newly arrived humanitarian migrants has been high in recent years, and that immigrants can become Swedish citizens relatively quickly, after only five years of legal residence in Sweden (or four years for refugees). This latter fact means that many immigrants are counted as third-country nationals only during their early years of stay, when many may not have managed to find a job. On the other hand, it is also obvious that municipalities and the public-employment agencies are barely coping with their task of assisting the newly arrived with internships, training and job-search services. This problem is most evident regarding immigrants who have arrived as asylum seekers or as a result of family-reunification policies, as the Swedish system for labor immigration implies that the migrants already have a job upon arrival.

In addition, there are also signs of a significant degree of "brain waste," with newly arrived migrants often performing work far below their qualification levels (Migrationsverket 2013: 21). This, among other aspects of the current situation, points toward a need to improve labor-market integration and recognition of qualifications that immigrants have acquired in other countries. Recently, the government increased funding for Swedish-language instruction and labor-market-related integration measures, and widened the scope and duration of existing programs, such as subsidized "step-in" jobs, apprenticeships, vocational training and "job guarantees," with a particular focus on helping young people.

If the Swedish municipalities, the central government, civil society and economic actors manage to resolve these challenges, the recent wave of immigration to Sweden may become a success story. The Scandinavian country could stand out as role model for absorbing and integrating a high number of migrants and for treating them fairly. However, if these actors fail to overcome today's difficulties, and if the rise in support for the xenophobic Sweden Democrats continues as it has for similar parties in neighboring Denmark and Norway, fair immigration policies in Sweden might give way to a much more restrictive and less idealistic approach, and some open doors might be closed.

References

Bevelander, Pieter, Henrik Emilsson, Karin Magnusson and Sayaka Osanami Törngren. *Världens öppnaste land, arbetskraftsinvandring efter reformen 2008*. Stockholm: Fores, 2014.

Bitoulas, Alexandros. "Asylum applicants and first-instance decisions on asylum applications: 2013." *Eurostat Data in focus 3/2014*. Brussels: Eurostat, 2014.

EC/EMN (European Commission/European Migration Network). *A Descriptive Analysis of the Impacts of the Stockholm Programme 2010–2013*. Brussels: EC, 2014.

EMN (European Migration Network). *Attracting Highly Qualified and Qualified Third-Country Nationals*. Brussels: EMN, 2013.

Eurostat. "Asylum in the EU28. Large increase to almost 435.000 asylum applicants registered in the EU28 in 2013." News release, March 24, 2014. Brussels: EC, 2014. http://europa.eu/rapid/press-release_STAT-14-46_en.htm.

GOS (Government Offices of Sweden). Migration Policy. *Fact Sheet* Ju 14.04e. Stockholm: GOS, 2014. www.regeringen.se/content/1/c6/24/55/93/625193d0.pdf.

LiS (Landsorganisationen i Sverige). *Fusk och utnyttjande – om avregleringen av arbetskrafts-invandringen*. Stockholm: LiS, 2013.

Migrationsverket (Swedish Migration Board). *Attracting Highly Qualified and Qualified Third-Country Nationals*. Norrköping: EMN Sweden, 2013.

Migrationsverket. *EMN Policy Report 2013*. Norrköping: EMN Sweden, 2014. http://ec.europa.eu/dgs/home-affairs/what-we-do/networks/european_migration_network/reports/docs/annual-policy/2013/27.sweden_national_policy_report_migration_asylum_2013_final_en_version.pdf.

OECD (Organization for Economic Co-operation and Development). *Recruiting Immigrant Workers – SWEDEN 2011*. Paris: OECD Publishing, 2011.

Parusel, Bernd. "'Spurwechsel' in Schweden: auf dem Weg zu einem flexiblen Migrationsrecht." *Terra Cognita* (25): 88–91, 2014. www.terra-cognita.ch/fileadmin/user_upload/terracognita/documents/Terra_Cognita_25.pdf.

SOU (Statens Offentliga Utredningar). *Cirkulär migration och utveckling – förslag och framåtblick. Slutbetänkande av Kommittén för cirkulär migration och utveckling. SOU 28*. Stockholm: SOU, 2011.

Lessons from Norway

Espen Thorud

Introduction

We have been challenged to reflect upon the following questions:
- Is the "fair management of migration" an issue in your country and is it factored into labor-migration policy? How is that done?
- Are there any model programs/initiatives that demonstrate best practices or from which lessons can be learned?
- How could the "fair management of migration" be improved?

It is tempting as a prelude to discuss what fair migration management might imply. What does fairness have to do with the management of migration? Fair for whom? For people, for employers or for states? For individuals in sending or in receiving countries? For migrants or for the natives in one or in both settings? Are we mainly concerned with fair process or fair outcome?

Migration has effects on the national, local and individual levels. Some gain from migration, while others experience loss. A fair(er) management of labor migration could perhaps be accomplished through a policy framework designed in such a way that the gains resulting from migration were distributed in a balanced manner between employers, individuals and society, while the "losers" were compensated. However, this belief that a "triple-win" outcome is in fact possible presupposes a model of the world's functioning based on wide-ranging harmony. Some would probably view this outcome as unrealistic, given existing national and global socioeconomic dynamics and class relations.

However, such philosophical and normative issues ought to be elaborated from an academic perspective. My task as a civil servant is to present a few relevant elements of Norwegian policies and initiatives, and to reflect upon them. My comments here take on the assumptions inherent to the RMP framework. These include:
- There is increasing competition for talent or highly skilled workers on the global market.
- The supply of such talent within Europe and the OECD countries is limited, even though Europe and many other countries in the OECD presently experience high unemployment rates.

Lessons from Norway

- A growing share of the global pool of talent will be concentrated in less-developed countries.
- It is not a viable solution for rich countries to "buy up" highly skilled trained persons from abroad.
- There is a need for international cooperation or partnerships to avoid a widening "talent gap."

Some may want to question such presumptions – and perhaps also an underlying assumption about the detrimental effects of "brain drain" for sending countries (Clemens 2013) – but these issues are not discussed in this paper.

Facts

Before discussing relevant policies, the presentation of a few facts will provide context to the issue of labor migration in Norway:

- Norway's population growth rate is one of the highest in Europe, largely due to the increase in immigration since 2004. The population recently passed the 5 million mark, with immigrants making up a share of around 13 percent. In addition, Norwegian-born children with two immigrant parents make up approximately 2 percent of the population.
- For the last decade, there has been considerable labor migration from new EU member states, especially Poland and Lithuania, but also from countries such as Sweden and Germany. This migration is regulated by supply and demand for labor in the open European labor market. These labor migrants are low, medium and highly skilled.
- Since 2006, labor migration has accounted for between 40 and 50 percent of all migration from countries outside the Nordic area. If migration from Nordic countries were also included in this category, labor migration's share would exceed 50 percent.
- Between 10 and 15 percent of all non-Nordic labor immigration was from third countries outside the EU/EEA. This group primarily comprises skilled workers, such as engineers and health professionals. India, the United States, the Philippines, Russia, Serbia and China have been the most significant countries of origin in recent years. In addition, there is some seasonal labor migration, mostly in the area of labor-intensive agriculture. Vietnam, Ukraine and Belarus are major sending countries in this regard. These individuals are not counted as immigrants in Norway's national statistics.
- There is considerable return migration among labor immigrants. Only around 50 percent of immigrants who arrived in 2002 remained in Norway 10 years later, for example.
- There is also some immigration from third countries based on an intention to study or take part in what is officially considered to be cultural exchange (mainly as au pairs). Some of these individuals shift status and become labor migrants, but the numbers have so far been small. Major countries of origin for individuals in this latter group are China, Russia and the Philippines.

Policies

In 2008, the then-serving government presented what remains today the most recent comprehensive policy report on Norwegian labor-migration policies (NMSLI 20008). There have been no indications of major changes to this policy in the political platform of the present government. However, employer and business representatives have identified a need for a more proactive policy to enable Norway to participate successfully in the intensifying competition for talent (OCC 2013).

Relevant principles in the 2008 policy report include the following:

- The first priority is to mobilize domestic labor resources or reserves to fill emerging needs and gaps. This includes increasing labor-market participation rates among immigrants already residing in Norway as well as among refugees and the families of migrants who might arrive in the future.
- Participation in an open European labor market through the European Economic Area (EEA) agreement with the European Union provides Norway with access to a large pool of labor. This will be the main external recruitment area for many years to come.
- When recruitment domestically or within the EEA proves insufficient, current policy facilitates recruitment from third countries that takes place as simply and efficiently as possible within a flexible regulatory framework. This is a demand-driven system for managing labor migration. The starting point is that a concrete job offer is the precondition for a permit to work in Norway.
- According to the regulations, labor migration from third countries is possible for types of work requiring either high or medium skill levels. The migration of low-skilled workers from third countries is considered an exception that is generally limited to seasonal work.
- The regulation of labor migration from third countries should be neutral and should not favor or disfavor specific countries. Generally, bilateral agreements with individual countries are not on the policy agenda, with the exception of a few special arrangements with neighboring Russia that form a part of broader cooperation agreements.
- The regulation of labor migration should be designed and implemented in such a way as to avoid "serious consequences" for poor countries. This indicates a concern for possible brain-drain effects.
- Demographic developments and the growing need for certain types of labor make it necessary to engage in long-term planning to ensure that the education system has the capacity to provide sufficient numbers of skilled health workers.
- Regulation of labor migration is necessary to avoid a crowding out of the domestic workforce and to avoid undermining labor standards. Therefore, labor migrants must be offered equal pay and working conditions. Social dumping is unacceptable, and measure preventing this are in place. The gains from migration should be distributed in a balanced way among employers, immigrants and the domestic population.
- Labor migrants who become residents are expected to integrate into Norwegian society, as are other immigrants. However, the extent of public financial support for integration is more limited for labor migrants than for other categories of immigrants.

Lessons from Norway

- The regulation of labor migration and the integration of immigrants are also seen as portions of a broader strategy for securing a sustainable welfare society.

Influenced by the strong focus on migration and development at the time, the report contains a special chapter on labor-migration and development policies. Some relevant points here are:

- Policies that might result in brain drain should be avoided. Meanwhile, the rights of individuals to emigrate must be safeguarded. For example, there should not be any special restrictions on individual health care workers from certain countries.
- The effects of labor-migration regulations should be monitored with regard to the potential for negative consequences for poor countries.
- The country intends to contribute to the establishment of standards avoiding the targeted recruitment of highly skilled persons in short supply in poor countries. The health sector has been a key focus in this regard, reflecting the process leading up to the implementation of the WHO Global Code of Practice on the International Recruitment of Health Personnel from 2010 (Helsedirektoratet 2007).
- The possibility of granting permits to low-skilled employees from developing countries – with this action linked to the implementation of specific development projects funded by Norway – should be examined. The aim should be to facilitate some form of circular migration for such workers.
- Remittances from immigrants should be facilitated, with costs lowered by reducing legal restrictions on money-transfer agencies and by establishing a Web-based service to compare different service providers (ICMPD 2013).
- Migrants' ability to export their pension benefits if they wish to return to their countries of origin is generally seen to be sufficient.
- The need to secure and improve the rights of international labor migrants overall is emphasized.

Implementation

The 2008 policy report, and the continued implementation of the elements cited, shows that some concern for fair management of labor migration has been an element in Norwegian labor-immigration policy. This policy is designed in a way that does not provide scope for a large volume of labor migration from third countries. The relatively few individuals who are admitted from third countries have to be highly or medium skilled. Seasonal labor comprises the primary exception to this rule. An independent report on the topic of facilitating circular migration among low-skilled workers from developing countries, linked to development-cooperation projects, was commissioned by the government and later published. However, none of this report's proposals have yet been followed up on (Seip, Reegård and Skaland 2010).

In addition, there has been an explicit expression of concern as to whether the existing labor-migration policy has negative consequences for poor countries, particularly concerning the issue of brain drain. As noted above, the 2008 report stated an intention to monitor the effects of migration policy in this regard. As far as I know, no systematic, general monitoring has been implemented. However, it can be argued that there is targeted monitoring in the health sector. The reporting system linked to the WHO Global Code of Practice can be seen as a form of such monitoring. The report produced by this system examines which countries health personnel are recruited from, with a special focus on vulnerable countries with few skilled health workers. There is very little recruitment from these countries to Norway. The rate of employment in Norway of health workers from the 57 countries with critical shortages of health workers is very low. India, Pakistan and Iraq are the most important source countries in this category. Some may have come as refugees, particularly from Iraq, or as family migrants. Norway also has very few health workers trained or born in Africa. The report also covers what is being done to fill the need for health care personnel in ways other than through international recruitment.

Occasionally, the issue of fairness in recruitment is also brought up within the EU/EEA context. For example, there is substantial recruitment of health care personnel from a few other European countries, which may have some negative effects within these countries. Such recruitment has mainly been from Germany, Sweden and Denmark. Furthermore, this is not part of Norway's managed migration flows, but rather the effects of the intended free flow of labor within the EU/EEA boundaries, which cannot be regulated by applying migration-management tools. However, it is still possible to consider whether or not the public health service ought to be involved in active recruitment from specific EU countries that may be more vulnerable than others.

As far as I can see, there are currently no model programs or initiatives in Norway specifically intended to "highlight best practices or lessons to be learned" with regard to the fair management of *labor* migration. There have been some attempts to stimulate the "return of talent" to certain countries in a post-war or post-conflict situation, but this has been conceived as part of a comprehensive refugee policy rather than being linked to the management of labor migration per se. For example, these efforts have been a part of return and reintegration programs for persons from countries such as Afghanistan and Iraq whose applications for asylum have been rejected (Strand et al. 2008 and 2011). Stimulation of entrepreneurship has been an element in such programs. Furthermore, there have been attempts to facilitate temporary return for young, skilled refugees who have been granted protection in Norway or for the children of such refugees (Norsk Fredssenter 2009). This project has also focused on the contribution of these migrants to dialogue and reconciliation in post-conflict situations. However, a very limited number of migrants have been involved.

A "whole of government" approach

Reforming specific policies for the management of labor migration is only one way to approach the issue of a fair deal on talent. Policies in several other fields are highly relevant, including, for example, various aspects of foreign policy. Support for better education and health care systems in developing countries, the promotion of balanced trade agreements, the facilitation of conflict resolution and the promotion of good governance, including the management of migration, may indirectly contribute to a fairer deal on talent globally. Efforts to involve diaspora organizations, groups and individuals in foreign-policy issues and in the design and implementation of specific (co-)development projects, as we have seen in Norway and many other countries, are also relevant.

In the domestic context, the supply and recruitment of skilled labor are complex issues that have many aspects beyond the management of labor immigration. As indicated in the description of present policies, there are other categories of migrants than labor migrants; for example, among the populations of refugees and migrant family members, there are both new arrivals and long-term residents who could – and should – participate more deeply in the domestic labor market. Some of these migrants have brought skills from abroad or have talents that could be tapped. Therefore, creating better systems for recognizing and utilizing such skills, while making training and "upgrading" options available, are measures that will increase access to highly demanded skills in states with many immigrants. In Norway, this approach recently resulted in an action plan focusing on the better use of immigrants' skills (MCESE 2013). It is also an important aspect of an ongoing Skills Strategy Project that is being undertaken in close cooperation with the OECD (OECD 2014).

Another element in a broad strategy of mobilizing skills that indirectly contributes to a fair deal on talent both globally and domestically is to ensure equal educational opportunities. This is important not only for immigrants, but also for persons born in Norway to immigrant parents. A clear trend toward higher levels of participation and stronger education outcomes for some groups of young people with an immigrant background has been evident (SN 2013 and 2014).

Perhaps the provision of opportunities for international students to receive tuition-free higher education in Norway could also be viewed as an indirect contribution to a fair deal on talent. As indicated, some of these students choose to convert their status following graduation and become labor migrants. However, the majority choose to return to their home country, bringing formal and informal skills with them. Some probably move on to other countries to use their skills, perhaps receiving higher wages than would be possible in Norway or their country of origin. In fact, an increasing number of international students, especially those affiliated with colleges in the northern part of Norway, choose to become online students while still residing in their home country. Some never even visit Norway during the course of their studies. Both the issue of free tuition for international students and the growing number of non-resident online students are being reviewed by the government. Finally, in designing and implementing strategies that may affect the outcome of labor-migration policies, it is a challenge for any government to take into consideration the full complexity of interrelations between relevant policy elements. Over the years, policymakers in Norway have aspired to develop a stronger "whole of government" approach in several policy fields, including migration. However, the necessary structural mechanisms and continuous political focus have often been lacking. Various holistic approaches of this kind may also have a tendency to compete for attention, priority and resources.

References

Clemens, Michael. "What Do We Know About Skilled Migration and Development?" *Migration Policy Institute Policy Brief September 2013.* Washington, D.C.: Migration Policy Institute, 2013. www.migrationpolicy.org/research/what-do-we-know-about-skilled-migration-and-development.

Helsedirektoratet. *Recruitment of Health Workers: Towards Global Solidarity.* Oslo: Helsedirektoratet, 2007. www.helsedirektoratet.no/publikasjoner/recruitment-of-health-workers-towards-global-solidarity/Sider/default.aspx.

ICMPD (International Centre for Migration Policy Development). *Migration and Development Policies and Practices. A mapping study of eleven European countries and the European Commission.* Vienna/Maastricht: ICMPD/ECDPM, 2013. www.icmpd.org/News-Detail.1668.0.html?&cHash=f2e25a052a&tx_ttnews%5Btt_news%5D=156.

MCESE (Ministry of Children, Equality and Social Inclusion). *Summary of the Action Plan 2013–2016: We need the competenece of immigrants.* Oslo: MCESE, 2013. www.regjeringen.no/en/dokumenter/summary-of-the-action-plan-2013-2016-we-/id735937/.

Norsk Fredssenter. *"Hjem for a bygge landet?" Artikelsammling on migrasjon, fred og forsoning.* Lillehammer: Norsk Fredssenter, 2009. http://peace.no/images/stories/pdf/hjem-for-a-bygge.pdf.

NMSLI (Norwegian Ministry of Labour and Social Inclusion). *Labour Migration. Main Contents of Report No. 18 (2007–2008) to the Storting.* Oslo: NMSLI, 2008. www.regjeringen.no/contentassets/c9929b2c805741a6b8bfbf6aa2769219/en-gb/pdfs/stm200720080018000en_pdfs.pdf.

OCC (Oslo Chamber of Commerce). "Kompetanseinnvandring – Hvordan gjør vi Norge til et forektrukket land?" Oslo: OCC, 2013. http://abelia.no/getfile.php/Bilder/Rapport%20kompetanseinnvandring%281%29.pdf.

OECD (Organization for Economic Co-operation and Development). *Five Key Actions to Maximise Norway's Skills.* Paris: OECD Publishing, 2014. http://skills.oecd.org/informationbycountry/norway.html.

Seip, Åsmund Arup, Kaja Reegård and Anne Marte Skaland. *"Sirkulær migrasjon. Midlertidig arbeidsinnvandring av ufaglært arbeidskraft fra utviklingsland."* Oslo: FAFO, 2010. www.fafo.no/media/com_netsukii/20173.pdf.

SN (Statistics Norway). *Employment and education among young people with immigrant background. 2011.* Oslo: SN, 2013. www.ssb.no/en/arbeid-og-lonn/artikler-og-publikasjoner/unge-med-innvandrerbakgrunn-i-arbeid-og-utdanning-2011.

SN. *Immigrants and Norwegian-born to immigrant parents in lower secondary school.* Oslo: SN, 2014. www.ssb.no/en/utdanning/artikler-og-publikasjoner/innvandrere-og-norskfodte-med-innvandrerforeldre-i-grunnskolen.

Strand, Arne, Synnøve Bendixsen, Erlend Paasche and Jessica Schultz. "Between two societies. Review of the Information, Return and Reintegration of Iraqi Nationals to Iraq (IRRINI) Programme." Bergen: CMI, 2011.

Strand, Arne, Arghawan Akbari, Torunn Wimpelmann Chaudhary, Kristian Berg Harpviken, Akbar Sarwari and Astri Suhrke. "Return in Dignity, Return to What? Review of the Voluntary Return Programme to Afghanistan." Bergen: CMI, 2008.

Lessons from Denmark

Maria Nørby

Introduction

Denmark experienced a labor shortage in the 1960s, with the country's first so-called guest workers arriving in the middle of that decade, primarily from Turkey, Pakistan and what was then Yugoslavia. During the same period, refugees from Spain, Portugal and Greece, as well as from Latin American and African countries, came to Denmark. In the 1970s, immigration emerged as a powerful political issue and, in 1973, Denmark implemented an immediate stop to its guest-worker program, while remaining relatively open to refugees.

The Danish parliament passed the country's first Alien Act in 1983. The parties that favored this act called it a very humanitarian and liberal policy on asylum, while critics charged that the measure made it too easy to gain access to Denmark. The most significant portions of the act addressed the rights of asylum seekers and the right to family reunion. Since that time, the provisions of the act have been made more restrictive.

Beginning in 2001, Denmark gradually introduced new programs to allow qualified workers to apply for residence and work permits. From 2001 onward, two different regimes developed: a policy on asylum and family reunification called "firm and tight," and a policy on labor migration that has been relaxed since 2001 (OECD 2013).

Labor immigration is today handled by the Ministry of Labor, while asylum and family reunification issues are handled by the Ministry of Justice.

The proportion of highly educated immigrants among recent immigrants to Denmark increased between 2001 and 2009 (OECD 2012).

In 2008, the then-serving government introduced a jobs plan containing new labor-market provisions. The aim was to ensure that highly qualified labor had easy access to the Danish labor market. In April 2014, the government proposed a new labor-migration reform. The goals of this measure were to:
- make it easier for Danish companies to recruit internationally
- attract and retain more international students
- make foreign workers and their families feel more welcome, and

- ensure that the salaries and working conditions of labor migrants and native Danes were commensurate.

In 2013, there were approximately 118,000 foreign workers employed on a full-time basis in Denmark, accounting for about 5 percent of the total economically active labor force. Half of these individuals were from European Union countries, and a smaller number were from the Nordic countries. One-third of the foreign workers, or about 39,000 persons working full time, were from outside the European Union. According to the Danish national statistics office (www.jobindsats.dk), this number has remained stable since 2008, even during the ongoing economic and financial crisis.

Receiving country benefits

In a triple-win situation, the receiving country is deemed to benefit because it attracts the skilled workers needed and integrates them successfully into its labor market and society. However, it is not always easy to determine when this condition is filled and, thus, to determine how a receiving country actually benefits from migration.

The impact of labor migration is a complex issue. Impacts on salaries, prices, productivity, state budgets and welfare policies might differ over time and between receiving countries. Empirical studies differ in their findings on these issues, and there are no simple explanations for variations between countries with regard to migration's impact. In addition, the effects of labor migration may vary across labor-market sectors, and short- and long-term effects may differ.

A review of international recruitment that examines empirical studies on migration to and from Western Europe and the United States after 1945 finds that, in general, there is no clear evidence of wage effects or the extent to which labor migrants are supplementary to domestic labor (increasing productivity and wages overall) instead of serving as a substitute for domestic labor (Malchow-Møller 2013).

Some empirical studies indicate that the average migrant has little effect on the economy in general. These studies focus on the differences in net contributions made by migrants from Western countries and those from other countries. This is mainly due to the fact that migrants from less-developed countries have lower employment rates than do migrants from Western countries (CEPOS 2011; Schultz-Nielsen 2014).

Studies on labor migration

One recent study found that increased labor immigration can contribute to the resolution of future economic problems related to demographic developments. More than half of the labor migrants residing in Denmark are between 26 and 45 years of age, and the total employment rate within this population is about 82 percent. Forecasts hold that another net 5,000 labor migrants would increase gross domestic product by 1.7 percent, and that a net migration of 10,000 persons would increase GDP by 3.3 percent. This is in part due to the fact that labor migrants typically use public services to a lesser extent than do native Danes, while still paying taxes in Denmark (Rambøll 2012).

Another study concludes that highly skilled migrants make a positive net contribution to the financing of the Danish welfare state, since they pay taxes but make comparatively little use of day care, social and health services (Jacobsen, Junge and Skaksen 2011). This research found that an average highly skilled migrant traveling with his or her family stays in Denmark for an average of eight years and makes a net contribution of DKK 1.9 million. A typical highly skilled migrant without family stays for an average of six years and makes a net contribution of DKK 900,000.

A study on Denmark's preferential foreigner tax system (a program that allows new migrants with high incomes to be taxed at a low flat rate for a duration of three years) shows that the measure has doubled the number of highly paid foreigners in Denmark relative to foreigners receiving slightly less remuneration, who are therefore ineligible (Kleven et al. 2013). The study also indicates that foreigners' salaries have declined as a consequence of the reduced taxes. Finally, it shows that highly paid migrants do not have a positive effect on the wages or productivity levels of Danish residents.

Other studies indicate that companies employing highly skilled migrants were 5 to 7 percent more productive than companies that did not employ foreigners in the same period. That indicates a positive spillover effect on domestic labor (Malchow-Møller, Munch and Skaksen 2009).

A study on the effect of unskilled immigrants on the labor-market outcomes of similarly educated natives concludes that, in the private sector, an increased supply of non-EU immigrants in a Danish municipality pushed less-educated native workers to pursue more complex and less-manual-labor-intensive occupations. This reallocation took place mainly through the movement of individuals across firms and resulted in higher or unchanged wages. Immigration thus increased natives' mobility, but it did not increase their probability of unemployment (Foged and Peri 2013).

In sum, evidence as to whether labor migrants are supplementing domestic labor (increasing productivity and wages) or, instead, serving as a substitute for domestic labor remains mixed. Empirical studies indicate that highly skilled foreigners primarily supplement (highly skilled) Danish labor, while low-skilled foreign labor primarily acts as a substitute for Danish (low-skilled) workers.

Further analyses of the impacts of migration remain in progress, and studies vary with regard to methods and findings. Although the effects of labor migration are complex, existing analyses appear to support the case that highly skilled labor migration has primarily positive effects. In general, Denmark as a receiving country benefits from the migration of highly skilled workers. As work permits are increasingly being targeted toward highly skilled labor migrants, these benefits are likely to increase over time.

Highly skilled immigrants

Classic economic theory focuses on differences in wages as the primary driver for international (and national) migration, as labor moves to where wages are highest. Over time, that should in theory make wages more equal between areas and countries. More individual-oriented theories focus more on explaining individual choices to migrate. Possible benefits from migration may include a higher lifetime income, a calculus that includes the possibility of public benefits in the receiving country. Associated disadvantages can include costs related to integration in a new country and the costs of living apart from family and friends in a new culture. In general, actual and perceived costs and benefits may vary between individuals from the same country, for example, due to their education and skills, families and networks (Malchow-Møller 2013).

An individual person might perceive conditions as "fair" when expectations for migration are met with regard to wages, work and career conditions, quality of life and other such issues. The second dimension of fairness noted above, in which migrants are deemed to benefit because they can work commensurate to their qualifications and can integrate with their families, focuses on some of these issues; however, other issues, such as equal treatment and individual rights compared to native citizens, may also be relevant.

Programs for residence and work permit

The design of residence- and work-permit programs influences how migrants benefit and whether they can engage in work commensurate to their qualifications.

Most Danish programs are demand-driven, and the granting of work permits depends foremost on qualifications. Family, spouses or partners, and children under 18 can also obtain residence permits. In general, applicants for work permits need to have a written contract or a job offer. Salary and work conditions must correspond to Danish standards. This is a subject of review in applications, and some follow-up oversight of salaries is performed. Extensions to work permits can only be issued if salaries and working conditions are found to accord with Danish standards.

The Danish Greencard program is supply-driven and based on a point system. If applicants have the required qualifications, they can come to Denmark to look for work. However, evaluations indicate that migrants under this program have difficulties finding jobs, and that they often find work in sectors of the labor market normally associated with unskilled labor.

In the Danish context, demand-driven programs for residence and work permits have been more likely than supply-driven programs to ensure benefits for labor migrants.

A reform of international recruitment practices has been proposed, with the aim of ensuring equal conditions for labor migrants. Moreover, it focuses on the transparency of information within the Danish labor market so that migrants will know their rights and employers their obligations, and it additionally makes changes to some of the work-permit programs and improves oversight practices.

Initiatives that help migrants and families integrate

Providing foreign workers with access to the labor market does not in itself enable workers and their families to integrate into local society. Denmark has a variety of initiatives aimed at helping migrants settle down and integrate. These include:

- International Citizen Service (ICS) centers, where migrants can find representatives from all official agencies they will typically need to contact. These representatives can help migrants with paperwork and provide guidance on seeking jobs, Danish language courses and the Danish tax system. In addition, the centers provide information on living and working conditions, schools and day care.
- Migrants can take free Danish language courses.
- Various actors have developed program for spouses, helping them integrate into the labor market, developing welcome packages, creating expat organizations and so on.
- At the regional and local levels, there are several projects aimed at helping migrants and their families integrate.
- Educational institutions provide activities and career centers for foreign students.
- The Work in Denmark portal (www.workindenmark.dk) provides information on integrating in Denmark, the Danish labor market and other relevant topics.

The government has launched an action plan aimed at attracting and retaining international students. Moreover, the proposed international-recruitment reform is in part intended to make international labor feel more welcome, thus improving retention.

Sending countries and their benefits

The issue of sending countries and their potential benefits from labor migration is not an element explicitly considered within Danish immigration policy. In the current debate, no political actors have raised the issue of effects on sending countries, and the electorate may not hold strong sentiments on this topic.

Trade policy and negotiations on trade agreements do contain elements related to migration, but international-trade policy fundamentally aims at enabling more free trade on a global basis and is conducted in close cooperation with other EU countries.

Denmark's development cooperation aims to fight poverty, primarily through the support of human rights and economic growth (DMFA 2012). Danish development assistance has remained above the UN spending target (0.7 % of GNI) since 1978. Assistance efforts have been focused on some of the world's poorest countries.

Pakistan provides an illustrative example in this regard. With regard to migration, Pakistan is a sending country for Denmark and is also a partner country for development cooperation. China, another sending country, is granted development assistance in areas of democracy and human rights as well as on issues of climate and the environment (www.danida.dk).

Questions and policies regarding sending countries are not linked directly to migration policy, but are typically handled in the context of trade relations, development policies or cooperation within the educational area. These are policies in their own right and are not necessarily closely linked to sending countries.

Conclusion

This paper has offered examples from the Danish context related to the fair management of migration. Although the impact of labor migration is complex, existing analyses support the conclusion that the migration of highly skilled laborers has primarily positive effects. In general, Denmark as a receiving country benefits from the migration of highly skilled workers.

With regard to benefits for migrants themselves, at least within the Danish context, demand-driven programs for residence and work permits have been more likely than supply-driven schemes to provide benefits for labor immigrants.

To achieve greater benefits for both Denmark and its immigrants, initiatives are needed that help immigrants and their families settle down and integrate into society. Examples of programs that already work toward this goal include the International Citizen Service centers, programs that help spouses find jobs and the provision of welcome packages.

Migration's impact on sending countries does not play a direct role in the formulation of Denmark's immigration policies.

References

CEPOS (Center for Politiske Studier). *Negativt nettobidrag på 16 mia. kr. på de offentlige finanser fra indvandrere og efterkommere fra mindre udviklede lande – potentiale for forbedring.* Copenhagen: CEPOS, 2011.

DMFA (Dutch Ministry of Foreign Affairs). *The Right to a Better Life: Strategy for Denmark's Development Cooperation.* Copenhagen: Danida, 2012.

Foged, Mette, and Giovvani Peri. "Immigrants and Native Workers: New Analysis Using Longitudinal Employer-Employee Data." *NBER Working Paper* No. 19315. Cambridge, MA: NBER, 2013

Jacobsen, Højbjerg, Martin Junge and Rose Skaksen. *Højtuddannede indvandreres bidrag til det danske samfund.* Copenhagen: CEBR, 2011.

Kleven, Henrik Jacobsen, Camille Landais, Emmanuel Saez and Esben Anton Schultz. "Migration and wage effects of taxing top earners: Evidence from the foreigners tax scheme in Denmark." *NBER Working Paper* No 18885. Cambridge, MA: NBER, 2013.

OECD (Organisation for Economic Co-operation and Development). *Settling In – Indicators of Immigrant Integration.* Paris: OECD Publications, 2012.

OECD. *International Migration Outlook.* Paris: OECD Publications, 2013.

Malchow-Møller, Nikolaj. *Forskningsrewiew om international rekruttering.* Copenhagen: CEBR, 2013.

Malchow-Møller, Nikolaj, Jakob Roland Munch and Jan Rose Skaksen. "Det danske arbejdsmarked og EU-udvidelsen mod Øst." Copenhagen: Rockwool Fondens Forskningsenhed, 2009.

Rambøll. *Arbejdsindvandring i Danmark.* Copenhagen: Danish Agency for Labour Market and Recruiting, 2012. http://star.dk/da/Om-STAR/Publikationer/2012/06/Arbejdsindvandring-i-danmark.aspx.

References

Schultz-Nielsen, Marie Louise. "Indvandrere og danskeres nettobidrag til de offentlige finanser, Rockwool Fondens Forskningsenhed." *Rockwool Fondens Forskningsenhed Arbejdspapir* 30. Copenhagen: RFF, 2014.

Lessons from Canada

Triadafilos Triadafilopoulos

The issue of fairness is omnipresent in debates over immigration policy. In a world of mutually exclusive, sovereign nation-states, the admission of outsiders is bound to provoke profound unease. Yet it is important to note that the forms of this unease vary. Employers keen on securing a pliable workforce and reducing labor costs tend to be positively disposed to foreign workers, while organized labor (and native workers more generally) tend to see outsiders as a potential threat to their hard-won gains. At the same time, defenders of the nation may see immigrants as a threat to the prevailing national identity – to those things about "us" that make us ourselves. Conversely, cosmopolitans may embrace immigration precisely because it promises to open society up to a broader, global community.

Policymakers must contend with each of these poles of contention. Where governments are composed of moderate parties of the center-left or center-right, their efforts typically resemble a balancing act, for example, by enabling immigration for economic ends while simultaneously placing limits on entry (or the rights of foreign workers) to protect domestic labor and mollify the concerns of nationalists. When we look beyond the selfish interests of national governments and pose the issue of fairness at a global scale, as proponents of "triple-win" migration strategies have done, the quest for fairness becomes even more challenging. How might states committed to serving the interests of their societies also provide opportunities for improving the lives of outsiders through access to their labor markets?

The Canadian model

Canada has emerged as something of a model for states attempting to craft fair managed-migration systems. The "Canadian model" features an active immigration policy that admits (on average) 250,000 well-qualified immigrants per year, an official policy of state multiculturalism that enables newcomers and natives to partake of a common national identity and, more recently, an expansive Temporary Foreign Worker Program that provides outsiders with access to the Canadian labor market and an opportunity to provide assistance to those back home through remittances and knowledge transfer. When surveyed, Canadians – unlike their peers in almost every other industrialized country – express satisfaction with their government's immigration policies (for background on this, see Triadafilopoulos 2014).

I do not wish to contribute to this mythologizing of the Canadian case. Rather, I will use this opportunity to explore the degree to which Canada meets the demands of fairness, as proponents of the triple-win strategy understand it (for background, see Angenendt 2014). Specifically, I will consider the following questions:
1. Do Canadians benefit from the admission of skilled workers who integrate successfully into the majority society?
2. Do immigrants benefit by finding work that is commensurate with their qualifications and otherwise integrating successfully with their families?
3. To what degree can large temporary foreign worker (TFW) programs, which ostensibly promote migration and development in sending states, be successfully administered?

Canada does indeed benefit from the admission of skilled immigrants, but the economic fate of recent cohorts of immigrants suggests that they are not faring as well today as they have in the past. Paradoxically, while education and training levels among highly skilled immigrants have never been higher, these individuals' outcomes with respect to employment, wages and overall economic success have never been worse. As for the third question, we do not know the degree to which Canada's migration policies, especially concerning TFWs, benefit sending states. Even if we assume that remittances are substantial, we must recognize that these benefits come at a high cost, borne in the main by TFWs who are denied rights, such as labor mobility, as part of their contracts and often languish in poor conditions despite the official guarantees contained in their work agreements. Moreover, the expansion and misuse of TFW programs has catalyzed significant concern among Canadian workers who believe their government is enabling employers to prosper at their peril. In short, even high-capacity liberal-democratic states like Canada have a hard time administering "fair" guest-worker systems that respect the rights of foreign workers and prevent abuses by employers. I elaborate on each of these points below.

The paradox of immigration policy for the highly skilled in Canada

Since the 1970s, Canada has relied on immigrants selected through its Federal Skilled Worker Program (FSWP). Prospective immigrants submit an application that is evaluated by officials at Citizenship and Immigration Canada, the federal ministry tasked with immigration and citizenship policymaking. Successful applicants are admitted to Canada as permanent residents, with no subsequent need to renew a temporary visa; permanent residents are "welcome on arrival" and are ultimately expected to naturalize (Triadafilopoulos 2012). Immigrants have the right to bring along their spouses and minor-age children (up to the age of 18) and can also sponsor other relatives, including their parents and grandparents, through the Family Class stream (for background, see Reitz 2004).

Since the 1990s, the emphasis has been placed on selecting highly educated immigrants likely to be able to adjust to changing labor-market conditions by virtue of their abundant human capital. This led to a spike in the admission of immigrants with advanced degrees, professional designations and extensive foreign work experience. There has also been a steady decline of admissions under the Family Class stream, with reciprocal increases under the Economic Class. Simply put, Canada has never attracted so many well-qualified individuals. There is no gainsaying that immigration policy provides a benefit for Canada.

However, recent cohorts of immigrants admitted under the FSWP have experienced high rates of unemployment and falling earnings relative to native-born Canadians and previous immigrant cohorts (Boyd 2013; Hawthorne 2013). It appears that Canada is very good at attracting exceptionally well-qualified individuals, but rather less successful when it comes to providing them with access to work commensurate with their qualifications.

Part of the problem is attributable to barriers placed on foreign-trained professionals who lack Canadian licenses and work experience. As Monica Boyd has noted: "The collision of migration policies with domestic requirements of professional accreditation creates a paradox: While recruited on the basis of their potential professional contributions, migrants often face re-accreditation requirements that act as barriers to the full utilization of their skills [...] Foreign-trained doctors and engineers are less likely to be employed in occupations that correspond to their training; they earn less; and part of their lower earnings reflects the mismatch between their training and the occupations where they work. These patterns are accentuated for persons who have recently immigrated to Canada and for those who are from areas such as Eastern Europe and Asia" (Boyd 2013: 185).

A system that benefits the receiving state but leaves immigrants scrambling to find appropriate work is obviously not fair. To their credit, Canadian officials have (belatedly) acknowledged the severity of this problem and have attempted to deal with it through the introduction of "bridging programs" and other measures (including the establishment of a federal Foreign Credentials Referral Office and a Fairness Commissioner in the province of Ontario). A series of changes to Canada's immigrant admissions system have also been implemented. Among the most important has been the restructuring of the economic-immigration stream through the introduction of an "Express Entry" model through which employers play a more prominent role in the selection of immigrants.

Beginning on 1 January 2015, would-be immigrants will submit a "preliminary expression of interest" for admission under the FSWP, the Federal Skilled Trades Program and the Canadian Experience Class (an immigration program that enables graduates of Canadian post-secondary institutions, such as universities and colleges, to transition from temporary visas to permanent residency). Potential candidates' applications will then be screened by the federal government in accordance with "a points-based system called the Comprehensive Ranking System" (CIC 2014c). Points will be awarded based on a job offer, nomination from a province or territory,[5] skills, work experience, language ability, education and other factors (CIC 2014a). Candidates who score well will then be placed in a pool from which the highest-ranking can-

---

5 The Provincial Nominee Program (PNP) was established in 1995. The aim of the program was to allow provinces that did not receive significant shares of immigrants to select their own in accordance with their particular labor-market needs. Manitoba was the first province to come to an agreement with the federal government to administer its own PNP. By 2007, all other provinces, with the exception of Quebec (which already had the power to select immigrants through a seperate agreement) and two of Canada's three northern territories, had enacted PNP agreements with the federal government (Banting 2012).

didates will be invited to apply to immigrate as permanent residents on the basis of regular "draws." Candidates will have 60 days to submit their applications. The government has stated that applications will be processed in six months or less (CIC 2014b). Assuming applicants meet other eligibility and admissibility requirements under the Immigration and Refugee Protection Act (2001), they will be able to immigrate to Canada.

The Express Entry system is meant to be more responsive to labor-market needs; while a job offer is not required for admission under this program, it certainly helps boost the applicant's overall score. An unstated aim of the reform is to limit brain waste by taking greater care to select immigrants who are most likely to succeed in the Canadian labor market. The new system is also meant to enhance fairness by being more efficient. The six-month processing pledge is aimed at avoiding the long backlogs that have perennially plagued Canada's immigration system and added to the frustration of immigration applicants.

While this attempt to improve the employment prospects of economic immigrants through a shift in admission procedures is laudable, the move came at a high cost. Tens of thousands of applications that had been received under the previous system and were languishing in the backlog were returned without having been processed, even though some potential immigrants had waited several years for a decision on their files (CIC 2013). Ironically, actions taken to deal with the unfair outcomes of the previous policy – namely, the difficulty that skilled economic immigrants experienced in finding work in line with their qualifications and the long wait times for the processing of FSWP applications – have produced a new set of injustices. Moreover, these changes to the admissions procedures do not provide assistance to immigrants already in Canada who are experiencing difficulties obtaining appropriate jobs. Much more remains to be done if Canada's immigration policy for the highly skilled is to meet the standards of fairness.

The challenge of managing TFW programs fairly

While Canada has accepted TFWs since the 1960s, the size of the flow has increased markedly since the mid-2000s, especially after the Conservative Party assumed office in 2006. Whereas the total number of TFWs stood at 101,099 in 2002, it ballooned to 300,111 in 2011, marking a 180 percent increase (Alboim and Cohl 2012: 46). All of the streams that fall under the TFW class, including the Seasonal Agricultural Worker Program, the Live-In Caregiver Program and the Low-Skill Pilot Program, experienced significant increases.

This was accomplished in part by introducing a list of so-called regional occupations under pressure, which by 2010 included some 200 occupations "ranging from nurses and managers to hotel clerks, food and beverage servers, and gas-station attendants" (Foster 2012: 26). The Low-Skill Pilot project, introduced by the governing Liberal Party in 2002, went from admitting 1,304 TFWs in 2002 to 28,930 in 2010 – a 2,119 percent increase. Whereas the top five occupations for TFWs (excluding live-in caregivers) in 2005 were musicians and singers; actors and comedians; producers, directors and related occupations; specialist physicians; and other technical occupations in motion pictures and broadcasting, by 2008 the top five included food-counter attendants and kitchen helpers; cooks; construction-trade helpers and laborers; and light-duty cleaners. Only musicians and singers retained their position in the top five (ibid.: 29). As Jason Foster has noted, lower-skilled occupations in the TFW stream have experienced "exponential growth," while higher-skilled categories – the former mainstays of the program – have remained flat or experienced declines (ibid.: 33–35).

The Conservative government has maintained that it has expanded the TFW stream to meet "acute and short-term needs in the labor market that could not easily be filled by the domestic labor force" (CIC 2011: 19). Yet there is evidence that the program has changed labor markets in a more fundamental way. Under the Conservatives, the TFW program "opened up a new avenue of available workers for employers in industries traditionally restricted to a domestic labor pool, such as retail and restaurants," effectively "regulating labor supply in a fashion optimal for employer bargaining power" (Foster 2012: 42). The draw for employers is clear: TFWs do not have labor-mobility rights and are tied to a single employer (Nakache and Kinoshita 2010). They do not have access to settlement and integration programs, and hence are also at a distinct disadvantage with respect to their ability to communicate and avail themselves of whatever opportunities are available for redressing abusive workplace situations. Finally, low-skilled TFWs have no access to permanent residency and citizenship, and are expected to leave after no more than four years in Canada. Those who opt to stay will join the ranks of a highly precarious class of undocumented migrants.

This shift in migration and labor-market policy has occurred in the absence of parliamentary debate or even broad-ranging consultation. This is not terribly surprising: One would expect that many Canadians would have reservations about competing with a rapidly growing class of TFWs for jobs in what remains a fragile economic environment marked by high unemployment rates, especially among youth. The potential for backlash was made clear when the media reported on a major Canadian bank's efforts to fill positions held by recently laid-off workers with TFWs (Donkin 2013). Public condemnation was swift and fierce, forcing the Conservative government to announce changes to the program, including rolling back a policy introduced in 2011 that allowed employers to pay TFWs 15 percent less than the prevailing wage (Whittington and Campion-Smith 2013). The discovery of yet more abuse by employers has led to further changes to the program, including an outright moratorium on TFW hiring in the restaurant sector (Goodman 2014). The government's efforts to staunch public discontent have led restaurateurs and other employers to claim that they are being treated unfairly (Giovannetti and Curry 2014). Interestingly, diplomatic representatives of key migrant-sending states and organizations representing TFWs have also criticized the new policies, fearing the elimination of access to the Canadian labor market for their compatriots and members (Curry 2014).

Conclusion

As the Canadian case demonstrates, managed-migration fairness is difficult to achieve even in countries where policies are well established and outcomes have been positive in the past. Two points are worth highlighting:
1. It is not enough to attract highly skilled immigrants. Serious thought must also be devoted to devising means for meeting highly skilled immigrants' particular integration challenges. These include the recognition of foreign credentials, but also the need to fight dis-

crimination among employers who may be put off by an accent or a lack of in-country work experience. Admissions and integration policies must go hand in hand; otherwise, the receiving society may indeed benefit from the admission of talented newcomers, but at the cost of a massive and regrettable waste in talent and the crushing of immigrants' hopes and expectations.

2. The ability of even high-capacity states to administer extensive TFW programs successfully is open to question. This may not come as a surprise to citizens in states, such as Germany, that have had large-scale guest-worker programs in the past, but it seems to have been ignored or seriously downplayed by advocates of temporary- or circular-migration schemes. As the Canadian case makes clear, employers will push for more foreign labor when it is in their interests to do, leading some to abuse the system. This can provoke a backlash that imperils not only the continuation of TFW programs, but also the public's confidence in managed migration more generally. We must also expect that foreign workers might try to stay in the country when their contracts are up; indeed, many only agree to the terms of their agreements in order to gain a foothold in countries that are otherwise off-limits to them. Advocates of TFW programs should recognize that even when they are relatively well designed, these programs are susceptible to individuals' all-too-human tendency to act in their own self-interest.

My intention is not to argue that a fair migration system premised on a triple-win strategy is impossible. Rather, I wish to point out potential obstacles in achieving this aim. Migration provokes deep disagreements about fairness and will continue to do so. And given that all political decisions necessarily create winners and losers, no set of policy prescriptions will be entirely fair to all involved. The aim is to find a workable balance and seek to make improvements when the need arises. On this point, the willingness of Canadian policymakers to revise their now-famous immigration "model," even if at times unsuccessfully, is worth noting.

References

Alboim, Naomi, and Karen Cohl. *Shaping the Future: Canada's Rapidly Changing Immigration Policies.* Toronto: Maytree Foundation, 2012. http://maytree.com/wp-content/uploads/2012/10/shaping-the-future.pdf.

Angenendt Steffen. *Triple-Win Migration: Challenges and Opportunities. Migration Strategy Group on Global Competitiveness.* Stuttgart/Berlin: Robert Bosch Stiftung and German Marshall Fund of the United States, January 2014.

Banting, Keith. "Canada." *Immigrant Integration in Federal Countries,* edited by Christian Joppke and F. Leslie Seidle. Montreal/Kingston: McGill-Queen's University Press, 2012: 88–89.

Boyd, Monica. "Accreditation and the Labor Market Integration of Internationally Trained Engineers and Physicians in Canada." *Wanted and Welcome? Policies for highly Skilled Immigrants in Comparative Perspective,* edited by Triadafilos Triadafilopoulos. New York: Springer, 2013: 165–198.

CIC (Citizenship and Immigration Canada). *Annual Report to Parliament on Immigration.* Ottawa: CIC, 2011.

CIC. "Notice – Fee Returns for Federal Skilled Worker Applicants Affected by the Backlog Elimination Measure." Ottawa: CIC, 2013. www.cic.gc.ca/english/department/media/notices/notice-returns.asp.

CIC. "Entry Criteria and the Comprehensive Ranking System." Ottawa: CIC, 2014a. www.cic.gc.english/express-entry/criteria-crs.asp.

CIC. "Getting Ready to Launch Express Entry." Ottawa: CIC, 2014b. http://news.gc.ca/web/article-en.do?nid=910619.

CIC. "How Express Entry Works." Ottawa: CIC, 2014c. www.cic.gc.english/express-entry/index.asp.

Curry, Bill. "Top Filipino Diplomat Defends Ottawa's Foreign Worker Program." *The Globe and Mail,* April 29, 2014.

Donkin, Karisa. "RBC Defends Plan to Replace 45 Canadians, Outsource their Jobs." *Toronto Star,* April 7, 2013.

Foster, Jason. "Making Temporary Permanent: The Silent Transformation of the Temporary Foreign Worker Program." *Just Labour* (2) 19: 22–46, 2012.

Giovannetti, Justin, and Bill Curry. "Restaurants Warn of Closures in Wake of Temporary Foreign Workers Ban." *The Globe and Mail,* April 24, 2014.

Goodman, Lee-Anne. "Jason Kenney Suspends Restaurants from Scandal-Plagued Temporary Foreign Worker Program." *National Post,* April 24, 2014.

Hawthorne, Lesleyanne. "Skilled Enough? Employment Outcomes for Recent Economic Immigrants in Canada Compared to Australia." *Wanted and Welcome? Policies for Highly Skilled Immigrants in Comparative Perspective,* edited by Triadafilos Triadafilopoulos. New York: Springer, 2013: 219–256.

Levitz, Stephanie. "Would-be Immigrants Take Ottawa to Court over Cancelled Applications." *Toronto Star,* May 16, 2012.

Nakache, Delphine, and Paula J. Kinoshita. "The Canadian Temporary Foreign Worker Program: Do Short-Term Economic Needs Prevail over Human Rights Concerns?" *IRPP Study* No. 5, May 2010.

Reitz, Jeffrey. "Canada: Immigration and Nation-Building in the Transition to a Knowledge Economy." *Controlling Immigration: A Global Perspective,* edited by Wayne A. Cornelius. Stanford: Stanford University Press, 2004: 96–139.

Triadafilopoulos, Triadafilos. "Willkommen bei der Ankunft: Die Bedeutung des unbefristeten Aufenthaltsrechts für die Integration von Zuwanderern in Kanada." *Deutschland, öffne dich! Willkommenskultur und Vielfalt in der Mitte der Gesellschaft verankern,* edited by the Bertelsmann Stiftung. Gütersloh: Verlag Bertelsmann Stiftung, 2012: 93–106.

Triadafilopoulos, Triadafilos. "Zwischen Kontinuität und Wandel – was Deutschland von der kanadischen Zuwanderungspolitik lernen kann." *Vielfältiges Deutschland. Bausteine für eine zukunftsfähige Gesellschaft,* edited by the Bertelsmann Stiftung. Gütersloh: Verlag Bertelsmann Stiftung, 2014: 469–495.

Whittington, Les, and Bruce Campion-Smith. "Conservatives Crack Down on Abuses of Foreign Worker Program." *Toronto Star,* April 29, 2013.

Lessons from New Zealand

Ramasamy Kone

New Zealand's migration context

Fairness in international migration can simply mean better, mutually beneficial outcomes for all involved. Put another way, this means that no one participant or stakeholder corners all benefits or faces too many costs along the migration pathway. In this sense, challenges to the fair management of migration within New Zealand cut across several policy domains, including non-discriminatory selection and admission, facilitation of movement, regulation of supply-chain processes and actors, the safeguarding of workers' interests and rights, and considerations of the development impact on sending countries.

New Zealand is a traditional country of destination for migrants. However, it is sometimes described as an OECD country with a high brain-drain rate (Groysberg and Bell 2013), though it probably enjoys brain exchange and even brain gain, as well (Stillman and Velamuri 2010). Migrants make a significant contribution to New Zealand's labor market, with around 27 percent of the working-age population born overseas.

New Zealand has reasonably good settlement outcomes, as it tends to target people who will integrate well into the current society (e.g., those who speak English or have previously spent time in New Zealand). As a result, immigrants are overrepresented among the highly educated population, and their labor-market outcomes are favorable in international comparison.

Why development issues don't dominate

The first-order effect of emigration for sending countries is a brain drain or a reduction in highly skilled human capital. Traditionally, most migration to New Zealand has come from European OECD countries, particularly the United Kingdom. However, flows in recent years have been dominated by citizens of Asian countries, in particular India, China and the Philippines. The Pacific Islands remain an important additional source of labor migration. It is unlikely that flows to New Zealand are having a significant impact on source countries. For instance, in China and India, a study conducted by Gibson and McKenzie (2010: 3) showed that less than 5 percent of the population holding a tertiary degree lives abroad, while the Philippines specializes in skills export. The same study of countries with high emigration rates, including Tonga and Samoa, two countries that have preferential migration arrangements with New Zealand, showed some degree of return migration among those countries' best and brightest. This might help explain why the explicit consideration of impact on sending countries is not given a high priority in New Zealand.

What about admission policies?

Fairness may mean giving all qualifying migrants with identical attributes or qualifications an equal chance to gain admission to the country. Migrant workers require transparent criteria and a predictable process. As long as there are sufficient jobs available and policy criteria are met (e.g., labor-market tests or skill levels), the only condition that should matter is that the right workers are matched with the right skill needs.

The Expression of Interest system, pioneered by New Zealand as a second-stage filter to the points-based system, provides the ability to select those who are most likely to succeed. This policy provides clear, up-front signals to potential migrants with regard to their likelihood of selection so that marginal candidates won't wait endlessly for a decision or enter the system only to fail. It thus satisfies the test of fairness and efficiency.

There are always policy exceptions, however. For instance, New Zealand specifies "comparable" labor-market experience as a requirement within its skilled-migrant category, a factor that may appear to privilege some nationalities.[6] Yet this seems to be a decision based on the likelihood that individuals from comparable markets will have better labor-market outcomes. India and China are not considered comparable in this regard, but continue to serve as top source countries for permanent (and temporary) workers thanks to other criteria in the points-based system as well as other immigration pathways. The key point here is that the rationale underlying policy features must be reasonable and self-evident.

Facilitation and supply-chain regulation

The immigration-advice industry is regulated by the New Zealand Immigration Advisory Authority. Aside from lawyers, no one can provide immigration advice without having a license to do so. This regime is now being examined more closely, with a particular focus on people at the fringes of the advice industry, such as employment agents and recruitment firms. Moreover, the insidious issue of large fees taken by third parties demands attention. This concerns not just placement fees charged by authorized recruitment agents, but also other fees and charges faced by migrant workers, such as documentation fees, airfares and so on.

---

6   Points may be awarded for work experience in countries that do not have "comparable" labor markets, but only in cases involving a multinational commercial entity domiciled in one of these listed countries or in cases of an absolute skill shortage.

The agreement currently under development with the Philippines serves as a useful example of international cooperation. As of the time of writing, proposals for this agreement were still focused on the area of intergovernmental information exchange as well as the provision of pre-departure information and training for Filipino migrant workers with regard to their employment rights and obligations in New Zealand. However, the agreement may ultimately be expanded to other areas.

Improving compliance and protection

According protection to international students has been one area of considerable policy concern. In addition to generating education export revenues, students are both a supplementary labor force and a future reserve of skilled workers. However, as students also have comparatively little bargaining power in a new labor market, compliance efforts overseeing local employers must be strengthened

The Canterbury region suffered a devastating earthquake in 2011. There is considerable concern that migration associated with the reconstruction efforts be handled on fair terms. The number of incoming essential-skills workers in New Zealand overall is beginning to rebound, with the Canterbury region showing the most significant increase. The government is therefore putting more compliance officers on the ground, and a senior bureaucrat will be responsible for coordinating the Immigration and Labor Inspectorate's workplace health-and-safety compliance work.

In 2013, a ministerial inquiry on the issue of foreign chartered-fishing vessels resulted in significant changes to policies in this area. The legal change will mean that foreign crew members temporarily working in New Zealand will have the same policy protections as domestic crew members. For immigration policy specifically, this will mean employers of migrant crew members will be subject to new requirements with regard to employment, immigration and health-and-safety laws (NZMPI 2013).

An end-to-end migration management

The New Zealand Recognized Seasonal Employer (RSE) policy is held up as a model with regard to attaining a so-called triple win for migrants, destination countries and sending countries. The RSE combines a variety of different policy options, establishing best practices with regard to the employment of foreign workers by making recruitment agencies and employers accountable, mandating pastoral care and facilitating return migration. In addition, it provides an example of bilateral agency-to-agency arrangements, investment in furthering workers skills and literacy, and direct work aimed at strengthening institutional capabilities in the Pacific sending states.

The RSE is a case in which government regulatory action, government labor-market policies, World Bank advice and the actions of private employers have all combined to result in one of the most effective development policies evaluated to date. A 2010 World Bank/Waikato University study provided the first rigorous evaluation of the impact of the seasonal-migration policy on households in sending countries, and it found gains in household well-being that greatly exceeded those associated with other popular development interventions, including microfinance and conditional cash transfers. It should be noted that when coupled with analysis showing very low rates of overstaying and only modest impacts on the native labor force (NZDoL 2010), these results suggest that more countries should give seasonal-worker programs a chance.

In addition, the International Labour Organization's (ILO) good-practices database states: "The comprehensive approach of the RSE scheme toward filling labor shortages in the horticulture and viticulture industries in New Zealand and the system of checks to ensure that the migration process is orderly, fair, and circular could serve as a model for other destination countries."

What motivates New Zealand?

Competing in a global marketplace for talent and skills requires that New Zealand demonstrate a reputation for fair admission processes and effective oversight of its supply chain and workplaces. This is important for several reasons: First, it protects New Zealand's export industries in cases where their trading partners demand ethically produced goods and services. Secondly, highly skilled people in particular will not want to come (or return) to New Zealand if is not a good place to work and live. Reputational risk and economic consequences matter as much as ensuring rights per se.

New Zealand also appears to be guided by pragmatism in its policy focus on fairness. It may choose to prioritize compliance and protection of workers within its domestic labor market because that is where the government has most reach and ability to make a difference.

Conclusion

Applying the test of fairness is never easy. New Zealand's experiences provide at least two examples of just such challenges. For example, it has been difficult to be guided completely by the principle of equity in the selection of seasonal workers when employers clearly prefer that the same workers return year after year, while the sending countries simultaneously desire that opportunities be rotated across communities or regions. Balancing these issues involves an apparent trade-off between equity and efficiency.

Moreover, not all actors have equal access to international migration. For instance, larger employers enjoy economies of scale and the ability to develop specialized recruitment channels and in-house staff. Since skills shortages are equally or especially acute in smaller local businesses, ensuring that these employers have equal access to the migration system is a reasonable objective, though it may be difficult to operationalize.

More broadly, New Zealand and other countries must ask themselves how they can explicitly or implicitly address the issue of fairness in their policies. Answering this question will inevitably involve knowing how to set priorities among the many interlocking issues and determining whose perspectives and values will ultimately be considered in this mix.

References

Gibson, John, and David McKenzie. "The Economic Consequences of "Brain Drain" of the Best and Brightest: Microeconomic Evidence from Five Countries." *World Bank Policy Research Working Paper No. 5394*. Washington, D.C.: World Bank, 2010.

Groysberg, Boris, and Debora Bell. "What Boards Can Do About Brain Drain." Harvard Business Review Blog Contribution from December 17, 2013. https://hbr.org/2013/12/what-boards-can-do-about-brain-drain/, www.stats.govt.nz/browse_for_stats/population/myth busters/brain-drain.aspx.

NZDoL (New Zealand Department of Labor). *Final Evaluation Report of the Recognised Seasonal Employer Policy (2007–2009)*. Wellington, New Zealand: Evalue Research/New Zealand Department of Labour, 2010. http://dol.govt.nz/publications/research/rse-evaluation-final-report/rse-final-evaluation.pdf.

NZMPI (New Zealand Ministry for Primary Industries). Fisheries (Foreign Charter Vessels and Other Matters) Amendment Bill, May 2013. www.parliament.nz/resource/mi-nz/50SCPP_ADV_00DBHOH_BILL11820_1_A325972/f5c5fc867849ec99bd6162e6ddaf5d9f9db4bc73.

Stillman, Steven, and Malathi Velamuri. "Immigrant Selection and the Returns on Human Capital in New Zealand and Australia." Wellington: NZDoL, 2010.

Perspectives from Regions of Origin

Lessons from Poland
Paweł Kaczmarczyk

Introduction

Poland is undoubtedly a country of emigration. From the middle of the 19th century onward, international migration has played an important – at some points critical – role in Polish history. Nonetheless, even considering previous massive waves of migration, the country's accession to the European Union (2004) marked a turning point regarding mobility trends among Poles. The early post-accession years saw a spectacular increase in the scale and dynamics of international mobility among Poles (which, in regional perspective, was comparable only to Romanian citizens' propensity toward migration). In 2007, the peak year for this trend, the stock of Polish citizens residing temporarily abroad was estimated at around 2.3 million individuals (6.6% of the total population); this figure remained at a relatively high level even after the onset of the Europe-wide economic crisis. Traditionally, the mobility of persons endowed with relatively high levels of human capital has played an important role in Polish migration patterns.

Against this background, this paper seeks to assess recent mobility trends among well-educated Poles while examining risks and challenges related to migration among the highly skilled from the perspective of the sending country. The structure of the paper is as follows: The first section looks at mobility among well-educated Poles in a historical perspective, but with a particular emphasis on recent outflows and their consequences. The second section attempts to assess the underlying factors, while the third section provides conclusions and recommendations.

Before going into details, it will be useful to define the term "highly skilled" as used in this paper as well to comment on the recent theoretical debate over the issues of brain drain and brain gain. With respect to the definition, it is common practice to identify skilled individuals with highly educated workers, as it is difficult to gather reliable information on the extent of "on the job" experience or to measure something as fuzzy as innate ability, even though these two components are admittedly important factors in determining a worker's true skill level. For instance, the OECD (2002) has proposed a definition of highly skilled workers that includes workers who have completed tertiary education as well as workers who have not completed tertiary education but are employed in occupations where such a qualification is usually required. This definition is data intensive, and thus hard to implement. In this paper, I will use a definition of skilled worker that is based on the years of formal education acquired; this has the additional benefit of cohering with the approach to this issue taken in Poland, where highly skilled workers are defined as university graduates who have acquired at least a master's-level degree (5–6 level in ISCED classification).

The second controversy is related to the notion of brain drain. There are two distinctive strands of the literature on the consequences of mobility among the highly skilled. The first – let us call it a "traditional approach" (Grubel and Scott 1966; Bhagwati and Hamada 1974), offers a pessimistic view of the impact of mobility within this population. Emphasis here is placed on costs and losses, particularly for sending countries and economies; thus, fiscal effects, impact on factor productivity and other such effects are cited. In this regard, the term *brain drain* is used to emphasize the negative effects of the outflow. Nonetheless, since the mid-1990s, a "modern approach" to the issue has been represented more strongly in the literature (Stark, Helmenstein and Prskawetz 1997; Mountford 1997; Beine, Docquier and Rapoport 2001). In the *new economics of brain drain*, migration is presented as a probabilistic event – thus, as the outcome of a lottery where the would-be migrant has a positive probability p of actually migrating (where $p<1$). Next, it is assumed that the decision to invest in education is driven by the expected return to human capital, with the positive probability p of migrating increasing the expected return to investment in human capital as compared to the no-migration situation. If this calculus increases the overall amount of education received, migration among the well-educated could theoretically lead to an increase in the optimal level of human capital achievable within a given country (we call this situation *brain gain* or *beneficial brain drain*). Following this line of reasoning, while continuing to use the term brain drain, I will not attempt to assess the impact of this phenomenon, but will instead make reference only to the selectivity of migration in terms of the statistical overrepresentation of the well-educated among migrants. In fact, this phenomenon is difficult to assess fully using the traditional means employed within the economic literature: A positive selection of migrants with respect to education might be regarded as a worrisome signal, for example, but it may also be matched by a substantial increase in educational investment by prospective migrants. This critical factor is not well captured by simple descriptive statistics on skill composition.

Migration among highly skilled Poles

Traditionally, the emigration of individuals with high-quality human capital has played an important role in Poles' mobility. In the communist period, the phenomenon of brain drain was evident in at least two periods: between 1968 and 1971, when approximately 13,000 Polish citizens of Jewish nationality were expelled, and in the 1980s, when a large wave of emigration followed the introduction of martial law. According to Sakson (2002), of almost 700,000 emigrants who left Poland between 1981 and 1988, 15 percent had advanced degrees, and an additional 31 percent had completed secondary school. In the same period, the share of people in the total population holding university degrees was around 7 percent; thus, there was significant overrepresentation of emigrants with high-quality human capital relative to the population of Poland as a whole.

Various data indicate that the situation has changed during the country's post-communist socioeconomic transformation. For instance, it was estimated in 1991 that the number of scientists employed in the country would have been 25 percent higher if an outflow of employees from scientific institutes had not taken place in the 1980s (Hryniewicz, Jałowiecki and Mync 1992, 1997; Jałowiecki, Hryniewicz and Mync 1994). This outflow, however, included both emigration and outflow from the scientific sector to other economic sectors within Poland; surprisingly or not, the latter phenomenon turned out to be the major driver. According to official data, the share of the migrants having completed only the lowest level of education has been increasing since 1990, while the share of migrants with the highest level of educational attainment has been decreasing. On the eve of economic transition, in 1988, a total of 9 percent of migrants held university degrees (as opposed to 37% who had completed only primary education), whereas in 2003, 15 percent had completed university degrees. Similar results were derived from studies conducted in Poland and in the receiving countries (Kaczmarczyk and Okólski 2005). Most of the studies found that people with low cultural skills, often without knowledge of foreign languages and unfamiliar with the institutional environment of destination countries and thus generally able to perform only low-skilled work, had the highest propensity toward migration (in the Polish literature, this type of emigrant is commonly referred to as an "incomplete migrant;" Kaczmarczyk 2011).

However, the structure of migration changed in the second half of the 1990s as a consequence of educational advancements, the economic crisis and, most specifically, the deteriorating situation on the Polish labor market. According to the 2002 population census, educational attainments of people residing outside Poland for more than two months was far higher on average than that of the population as a whole (aged 15 and over). At this time, the share of migrants with a scientific degree was double that of the full population, the share of migrants with a professional master's degree (or the equivalent) was 2.7 percentage points (36%) higher than in the full population, and the percentage of migrants having another type of advanced degree (e.g., engineers) was greater than that within the full population by 0.7 percentage points (26%). The changes after 1997 were accompanied by substantial changes in the composition of receiving countries, observed especially among the people with the highest educational attainments.

As stated in the introductory section, the post-2004 period saw a radical increase in the scale of migration from Poland. The stock of Polish (permanent) citizens residing temporarily abroad increased from around 1 million in 2004 to over 2.3 million in 2007 and declined only slightly during the Europe-wide economic crisis (according to the most recent data, totals remain as high as 2.13 million). Importantly, recent Polish migrants differ significantly from those who moved abroad in previous decades. Post-2004 migrants are generally younger, more often come from urban areas and are much better educated than their predecessors. As shown by the Labor Force Survey (LFS) data, recent Polish migrants are relatively well educated, with almost 20 percent of emigrants holding a university degree (as compared to 15% in the pre-accession period; see Table 1). This is particularly evident among female migrants, 27 percent of whom were highly skilled in the post-accession period. The most numerous group is migrants with vocational education, but there is a clear overrepresentation of individuals with tertiary education (Brücker 2009).

Lessons from Poland

Table 1: The education structure of Polish migrants pre- and post-accession (first post-accession phase) by gender, in %

Level of education	Pre-accession			Post-accession		
	Total	Men	Women	Total	Men	Women
University degree	14.7	12.0	18.3	19.8	15.6	27.0
Secondary	14.0	7.1	23.1	14.2	8.8	23.8
Secondary vocational	26.1	26.0	26.3	28.1	29.8	25.1
Vocational	34.8	45.4	20.9	30.9	39.2	16.2
Primary	9.9	9.3	10.9	7.0	6.6	7.8
Unfinished	0.4	0.2	0.5	0.0	0.0	0.0
Total	100.0	100.0	100.0	100.0	100.0	100.0

Notes: Pre-accession population refers to those aged 15 and over who were abroad for at least two months in the 1999–2003 period; post-accession period refers to those aged 15 and over who were abroad for at least two months in the period between May 1, 2004, and December 31, 2006. The university degree category includes bachelor's, master's and Ph.D. degrees.

Source: Brücker 2009

Figure 1: Percentage of persons with tertiary education in the new member states' resident and migrant populations, 2006

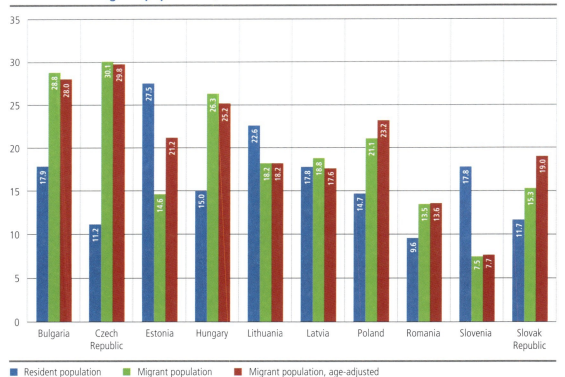

Note: Age-adjusted refers to the fact that the age structure of the migrant population commonly differs from that of the sending population.

Source: Own elaboration based on Brücker 2009

This picture is consistent with the situation in most of the European Union's new member states. Figure 1 presents the shares of individuals with tertiary education in resident populations as compared to migrant populations. Additionally, it takes into consideration the fact that the age structure of migrants and the overall sending population usually differs (thus employing an age-adjusted calculation). From the picture presented, it follows that positive selection with respect to human capital is a common phenomenon in Central and Eastern Europe, with Poland as a prominent example of this trend.

Interestingly enough, there is no single common pattern of migration from Poland with regard to destination and educational attainment. LFS data reveals a complex picture with regard to the selection of migration destinations (see Figure 2).

Figure 2: Share of persons with tertiary education among migrants, by destination, post-2004 migration

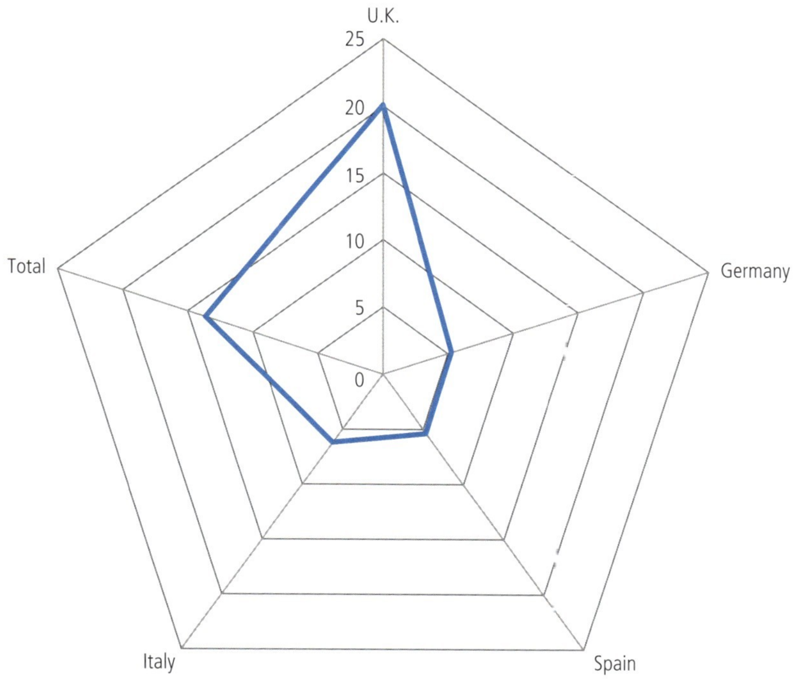

Source: Own elaboration based on the LFS data

While there is a clear overrepresentation of the highly skilled among all migrants from Poland, this picture is even clearer in the case of the United Kingdom. In contrast, countries such as Germany, Spain and Italy attract comparatively less-educated Polish citizens. Against this background, the case of Polish migrants in the United Kingdom seems extremely interesting.

Lessons from Poland

As shown by Kaczmarczyk and Tyrowicz (2013), in the case of the British labor market, all immigrant groups are on average better educated than the natives (particularly when it comes to tertiary education). The same holds true for A8 immigrants (those from the eight East European countries that joined the European Union in 2004) and Polish citizens residing in the United Kingdom. In this last case, almost 32 percent of Poles resident in the United Kingdom have completed tertiary education, as compared to 21 percent of natives (this share is higher than shown above due to the fact that the sample encompasses the 2004–2009 period). Additionally, Polish migrants in the United Kingdom are on average better educated than their counterparts on the Polish labor market. Unfortunately, this does not translate into relevant occupational positions or wages that reflect investments in education. Clearly, as shown below for the British labor market, natives tend to concentrate in the upper part of the occupational ladder, while immigrants' occupations are skewed toward the lower end of the distribution. A large majority of Polish migrants are employed in basic occupations (as compared to just over 50% within the Polish labor market) and thus, on average, earn considerably lower salaries than their British counterparts. This observation is consistent with recent studies (Dustmann, Frattini and Halls 2010; Fihel et al. 2009) that suggest Polish migrants abroad tend to be employed in positions far below their skill levels (severe over-education). Additionally, as Kaczmarczyk and Tyrowicz (2013) argue, the rate of return to education in the case of well-educated Polish migrants choosing the United Kingdom as their destination was among the lowest on the British labor market and, in addition, was lower abroad than on the domestic labor market. This signifies that the outflow of skilled workers from Poland has the characteristics of a "brain waste," which undermines the theoretical argument for migration based on its power to increase human-capital formation (see introductory section).

Table 2: Occupational structure of the British and Polish labor markets, in %

Occupation	British labor market								Polish labor market
	Natives	EU14 + EEA migrants	A8 migrants	Polish migrants	African migrants	American migrants	Asian migrants	Other migrants	Natives
High	28.9	39.0	7.9	7.1	25.6	22.4	27.6	24.3	21.0
Skilled	14.4	16.5	4.4	3.7	17.2	13.0	14.1	17.3	10.7
Low-skilled	22.8	15.1	20.2	20.9	12.0	15.5	13.4	16.2	18.2
Basic	33.8	29.5	67.5	68.2	45.1	49.1	45.0	42.2	50.1
N	779,540	14,240	12,755	1,119	7,421	2,230	12,589	1,139	100,749

Source: Kaczmarczyk and Tyrowicz 2013

One of the most controversial issues in the global public debate over migration is related to the emigration of medical professionals. This phenomenon is a consequence of the ongoing demand for this type of migrant within highly developed states, mainly due to unfavorable demographic trends and fluctuations within destination-country labor markets. Additionally, this field represents a typical example of intangible services, where the mobility of goods and services cannot easily substitute for a flow of individuals with high-quality human capital. In effect, potential immigrants in this field may expect highly beneficial financial and social conditions, integration support and, in at least some receiving countries, simplified immigration procedures. Strong pull factors are regarded as inflating migratory potential among medical professionals from the new member states to a significant degree. While there is no reliable data on the emigration of medical professionals from Poland, some indication of the scale of potential migration among medical professionals is provided by the issuance of certificates confirming qualifications and professional experience as required by employers in Western European states. In the most active period of post-accession migration (until the end of 2007), the number of certificates issued – 6,724 – amounted to 5.7 percent of the total number of medical doctors in Poland. With regard to semi-skilled medical staff, around 9,300 certificates were issued to nurses and midwives, amounting to 0.3 percent of this professional group in Poland.

From the data presented, it follows that migration among this category of highly skilled worker is a notable phenomenon, but its scale is not so large as to pose a threat to the Polish health care system in the short term. This threat is not dangerous because, in the experts' opinion, the Polish educational system turns out medical professionals at a rate that continues to exceed the outflow to other states. In fact, to some extent, the migration of medical specialists may be viewed as brain overflow rather than brain drain, particularly among the young professionals trapped in Poland's "feudal" medical-profession organizational structures, with its limited chances for promotion. Nonetheless, the outflow of medical doctors appears more critical in the case of certain specializations. This is particularly true within the field of anesthesiology (where the share of potential migrants amounted to almost 16% of Poland's total), chest surgery (12.8%), plastic surgery (14.7%) and radiology (7.7%). Outflow is thus most significant within specializations receiving the lowest average incomes within Poland's medical labor market (anesthesiologists, radiologists) and those for which there is high demand within foreign labor markets (plastic surgeons). Moreover, a temporary or permanent imbalance in local and regional labor markets is likely to appear (or has already appeared) (Kaczmarczyk and Okólski 2005; Kaczmarczyk and Okólski 2008; Ministry of Health data).

Underlying factors

As shown in the previous section, one of the most important structural features of recent Polish migration patterns is the positive selection of migrants with respect to tertiary education. Several possible explanatory factors might be identified, as follows:
- First, the picture presented above can be misleading without an accompanying assessment of the structure of the Polish population as a whole. In the last 20 years, Poland experienced a true educational breakthrough. Between 1970 and 2001, the share of university graduates among the Polish population increased from 2 to 12 percent. At the end of the 1990s, the number of students was 2.6 times higher than in 1990. Today in Poland, there are over 1.8 million students, and data from the Central Statistical Office shows that, in the early 2000s, the gross enrollment ratio (the ratio of current students within a given age

cohort) in the 19–24 age group was close to 50 percent, which means that Poland has almost reached developed-country standards with regard to the universality of higher education. If we take into consideration that relatively young persons (aged 18 to 35) have a higher propensity to migrate than do their older peers, the recent increase in migration among the highly skilled is to a large extent attributable to the country's general improvement in terms of human capital (see Figure 3). In this context, the increase in the share of relatively well-educated migrants should be perceived as a natural consequence of educational developments in Poland.

Figure 3: Share of persons with tertiary education in the total population, in %

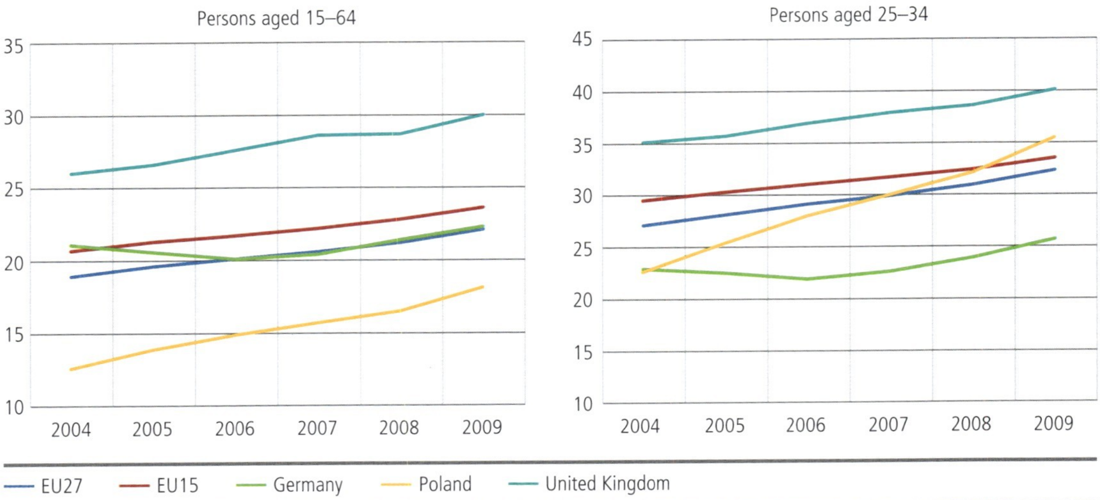

Source: Own elaboration based on Eurostat data

- Second, the high propensity to migrate among well-educated Poles is partially attributable to the low absorptive capacities of the Polish labor market. In fact, the development of the labor market (particularly within certain segments) has been much slower than the development of the educational sector described above. As a consequence, (well-educated) young persons have had difficulties finding employment within the domestic labor market since the late 1990s (see Figure 4). The very high unemployment rates among persons aged 25–29 with tertiary education must be viewed as one of the most important push factors in the post-2004 period.

Moreover, this set of circumstances implies that the outflow of persons with tertiary education who face serious difficulties finding work within the Polish labor market can be interpreted as brain overflow rather than brain drain. This process does not necessarily have to be negative for Polish economy, as those who leave stand a better chance of finding work and accumulating money that may subsequently be used in the sending country (if they return). Additional benefits may result from gaining professional and cultural experience abroad.

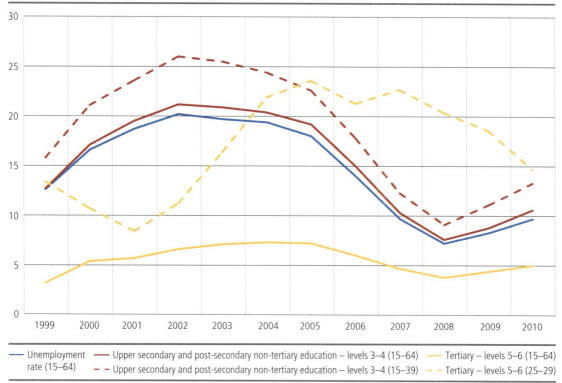

Figure 4: Unemployment rate in Poland, 1999–2010, in %

Source: Own elaboration based on Eurostat data

- Apparently, all the factors mentioned above continue to be accompanied by severe wage gaps and differences in the standards of living between Poland and the most frequently chosen destination countries. These wage gaps surely remain one of the major drivers of migration; however, their importance should not be exaggerated (Kaczmarczyk and Tyrowicz 2013).
- Lastly, it is worth noting that the relatively massive outflow of well-educated Poles has not been the result of any institutionalized recruitment process. On the contrary, several recruitment campaigns by German or Scandinavian employers have faced significant problems and have ultimately been viewed as failures. This demonstrates that for many young Poles, the experience of migration itself has begun to play an important part in overall life projects. Moreover, those projects have become increasingly complex, both in terms of content and spatial patterns.

Conclusions

The most common assessment of migration and its outcomes is as follows: Migration projects are positive for migrants and their families (particularly in the short term), while mobility is neutral or negative for regions and mostly negative for countries of origin. The analysis presented above shows indirectly that the picture is far more nuanced in Poland's case and does not lend itself to such a simplistic explanatory scheme.

For a country with a relatively large stock of well-educated labor, outflow among the highly educated does not have to be harmful. In fact, in such an environment, migration would be associated with relatively low opportunity costs (at least in the short term) while potentially leading to a better allocation of labor on the domestic market in the long term (see Kaczmarczyk and Okólski 2008). The Polish case demonstrates that the most critical factor is the way the human capital is utilized abroad.

Despite emigrants' relatively high level of human capital (or even very high in certain cases, as in the United Kingdom and Ireland), migration among Poles does little to improve individuals' occupational positions. On the contrary, the most common pattern of employment abroad involves serious over-education and skill mismatches. This situation is only partially attributable to the (low) quality of education in Poland, the lack of transferability of skills (e.g., due to low language skills) or the effects of migrant networks (employment in certain migrant niches). Rather, the available empirical research points to the importance of the structure of demand for foreign labor in destination countries, which is strongly concentrated at the low-skilled end of the occupational ladder. It shows that contrary to official rhetoric, Western European economies desperately need low-skilled workers to fill niches within their labor market, and that the importance of this category of workers is far higher than that of highly skilled migrants.

Importantly, taking employment below one's skill level – a common occurrence among migrants – can have very serious long-term consequences. First, it leads to the inefficient utilization of human capital (on the EU level), a phenomenon commonly recognized as brain waste. Second, it diminishes incentives to invest in human capital, an issue important in the context of so-called brain gain, as described above. Third, it may have a (negative) impact on resident immigrants' future integration prospects.

The post-enlargement migration experience shows that while destination countries are on average net beneficiaries from immigration, countries of origin tend to bear the relatively high costs of the outflow (particularly in the long term). In fact, considering the costs and benefits of migration as a whole, post-2004 mobility patterns present an evident case of free riding by the most developed countries. Against this background, one could argue that we need a pan-European approach to internal mobility and cooperation between migrant-sending and migrant-receiving countries in order to create win-win situations with regard to migration. For instance, such an approach could involve giving destination countries access to well-educated or well-trained labor from less-developed countries in exchange for origin countries' access to technology or capital.

Granting the freedom of movement is expected to increase the scale of overall mobility, but it does not necessarily entail dramatic effects in terms of permanent migration. Migrants tend to use "well-trodden social spaces" and engage in well-known migration strategies, including the short-term or circular movements so common in Central and Eastern Europe. This demonstrates that in contemporary Europe, there is ample space for so-called brain circulation, a pattern often described as a win-win situation.

Nonetheless, several policy measures can be recommended. This list would include improving the efficiency of skills recognition (diplomas), facilitating mobility among students (in part through exchange programs) and providing labor-market assistance for immigrants. Recent experience has shown that intra-EU migrants face severe problems in accessing destination-country labor markets, in finding (proper) jobs and in integrating in both a social and economic sense. Thus, innovative labor-market measures (training, coaching, labor-market assistance) are needed in order to amplify the developmental impacts of migration. The same is true within countries of origin, particularly with regard to returnees.

References

Beine Michel, Frederic Docquier and Hillel Rapoport. "Brain Drain and Economic Growth: Theory and Evidence." *Journal of Development Economics* (64) 1: 275–289, 2001.

Bhagwati, Jagdish, and Koichi Hamada. "The Brain Drain, International Integration of Markets for Professionals and Unemployment." *Journal of Development Economics* (1) 1: 19–42, 1974.

Brücker, Herbert (ed.). *Labour mobility within the EU in the Context of Enlargement and the Functioning of the Transitional Arrangements.* Nuremberg: IAB, 2009.

Docquier, Frederic, and Abdeslam Marfouk. "Measuring the International Mobility of Skilled Workers (1900–2000) – Release 1.0." *Policy Research Working Paper No. 3381.* Washington, D.C.: World Bank, 2004.

Dumont, Jean-Christophe, and Georges Lemaître. *Counting Immigrants and Expatriates in OECD Countries: a New Perspective.* Mimeo: OECD, 2005.

Dustmann, Christian, Tommaso Frattini and Caroline Halls. "Assessing the Fiscal Costs and Benefits of A8 Migration to the UK." *Fiscal Studies* (31) 1: 1–41, 2010.

Fihel, Agnieszka, and Pawel Kaczmarczyk. "Migration: A Threat or a Chance? Recent Migration of Poles and its Impact on the Polish Labour Market." In *Polish Migration to the UK in the 'New' European Union: After 2004,* edited by Kathy Burrell. London: Ashgate, 2009: 23–49.

Fihel, Agnieszka, Pawel Kaczmarczyk, Nina Wolfeil and Anna Żylicz. "Brain Drain, Brain Gain and Brain Waste." *Labour Mobility within the EU in the Context of Enlargement and the Functioning of the Transitional Arrangements,* edited by Herbert Brücker. Nuremberg: IAB, 2009: 89–103.

Grubel, Herbert G., and Anthony Scott. "The International Flow of Human Capital." *American Economic Review* (56) 1/2: 268–274, 1966.

Hryniewicz, Janusz, Bohdan Jałowiecki and Agnieszka Mync. *Ucieczka mózgów ze szkolnictwa wyższego i nauki. Raport z badań.* Warsaw: Europejski Instytut Rozwoju Regionalnego i Lokalnego, 1992.

Hryniewicz, Janusz, Bohdan Jałowiecki and Agnieszka Mync. *Ruchliwość pracowników naukowych w latach 1994–1997.* Warsaw: Europejski Instytut Rozwoju Regionalnego i Lokalnego, 1997.

Jałowiecki, Bohdan, Janusz Hryniewicz, and Agnieszka Mync. *Ucieczka mózgów z nauki i szkolnictwa wyższego w Polsce w latach 1992–1993.* Warsaw: Europejski Instytut Rozwoju Regionalnego i Lokalnego, 1994.

Kaczmarczyk, Paweł (ed.). *Migracje i mobilność w dobie zmian: wyzwania metodologiczne.* Warsaw: Scholar, 2011.

Kaczmarczyk, Paweł, and Marek Okólski. *Migracje specjalistow wysokiej klasy w kontekscie czlonkostwa Polski w Unii Europejskiej.* Warsaw: UKIE, 2005.

Kaczmarczyk, Paweł, and Marek Okólski. "Demographic and Labour Market Impacts of Migration on Poland." *Oxford Review of Economic Policy* (24) 3: 600–625, 2008.

Kaczmarczyk, Paweł, and Joanna Tyrowicz. "Winners and Losers among Highly Skilled Polish Migrants." *WNE UW Research Seminar Paper.* Warsaw: UW, 2013.

Mountford, Andrew. "Can a Brain Drain be Good for Growth in the Source Economy?" *Journal of Development Economics* (53) 2: 287–303, 1997.

OECD (Organization for Economic Co-operation and Development). *International Mobility of the Highly Skilled.* Paris: OECD Publishing, 2002.

Rapoport, Hillel, and Frederic Docquier. *Skilled Migration and Human Capital Formation in Developing Countries: a Survey.* Stanford: Stanford Center for International Development, 2004.

Sakson, Barbara. *Wpływ "niewidzialnych" migracji zagranicznych lat osiemdziesiątych na struktury demograficzne Polski.* Warsaw: Szkoła Główna Handlowa, 2002.

Stark, Oded, Christian Helmenstein and Alexia Prskawetz. "A Brain Gain with a Brain Drain." *Economics Letters* 55: 227–234, 1997.

Lessons from Eastern Europe
Martina Lubyova

In this article, I try to shed light on the question of whether any programs or initiatives are in place that allow regions of origin (and their societies) to benefit from labor migration to OECD and non-OECD countries. However, before going more deeply into the issue, it is important to distinguish between beneficial impacts for the sending regions and societies, on the one hand, and benefits to individual migrants or sending-country nationals, on the other. Likewise, it is also necessary to distinguish between differing elements within the sending societies and their individual perspectives – thus, between the perspectives of workers and employers, those of skilled workers and unskilled workers, those of returning migrants and the broader population, and so on. These distinctions make it clear that the proposed question refers to a complex and multifaceted set of conditions that does not allow for simple answers.

In this brief contribution on the topic of fair migration, we would like to discuss only a few of the many issues that are of concern to origin countries in the East European and Central Asian regions as well as to the migrants originating from these countries. We also provide examples of programs and policies that can help alleviate the problems identified, along with some examples of good practices. In particular, the following issues are discussed in the next four subsections:

1. The mass emigration of sending-country nationals
2. The pro-cyclical nature of temporary labor migration
3. The loss of human capital and skills and
4. Migrants' vulnerability and informality in destination countries.

Within each subsection, we illustrate the nature of the problem from the perspective of the origin countries and then propose measures and programs that could allow these countries and their citizens to benefit from labor migration.

In general, let us start with the premise that it is not optimal for any society to lose its population, as this represents its human capital, its future potential and its most important resource. However, there are economies that are not in a position to provide access to gainful activities to all their people. They have to rely on labor emigration as a "valve" that helps mitigate labor-market pressures and social tensions, provide workers with employment opportuni-

Lessons from Eastern Europe

ties and secure a flow of remittances for those who stay at home. Central Asia and South Asia are prominent examples of such regions. Of course, the first-best strategy of such countries would be to support growth and employment opportunities at home, thus allowing the domestic labor force to be retained. However, when the first-best strategy fails, the set of usual "second-best" policies typically includes pre-departure training, support services for migrants in their host countries and trying to recapture migrants' potential either by reaching out to diaspora communities or by encouraging return migration and repatriation. In this regard, the South Asia region has a long-standing tradition of organizing and institutionalizing the "overseas" employment of its nationals.

The traditional sending countries of Central Asia, such as Tajikistan and Uzbekistan, have been supplying their excess labor force to other nations since the onset of the post-Soviet transition, mainly to the Russian Federation. These origin countries have undertaken some limited efforts aimed at the protection of their nationals abroad. The initiatives include pre-departure orientation, general civil orientation, liaison with diaspora communities and support for migrants' association-building in their host countries. These efforts and initiatives undoubtedly benefit sending regions' nationals as they move and live abroad; however, their scope and effectiveness continue to be rather limited. More effective protection can be provided by the host countries themselves. There are instances of such measures, although they largely lack a systematic approach and broad coverage. An interesting example in this regard is an initiative sponsored by several Russian trade unions that provides help and support to immigrant workers from selected origin countries (notably to Tajik and Uzbek workers in the construction sector, including those in informal working arrangements). Such activity benefits not only the migrant workers, but also the national unions, whose members benefit from support of their professional standards in terms of pay, working conditions and so on.

Mass emigration of sending-country nationals

The first issue of serious concern for countries of origin in Eastern Europe and Central Asia is the mass emigration of their national citizens. Several Commonwealth of Independent States (CIS) countries, including Tajikistan, Uzbekistan, Ukraine and Armenia, have lost a large share of their labor forces to foreign destinations. A mass emigration leading to substantial losses in terms of population and labor-force resources has also taken place over the past two decades in several of the new EU member states, particular in the Baltic states, Romania, Bulgaria and, to some extent, Poland (Note: Data on emigration referred to in this section originate from the OECD's continuous reporting system on migration (SOPEMI) reports for Russia, Bulgaria, Romania, Lithuania, Poland and Hungary). Although emigration rates have recently subsided in some of these countries (e.g., in Poland and Slovakia), in others the trend has continued unabated (Romania, Bulgaria) or even intensified (Lithuania). For example, in Bulgaria, it is estimated that emigration during the past two decades has led to the loss of 6.1 percent of the country's population and 10.1 percent of its labor force. Similarly, expert estimates for Romania suggest that the country has lost about 10 percent of its total population due to emigration. In Lithuania, where massive emigration flows originally targeted CIS states in the aftermath of the breakdown of the U.S.S.R., outflows have recently accelerated and gained a new orientation toward EU member states (e.g., the United Kingdom and Ireland received more than 65 % of Lithuania's outflow in 2010). It is estimated that approximately 1.3 million persons of Lithuanian descent, including 400,000 current citizens of Lithuania, live abroad. Similarly, the Polish Central Statistical Office estimated that the number of Polish citizens residing abroad for more than three months rose to 2.13 million in 2012 (compared to 2.06 million in 2011). Of these, 500,000 persons were residing in Germany, and 637,000 in the United Kingdom. Some developed countries, such as Ireland, Luxembourg and New Zealand, have also experienced sizeable outflows among their nationals and have considered measures aimed at their retention or return. Thus, the large-scale emigration of nationals remains a serious concern for these countries, which have increasingly sought to encourage their nationals to return home by means of various programs aimed at supporting return migration and repatriation. Examples of overarching national repatriation and naturalization programs can be found in Russia, Lithuania, Poland and Hungary.

Russia has also tried to encourage its emigrants to return by means of naturalization and repatriation programs. Although the country continues to tighten its relatively simple naturalization procedures (i.e., it discontinued in 2012 international agreements with Kazakhstan, Kyrgyzstan and Belarus that had enabled shorter waiting periods of three months after arrival), it provides favorable treatment to Russian-speaking descendants of past emigrants and to the so-called affiliates of Russian culture. The State Program of Assistance in the Voluntary Return of Compatriots Living Abroad is gradually becoming one of the primary routes to naturalization in Russia; the total number of program participants and their family members doubled in 2012, exceeding 125,000 persons. The repatriation program is targeted at 12 regions located in areas with severe climatic conditions (Kaliningrad, the westernmost of these regions, receives most of the repatriates).

The Lithuania 2030 national strategy, approved by the Lithuanian Seimas in 2012, identifies the problem of emigration as one of the country's most serious issues, and one that requires a major national initiative to address. As a consequence, the Lithuanian government supported the development of an interagency action plan focused on implementing the Global Lithuania program (Involvement of Lithuanian Emigrants into the Life of the State) during the 2011–2019 period. Under this initiative, efforts are being made to involve Lithuanian emigrants in the creation of a welfare state while strengthening their ties with Lithuania and ultimately encouraging them to return to their homeland. The measures implemented include support for Lithuanian communities and organizations abroad, efforts to strengthen ties with recognized professionals able to make specific contributions to Lithuania's welfare, and encouragement for Lithuanians living abroad to study in Lithuania.

Hungarian authorities have recently implemented initiatives aimed at fostering ties with ethnic Hungarians abroad by granting them preferential treatment in naturalization procedures. Nearly 440,000 persons have received Hungarian citizenship under this program since its introduction in January 2011. It is important to note that the majority of these naturalized persons do not in fact move to Hungary. At the same time, Hungarian citizenship was granted to 867 persons in 2012 under the framework of a general naturalization procedure.

The massive emigration of Polish citizens continues to be an issue of serious concern for the national authorities of that country. A strategic migration document called the Migration Policy of Poland – the Current State of Play and Future Actions, prepared by the country's Inter-Ministerial Committee on Migration and adopted by the Polish government in July 2012, is aimed at bolstering the competitiveness of the Polish economy, thus providing more domestic employment opportunities.

Pro-cyclical nature of temporary labor migration

The second issue of concern for many origin countries is the pro-cyclical nature of temporary labor migration. The problem is also serious in the context of labor migration from the new EU member states to their older counterparts. On the one hand, the increased labor mobility within Europe is a desirable phenomenon that allows for greater flexibility in terms of filling vacancies and securing a larger pool of job applicants, thus better matching employment opportunities with applicants. On the other hand, in the case of job loss, labor migrants tend to return to their country of origin, where they add to labor-market tensions, burden social-assistance programs and so on. This makes the benefits of intra-EU labor migration rather asymmetric: Recipient countries benefit from the availability of labor when times are good, while origin countries receive the return flow of migrants who have lost their jobs when times turn bad. The situation also contributes to a self-perception of being "second-class" EU citizens among the labor migrants from these origin countries.

In terms of figures, according to the Polish labor force survey, the number of Polish temporary migrants residing abroad for more than three months reached almost 300,000 people as of mid-2013 (60% of whom were males, and 90% of whom had gone abroad for the purposes of employment). Moreover, it seems that the old member states' transitional migration measures regarding citizens of the new member states did have an effect in terms of redirecting the flows of labor migrants. For example, when the United Kingdom opened its labor market to nationals of the new EU member states in 2004, it overtook Germany as the most significant host country for Polish labor migrants. Between 2002 and 2012, the number of Poles in Germany increased from 294,000 to 500,000 persons; in the same period, this figure increased from 24,000 to 637,000 in the United Kingdom.

However, due to the recession, return migration has recently been on the rise in many countries of origin, particularly in Eastern Europe. In Lithuania, the country's own citizens accounted for 80 percent of immigration inflows in 2010. Polish immigration has risen since 2006 due to return migration, and in Bulgaria, return migration increased by 17 percent in 2010 compared to the previous year. The main factor behind this return migration may be the effects of the economic crisis rather than successful return-migration policies. In Bulgaria, for example, a 2010 survey among return migrants indicated that more than two-thirds intended to emigrate again. In Poland, registration data confirms the return flow of Polish citizens, with the main origin countries continuing to be the United Kingdom, Germany, the United States and Ireland, which have traditionally been the main destination countries for Polish emigrants.

A number of measures cushioning the adverse effects of these flows on countries of origin and/or their nationals are possible, including the harmonization of social-security schemes (notably unemployment insurance), the transferability of benefits, active labor-market measures targeted at migrants, support during job-search periods in host countries following the loss of employment, and labor-market integration programs. For example, active labor-market measures facilitating labor-market integration within host countries following job loss could provide a partial remedy. This could be done by opening active programs to labor migrants or by specifically targeting migrant workers with active measures. Spain, for example, enacted labor-market measures targeted specifically at migrant workers through its Fund for the Reception and Integration of Immigrants and Educational Support, created in 2005. However, due to the country's fiscal limitations in recent years, cuts have been made to all active-labor-market programs, including the immigrant-integration measures. The fund was suspended in 2012, along with a program providing free access to basic health services for irregular migrants. At the same time, a program (the Prepara Plan) that provided vocational training for unemployed workers who had exhausted their unemployment benefits was extended till 2013. Although the training measures were not targeted specifically at migrants, the plan's universal coverage encouraged the participation of migrant workers.

The Scandinavian countries maintain a more complex system of labor-market integration. For example, the national integration program in Denmark involves offers of active employment based on three types of active labor-market measures: guidance, job training and internships, and employment with wage subsidies. The integration programs are implemented by local authorities and cover all refugees and persons entering under the country's family-reunification program. A new initiative called We Need Everyone was launched in 2012 to aid recipients of cash benefits who were not participating in integration programs for newly arrived migrants and who were not able to find jobs due to various personal and social problems.

Other partial but useful measures in this group of countries include provisions that allow migrants to engage in a job search upon loss of employment in the host country. This measure is particularly relevant for third-country nationals who would otherwise have to leave the country or join the ranks of illegal workers. This type of measure has been increasingly popular as host countries have sought to retain their existing migrant labor force rather than recruiting newcomers from abroad.

Loss of human capital and skills

The third issue of concern we address here is the diminution of the skilled labor force within sending countries and the deskilling of migrant workers. At times of global competition for talent and skills, the emigration of skilled workers represents a net loss for the country of origin. The damage is aggravated further when migrant workers accept positions for which they are overqualified in the host countries. Such a situation results in a "triple loss": the waste of resources for the origin country, a waste of foreign workers' potential for the host country, and the loss of skills and career prospects for individual migrant workers. This situation can be prevented or ameliorated through anti-social-dumping programs or measures that enable migrants to participate in lifelong-learning opportunities within host countries. Moreover, more support can be provided to knowledge-transfer and R&D opportunities within origin countries as a means of helping retain skilled workers at home.

With regard to lifelong learning (LL) opportunities in Europe, the Adult Education Surveys carried out in 2007 and 2011 indicated that LL participation takes place mainly through on-the-job training rather than though other forms of learning, such as seminars, classroom work, courses or distance learning. This fact exposes a lack of inclusive mechanisms in LL programs, as the predominance of on-the-job training excludes jobless people from participation in LL programs. A broader opening of LL processes to unemployed or economically inactive people, including migrants, would enable migrants to retain or even expand their skills as a side benefit of labor migration.

A first-best strategy for origin countries seeking to retain their skilled labor force would be to increase national support for knowledge transfer and R&D opportunities. To this end, the Europe 2020 strategy aims at national research-and-development expenditure of 3 percent of GDP for each member state. However, this goal has no enforcement mechanism, and it is largely being neglected by many countries that typically serve as countries of origin for high-skilled migrant workers. The recent fiscal crisis, which has been accompanied by the global relocation of research and production capacities, may further aggravate the problem, particularly in Central and Eastern Europe.

Migrant vulnerability and informality

Finally, another issue of serious concern for origin and host countries alike is the prevalence of migrant labor in the informal economy and the related vulnerabilities suffered by migrant workers. It should be noted that although informal work and the informal economy are related dimensions of informality, they are not identical categories. It is possible to work under formal arrangements in the informal economy, and it is possible to be informally employed by a formally incorporated enterprise. Migrant workers are particularly prone to end up in informal working arrangements. There have been instances in Eastern Europe in which easy entry and residence regimes for foreigners, combined with strict labor-market protections against foreign workers, resulted in the concentration of migrant workers in the informal economy. Examples of such situations include the pre-2004 European Union regime with regard to nationals of the newly acceding countries or the current practice of applying transitory measures to citizens of the new member states (the combination of free movement with a work-permit requirement). Another example is the current regime in Russia with regard to nationals of CIS countries. Furthermore, migrant workers tend to be overrepresented in the labor-market segment denoted as domestic labor (i.e., workers in private households, where they are in the position of hired workers rather than household members or relatives). Domestic work is characterized to a large degree by informality and worker vulnerability.

Any measures aimed at combating informality thus also help reduce migrant workers' vulnerability and can be considered as benefiting the nationals of sending countries at the individual level. Examples of such national programs and initiatives include the regularization programs (amnesties) that grant full or at least partial access to the labor market for informal workers. Poland and Luxembourg have both adopted regularization programs of this kind in recent years. A partial remedy has also been provided in Russia through the introduction of "patents" for migrant workers employed by private households, which help regulate the total flow of such workers. Finally, a major international initiative in the field was recently undertaken by the International Labour Organization through the adoption of the Convention on Domestic Workers.

Luxembourg's government introduced its program in 2013 with the aim of regularizing illegal workers who had worked in the country for at least nine consecutive months in the course of the previous 12 months. Applicants have to prove the existence of an indeterminate-period work contract for at least 40 hours per week with a salary that is at least the level of minimum wage. Similarly, Poland implemented a third round of regularization in 2012, granting two-year residence permits to more than 4,500 foreigners primarily originating from Ukraine, Vietnam and Armenia.

Russia's program of patents (essentially a form of license) for foreigners working for private households offers a partial remedy with regard to alleviating the risks resulting from informality. The scheme was launched in 2010 and allows foreign workers to gain legal working status by purchasing a patent. However, the patents do not grant access to health insurance, social insurance or other programs that might facilitate migrants' integration into Russian society. Nevertheless, the program has taken on considerable significance in Russia, where out of a total inflow of 2.7 million temporary migrant workers in 2012, 1.4 million obtained regular work permits and almost 1.3 million purchased patents. More than half of all patents were acquired by Uzbek nationals.

Finally, a coordinated international effort aimed at combating informality and vulnerability among domestic workers (a population that accounts for a large share of the overall migrant labor force) was recently launched by the International Labour Organization, which adopted its Domestic Workers Convention (No. 189) in 2011. The relevance of this initiative to migrants stems from the fact that migrant workers often work in private households, for example, as caretakers, domestic helpers, guards, drivers and so on. The convention aims to uphold working standards for domestic workers, for example, in terms of minimum wages, minimum allowed durations of leave, the worker's right to choose his or her living place, and the right to have working conditions clarified, preferably in writing. In the case of migrant workers, future working conditions should be made clear in writing as they are being recruited and before they have immigrated. To date, 13 countries have ratified the convention, mainly from Latin America and Asia. Germany and Italy are the only two countries that have ratified the convention in Europe. The regulations came into force in January 2014 in Italy, and in September 2014 in Germany.

References

Bobeva, Daniela. *National SOPEMI Report for Bulgaria, Annual Reunion of SOPEMI Correspondents.* Paris: OECD Publishing, December 2012.

Chudinkovskikh, Olga. *National SOPEMI Report for Russian Federation, Annual Reunion of SOPEMI Correspondents*. Paris: OECD Publishing, December 2013.

Hussmanns, Ralph. "Measuring the Informal Economy: From Employment in the Informal Economy to Informal Employment." *Working Paper No. 53*. Policy Integration Department, Bureau of Statistics, International Labour Office. Geneva: ILO, 2005.

ILO (International Labour Organization). "Resolution Concerning Decent Work and the Informal eEconomy, Governing Body 285th Session, Seventh Item on the Agenda." Geneva: ILO, 2002.

ILO. *Global Employment Trends for Women*. Geneva: ILO, 2009.

ILO. "Global and Regional Estimates on Domestic Workers." *Domestic Work Policy Brief No. 4*. Geneva: ILO, 2010.

ILO. *Effective Protection for Domestic Workers: A Guide to Designing Labor Laws*. Geneva: ILO, 2012a.

ILO. *Global Employment Trends* 2012. Geneva: ILO, 2012b.

Kaczmarczyk, Paweł. *National SOPEMI Report for Poland, Annual Reunion of SOPEMI Correspondents*. Paris: OECD Publishing, December 2013.

Maresova, Jarmila. *National SOPEMI Report for the Czech Republic, Annual Reunion of SOPEMI Correspondents*. Paris: OECD Publishing, December 2013.

OECD (Organization for Economic Co-operation and Development). *International Migration Outlook 2011*. Paris: OECD Publishing, 2011.

OECD. *International Migration Outlook 2012*. Paris: OECD Publishing, 2012.

OECD. *International Migration Outlook 2011*. Paris: OECD Publishing, 2013.

Sipavicienne, Audra. *National SOPEMI Report for Lithuania, Annual Reunion of SOPEMI Correspondents*. Paris: OECD Publishing, December 2011.

Lessons from MENA

Jad Chaaban

Profile and destinations of migrants from Arab Mediterranean countries

Arab Mediterranean countries (AMCs) can be classified into two distinct groups: The first are countries in the Maghreb (Morocco, Algeria, Libya and Tunisia), which in 2013 sent almost 5.5 million migrants abroad (Table 1). Most of these migrants (more than 80%) went to countries in the European Union (Figure 1). In general, migrants from the Maghreb had low skill levels (to a large extent, with primary education as the highest level attained; see Figure 2). The second group comprises the countries of the Mashreq (Egypt, Jordan, Lebanon and Syria), which primarily sent migrants (about 5.7 million in 2013) to other Arab countries, mainly those in the Gulf Cooperation Council (GCC). Migrants from Egypt and Jordan were mostly highly skilled, while migrants from Lebanon and Syria showed a mix of educational backgrounds (Figure 2).

Table 1: Migrants originating from AMCs by region of residence (2013)

	European Union	Arab countries	Other	Total
Algeria	877,398	11,209	73,243	961,850
Libya	43,646	8,963	10,947	63,556
Morocco	3,056,109	214,438	101,432	3,371,979
Tunisia	911,400	154,900	31,900	1,098,200
Maghreb total	*4,888,553*	*389,510*	*217,522*	*5,495,585*
Egypt	199,153	2,783,000	238,770	3,220,923
Jordan	24,158	158,284	84,591	267,033
Lebanon	148,717	162,663	290,900	602,280
Syria	131,108	1,387,806	124,833	1,643,747
Mashreq total	*503,136*	*4,491,753*	*739,094*	*5,733,983*
Grand total	**5,391,689**	**4,881,263**	**956,616**	**11,229,568**

Source: www.eui.eu/RSCAS

Lessons from MENA

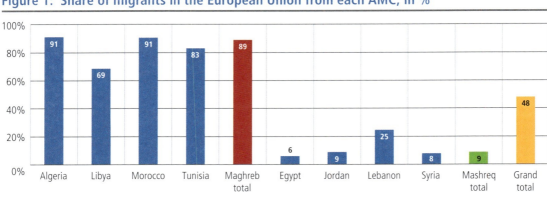

Figure 1: Share of migrants in the European Union from each AMC, in %

Source: Fargues 2013

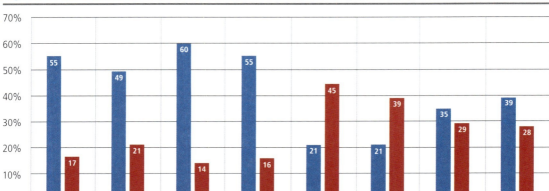

Figure 2: Educational attainments within the emigrant population, in %

Source: Dumont, Spielvogel and Widmaier 2010

One can therefore safely conclude that outward migration from the AMCs to the European Union is primarily a Maghreb phenomenon, while the volume of migrants from the region to other OECD countries (such as the United States or Canada) is very small compared to that of other regions (such as India or China).

The role of remittances

Remittances sent home by migrant workers constitute a sizeable benefit for AMCs. Recent World Bank data (2011) shows that remittances in fact constitute between 5 and 15 percent of

GDP for countries in this region, serving as the highest share of national income in Lebanon and Jordan. Although these remittances constitute a good source of foreign currency and contribute positively to the balance of payments, they are primarily spent on consumption in the origin country rather than on investment in productive activities. However, some exceptions to this rule do exist in countries such as Jordan, where remittances have contributed to increases in educational attainment by easing the financial constraints linked to school attendance (Mansour, Chaaban and Litchfield 2011).

Most AMC governments have focused on facilitating the flow of remittances, but have given little attention to creating incentives that might channel them into productive investments. Typical measures have included the establishment of bank branches and post offices overseas and the provision of tax breaks on remittances. In Egypt, migrants remitting through banks receive tax breaks for up to 10 years from the time of the first formal transfer.

However, some initiatives designed to channel remittances more productively are appearing in the region. For example, Live Lebanon (www.livelebanon.org) aims to mobilize Lebanese living abroad to help support local development efforts in the country's most deprived areas. An online platform has been created with the aim of engaging expatriates, providing them with an opportunity to donate money online that will be used to support local community and development projects in four regions of the country.

Return migration

Return migration can have substantial benefits for countries in the region. Migrants often bring back upgraded skills, command wage premiums in their home country's labor market and contribute to the creation of a more dynamic entrepreneurship environment. Although evidence is still scarce, recent research on Morocco and Egypt provides interesting insights into this issue.

In the case of Morocco, Hamdouch and Wahba (2012) use the 2004 population census to show that return-migration rates have been stable since the 1990s, at around 33,000 returnees a year. This accounts for less than 1 percent of the country's overall diaspora and is slightly lower than the number of new emigrants, which totals about 38,000 a year. Since 2008, the global financial crisis has evidently prompted a higher rate of return, although limited empirical evidence exists on this trend. Moroccan returnees are mostly men in urban areas, are older than the Moroccan population and have higher average educational levels than does the country's general population. Moreover, 46.8 percent of return migrants are economically active, a figure considerably higher than the 35.9 percent average among the general Moroccan population. A significant proportion of returnees (35.5%) act as entrepreneurs (12% as employers and 23.5% as self-employed workers), compared to 31.9 percent among non-migrants (1.8% as employers and 31.9% as self-employed workers) (ibid.). Yet despite these trends, very few initiatives helping to integrate and reinsert returnees into the Moroccan labor market have been implemented. The implementation of a focused return-migration policy could enable the country to derive stronger socioeconomic-development returns from its return-migration flows.

In Egypt, Giuletti, Wahba and Zimmerman (2013) find that male return migrants earn around 14 percent more on average than do non-migrants, controlling for various factors affecting migration. They also find that this wage premium differs by educational level; comparatively less-educated returnees earn an average of 8 percent more than non-migrants, while university graduate returnees earn 20 percent more. Moreover, they find that overseas training is positively correlated with the probability of returnees investing in the Egyptian market or becoming entrepreneurs. It is therefore vital for any migration policy seeking to address skills shortages in sending countries to tap the dynamism of this circular mobility.

Migrant, professional and student diaspora associations

Sending countries can also benefit from the skills and expertise of their migrants by enabling civil society associations to create links with the country's diaspora. Many such migrant associations exist in the region, but evidence able to illuminate the success or failure of their programs and interventions is scarce.

In Morocco, for instance, organizations such as the Association des Jeunes Marocains de France (AJMF), Migrations et Développement, and the Club des Investisseurs des Marocains Résidant à l'Étranger (CIMRE) focus on fostering and consolidating links within Moroccan diaspora communities, safeguarding migrant rights in destination countries and contributing to development efforts within Morocco. In Tunisia's case, the Association des Tunisiens des Grandes Écoles (ATUGE) was created in 1990 as non-profit organization with the aim of bringing together networks of Tunisian students and graduates of French engineering and commerce graduate schools. It has offices in Paris, Tunis, London, Bordeaux, Lyon, Grenoble, Lille, Toulouse and Nice. The ATUGE has over 4,500 members in its network and regularly organizes events and conferences that bring together recent graduates and experts in various sectors. Conferences in 2009, for instance, were dedicated to the issue of entrepreneurship, with the theme "Doing Business in Tunisia" aiming to provide an overview of the Tunisian business environment. Participants benefited from the views and experiences of investors and field experts in addition to knowledge-sharing by ATUGE members who had already established businesses in Tunisia.

On the multilateral level, the most well-known program supporting the mobilization of diaspora-community skills is the United Nations Development Program's (UNDP) Transfer of Knowledge Through Expatriate Nationals (TOKTEN) program, which has been active since 1977. TOKTEN experts are sent to their home country on a temporary basis to take on assignments for which international consultants would otherwise be hired. The program has been implemented in several AMCs (Egypt, Lebanon, Morocco and Syria), which have benefited from the knowledge and skills provided by qualified members of their diaspora communities. In some cases, the program has led to the permanent return of individuals who have taken up senior positions in the government or private sector.

References

Dumont, Jean-Christophe, Gilles Spielvogel and Sarah Widmaier. "International Migrants in Developed, Emerging and Developing Countries: An Extended Profile." *OECD Social, Employment and Migration Working Papers No. 114*. Paris: OECD Publishing, 2010. www.oecd.org/els/workingpapers.

Fargues, Philippe. "Demography, Education and International Migration in the Arab Countries." Tunis: EUI, 2013. www.oecd.org/els/mig/PPT_Philippe%20Fargues.pdf.

Giulietti, Corrado, Jackline Wahba and Klaus F. Zimmermann. "Entrepreneurship of the Left-behind." *Res Labor Econ* (37): 65–92, 2013.

Hamdouch, Bachir, and Jackline Wahba. "Return Migration and Entrepreneurship in Morocco." *ERF Working Paper 666*. Cairo: Economic Research Forum, 2012.

Mansour, Wael, Jad Chaaban and Julie Litchfield. "The Impact of Migrant Remittances on School Attendance and Education Attainment: Evidence From Jordan." *International Migration Review* (45) 4: 812–851, 2011.

World Bank. *Migration and Remittances Factbook 2011*. Washington, D.C.: World Bank, 2011. http://go.worldbank.org/QGUCPJTOR0.

Lessons from Africa
Jonathan Crush

Introduction

Africa has become an increasingly important source of migrants for OECD countries in recent years. Of the approximately 24 million Africans residing outside their country of birth, around 7.5 million live within the OECD. The remainder live in non-OECD countries within Africa itself (14 million) or outside the continent (3 million) (Table 1). These figures are the cumulative result of different kinds of migrant flows over several decades, including refugee movements, migration among skilled workers (the so-called "brain drain"), and regular and irregular migration among those with lower skill levels. The majority of skilled migrants have settled permanently in OECD countries. However, many maintain backward linkages to their countries of origin, and some eventually return. The migrant stock within the OECD of the three African countries discussed in this paper is shown in Table 1. The numbers vary considerably from destination to destination, reflecting both the legacy of colonial and post-colonial ties and the current-day preferences of refugees and economic migrants. With only three exceptions, there is at least one migrant from these African countries in every OECD state.

The long-standing pattern of permanent emigration from Africa and settlement in the OECD has been augmented over the last decade by the "resurrection" of temporary labor migration (Castles 2006). In Australia, Canada and the United States alone, for example, the number of legal temporary migrants reached 2.4 million in 2011 (up from 1.8 million in 2005). How many of these were from Africa is less certain. In addition, there are unknown numbers of irregular migrants from Africa in the OECD. De Haas (2008) argues that while the numbers are often exaggerated for popular consumption, and sometimes even painted as an apocalyptic "invasion," they do in fact represent a significant governance challenge. More controversially, he claims that "despite lip service being paid to 'combating illegal migration' for political and diplomatic reasons, neither European nor African states have much genuine interest in stopping migration." What they do increasingly share is an interest in legal temporary labor migration to meet their respective and differing needs: one to meet growing labor shortages at the lower end of the labor market, the other to cope with burgeoning domestic unemployment and the need for foreign exchange in the form of remittances.

Lessons from Africa

Hugo (2009) provides a useful eight-part typology of the temporary labor migration movements that are now augmenting and, in some cases, outpacing more permanent forms of migration (Table 2). This typology is applicable to temporary migration from Africa to the

Table 1: African migrant stock in OECD countries

	Africa Total	South Africa	Ghana	Mauritius
France	2,833,894	3,202	4,681	32,913
Germany	928,615	34,674	21,758	11,420
USA	689,994	70,465	69,995	1,913
UK	555,584	142,416	57,172	27,331
Spain	381,499	1,372	3,189	142
Canada	338,880	37,725	18,640	9,085
Israel	315,024	583	724	124
Portugal	304,436	11,197	54	12
Italy	298,724	758	2,282	7,431
Netherlands	251,725	11,286	11,201	299
Belgium	238,934	2,727	2,689	2,623
Australia	212,723	90,810	2,488	17,810
Switzerland	73,244	5,204	2,009	2,206
Sweden	57,582	1,408	1,189	144
Greece	44,317	5,550	412	53
New Zealand	37,538	26,069	253	163
Norway	28,438	787	1,176	142
Denmark	28,014	1,008	1,085	114
Austria	18,330	2,038	59	38
Ireland	10,299	6,277	407	136
Finland	8,831	208	295	26
Turkey	6,605	296	144	7
Luxembourg	5,410	178	23	89
Japan	3,958	248	1,322	20
Poland	1,900	277	49	9
Estonia	1,611	67	41	14
Czech Republic	1,591	154	42	4
Hungary	1,590	94	58	5
Mexico	712	75	12	5
Chile	556	250	9	3
Iceland	388	76	9	1
Slovakia	268	16	4	0
Slovenia	41	2	1	0
Korea	37	2	6	0
Total	7,418,966	457,499	203,521	113,612

Source: Migration DRC 2010

countries of the OECD. The value of the typology is that it distinguishes between types of migration in terms of skill levels, legal status, the migrant's ability to shift to a permanent residence status or to bring their dependents with them, and the rights they can expect in the destination country. What the typology does not do is distinguish between the different types of immigration regime and migration-management styles that govern these movements. Nor does it capture the character of the formal and informal reception that temporary migrants receive from employers and citizens.

Table 2: Temporary labor migration typology

Type	Status in destination	Potential to move to permanent residence	Ability to bring family	Rights
1. Less-skilled contract labor temporary migration	Documented and undocumented	Very low	Not possible	Very limited
2. Highly skilled temporary labor migrants	Mostly documented	High	Allowed	Substantial
3. Low-skilled seasonal labor migration	Documented and undocumented	Low	Not possible	Very limited
4. Working holiday makers	Mostly documented	Moderate	Possible	Substantial
5. Student migration	Documented	High	Allowed	Substantial
6. Trainee migration	Initially documented, but many become undocumented	Low	Not possible	Limited
7. Border commuters/circulatory	Documented and undocumented	Low	Not necessary in many cases	Limited
8. Project-tied labor migration	Documented	Low	Possible	Limited

Source: Hugo 2009

This paper focuses on Type 1 migration from Africa. Temporary labor migration is increasingly viewed in forums such as the Global Forum on Migration and Development and elsewhere as the developmentally optimal form of migration and as a "triple win" for countries of destination, countries of origin and migrants themselves (Wickramasekara 2011). Implicit in this argument is that all three parties are receiving a "fair deal." But is this in fact the case? Only by looking at particular examples can we identify the challenges and obstacles to fairness and the kinds of best practices that might enable a fairer deal for all.

A key area in migrant-mobilization systems, and one in which fairness issues are often ignored, is the series of mechanisms by which employers are matched with prospective employees. The growth of the global recruitment industry has been dramatic in the last two decades, but it generally operates without significant scrutiny by researchers and policymakers. The labor-recruiting industry (or "international labor-services trade," in the words of the International Organization for Migration (IOM)) plays a crucial intermediary role in facilitating temporary labor migration (Boyd 2014). As Rahman and Fee (2012) note, the industry is "vital in the channeling of migrant workers, [as] without it few migrants would have the information or contacts needed for successful migration."

The main focus of this paper is therefore not so much on whether temporary labor migration from Africa offers a "fair deal" for all, but rather on whether those who deal in labor (such as labor recruiters, agents and brokers) provide a fair service to migrants. While highly skilled migrants generally have a much broader range of information sources regarding employment opportunities overseas and a choice of migration channels, lower-skilled migrants generally lack these options. This latter group is thus highly dependent on labor dealers for information about job opportunities and assistance in accessing other labor markets. In exchange, many are forced to pay for these services, and tales of exploitation, false representation and corruption are legion. These excesses can be curbed where licensing procedures and other industry regulations are in place. However, most dealers are private-sector operators and resist heavy-handed regulation or find ways around it.

This paper examines three contrasting examples of labor recruitment from and within Africa, looking at South Africa, Ghana and Mauritius. It examines the recruitment apparatus for temporary medium- and low-skilled migrants in each country, draws contrasts between them and asks to what extent these operate in a way consistent with the idea of the triple win in general and with the interests of migrants in particular.

Worst-practice labor recruiting: The South African case

South Africa is both a (skilled) labor-exporting country and a (lower-skilled) labor-importing country. The contract-labor system for workers from other African countries (notably Lesotho and Mozambique) is one channel through which labor for South Africa's gold, coal and platinum mines is imported. This came into existence in the late 19th century and has persisted into the present. The system was established and run by the mining companies with minimal government oversight through a single monopolistic recruiting agency, TEBA. At its peak in the 1970s, the system delivered over 500,000 male contract workers to the mines every year. Miners were sequestered in single-sex barracks cut off from the outside world and were treated as disposable labor units. All skilled and supervisory jobs were reserved for whites (often immigrants from Europe). Wages were pitiful, accident rates astronomical and occupational diseases, such as lung cancer, silicosis, TB and (latterly) AIDS, decimated the workforce. Incapacitated workers were simply shipped back to where they came from with minimal compensation. With reason, this migrant-labor system has been described as the modern world's most exploitative temporary work program (Crush, Jeeves and Yudelman 1992).

The post-apartheid South African experience demonstrates how difficult it is for government, even with the best intentions in the world, to reform an entrenched "worst-practice" system (Crush 2014). Three main strategies have been tried. The first was motivated by the desire to completely abandon the system by offering foreign migrants the chance to "opt out" and settle in South Africa. They were offered permanent residence upon application, which meant that for the first time in 100 years, their families could join them in South Africa. Around 50,000 miners, around a third of those eligible, applied for permanent residence (far fewer than expected). Research showed that they took the offer as a form of insurance against job loss, but continued to engage in circular migration via TEBA since the underlying system itself remained unchanged.

The second strategy adopted by government was to try to "normalize" the mining sector's migrant-labor system by removing the special privileges afforded by the apartheid government to the mining companies through TEBA to recruit foreign labor at will, a privilege not enjoyed by any other South African employer. Rather than allowing the same unfettered access to foreign labor by all employers, the government instead initially proposed that the mines, like all other employers, should have to apply for permits for each foreign worker on an individual basis. This loss of discretion and privilege was vigorously contested by the mining companies as highly damaging to their operations. They forcefully argued that the existing privatized system worked well and should be left intact.

Negotiations led to a compromise that would give the government more say in recruitment strategy and eliminate the mining companies' special privileges, while also maintaining a fast-track processing system for employers who wished to hire significant numbers of foreign migrants. This compromise was embodied in the 2002 Immigration Act, the country's first post-apartheid immigration legislation. The Act introduced a new "corporate permit" system that allowed employers to apply for group work permits for a predetermined number of workers. Recruiting and processing continued to be handled by TEBA.

For the first time, the government, through its control over the issue of corporate permits, could exercise some oversight over the system. This became ever more imperative as unemployment rates within South Africa continued to rise, and the government argued that the mining industry should give preference to South Africans. As a direct result, the numbers of foreign-migrant miners fell from 160,000 in 1994 to 65,000 in 2012 (Figure 1). Proposed 2014 amendments to the 2002 Immigration Act would require a company applying for a corporate permit to demonstrate that at least 60 percent of its workforce is South African, putting further pressure on companies to reduce their use of foreign migrants.

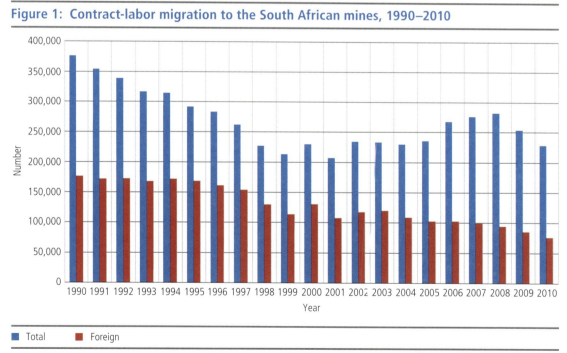

Figure 1: Contract-labor migration to the South African mines, 1990–2010

Source: www.teba.co.za

However, this reform of a historically entrenched temporary labor migration system, and the parallel reduction in the number of approved foreign migrants, has had a major unintended consequence in the form of a massive upsurge in irregular migration from source countries outside legal recruiting channels. Unemployed male contract miners are being "replaced" by migrant women from the same households who are migrating to South Africa on visitor's permits and then seeking employment as domestic workers and farmworkers. Other unemployed miners have joined the booming illegal-mining industry in which gangs of migrants spend weeks and sometimes months underground working disused and abandoned mine shafts. Working conditions are extremely hazardous, and there are regular fights between rival gangs and between the illegal miners and the authorities, who are trying to crack down on the phenomenon.

Unregulated private-sector labor recruiting: The case of Ghana

An estimated 200,000 Ghanaian migrants live within the OECD countries. This is primarily the result of post-1990 migration among skilled individuals to countries such as the United States, the United Kingdom, Germany, Canada and the Netherlands. However, Ghanaian migrants are widely dispersed throughout the OECD, with every country having at least one resident from Ghana (Table 1). According to the IOM (2009), Ghana has West Africa's highest rate of emigration among the highly skilled (46%). Over one-half of doctors trained in Ghana, as well as one-quarter of the nation's domestically trained nurses, live and work abroad. The Ghanaian diaspora maintains close ties with the country, and annual remittances exceed $1.5 billion per annum. Despite robust economic growth, Ghana has experienced rising levels of unemployment among its increasingly well-educated population, leading growing numbers of low- and semi-skilled people to seek work outside the country. According to the Development Research Centre on Migration, Globalisation and Poverty, over 70 percent of Ghana's 950,000 migrants outside the country are in West Africa (Migration DRC 2010). But the countries of the OECD are an increasingly attractive destination for migrants in search of temporary work.

The incidence of irregular migration from Ghana to Europe has increased, but local and international recruiting agents and companies have sought to take advantage of the legal temporary-work programs that are becoming increasingly common in the OECD. Ghana has become a target country for outside recruiters, and a number of local companies have sprung up, forging partnerships with their international counterparts. These include companies such as Africa Manpower, Rectrain, KenCon Recruitment, Paulson Ventures, Bonnie Lee Recruitment Agency, SOS Labour and the Christian Labor Association of Ghana (all based in Accra). Local labor recruiters connect aspiring migrants in Ghana with prospective employers in a number of OECD countries or the Gulf region for a fee (usually paid by the employer, but sometimes by the migrants themselves) and, at a minimum, facilitate the paperwork necessary to obtain work permits in destination countries. Others offer a much broader suite of services. This new and growing industry appears to be largely unregulated, a fact that partially explains the relative dearth of public information on its structure and activities. A 2013 survey of changing Ghanaian migration patterns, for example, makes no mention of this phenomenon (Schans et al. 2013).

One of the higher-profile agencies is SOS Labour Ghana Ltd, a local recruitment company founded and run by an American-educated Ghanaian businesswoman and philanthropist, Naa Asie Ocansey. SOS Labour advertises itself as a "job placement specialist company" facilitating the employment of "redundant and excess African workers in excellent and well-paid job positions overseas" (www.soslabour.com/about-us). The company began by placing Ghanaian services-industry workers at several tourist resorts in the United States. In 2006, it turned its attention to western Canada following a series of consultations with government officials, employers and Canadian recruiters designed to better understand the Canadian Temporary Work Program and Canadian certification procedures. SOS Labour works closely with Canadian recruiters, such as Calgary-based Xela, and claims to have 11 client companies in Canada. More recently, the company has created ties with recruitment agencies and employers in countries such as Spain and Norway, as well as in the Gulf region.

SOS specializes in the placement of welders, pipefitters, instrument technicians, heavy-equipment mechanics, heavy-equipment operators, iron workers (reinforcing or structural), plumbers, construction workers, crane operators and hospitality workers. Applicants to SOS Labour (which actively advertises its services on radio) submit a comprehensive application detailing qualifications and experience with supporting documentation. Those who pass the initial screening are added to a skills and experience database. When the applicant is matched with an overseas employer (either directly or via an overseas recruiting agency), they are assisted in applying for immigration documentation and are required to attend a training, cultural-familiarization and induction course, the Global Workers Certificate Program, run by an affiliate (Prosperity College). Course modules include advice on remitting as well as on property investment and small-business development back in Ghana. SOS Labour receives a capitation fee from the employer as payment.

In contrast to the relatively unproblematic Ghanaian experience of temporary migration to the OECD, migration to the Gulf region has been plagued with problems. In 2004, Ghana and Qatar signed a bilateral economic-cooperation agreement, resulting in an immediate increase in temporary migration from Ghana to Qatar for the purposes of employment. In 2006, reports surfaced of extremely poor treatment of Ghanaians working in the Qatar construction industry, including overcrowded living conditions, inadequate diets, non-payment of wages and confiscation of personal-identity documentation, such as passports. A Ghanaian government fact-finding mission went to Qatar to meet with Ghanaian workers and Qatari employers, and largely confirmed these reports.

In 2013, the CEO of SOS Labour, Ocansey, was arrested by the Anti-Human Trafficking Unit of the Ghana Police Service and charged with human trafficking. This followed reports from Ghanaian migrant women that they had been promised jobs by SOS Labour as shop assistants in supermarkets in Kuwait and the United Arab Emirates, but when they arrived, they were forced into manual labor and, in some cases, prostitution. Ocansey denied all charges and was released on bail. Eventually all charges against her were withdrawn. However, the treatment of Ghanaian workers in the Gulf region has led the country's government to take a much more active interest in the recruiting and treatment of Ghanaian workers for temporary employment outside the country.

In 2012, an Inter-Ministerial Committee on Migration (IMSCM) was convened by the Ministry of the Interior and charged with formulating a national migration and development policy for Ghana. The UNDP and IOM have observer status on the IMSCM. An initial draft policy was commissioned from the Centre for Migration Studies at the University of Ghana. However, as of the time of writing, the proposed National Migration and Development Policy had not yet been approved by the cabinet or released as official policy. In addition to laying out a strategy for greater engagement with the diaspora, the document proposes greater regulation and oversight of temporary labor migration.

Recruiting under bilateral agreements: The case of Mauritius

Mauritius is a small but relatively robust island economy in the Indian Ocean off the coast of mainland Africa with a population of 1.3 million. Over the years, it has been both an importer and exporter of migrant labor. Much of the island's population is made up of descendants of the half-million indentured workers from India who were imported by colonial Britain between 1830 and 1920 to work on the island's sugar-cane plantations, which had previously been run by France with imported slave labor.

After independence in 1968, the Mauritian economy became far more diversified. Sugar exports remained a mainstay, but tourism, financial services and light manufacturing (mainly textiles in an economic processing zone (EPZ)) propelled the country into middle-income status. At the same time, like many other African countries, Mauritius experienced a significant outflow of skilled migrants and professionals. According to the Migration DRC, over 100,000 migrants from Mauritius now live in the diaspora outside the country, primarily in OECD countries including France (38,000), the United Kingdom (24,000), Australia (18,000), Germany (11,000), Italy (10,000) and Canada (9,000) (Migration DRC 2010). The government is actively courting its diaspora with an eye toward encouraging investment in the country.

To some degree, the skills outflow was compensated for by an immigration policy that encouraged the temporary importation of scarce skills. Between 2006 and 2012, 10,000 three-year occupational permits were issued, the majority of which went to professionals from OECD countries, especially France and the United Kingdom, as well as to nationals of non-OECD countries, such as India and South Africa. The most important sector in this regard was hospitality (tourism), followed by professional services, ICT and media, trade, financial services and manufacturing. Mauritius has also consistently imported temporary semi-skilled labor to work in the EPZ factories and in construction, primarily from India, China, Sri Lanka and Bangladesh. These numbers peaked at 35,000 in 2007.

In recent years, layoffs in the sugar and textile industries have contributed to rising unemployment rates among local workers, prompting the conclusion that the country could gain from becoming an exporter of lower-skilled labor through temporary migration to various countries in the OECD. The government-led Circular Migration Programme grew out of an IOM-funded project called Enhancing the Development Impact of Migration: Developing an Overseas Employment and Diasporas Mobilization Strategy in Mauritius, which in 2008 mapped the location and profile of the Mauritian diaspora and highlighted opportunities for labor migration abroad for Mauritian nationals. The primary aim, from the Mauritian point of view, is for Mauritians to use their trade-sector skills to earn sufficient money overseas to set up small, medium- or micro-sized enterprises (SMMEs) upon their return. The IOM views the program as a best-practice pilot.

The Circular Migration Programme has a number of components, including the following:

- *The Mauritius Circular Migration Database.* This is managed by the National Empowerment Foundation (under the Ministry of Social Integration and Economic Empowerment) and a Migration Resource Center housed at the IOM Office in Mauritius. This project aims to enhance the labor-migration program by setting up an online registration tool for Mauritians interested in temporary employment abroad and by providing informative assistance to potential and actual Mauritian migrants in the migration and decision-making process. Moreover, it assists returning migrants to Mauritius by providing information on options, procedures and reliable contacts.
- *A bilateral agreement with France.* Signed in 2008, this facilitates the employment of skilled French nationals in Mauritius and enables up to 500 Mauritian migrants to be provided with temporary employment in France (the first cohort was recruited for work in France in 2011).
- *A bilateral agreement with Italy.* Signed in 2012 and funded by the European Commission and the Italian Ministry of Labor and Social Policy, this includes funding for the agro-industry training of Mauritians in Italy as well as job placements in the Italian tourism and fishing industry. In late 2013, an initial cohort of 70 migrants was recruited to work in Italy.
- *The IOM Mauritius-Canada pilot project.* This project facilitates the recruitment of Mauritians in three Canadian provinces under the Canadian Temporary Work Program in partnership with the Mauritian government and a Canadian labor-recruiting company, Prudhomme International. The IOM undertakes recruiting, medical examinations, visa applications and transport arrangements, in effect operating as a quasi-recruitment agency. Spouses can accompany migrants and also seek employment.

According to the IOM, this is an excellent example of collaboration between the government, civil society, the private sector and an international organization on legal-migration initiatives that benefit migrants, destination countries and source countries. It also benefits the private sector, as it is able to define its labor needs for the mid to long term.

Conclusions

The management of temporary labor migration among semi- and low-skilled workers poses considerable challenges to governments both in countries of origin and destination. By its very nature, temporary migration needs to be especially responsive to labor-market demands, which means that top-heavy government regulation is likely to inhibit rather than facilitate migration flows. On the other hand, as the Canadian government has recently discovered with its Temporary Foreign Worker Program, a light-touch policy approach to matching supply and demand can give employers too much discretion, leading to abuse of the system.

From the perspective of migrants, entitlements to good treatment, decent work, fair wages, legal protection and other basic freedoms obviously vary from country to country and program to program. The Qatari construction industry has achieved global notoriety over the course of the last year for the way in which migrants have been exploited by unscrupulous employers. But this is really only one end of a spectrum on which we would also place the South African migrant-labor system. One of the recurrent complaints of civil society and migrant organizations at the GFMD is that temporary work programs, by their very nature, leave migrants vulnerable to exploitation and abuse. If a recipient state is not prepared to intervene, then the government of the supplier country (as the Ghana case suggests) has little bargaining power, despite sending missions of inquiry, short of refusing to allow its citizens to accept work. Ghana's bilateral agreement with Qatar, for example, has certainly not prevented the poor treatment of Ghanaian migrants.

A global study of the operation and practices of the recruitment industry is urgently needed to provide better evidence on its structure and role in matching positions and employers with potential employees. Such an exercise would also identify the range of different types of institution, their recruiting strategies, the costs and benefits to migrants, and possible best practices. This paper has identified three different "types" of intermediary structure with very different operating parameters. In South Africa, all mining-sector recruiting is organized through a single monopolistic private company (TEBA). In Ghana, a growing number of small recruitment companies are jostling for business. The Mauritius case features an attempt to bypass private recruiters altogether and operate entirely on a government-to-government basis. However, the role of the job-matching intermediary cannot be entirely dispensed with. In this third case, an international organization, the IOM, has taken on the role; but this can only be a stopgap, as it is difficult to imagine the organization playing such a role on an ongoing basis. In addition, the program is donor-funded (at considerable cost), so its sustainability must also be called into question.

References

Boyd, Monica. "Recruiting High Skill Labour in North America: Policies, Outcomes and Futures." *International Migration* (52) 3: 40–54, 2014. doi: 10.1111/imig.12139.

Castles, Stephen. "Guestworkers in Europe: A Resurrection?" *International Migration Review* (40) 4: 741–766, 2006.

Crush, Jonathan. "Southern Hub: The Globalization of Migration to South Africa." *International Handbook on Migration and Economic Development,* edited by Robert Lucas. Cheltenham: Edward Elgar, 2014: 211–240.

Crush, Jonathan, Alan Jeeves and David Yudelman. *South Africa's Labor Empire: A History of Black Migrancy to the Gold Mines.* Boulder: Westview, 1992.

de Haas, Hein. "The Myth of Invasion: The Inconvenient Realities of Migration from Africa to the European Union." *Third World Quarterly* (29) 7: 1305–1322, 2008.

Hugo, Graeme. "Best Practice in Temporary Labour Migration for Development: A Perspective from Asia and the Pacific." *International Migration* (47) 5: 23–74, 2009.

IOM (International Organization for Migration). *Migration in Ghana: A Country Profile.* Geneva: IOM, 2009.

Migration DRC (Development Research Centre on Migration, Globalisation and Poverty). Global Migrant Origin Database. Ghana, 2010. www.migrationdrc.org/research/regions/ghana_africa.html.

Nayeck, Joyker. "Circular Migration: The Case for Mauritius." International Conference on Diaspora for Development, Washington, D.C., July 13–14, 2009.

Rahman, Mizanur, and Lian Kwen Fee. "Changing Patterns of Ghanaian Migration: Interplay Between Institutions and Networks." *Asian Migration Policy,* edited by Mizanur Rahman and AKM Ahsan Ullah. New York: Nova, 2012: 251–270.

Schans, Djamila, Valentina Mazzucato, Bruno Schoumaker and Marie-Laurence Flahaux. "Changing Patterns of Ghanaian Migration." *MAFE Working Paper* No. 20, 2013.

Wickramasekara, Piyasiri. "Circular Migration: A Triple Win or A Dead End." *Global Union research Network Discussion Paper* No. 15. Geneva: ILO, 2011.

Lessons from Asia

Nilim Baruah

Introduction

Creating a "fair deal" with regard to talent implies the institution of migration policies and programs that benefit migrants, countries of origin and countries of destination alike (employers and society). This is particularly important for countries of origin. While countries with liberal-democratic constitutions recognize the freedom of movement, thus giving people the choice of working abroad, countries of origin may lose public investment in education through the emigration of their skilled human resources (although this may be partially recouped through subsequent monetary and skills transfers).

The United Nations has estimated that the world's stock of migrants, defined as persons residing outside their country of birth, amounted to 232 million individuals in 2013, 48 percent of whom were women. An estimated 30 percent of migrants (71 million) live and work in Asia. Since 2000, Asia has added a total of 20 million migrants, or 1.6 million per year, more than any region (UN DESA 2013). Yet these numbers still do not fully reflect the significance of the migrant workforce in destination countries and economic sectors.

Labor-migration flows in Asia are primarily intraregional (including the Middle East). Such migration occurs largely on the basis of temporary-migration regimes, with a focus on comparatively low-skilled work. Women comprise 42 percent of the migrant population in Asia and are concentrated in domestic work. The region is marked by substantial remittance inflows. Indeed, six Asian countries were among the top 10 remittance-receiving countries in 2013 (World Bank 2013).

Migration from Asia is a major and growing component of flows to OECD countries, representing a third of all such migrants in 2011. Skilled-labor flows are particularly strong from India, the Philippines and China, and student migration is significant. In the mid-2000s, more than 50 percent of migrants from Asia in OECD countries were highly educated, while this figure was less than 30 percent for migrants from other regions. In OECD countries, a total of 80 percent of these highly educated male migrants and 66 percent of highly skilled female migrants from Asia are employed and making pivotal economic contributions to the region (ADBI 2014).

Lessons from Asia

While Asia has for decades been a source of skilled workers and student migration for traditional immigration-destination countries and the United Kingdom, the implementation of policies and programs addressing skilled migration within the region is a recent phenomenon, except in Singapore. The economic transformation to high-value manufacturing and services in Japan and the Asian tiger economies has led to a high level of demand for a skilled workforce that the native population has not been able to meet in full (Ducanes 2013). This factor, along with the global competition for talent, has compelled Asian countries, which (apart from Singapore) have traditionally had only temporary or fixed-term labor-migration programs, to introduce programs to attract and retain skilled workers.

ASEAN member states have set a goal of achieving the freer flow of skilled labor within ASEAN by 2015. This objective is embodied in the Economic Blueprint, one of three blueprints adopted for the ASEAN Economic Community (AEC).

Mechanisms

Mechanisms appropriate to the achievement of a "fair deal" on the issue of talent (for migrant workers of all skill categories) include national legislation; bilateral agreements; and regional, interregional and global frameworks.

National legislation

Clear, simple and consistent immigration laws and regulations facilitate skilled migration. Singapore has proved skillful at achieving this goal. In East and Southeast Asia more generally, legal regimes tend to provide for equal treatment between nationals and migrants in terms of remuneration and labor protection. Incentives to attract and retain skilled workers have become more mainstream. In Japan, for example, for those working in select occupations and in possession of certain skills, there are now routes to permanent residency. Spouses are also provided with labor-market access, family unification for parents has been introduced, and employment services for students and foreign workers have been created.

At the lower skills end, however, recently admitted migrants are often concentrated in low-wage and difficult jobs that nationals do not want. Recruitment costs are high across most migration corridors.

Bilateral agreements and MOUs

Memorandums of understanding (MOUs) have not always adequately served their intended purposes. In some countries, the flow of undocumented migrant workers is greater than that taking place through MOU-created processes. This can be partially explained by slow emigration procedures in the countries of origin. Nevertheless, MOUs and bilateral agreements are important tools in Malaysia, the Republic of Korea, Thailand and elsewhere, both in terms of setting an orderly migration process and facilitating agreement on standards for the employment of migrant workers. Countries of origin are eager to pursue and review agreements that protect their migrant workers and secure admission.

Recently, India and the United Kingdom signed an MOU on cooperation in the health care sector. This agreement goes beyond recruitment of health workers to include human resources within the sector, primary health care (PHC), the strengthening of public infrastructure, capacity development and technology development. Similarly, Germany and the Philippines struck an agreement in March 2013 governing placement in the health care professions. This agreement focuses on job-placement procedures and working and employment conditions. However, one article states that "both parties will explore projects to sustain and promote human resource development (HRD) in the Philippines."

On a related topic, India has signed 15 social security agreements (SSAs) governing the transfer and portability of social security, four of which are in force.

Multilateral agreements

The ASEAN community has recognized the importance of labor migration in the region. The topic is included in two of the three ASEAN blueprints, including the Economic Community Blueprint and the Social-Cultural Community Blueprint. The economic blueprint calls for the free flow of skilled labor, while the socio-cultural blueprint provides for the protection and promotion of the rights of migrant workers.

The International Labour Organization's (ILO) Multilateral Framework on Labor Migration (2006) is perhaps the only representative global framework of principles and guidelines that takes a rights-based approach to labor migration. This framework is anchored within ILO conventions and standards, and promotes best practices, but it is also based on tripartite negotiations and consensus among origin and destination countries. The framework contains nine thematic areas consisting of 15 broad principles and corresponding guidelines. Aspects relevant to the current topic include the Effective Management of Labor Migration and the Migration and Development sections.

Examples of programs benefiting migrants and countries of origin

Regional economic integration within ASEAN

The January 2007 adoption of the ASEAN Declaration on the Protection and Promotion of the Rights of Migrant Workers was a milestone in this regard. While implementation of the declaration remains a work in progress, commitments by labor-sending and labor-receiving states provide a good framework for action. ASEAN has also created the ASEAN Forum on Migrant Labor (AFML), a tripartite forum (with additional participation by civil society organizations) that provides a platform to share good practices and assess the ongoing implementation of the declaration of migrant workers' rights. The AFML has been supported by the ILO since the forum's inception.

ASEAN member states aim to realize the freer flow of skilled labor within ASEAN by 2015, a goal embodied in the community's Economic Blueprint. Thus far, mutual recognition arrangements (MRAs) have been agreed upon among ASEAN countries to cover seven professional occupations: architectural services, surveying, medical practitioners, dental practitioners, engineering services, nursing and accounting services. All 10 ASEAN member states are active participants in these MRAs, and a variety of mechanisms are being established to administer their implementation. An eighth MRA, in the area of tourism services (MRA-TP), aims to facilitate the mobility of tourism professionals within ASEAN on the grounds of competency-based tourism qualifications. However, while MRAS have been established in seven areas, more work needs to be done on defining competency-based qualifications and benchmarks. ASEAN member states are also currently supporting the establishment of an ASEAN Regional Qualifications Framework (ARQF), which has the potential to simplify the recognition of skills by educational authorities across borders, as has been accomplished to a significant extent in Europe. Employers' and workers' organizations are also collaborating at the ASEAN level, although this cooperation is in the early stages of development.

Pakistan Remittance Initiative (PRI)

In 2009, the State Bank of Pakistan, along with the country's Ministry of Overseas Pakistanis and Ministry of Finance, launched a joint initiative called the Pakistan Remittance Initiative (PRI) (Sattar 2013). Before the PRI was introduced, the country's remittances market suffered from the following problems:
- Banks were not significant participants in the remittances business.
- Banks received no assistance in developing remittance products.
- Banks did not develop customized remittance strategies.
- No specialized IT platform designed to handle remittance business existed.
- Market participants received no help in developing necessary skills for handling remittance services.

The PRI initiative was launched with the aim of facilitating a faster, cheaper, more convenient and more efficient flow of remittances and of creating investment opportunities in Pakistan for overseas Pakistanis. The main competitor to PRI and other formal channels are informal channels (Hundi), which can transfer remittances within 10 minutes, with funds delivered to the remittance receiver's doorstep and without significant paperwork. PRI's challenge is to meet that timeline and cost (Sattar 2013).

According to Sattar, PRI's achievements thus far include the following:
- On the policy level, the initiative has emphasized the remittance business case for banks. Twenty-four banks now have a dedicated home-remittance division.
- A large number of bilateral agreements have been struck. Bank representatives have been placed in overseas banks (eight to 10 representatives have been sent to Gulf Cooperation

Council (GCC) countries, for example), and PRI itself has arrangements with 400 overseas entities.
- Remittance-rich areas have been identified. Between 40 and 50 cities account for 80 percent of all remittances to Pakistan; similarly, between 400 and 500 bank branches serve as conduits for 85 percent of remittances.
- Domestic remittance centers have increased flexibility. Opening bank branches in rural areas can be costly; therefore, state banks have been allowed to open remittance booths engaging only in remittance disbursement. If banks find these entities to be cost-effective, they can be converted to a full branch office later.
- New remittance channels have been established. These include automated deposit into beneficiary accounts (available immediately); cash-over-the-counter (COC) payments; real-time gross settlements (RTS) (available on the same day, an improvement from the previous four days); and interbank fund transfers (IBFT; available within 30 minutes).
- Monetary penalties have been imposed for delays. Thus, banks are fined if remittance delivery is slow. The current fine is comparatively low so as to encourage banks to enter the market, but it will gradually be increased.
- Complaint handling has been made more robust. The PRI itself maintains a round-the-clock call center, and banks have their own dedicated call centers.
- The introduction of Pardes (debit) cards has allowed remittance beneficiaries to make withdraws from ATM machines. Two banks have launched this product, and three additional banks are planning to launch it soon.

The Republic of Korea's Employment Permit System and Happy Return Program

South Korea's Employment Permit System (EPS) was introduced in 2004 as the primary system managing the entry and residency of foreign workers in Korea. The EPS program involves the recruitment of workers by government agencies, pre-departure training, skills and job matching, processes for issuing visas and employment contracts, protected employment conditions (Korean labor law), complaints mechanisms, health and accident insurance, and cross-cultural workplace programs. Support services include the Foreign Workers' Support center and a counselling hotline with translation available into 15 languages. Interstate cooperation is governed by an MOU. National and regional workshops tasked with reviewing implementation of the MOUs have been organized in partnership with the ILO.

Introduced in 2009, the related Happy Return Program offers migrant workers a series of programs focused on their return to and reintegration into their countries of origin. The Happy Return Program is intended to provide an incentive for workers to return voluntarily upon completion of their employment contracts, thus completing the temporary labor-migration cycle through a successful reintegration and transfer of skills. While migrants are still in Korea, services include pre-return seminars, skills training and the issuing of career certificates. A career certificate attests to a returnee's work experience and vocational competencies, and makes it easier to apply successfully for a job at a Korean company or a multinational corporation. The Human Resources Development Service of Korea (HRD Korea) also notifies migrant workers of the expiration of their employment periods and offers information on return requirements. In their countries of origin, former migrant workers have access to job-matching services, returnee networks and job fairs jointly organized by HRD Korea and local ministries of labor, which are intended to introduce former migrants to local branches of Korean-owned enterprises. Although the return program does not provide a solution for all returnees and some migrants continue to overstay their visas, it is a good example of a destination country being innovative and proactive in all stages of the temporary-labor-migration cycle.

While containing benefits for migrants and origin countries, these programs are clearly designed to benefit South Korea as a destination country, as well.

Public information campaigns

Although host populations within Asia are more open to skilled than to unskilled migration, public attitudes are essentially conservative, varying depending on the size of migrant populations and the intensity of flows. The U.N. secretary-general's eight-point agenda on migration and development calls for improving public perceptions of migrants, noting that both information and leadership are necessary to reinforce positive messages about the benefits of migration. A positive image of migrants should be generated in line with their contribution to development.

In this regard, a 2010 ILO study on public attitudes toward migrant workers in four Asian destination countries informed the development of subsequent public-information campaigns, including:

- The Bridge of Voices (Saphan Siang) campaign in Thailand, which was led by the ILO in partnership with the International Organization for Migration, the United Nations Economic and Social Commission for Asia and the Pacific, and World Vision International.
- The Migration Works campaign in Malaysia, which was led by ILO in partnership with a variety of U.N. agencies.

The campaigns focused on promoting better understanding between nationals and migrants by countering misconceptions and informing the public about migrants' positive social and economic contributions. Activities included the creation of online communities; a photo competition and exhibition called "A Positive Image"; the development of a public service announcement (PSA) in Malaysia; and events for International Migrants Day.

References

ADBI (Asian Development Bank Institute). *Labor Migration, Skills & Student Mobility in Asia*. Tokyo: ADBI, 2014.

Ducanes, Geoffrey. *Labor Shortages, Foreign Migrant Recruitment and Portability of Qualifications in East and South-East Asia*. Bangkok: International Labour Organization, 2013.

Sattar, Arshad. "Overview and Lessons Learnt from Pakistan Remittance Initiative." Paper presented at the ILO-Korea multi-country dialogue: Effective implication of the employment permit system. Bangkok, December 3–4, 2013.

UN DESA (U.N. Department of Economic and Social Affairs, Population Division). "The Number of International Migrants Worldwide Reaches 232 Million." *Population Facts* no. 2013/2, September 2013. http://esa.un.org/unmigration/documents/The_number_of_international_migrants.pdf.

World Bank. "Migration and Remittance Flows: Recent Trends and Outlook, 2013–2016." *Migration and Development Brief* 2, October 2013. Washington, D.C.: World Bank, 2013.

Lessons from Latin America

Jean-Baptiste Meyer

The following paper addresses two basic mobility-policy questions in examining recent and present-day Latin American policies:
- What programs have origin countries developed in order to take advantage of migration?
- What kind of tools might be developed to manage mobility in a more positive manner?

The answers provided to these questions are drawn largely from the results of the CIDESAL project focusing on skilled mobility and expatriate communities (CIDESAL 2013). For this reason, the paper's conclusions are evidence-based and suggest very concrete options. In the two sections to come, we first describe migration-focused programs that have appeared in the region over the course of the last two decades, and then present some innovative, recently implemented tools designed to address the challenge of diaspora management.

Existing programs/initiatives designed to foster migration benefits for countries of origin in Latin America

Countries in Latin America – a traditional region of both in- and out-migration – have without doubt experimented and developed a number of national policies designed to take advantage of mobility in recent years (Koolhaas, Pellegrino and Bengotchea 2015). Many such programs have been developed since 1990, when the region was a pioneer in this policy area (Meyer 2005). Most have been conceptualized and specifically identified as diaspora policies, thus relying on talented expatriates to contribute to development processes at home. A review of these initiatives reveals a broad diversity of policy options as well as considerable variance in sequence, with some countries having entered this policy arena as long as 25 years ago and others quite recently. As a consequence, a variety of lessons may be derived from these case studies.

Argentina, Colombia, Uruguay: The pioneers

Argentina has implemented several mobility-focused programs since the 1980s, following the end of military dictatorship and the integration of many expatriate intellectuals into the domestic democratic process (Luchilo 2015). The most recent and most elaborate such measure is the RAICES program (a term that both means "roots" and serves as an acronym for the Network of Argentina Scientists and Researchers Abroad) led by the Ministry of Science, Technology and Productive Innovation (MINCYT 2014), which over the course of the last decade has managed to bring back 1,000 researchers to Argentina, sponsor hundreds of short-term stays in Argentina by prominent scientists based in Europe and the United States (Cesar Milstein grants), create 30 thematic digital communities or networks that connect teams and individuals sharing common interests abroad and in Argentina, and involve dozens of researchers based overseas in Argentine projects.

Colombia has also developed several programs over the course of the last two decades. The Red Caldas, a Colombian network of scientists and engineers abroad, drew considerable attention during its period of activity from 1991 to 2005 (Charum and Meyer 2000; Chaparro, Jaramillo and Quintero 2006; Pellegrino 2015). Its dynamics and results were described as extremely innovative and promising, but also as hectic and inefficient. During the mid-2000s, a number of attempts to overcome the program's perceived limits were made, including a round of "scientific diplomacy" (making connections between expatriates with the aim of international cooperation) and the "boomerang" program, in which talented young people were sent abroad but expected to return. In the late 2000s, the Colombia Nos Une program (meaning both "Colombians unite" and "Colombia unites us") emerged (MRE 2014). These initiatives were initially overseen by Colciencias (originally an agency-level body, now the Department of Science, Technology and Innovation) and, later, by the Ministry of Foreign Affairs (Ministerio de Relaciones Exteriores). However, another recent Colciencias program offers grants to excellent young researchers and engineers to pursue studies and careers abroad; return is not necessary, though a strong commitment to future cooperation with Colombia, wherever the grant recipient may wind up, is expected (Caplan 2015).

As a small country – though one with a very high rate of expatriation and a central position in South America – Uruguay has experimented on the strictly national level and on the regional level with reconnection and return programs (Lema 2015). During the 1980s and 1990s, the Basic Sciences Development Program (Programa de Desarrollo de las Ciencias Basicas, PEDECIBA), the Franco-Uruguayan Association for Scientific and Technical Development (AFUDEST) and the Association of Latin-American Scientists (ALAS) all sought to build and strengthen international connections; today, with its booming economy, the country has sought to promote the return of migrants through short-term appointment programs, encouraging international recruitment of highly skilled as well as mid-skilled workers (plumbers, technicians and so on) to fill shortages on the local labor market.

These three pioneers of diaspora-community policies in Latin America have continued to experiment with outreach programs throughout the last several decades. Through the implementation and improvement of a number of programs with differing results, they have developed considerable experience that has inspired policies in other countries.

Existing programs/initiatives designed to foster migration benefits for countries of origin in Latin America

Early adopters (Mexico, Chile) and newcomers (Ecuador, Peru, Brazil)

During the last decade, in cooperation with the World Bank, Mexico and Chile have each developed official networking programs targeted at their diaspora communities (MICAL, Observatorio de las diásporas calificadas). Mexico's Network of Mexican Talent Abroad (Red de Talentos Mexicanos en el Exterior) is overseen by the country's Secretary of Foreign Affairs and comes as the result of a long process of developing linkages with skilled expatriates, led by the Institute of Mexicans Abroad (IME). Mexico (along with Morocco) has recently been praised for providing an example of constructive migration policy (Iskander 2011). The networking program has developed nodes or significant groups in the United States and in Europe, especially in Germany.

The Chile Foundation (La Fundacion Chile), a private foundation with business-community support, and the Directorate of Chilean Communities Living Abroad (La Dirección para la Comunidad de Chilenos en el Exterior, DICOEX), a part of the Department of Foreign Affairs, have together established the Chile Global network, which has created digital connections as well as a significant physical presence in the United States, Canada, Germany and elsewhere. A number of success stories related to the network's work have been documented (Kuznetsov 2006). It focuses on enlisting prominent entrepreneurial talents in the diaspora community for concrete projects and knowledge-transfer efforts within Chile.

Ecuador has recently shifted to an active diaspora policy from its traditionally passive position with regard to migration. The country's national expenditures and number of grants for advanced students to study abroad have increased tremendously since the late 2000s. A network seeking to form connections among these skilled expatriates has been established. Prometeo, a program sponsoring short-term visits (providing travel expenses and a bonus of $4,000 in return for a commitment of at least three months) by expatriate scientists and engineers, has been operating successfully since 2011. Funding for this program was expanded from $3 million in 2012 to $19 million in 2013 (SENECYT 2014).

With similar aims, if different means, Peru has created a reintegration grant program, offering to pay resettlement costs and an income bonus to returnees who make at least a four-year commitment. The Peru 2040 plan has led to the creation of links with many of the country's highly skilled expatriates and diaspora communities.

Brazil launched its Science without Borders (Ciencia Sem Fronteiras) program in 2011. Considered a country with a relatively low expatriation rate (less than 3% of its skilled population seeks work abroad), Brazil is seeking to boost circular migration through various means, including a massive expansion of subsidies given to excellent students for studies abroad, rewards given to expatriate scientists who return to Brazil or reconnect with the country's scientific community, and the provision of attractive incentives to work in Brazil for foreign researchers at both the junior and senior levels. Brazil thus intends to boost its domestic science and technology capacities, driving a new knowledge-based phase of economic growth (Meyer 2012).

Lessons from Latin America

Are these programs sustainable? How can they be supported?

Some observations and policy lessons may be derived from the above-noted experiences. First, there have been a number of new and original features in these programs. In general, there has been a proactive move to implement mobility-oriented and diaspora policies. Moreover, this trend remains on the upswing, as an increasing number of countries with different economic and social conditions are beginning to take a positive approach toward migration and its potential benefits. Countries that started relatively early in this process have continued to try to improve their methods and forge new tools to reconnect with diaspora communities and involve them in development projects. Countries that have come more recently to the issue are implementing active circular-migration strategies, intentionally sending talented people abroad in order to expose the country, through these individuals, to fertile ideas outside their borders. This marks a complete break from former approaches in which outflows were considered to be predominantly negative and migration was discouraged so as to prevent brain drain. Such new approaches – aiming at deliberate investment in skilled expatriation – have alternately been dubbed brain-export or diaspora policies (Caplan 2015; Gamlen 2011; Larner 2007).

Nor are these initiatives stemming solely from countries of origin. Germany's official development-cooperation institutions, for example, have also served as pioneers in this field. This includes governmental or parastatal organizations, such as the German Academic Exchange Service (DAAD), the Centre for International Migration and Development (CIM), the Deutsche Gesellschaft für Internationale Zusammenarbeit (GIZ) and the Alumni Portal Deutschland, as well as institutional initiatives, such as those of the Katolischer Akademischer Ausländerdienst (KAAD), the Karlsruhe Institute of Technology (KIT), the Humboldt Foundation and the Brandt Foundation. Each of these has systematically created links with high-skilled returnees in most Latin America origin countries. To some extent, these links between scattered groups connected to their mother institutions in Germany may be called "inverted diasporas" (in these case, the central point of reference is the former host country). The challenge is to ensure a synergetic dynamic between initiatives led from origin countries and those from host-country institutions and programs.

In Latin America, as well as in other parts of the world, the nexus between diaspora-community activity and migration policy has become a major focus of international cooperation. Institutional and organizational recommendations are often made with the aim of ensuring that mobility has a positive impact on development (IOM/MPI 2011). However, these recommendations often remain at the level of abstract, mostly administrative tasks, such as making a skills inventory, implementing twinning exercises, mapping diaspora organizations and so on. Thus, the road map often remains in the form of a general reference scheme that is not easy to translate into actual steps in the effective realization of engagement and mobilization.

The CIDESAL project, which creates diaspora incubators for Latin America, has provided tools for this translation. It aims at nurturing links between potential diaspora and domestic partners with four successive steps, including the discovery, description, mobilization and involvement of actors.

As a part of this process, a software package called Unoporuno has been developed that searches for relevant actors and then characterizes them and their skills (social, professional) (Turner, Garcia Flores and de Saint-Léger 2014). Moreover, interactive platforms allowing encounters and collaborative work between dispersed individuals and groups have been designed and tested (Blanco 2015). Policy and organizational options have been suggested that will strengthen and develop these linkages by deepening infrastructure and other substantive resources.

With tools available that can reach out to expatriate communities, exploring their various strands and weaving ad hoc relationships, the diaspora becomes more than a hypothetical concept in which linkages are conditional upon good will and random encounters. Rather, it becomes a genuine resource, enabling opportunities to be expanded according to a given county's concerns, interests and objectives.

Conclusion

A number of tools can be designed that promote a fair deal on migration. Some of these are primarily organizational measures that take the diaspora into account without actively creating bridges to reach it. However, technological devices may also be developed that express and sustain the relationships between actors. The natural way to engage in proactive diaspora policies is to provide transnational civil society groups with enhanced possibilities for interaction. States, by contrast, traditionally rely on administrative measures to manage their constituencies. However, the diaspora is not a traditional constituency. It is an artificial hybrid entity whose existence depends upon technology; thus, links can be forged and deepened through the implementation of technology. Therefore, the next step in creating proactive policies, such as those under development in Latin America, is to invest in the creation of CIDESAL-style mechanisms that facilitate and sustain links between the state's domestic policies and its extraterritorial initiatives.

References

Blanco, Alejandro. "Incubating Diaspora Knowledge Networks." *Diaspora, the New Frontier... and How to Reach It,* edited by Jean-Baptiste Meyer. Marseille/Montevideo: IRD and Udelar, 2015.

Caplan, Caroline. "Diaspora Networks and Associations." *Diaspora, the New Frontier... and How to Reach It,* edited by Jean-Baptiste Meyer. Marseille and Montevideo: IRD and Udelar, 2015.

Chaparro, Fernando, Hernan Jaramillo and Vladimir Quintero. "Promise and Frustration of Diaspora Networks: Lessons from the Network of Colombian Researchers Abroad." *Diaspora Networks and the International Migration of Skills,* edited by Yevgueny Kuznetsov. Washington, D.C.: World Bank Institute, 2006: 187–198.

Charum, Jorge, and Jean-Baptiste Meyer (eds). *International Scientific Migrations Today.* Paris/Bogota: IRD/COLCIENCIAS, 2000.

CIDESAL. "Creacion de diasporas de los saberes para America Latina (Creation of knowledge diaspora incubators for Latin America." Palma: CIDESAL, 2013. http://observatoriodiasporas.org.

Fundacion Chile. "La Red ChileGlobal." Observatory of Skilled Diasporas. Palma: MICAL, 2014. http://observatoriodiasporas.org/encuentro-internacional-diaspora-y-desarrollo.

Gamlen, Alan. "Creating and Destroying Diaspora Strategies." *Oxford Diaspora Programme, IMI Working Papers Series* No. 31. Oxford: Oxford University, 2011.

IOM/MPI (International Organization for Migration/Migration Policy Institute). *Developing a Road Map for Engaging Diasporas in Development: A Handbook for Policymakers and Practitioners in Home and Host Countries.* Geneva/Washington, D.C.: IOM/MPI, 2011.

Iskander, Natasha. *Creative State, Forty years of Migration and Development Policy in Morocco and Mexico.* Ithaca: Cornell University Press, 2011.

Koolhaas, Martin, Adela Pellegrino and Julieta Bengotchea. "Indicators and reflections about skilled migration from Latin-America." *Diaspora, the New Frontier... and How to Reach It,* edited by Jean-Baptiste Meyer. Marseille/Montevideo: IRD and Udelar, 2015.

Kuznetsov, Yevgeny (ed.). *Diaspora Networks and the International Migration of Skills.* Washington, D.C.: World Bank Institute, 2006.

Larner, Wendy. "Expatriate Experts and Globalizing Governmentalities: the New Zealand Diaspora Strategy." *Transactions of the Institute of British Geographers* (32) 3: 331–345, 2007.

Lema, Fernando. "Qualified Uruguayans, Connection Experiences and Policy Formulation." *Diaspora, the New Frontier... and How to Reach It,* edited by Jean-Baptiste Meyer. Marseille/Montevideo: IRD and Udelar, 2015.

Luchilo, Lucas. "Return and Reconnection Policies in Argentina: Shifts and Continuity." *Diaspora, the New Frontier... and How to Reach It,* edited by Jean-Baptiste Meyer. Marseille/Montevideo: IRD and Udelar, 2015.

Meyer, Jean-Baptiste. "Back to the Future: Brain Drain and the Diaspora Option in Latin America." Presented at OECD seminar on Latin America and international migration, held in La Coruña on June 9, 2005.

Meyer, Jean-Baptiste. "Skills Circulation and the Advent of a New World Order." *Diversities* (14) 1: 63–75, 2012.

MINCYT (Ministry of Science, Technology and Productive Innovation). RAICES 2014. www.raices.mincyt.gov.ar.

MRE (Ministry of Foreign Affairs). Colombia Nos Une 2014. www.redescolombia.org/colombianosune.

Pellegrino, Valentina. "A Story with Many Tales: the Colombian Experience of the Red Caldas Network." *Diaspora, the New Frontier... and How to Reach It,* edited by Jean-Baptiste Meyer. Marseille/Montevideo: IRD and Udelar, 2015.

SENECYT. "Movilidad en el fomento al talento humano en educacion superior en Ecuador." Observatory of Skilled Diasporas. Palma: CIDESAL, 2014. http://observatoriodiasporas.org/encuentro-internacional-diaspora-y-desarrollo.

Turner, William, Jorge Garcia Flores and Mathilde de Saint-Léger. "Computer supporting Diaspora Knowledge Networks: a Case Study in Managing Distributed Collective Practice."

Diaspora, the New Frontier... and How to Reach It, edited by Jean-Baptiste Meyer. Marseille/Montevideo; IRD and Udelar, 2015.

The Role of International Organizations and NGOs

The Role of the European Union in the Fair Management of Migration

Florian Trauner

Introduction

The European Union began developing its framework for external cooperation on the issue of migration in the wake of the Treaty of Amsterdam (1999), which provided the EU with legal competences in this area. Since the implementation of this policy, the EU's approach has included elements both of prevention and of migration control. According to Christina Boswell (2003), two rather distinct concepts can be discerned in the EU's external migration policy. A first approach seeks to externalize tools traditionally used to control migration at the domestic or EU level (e.g., border control) to the countries of migrant origin and transit. The second approach is preventive in nature and strives toward an elimination of the root causes of migration through channels such as trade relations, development aid and human-rights conditionalities. Achievement of a "triple win" situation, in which benefits from migration accrue both to sending and receiving countries as well to migrants themselves – a key interest of the present volume – is better accommodated under this second approach.

The more restrictive approach nevertheless came to dominate the EU's external cooperation activities in the early 2000s. Following the terrorist attack of 9/11, security concerns took on a greater importance in the development of EU migration policy, greatly informing its efforts to control unwanted migration. Cooperation on return and readmission issues, often in exchange for facilitated travel opportunities for bona fide travelers, became the cornerstone of the EU's external cooperation framework (Trauner and Kruse 2008). This direction changed somewhat in 2005 with the launch of the EU's Global Approach to Migration (Council of the European Union 2005). With this policy, the European Union announced it would develop a truly "comprehensive approach" aimed not only at better control over irregular migration, but also at addressing key migration push factors, such as poverty and the lack of job opportunities in countries of origin. According to the European Commission (2008: 3), "the Global Approach reflects a major change in the external dimension of the European migration policy over recent years, namely the shift from a primarily security-centered approach focused on reducing migratory pressures, to a more transparent and balanced approach guided by a better understanding of all aspects relevant to migration."

The Role of the European Union in the Fair Management of Migration

This chapter examines the initiatives and projects launched under the EU's Global Approach (and related fields) from the perspective of fair migration, seeking to determine whether its initial ambitious objectives have been achieved. Has the EU indeed managed to make migration "fairer" for all actors involved? And what challenges remain?

The Global Approach to Migration: Developing EU mobility partnerships

Although the Global Approach to Migration was initially focused on Africa and the Mediterranean region, it was quickly extended to other regions, notably Eastern and Southeastern Europe. One of the pilot projects launched under this initiative entailed the creation of a European Job Mobility Portal on the African continent (Frattini 2006). This job center, as the media quickly referred to it, was intended to demonstrate the EU's more "comprehensive" approach toward migration originating from Africa, and was to be accompanied by "packages of legal-entry quotas" for those countries willing to cooperate on the return of irregular migrants (ibid.). These were ambitious objectives – as it turned out, too ambitious for the EU member states involved. Funded by the European Development Fund, a first Migration Information and Management Center (CIGEM) opened in Bamako, the capital of Mali, in 2008. CIGEM was primarily tasked with addressing issues related to returned migrants in Mali, with policymakers stating at the time that "it is not foreseen that the center will help migrants find a job in Europe" (CIGEM 2008: 16). Rather, the center has informed Malians interested in emigration about opportunities for vocational training and employment in Mali (for details, see Trauner and Deimel 2013).

The transformation of the original job-center concept into the CIGEM's less-ambitious reality is illustrative of the challenges faced by the European Union as it seeks to move beyond a narrow focus on migration control. While the Commission has sought to realize a "comprehensive approach," it has had difficulties winning support for specific policies from the member states. A similar struggle has been evident with regard to the EU's mobility partnerships, the flagship project of the Global Approach to Migration.

In 2008, the first such partnerships were signed with an Eastern Partnership country, Moldova, and an African state, Cape Verde. In composing these agreements, the European Union sought to address its partner countries' priorities directly. In Cape Verde, for instance, priorities have included improving the border-management system, bolstering the security of identity and travel documents, and facilitating mobility for the nation's citizens. In Moldova, a high level of emigration (and the associated negative consequences) made policymakers eager to implement measures encouraging return migration (Commission of the European Communities 2009: 4–5). However, the mobility-partnership program did not have an altogether smooth start. In 2009, Senegal suspended negotiations over its agreement due to dissatisfaction with the EU's offer. From a Senegalese perspective, the partnerships offered little that was new or innovative. As Sandra Lavenex (2010: 473) maintained, "They largely summarize existing bilateral cooperation programs with individual member states under a new heading."

The Arab Spring was a game changer for the European Union's migration policy in the affected region. The field of migration and mobility featured strongly in European debates on how to reinvigorate Euro-Mediterranean relations in the wake of the revolutionary events (European Commission 2011b). The term "mobility" was added to the Global Approach to Migration in order to reflect the EU's intention of promoting person-to-person contacts. Other objectives of the renewed approach included fostering legal immigration, focusing more on migrants' rights, improving the international protection of refugees, and creating a closer nexus between development and migration policy. The Commission stated that mobility partnerships "should be upgraded and promoted as the principle framework for cooperation in the area of migration and mobility between the EU and its partners, with a primary focus on the countries in the EU Neighborhood" (ibid.: 10). Moreover, if a partner country preferred not to negotiate readmission and visa-facilitation agreements, the Common Agenda on Migration and Mobility was offered as an alternative framework. This cooperation framework was less ambitious and required a lower level of commitment (excluding cooperation on readmission), but it could be upgraded to a mobility partnership at a later stage.

Mobility partnerships hence became more flexible and adaptable to the particular commitments a country was willing to make. Today, signing a readmission agreement is no longer a precondition for entering into a partnership with the European Union; instead, the formal recognition of a willingness to cooperate on the return of irregular migrants now suffices (European

Table 1: EU migration agreements with third countries (as of November 2014)

	Negotiating mandate		Agreements signed	Start of visa-free dialogue	Visa-free travel	Mobility partnerships
	Readmission agreement	Visa-facilitation agreement				
Albania	Nov 2002	Nov 2006	Nov 2007	Jan 2008	Dec 2010	
Bosnia and Herzegovina	Nov 2006	Nov 2006	Nov 2007	Jan 2008	Dec 2010	
Serbia	Nov 2006	Nov 2006	Nov 2007	Jan 2008	Dec 2009	
Montenegro	Nov 2006	Nov 2006	Nov 2007	Jan 2008	Dec 2009	
Macedonia	Nov 2006	Nov 2006	Nov 2007	Jan 2008	Dec 2009	
Kosovo				Jan 2012		
Belarus	Feb 2011	Feb 2011				
Ukraine	Feb 2002	Nov 2005	Jun 2007	Oct 2008		
Moldova	Dec 2006	Dec 2006	Oct 2007	Jun 2010	Apr 2014	May 2008
Georgia	Nov 2008	Nov 2008	Nov 2010	Jun 2012		June 2009
Armenia	Dec 2011	Dec 2011	Dec 2013			Oct 2011
Azerbaijan	Dec 2011	Dec 2011	Nov 2013			Dec 2013
Russia	Sept 2000	Jul 2004	May 2006	Apr 2007		
Turkey	Nov 2002	Feb 2011	Jun 2012*	Jun 2012		
Cape Verde	Jun 2009	Oct 2012	Oct 2013			May 2008
Morocco	Sept 2000	Dec 2013				Jun 2013
Tunisia						Mar 2014
Jordan						Oct 2014

Note: The table does not include countries that have signed only a readmission agreement (Sri Lanka, Macao, Hong Kong, Pakistan).

* Only the readmission agreement was signed.

Commission 2011a: 8). Following the implementation of this new approach, Morocco, Tunisia and Jordan (in the EU's southern neighborhood), as well as Georgia, Armenia and Azerbaijan (in the eastern neighborhood), accepted mobility partnerships. In April 2013, an agreement based on the Common Agenda for Migration and Mobility was proposed to India, and another in October 2013 to Nigeria. The EU regards Egypt and (should the circumstances allow) Libya as high-priority countries for future migration-cooperation agreements (European Commission 2014b: 3, 6).

What added value do mobility partnerships offer? From the perspective of EU member states, they primarily provide for an enhanced toolbox in tackling the issue of irregular migration. The EU has the power to demand intense cooperation from its partner countries on curbing irregular migration, including "commitments to promote productive employment and decent work, and more generally to improve the economic and social framework conditions [as this may] contribute to reducing the incentives for irregular migration" (Commission of the European Communities 2007: 4). In exchange, the European Union provides opportunities for legal migration, albeit with two caveats: Such migration must be "based on labor needs of interested member states" and be undertaken with an "obligation to respect the principle of Community preference for EU citizens" (ibid.: 5).

Mobility partnerships also place a greater focus on the migrants themselves. Under the agreements' terms, individuals are to be provided with information on labor opportunities in EU member states and on the conditions governing emigration. A partnership may also include practical programs aimed at facilitating emigration or return to the origin country, including pre-departure linguistic and technical training for migrants with concrete employment offers; the development of a framework supporting the portability of social rights; support for economic and social reintegration among returning migrants; and the creation of easier means of transferring migrants' remittances (Commission of the European Communities 2007).

Mobility partnerships are legally nonbinding, but politically commit the member states to the implementation of certain projects and priorities. The level of participation differs. In the mobility partnership with Cape Verde, the first of its kind, only four member states signed the declaration (France, Spain, Luxembourg and Portugal). The Netherlands joined a few months after the document's ratification. This reflects the open nature of this instrument; member states may decide to participate after an agreement is in place, and new projects may be added over time.

Table 2: Member states participating in EU mobility partnerships (as of November 2014)

Third country	Conclusion	Participating member states (at signature)
Cape Verde	2008	E, F, LUX, P
Moldova	2008	BG, CY, CZ, F, GR, H, I, LVA, PL, P, RO, SLO, SK, SE
Georgia	2009	B, BG, CZ, DK, EST, F, D, GR, I, LVA, LT, NL, PL, RO, SE, UK
Armenia	2011	B, BG, CZ, F, D, I, NL, P, RO, SE
Azerbaijan	2013	BG, CZ, F, LT, NL, PL, SLO, SK
Morocco	2013	B, F, D, I,NL, P, E, SE, UK
Tunisia	2014	D, B, DK, E, I, F, PL, P, UK, SE
Jordan	2014	CY, D, DK, GR, E, F, I, H, PL, P, RO, SE

Source: Author research

Mobility partnerships focus in large part on circular migration. Certain migrant populations – such as students, researchers, workers with special skills, and people interested in participating in intercultural person-to-person exchanges – are therefore a prime audience for this instrument. Signatories to an agreement are expected to provide active incentives for circularity and return after a predefined period of time, for example, by giving migrants access to a "form of privileged mobility to and from the member states where they were formerly residing" (ibid.: 8). This may include expedited procedures for future admission and reentry, for example. Other policies encouraging temporary migration include the provision of more support for return migrants (e.g., special housing programs or assistance in establishing businesses in their countries of origin). However, not all measures are grounded in positive incentives; if a migrant does not return to his or her country of origin voluntarily after the expiration of a visa, then the EU will ultimately enforce such a return. This is one of the reasons why the EU places a strong emphasis on readmission agreements.

While the mobility-partnership concept foresees a fair distribution of gains and obligations between the EU and partner countries, the curbing of irregular migration has in fact remained a dominant theme of the cooperation framework (Reslow 2013; Carrera and Hernandez i Sagrera 2009). Mobility partnerships have not contributed to higher levels of immigration into the European Union. This is demonstrated in Figure 1, which compares the number of citizens of Cape Verde, Georgia and Moldova – the first three countries to sign mobility partnerships – emigrating to the European Union in the years before and after the conclusion

Figure 1: Immigration into the EU before and after the signature of a mobility partnership (MP)

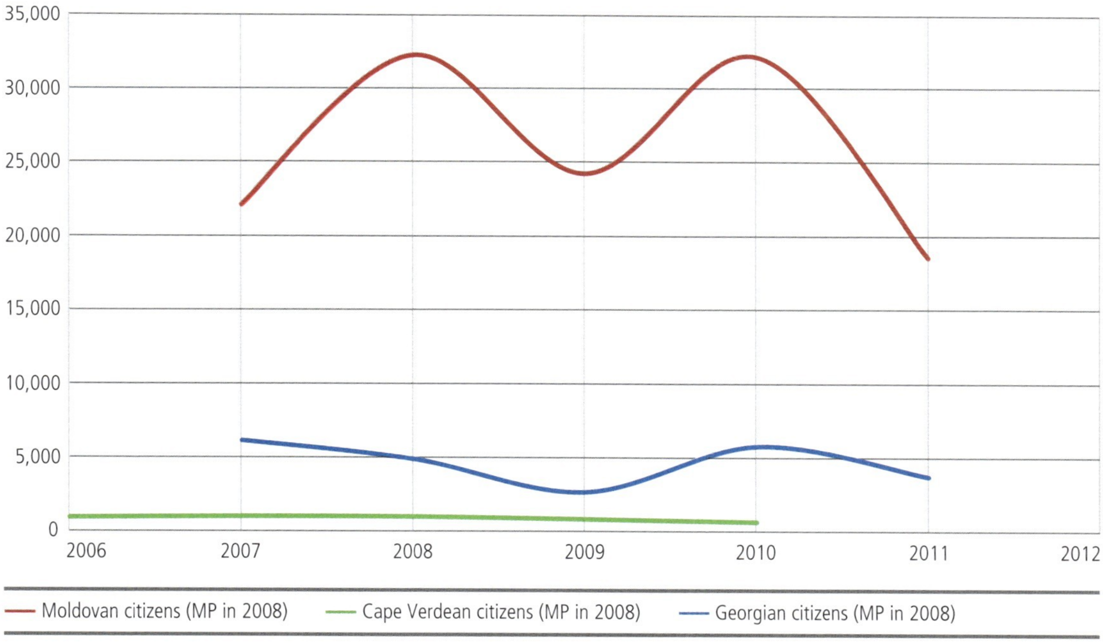

Source: Own research, drawing on Eurostat immigration data by member state (EU-28)

of each country's agreement. Interestingly, this data indicates stagnating if not declining numbers of migrants coming into the EU after the signature of the agreements.

Figure 1 reflects the fact that many EU member states have been reluctant to provide migrants from outside Europe with full access to the European labor market, in part due to high domestic unemployment rates (see also Maroukis and Triandafyllidou 2013). However, there has been an East-West divide, with Poland, the Czech Republic and Slovakia taking a more liberal approach than their western peers. Poland has gone furthest in opening up its labor market for (temporary) migration by citizens of countries that have signed a mobility partnership (Weinar 2013). Other projects developing out of this EU instrument have included a German initiative to offer its long-term non-citizen residents the ability to return to their home country for an extended period of time (up to two years) without losing their residence rights. In Cape Verde, an EU Common Visa Application Center has helped facilitate procedures for (short-term) travel into the European Union (ibid.).

The EU Blue Card Directive: Fostering ethical recruitment

In parallel with efforts to strengthen cooperation with migrants' countries of origin and transit, the European Union has adopted a range of directives defining the conditions of legal entry and residence for specific migrant populations, including family members qualifying for reunification rights (2003/86/EC), migrants residing long-term in the European Union (2003/109/EC), foreign students (2004/114/EC), researchers (2005/71/EC), intra-corporate transferees (2014/66/EU), and seasonal workers (2014/36/EU). The European Union has also agreed on a framework directive establishing a single application procedure for residence and work permits (the Single Permit Directive 2011/98/EU).

The flagship law in the field of labor migration has in recent years been the Blue Card Directive (2009/50/EC). This aims at attracting highly skilled migrants, with the goal of rendering Europe more competitive in the global race for the best and the brightest. Inspired by the United States' Green Card, the Blue Card program establishes a fast-track procedure for admitting highly qualified migrants. To become eligible, migrants require a recognized diploma, three years of professional experience and a job contract of (at least) one year with an enterprise operating in the European Union and with a salary at least three times the minimum wage. A Blue Card allows for a stay of two years and is renewable. The right to permanent stay is established after five years. The law is not applicable within the United Kingdom, Ireland and Denmark, all of which have opted out (Wolff and Trauner 2011).

The Blue Card law includes some innovative elements from the perspective of fair migration. It has two articles requiring member states to respect "ethical" standards when implementing the law. Article 3(3) of the Blue Card Directive states that the law will not pre-empt individual member-state policies that exclude certain professions from the Blue Card Directive on ethical grounds, seeking thereby to prevent recruitment within developing-country sectors that suffer from a lack of personnel. This stipulation implies that third countries may have a say in defining which sectors should be shielded from EU actors' recruitment activities. Furthermore, Article 8(4) maintains that "member states may reject an application for an EU Blue

Card in order to ensure ethical recruitment in sectors suffering from a lack of qualified workers in the countries of origin." With these two articles, the EU has sought to minimize the risk of brain drain in developing and middle-income countries. The directive commits member states to refrain from actively engaging in recruitment in target-country sectors that suffer from a lack of qualified personnel, as is often the case with health care, for example.

To date, the Blue Card policy has given no evidence of producing brain drain in developing countries. As of 2014, the European Commission (2014a: 4) had not been notified of any rejection of a Blue Card application on ethical grounds. Indeed, member states have used the directive's powers comparatively infrequently. In 2012, the first year of the policy's application, only 3,664 Blue Cards were issued in the whole EU. The top countries benefiting from Blue Cards were India (699), China (324), the United States (313), Russia (271) and Ukraine (149). The number of Blue Cards issued increased to 15,261 in 2013, with Germany alone issuing 14,197 (ibid.: 11). This is still a modest number in overall terms, demonstrating that many member states still prefer to work through their national-level policies if they seek at all to attract highly qualified migrants.

Fairness and EU asylum policy

Any discussion of fair migration in the EU must address the Dublin regime, a migration-governance system often criticized as being highly unfair. The Dublin Convention (1990) was initially signed as an intergovernmental treaty outside the EU's legal framework, and was only later incorporated into EU law (Dublin-II-Regulation 343/2003/EC). It is based on the principle that only a single member state – usually the first country of entry – is to be responsible for the examination of an asylum seeker's application. From the perspective of its advocates, the Dublin regime is essential in preventing asylum seekers from applying in multiple EU countries simultaneously, a phenomenon known as asylum "shopping" (Lavenex 2001). From the perspective of its critics, however, the Dublin regime is unfair to asylum seekers, as they do not have the opportunity to freely choose the country in which they are to make their application. This is problematic, as the EU's legal harmonization process has not yet resulted in a system of asylum procedures and standards comparable across the member states. In other words, it does matter where an asylum seeker submits his or her application. According a quantitative analysis by Toshkov and de Haan (2013: 662), "Asylum seekers from most countries of origin face substantially different chances of recognition depending on the destination country to which they apply."

Secondly, the Dublin system has been regarded as unfair to some member states because it institutionalizes a system of refugee burden-shifting instead of burden-sharing (on the issue of burden-sharing in the EU, see Thielemann 2008). As a consequence, the southern "frontier countries" feel excessively exposed to migratory pressure, with insufficient support from their northern EU partners. Italy has been outspoken in its call for more solidarity from Europe's north in the aftermath of the Arab revolutions and the Syrian civil war, as the number of migrants arriving in Italy from across the Mediterranean Sea has been increasing (e.g., EurActiv 2014). Several rulings by the European Court of Human Rights and the Court of Justice of the

European Union have highlighted the inadequacy and poor functioning of the asylum systems operated by some EU border countries, most notably that of Greece. On December 22, 2011, the Court of Justice of the EU delivered a landmark judgment ruling that an asylum seeker sent back to Greece under the Dublin rules "would face a real risk of being subjected to inhuman and degrading treatment" (joined cases C-410/10 and C-493/10). Yet even under the pressure of this and similar judgments, the EU has maintained the core elements of the Dublin regime. The Dublin III Regulation (Regulation No. 604/2013 of June 26, 2013) primarily sought to remedy the observed shortcomings by creating an early-warning mechanism and instituting ad hoc support for countries, such as Greece (Ripoll Servent and Trauner 2014).

Conclusion

Despite an initial external-cooperation framework that was security-driven and oriented toward controlling migration, since 2005 the European Union has developed a more "comprehensive approach" toward migration issues. Various initiatives – including the European Job Mobility Portal on the African continent and, most importantly, the mobility-partnership program – have reflected the EU's desire to embark on a proactive approach based on the understanding that well-managed migration can benefit all actors involved. The Blue Card Directive also commits the member states to respect "ethical" standards when seeking to attract highly skilled migrants from around the world. However, implementing and using these new instruments has been a challenge. Faced with difficult domestic economic conditions and rising unemployment, a majority of member states have been reluctant to follow the European Commission's lead in developing a comprehensive approach worth the name. Lacking the firm support of the member states, the Commission's scope for action has been limited, given that the EU has primarily worked through soft law (as in the case of mobility partnerships) or hard law that gives member states significant discretion and flexibility (as with the Blue Card Directive).

However, instruments such as mobility partnerships may be understood as works in progress. Even if they have not yet developed to their full potential, they do reflect an increasing level of pragmatism at the EU level and a stronger degree of recognition of origin countries' concerns and priorities (Cassarino 2009). The EU should continue and even expand this engagement with countries of origin, as well as its concern with individual migrants, and it should realistically assess what can be done to render migration a well-managed and overall more positive experience. This does not necessarily require the creation of new instruments and may indeed mean simply exploiting the potential of existing ones more fully.

The management of migration in the wider European region (and the way in which refugees are treated within Europe) has become a central criterion of the outside world's perception of the EU. Almost a decade ago, in a resolution on strengthening the European Neighborhood Policy, the European Parliament proposed taking "firm measures [...] to erase the image of a fearful Europe, more concerned with its own security and combating immigration than with the sustainable development that is both expected and necessary" (European Parliament 2006: Point 55). This advice has not lost any of its relevance.

References

Boswell, Christina. "The 'External Dimension' of EU Immigration and Asylum Policy." *International Affairs* (79) 3: 619–638, 2003.

Carrera, Sergio, and Raül Hernandez i Sagrera. "The Externalisation of the EU's Labour Immigration Policy: Towards Mobility or Insecurity Partnerships?" *CEPS Working Document No. 321*. Brussels: Centre for European Policy Studies, 2009.

Cassarino, Jean-Pierre. "EU Mobility Partnerships: Expression of a New Compromise." *Migration Information Source* September 15, 2009. www.migrationinformation.org/Feature/display.cfm?ID=741.

CIGEM (Migration Information and Management Center). Inauguration on October 6, 2008 in Bamako, Mali. Press Pack. Bamako, 2008.

Commission of the European Communities. "Communication from the Commission to the European Parliament, the Council, the European Economic and Social Committee and the Committee of the Regions. On circular migration and mobility partnerships between the European Union and third countries." Brussels: COM(2007)248 final, 2007.

Commission of the European Communities. "Mobility Partnerships as a Tool of the Global Approach to Migration." Brussels: SEC(2009) 1240 final, 2009.

Council of the European Union. "Global Approach to Migration: Priority Actions Focusing on Africa and the Mediterranean." Brussels: 15451/05 final, 2005.

EurActiv. "Italy pushes 'Frontex Plus' to tackle migration crisis." EurActiv.com, July 7, 2014.

European Commission. "Strengthening the Global Approach to Migration: Increasing Coordination, Coherence and Synergies." Communication from the Commission to the European Parliament, the Council, the European Economic and Social Committee and the Committee of the Regions. Brussels: COM(2008)611 final, 2008.

European Commission. "A Dialogue for Migration, Mobility and Security with the Southern Mediterranean Countries." Brussels: COM(2011) 292 final, 2011a.

European Commission. "The Global Approach to Migration and Mobility." Brussels: COM(2011) 743 final, 2011b.

European Commission. "Communication on the implementation of Directive 2009/50/EC on the conditions of entry and residence of third-country nationals for the purpose of highly qualified employment." Brussels: COM(2014) 287 final, 2014a.

European Commission. "Report on the implementation of the Global Approach to Migration and Mobility 2012–2013." Brussels: COM(2014) 96 final, 2014b.

European Parliament. "Resolution on the European Neighbourhood Policy." Brussels: P6_TA (2006)0028, 2006.

Frattini, Franco. "Migration and Development: Time for Creative and Courageous Approaches." Presented at the EU-Africa Ministerial Conference on Migration and Development in Tripoli on November 22, 2006.

Lavenex, Sandra. "The Europeanization of Refugee Policies: Normative Challenge and Institutional Legacies." *Journal of Common Market Studies* (39) 5: 851–874, 2001.

Lavenex, Sandra. "Justice and Home Affairs. Communitarization with Hesitation." In *Policy-Making in the European Union,* edited by Helene Wallace, Mark A. Pollack and Alasdair Young. Oxford: Oxford University Press, 2010: 458–477.

Maroukis, Thanos, and Anna Triandafyllidou. "Mobility Partnerships: a Convincing Tool for the EU's Global Approach to Migration." *Policy Paper No. 76*. Paris: Notre Europe Institute, 2013.

Reslow, Natasja. *Partnering for mobility? Three Level Games in EU External Migration Policy.* Maastricht: University of Maastricht Press, 2013.

Ripoll Servent, Adriana, and Florian Trauner. "Do Supranational Institutions Make a Difference? EU Asylum Law before and after Communitarisation." *Journal of European Public Policy* (21) 8: 1142–1162, 2014.

Thielemann, Eiko. "The Future of the Common European Asylum System." Need of a More Comprehensive Burden-Sharing Approach. *European Policy Analysis No. 1*. Stockholm: Swedish Institute for European Policy Studies, 2008.

Toshkov, Dimiter, and Laura de Haan. "The Europeanization of Asylum Policy: an Assessment of the EU Impact on Asylum Applications and Recognition Rates." *Journal of European Public Policy* (20) 5: 661–683, 2013.

Trauner, Florian, and Stephanie Deimel. "The Impact of EU Migration Policies on African Countries: The Case of Mali." *International Migration* (51) 3: 20–32, 2013.

Trauner, Florian, and Imke Kruse. "EC Visa Facilitation and Readmission Agreements: A New Standard EU Foreign Policy Tool?" *European Journal of Migration and Law* (10) 4: 411–438, 2008.

Weinar, Agnieszka. "Mobility Partnerships – What Impact do they Have on Legal Migration and Mobility?" Florence: Migration Policy Centre, European University Institute, 2013. www.migrationpolicycentre.eu/publication/mobility-partnerships-what-impact-do-they-have-on-legal-migration-and-mobility/.

Wolff, Sarah, and Florian Trauner. "A European Migration Policy Fit for Future Challenges." *Freedom, Security and Justice after the Lisbon Treaty and the Stockholm Programme*, edited by Sarah Wolff, Flora Goudappel and Jaap de Zwaan. The Hague: TMC Asser Press, 2011: 63–78.

Migration "is" Development:
The World Bank's Efforts to Facilitate Labor Mobility

Manjula M. Luthria, Casey Alexander Weston

Migration *is* development

While the phrase "migration and development" has garnered increased attention from the development community over the past several decades, policymakers have struggled to realize the potential links between the two phenomena. Careful scrutiny of remittance flows and "brain drain" has framed discussions about migration's role within development agendas, but an overemphasis on these flows distracts from the role of mobility in the lives of the individuals who actually choose to migrate. People migrate for a myriad of reasons, perhaps the foremost of which is increased access to employment and human-development opportunities. Examining flows of money or skills across borders supports a *place*-focused development model; shifting the focus to *human* development makes the role of migration in development much clearer. In fact, insomuch as voluntary migration is usually a choice made to facilitate individual or collective advancement, one might say that migration does not merely have a role in development. Migration *is* development.

When individual advancement comes to the fore, the migration impacts that have served as a focus for the development community over the past several decades lose their centrality to the migration story. Remittances – often viewed as a crowdsourced version of development aid – become something significantly less revolutionary when viewed through a human-development lens and, indeed, can be regarded simply as traditional intra-house financial transfers. Rather than focusing on remittance sums, the development community might instead examine the potential gains from increased labor mobility. Estimates suggest that economic gains from complete labor-market liberalization would surpass $65 trillion (Hamilton and Whalley 1984) – a sum that exceeds the total world GDP of a year as recent as 2006. Even much more modest and realistic labor liberalization could offer significant benefits for migrants, destination countries and labor source communities, thus producing a triple win. While remittance flows are an important piece of the migration story, labor-mobility policy formation should be guided by the desire to realize these much larger and more universal economic gains.

Similarly, "brain drain" discussions reflect a place-based development model owing to the assumption that countries should attempt to retain their skilled residents at all costs. This idea

Migration "is" Development: The World Bank's Efforts to Facilitate Labor Mobility

persists despite demographic projections that affirm the inevitability of increased mobility among skilled workers. Europe may lose 66 million workers by 2050 (World Bank 2009), while working-age populations will begin declining in China by 2020 (IMF 2013). Migration from regions with steadily expanding populations is perhaps the most reasonable option to mitigate the effects of working-age population declines in developed regions and continued population growth in less-developed ones. Thus, rather than attempting to prevent people from accessing personal-advancement opportunities for the sake of a given country's skill stock, the development community should try to encourage a greater abundance of skills overall. One way to do this is by ensuring that skill development remains attractive, which will certainly not be accomplished by limiting how, or where, people can benefit from the skills they acquire. From an individual's viewpoint, access to safe and legal migration channels represents a chance to capitalize fully on acquired skills, and the development community should attempt to strengthen those channels as a way to facilitate this process.

Barriers to labor mobility

If migration is seen primarily as a way for individuals to increase their access to more profitable employment, development questions become less about flows of money and skilled labor, and more about how to dismantle barriers to those flows. The numerous barriers that complicate individuals' attempts to access foreign labor markets have their roots in policy failures, institutional misalignments and perceptional biases. These barriers appear in migration corridors around the world and pose significant challenges to individuals hoping to access labor mobility's benefits, as well as to the policymakers and institutions attempting to support potential migrants' efforts. Members of the World Bank's Development Economics (DEC) unit, as well as the Global Knowledge Partnership on Migration and Development (KNOMAD), have conducted research to help describe some of these barriers quantitatively. Meanwhile, teams in the World Bank's Social Protection and Labor Global Practice, including the World Bank/Center for Mediterranean Integration's International Labor Mobility (ILM) Program, have spent some time trying to parlay this research into practical results through engagement with international partners. The ILM Program has worked on the following types of barriers and identified some potential strategies for overcoming them.

Policy failures

Policymakers in destination countries face the challenge of crafting migration policies that match ever-changing labor-market needs. However, due to the complexity of identifying and matching these labor needs, as well as the difficulty of designing politically popular migration regulations, many countries fail to create coherent policies at all. In those cases where policies do exist, they generally focus on high-skilled labor flows, ignoring the importance – and often even the existence – of low-skilled labor needs. Designing effective migration policies requires policymakers to frankly acknowledge supply-and-demand side pressures in the labor market.

In doing so, policymakers must distinguish clearly between labor migration and other migration issues, such as refugee flows, for example. Failing to do so will discourage a lucid conversation about labor needs and the migration policies that may be appropriate to meeting them.

It follows, then, that avoiding policy failures requires that policymakers place labor shortages at the center of their labor-migration policies. The identification of labor shortages allows policymakers to design legal pathways that encourage labor to move into affected sectors. To ensure that these pathways reach an appropriate scale, policy architects must utilize a combination of point-based and employment-based admission systems. While employment-based regulations ensure systemic alignment with labor-market needs, point-based systems prevent highly qualified workers, such as recent graduates, from being rejected. Thus, taking full advantage of the potential benefits of international labor mobility demands not only recognition of labor needs, but also policies designed flexibly enough to adapt to and anticipate those ever-changing needs.

Labor origin countries also frequently fail to create concrete or responsive policies as a result of efforts to avoid acknowledging migration patterns. By turning a blind eye to labor outflows, origin countries can avoid tense negotiations with neighboring labor destination countries over regulation enforcement or social protections, but migrants ultimately pay the cost for that avoidance. Sometimes, counterproductive policies actually emerge in the midst of this disengagement; for example, "ethical recruitment" limits mobility to the detriment of the migrant, the destination country and often even the origin country, as well. Increased acknowledgement of migration flows can lead to enhanced policy formation and improved institutional alignment in relevant migration corridors.

Institutional misalignment

Migration policies often have the specific goal of managing labor flows. By contrast, many institutions that affect migrants' employment were originally designed to focus on destination-country nationals. For example, the vocational-education institutions that measure and verify skill acquisition, the employment institutions that determine job eligibility, and the benefits institutions that manage pension and insurance programs often struggle to integrate migrants into their systems. The processes of verifying years of foreign work experience and ensuring pension portability pose challenges to destination-country institutions. As these are domestic institutions, they often lack the capacity or incentives necessary to cultivate transnational compatibility and institutional alignment.

Institutions in labor origin countries also frequently lack the capacity to design institutional standards and processes flexible enough to serve domestic and international labor markets. Training, migration and social-service institutions must consider and test adaptations of traditional procedures to ensure that they are appropriate for citizens who live or work abroad. Often, this adaptation requires the creation of new feedback channels accessible to citizens living abroad, foreign governments and foreign employers. If labor origin and destination countries are to maximize the benefits of migration for their citizens and societies, the institutional capacity to design flexible and compatible migration and employment systems is critical.

Migration "is" Development: The World Bank's Efforts to Facilitate Labor Mobility

Perceptional biases

While policy coordination and institutional alignment can provide the structural elements to facilitate successful migration management, migrants' labor-market entry also relies upon local actors, such as small-business owners, community organizations and city authorities. The decisions of these actors – to hire migrants, to facilitate their integration into neighborhood networks, to ensure their access to affordable housing – help determine migrants' ability to realize the gains associated with international labor mobility. These decisions, in turn, have their roots in individuals' perceptions of immigrants, which may suffer from a lack of personal exposure, subliminal biases or the over-politicization of migration in public discourse. Shifting the perceptions of local actors to prevent negative biases may help maximize the benefits of international labor-mobility arrangements in parallel with policy reforms and institutional support.

Breaking down barriers

Working collaboratively with governments, academics, employers and civil society organizations, the ILM Program has examined labor-mobility barriers and investigated potential strategies to overcome them. Fundamental to this process of investigation has been the willingness of key actors to critically analyze existing policies, institutions and perceptions, and to contribute to conversations about improvement. No universal solutions exist to these questions of migration management, which depend so heavily on the economic, political and cultural context of the countries in question. Nevertheless, the ILM Program has identified several processes that help dismantle these harmful labor-mobility barriers. Taken together, these processes may provide helpful lessons for governments and development bodies hoping to increase and improve international labor mobility.

Policy intermediation: Global Skills Partnership

Anti-brain-drain policies, such as the "ethical recruitment" of health care workers and scientists, discourage developed countries from accepting high-skilled immigrants from the Global South. Driving such policies is the assumption that in sourcing skilled labor from the Global South, developed countries would profit from developing countries' educational investments. Preventing high-skilled developing-country nationals from accessing employment opportunities that would utilize their skills, however, represents a serious loss for developed countries and – most importantly – skilled would-be migrants. The Global Skills Partnership concept creates a true triple win out of this scenario by asking developed countries to fund vocational-training programs in the Global South (Clemens 2014). Those graduates that choose to migrate would fill important skill gaps in the Global North at relatively low cost, while non-migrant graduates would contribute to skill stocks in the Global South. The ILM Program has discussed the feasibility of this intervention with several labor origin and labor destination countries as a fairly simple policy adjustment that creates important education, employment and labor-market improvement opportunities.

Institutional alignment: Intermediation for overseas employment in Tunisia and Morocco – from diagnostic to practice

The ILM Program identified a 2008 French-Tunisian bilateral labor agreement (Government of France 2008) as an ambitious and innovative tool for joint migration management with strong potential to support circular-migration schemes through triple-win development outcomes. However, the agreement's incomplete implementation and resultant unfulfilled potential instigated an in-depth review of the policy in conjunction with French and Tunisian counterparts during the course of 2012. This review identified implementation challenges rooted in institutional misalignments, and these findings subsequently informed labor-mobility intermediation efforts in other migration corridors, including those between Morocco and Germany.

The government of Morocco expressed interest in developing public institutional mechanisms for supporting individuals who chose to pursue overseas-employment opportunities, while simultaneously protecting their safety and potential to access human-development gains. To support these efforts, the ILM Program examined how public-intermediation services could be strengthened, how the functioning of bilateral agreements and other mobility programs could be improved, how market-assessment capacities and marketing strategies could be better developed, how the regulatory framework for private international-recruitment services could be restructured, and how protection mechanisms for overseas workers might be established. Following this analysis, the ILM team held regular discussions with the Moroccan and German governments aimed at translating these institutional diagnostics and recommendations into practice. These efforts materialized into a planned capacity-building pilot program in the hospitality and tourism sectors, where acute labor shortages are already evident in Germany and where supply-side synergies can be found in Morocco. The pilot program's outcome will not only demonstrate the potential for a large-scale labor-mobility scheme, but also provide an opportunity for Morocco to evaluate its improvements in migration-intermediation services.

Perception biases: Labor Integration Network of Cities and Urban Planners (LINC-UP)

The vast majority of international migrants move to cities, which offer more opportunities for employment and stronger social support networks than can be found in non-urban areas. Therefore, local authorities in these cities have a significant role to play in shaping communities that welcome migrants, for instance, by encouraging positive perceptions, facilitating access to labor markets and fostering social cohesion. LINC-UP convenes local leaders, academics, practitioners and employers to identify successful local-integration solutions and disseminate them throughout destination communities. Communities committed to the successful integration of migrants will reap economic and social benefits for themselves, labor origin communities and incoming migrants. The ILM Program is committed to helping community leaders identify strategies to realize these potential triple-win benefits.

This select sample of the ILM Program's activities demonstrates how efforts to tackle the three types of labor-mobility barriers can both improve and increase labor migration flows for the benefit of all parties involved. The informed design and coordinated review of policies that determine flows, the alignment of institutions that govern mobility processes, and the reduction of perceptional biases that prevent optimal migrant integration can all help realize the tremendous potential for economic and human development inherent in labor mobility.

References

Clemens, Michael A. "Global Skill Partnerships: A Proposal for Technical Training in a Mobile World." *CGD Policy Paper 40*. Washington, D.C.: Center for Global Development, 2014.

Government of France. Protocole Relatif A La Gestion Concertee des Migrations entre Le Gouvernement de la Republique Francaise et Le Gouvernement de la Republique Tunisienne, April 28, 2008. www.immigration-professionnelle.gouv.fr/sites/default/files/fckupload/TUNISIE%20-%20Protocole%20gestion%20des%20migrations.pdf.

Hamilton, Bob, and John Whalley. "Efficiency and Distributional Implications of Global Restrictions on Labour Mobility: Calculations and Policy Implications." *Journal of Development Economics* (14) 1: 61–75, 1984.

IMF (International Monetary Fund). "The End of Cheap Labor." *Finance and Development* (50) 2: 37–39, 2013.

World Bank. *Shaping the Future: A Long-Term Perspective of People and Job Mobility for the Middle East and North Africa*. Washington, D.C.: World Bank, 2009.

Approaches in Promoting Ethical Recruitment and Fair Migration

Lara White, Clara Pascual de Vargas

Rapid globalization, technological advances and demographic challenges have led to the emergence of a global labor market, with an unprecedented number of employers seeking workers internationally to fill labor gaps in all sectors and skill levels. Whether performed by temporary employment agencies, public employment services (PES), recruitment agents or employers themselves, recruitment intermediaries play an important role in facilitating labor migration. Indeed, it can be argued that in most cases, recruitment is the first step in the labor-migration process. When operating transparently and ethically, recruitment intermediaries minimize labor mismatches and facilitate labor mobility, thereby creating economic-development gains for migrants, as well as for their countries and communities of origin, through remittance transfers, and for employers in countries of destination.

However, unethical recruitment, including practices such as document retention or the imposition of excessive fees for recruitment services, can constitute labor exploitation and may lead to further abuse of migrant workers. It also brings negative consequences for governments, including the erosion of the integrity of immigration systems and a "race to the bottom" for domestic labor markets through downward pressure on wages and working conditions in destination countries. From a business perspective, unethical recruitment practices can precipitate reputational damage and, in some cases, lead to civil and criminal liability. Additionally, unethical recruitment can result in decreased worker productivity and skills mismatching, especially when workers are selected based upon their ability to pay recruitment fees rather than through competency-based hiring.

In response, many governments have attempted to regulate recruitment intermediaries using different approaches, ranging from basic licensing requirements to more robust frameworks that are linked to immigration and emigration management. Non-governmental actors have also created nonbinding guidance for the private sector on ethical recruitment practices, such as the Dhaka Principles for Migration with Dignity. Complementing these approaches, private-sector actors have worked to address unethical recruitment through industry-led codes of conduct and other self-regulatory initiatives requiring ethical recruitment practices within supply chains. However, despite these efforts, there is a lack of global policy coherence related to international recruitment, which creates governance gaps that leave migrant workers vulnerable to human rights violations and abuses as well as an uneven playing field for industry leaders who champion ethical recruitment.

Responding to the need to mobilize labor-migration stakeholders to address this problem, the International Organization for Migration (IOM) and partners launched the Public Private Alliance for Fair and Ethical Recruitment (PPA) to promote ethical international labor recruitment and thereby increase the transparency of the recruitment industry. The PPA is a forum for employers, recruitment intermediaries, governments, civil society organizations and other stakeholders to develop practical operational tools to address this issue. The first such tool is the International Recruitment Integrity System (IRIS), a certification system that enables employers to identify recruitment intermediaries who share a similar commitment to fair recruitment and labor practices.

This paper will discuss the main challenges in tackling unethical international recruitment, underscoring the need for global policy coherence among stakeholders and a coordinated multistakeholder approach to complement government regulation.

Types of recruitment intermediaries

Recruitment intermediaries include a variety of actors whose differences lie primarily in the types of services they provide and the nature of the relationship established with the workers. Recruitment intermediaries are commonly divided into:

1. Recruitment agents or agencies are any natural or legal person who provides services to match job seekers with offers of, or applications for, employment, without being party to the employment relationship.
2. Employment agents or agencies are any natural or legal person who employs workers with a view to making them available to a third-party end-user enterprise. These entities are often considered to be the employer of record under relevant employment legislation, thereby creating a triangular relationship between workers, agencies and employers.
3. Employers may also perform their own recruitment services without the use of any external intermediaries.
4. Informal recruitment intermediaries or sub agents are private-sector agents who may be involved in the provision of recruitment services. These intermediaries are often unregistered or unlicensed and may include family or community members, former or current employees, travel agencies and migrant associations.
5. Public employment services (PES) are employment services funded by governments that may offer a variety of labor-market programs, including job-matching or employment-referral services.

The labor-migration process may also involve other intermediaries – such as travel agents, language schools, vocational-training academies and medical clinics – with whom recruitment intermediaries often coordinate along with other service providers. While it is noted that these entities may charge fees, thereby increasing the overall costs of migration for the worker, the efforts described in this paper focus on the services that are directly related to job-matching between workers and their overseas employers.

What is ethical recruitment?

There are several key instruments in international law, notably from the International Labour Organization (ILO), that help identify benchmarks of ethical recruitment. Consistent with the U.N. Guiding Principles on Business and Human Rights, recruitment intermediaries should respect all applicable laws and have in place policies and procedures, including due diligence, to ensure that their recruitment activities are conducted in a manner that treats migrant workers with dignity and respect, free from harassment or any form of coercion or inhumane treatment. Additionally, the following key principles are recognized by stakeholders as being cornerstones of ethical recruitment practice:

1. *Prohibition of forced labor and human trafficking.* Recruitment intermediaries should neither promote nor use forced labor, human trafficking or any other slavery-like practice. To ensure compliance, they should establish measures of due diligence in their supply chain. Today, the two main international instruments on the eradication of forced labor and human trafficking are the Forced Labour Convention, 1930 (C029) – as well as the protocol and recommendation adopted in 2014, which specifically address recruitment practices – and the U.N. Protocol to Prevent, Suppress and Punish Trafficking in Persons, Especially Women and Children.

2. *Prohibition of recruitment fees to job seekers.* Excessive fee-charging is an indicator of forced labor linked to debt bondage. Workers, especially within the lower-skilled occupations where supply outweighs demand, are often required to pay fees to secure employment. When unable to pay these fees up front, loans from banks or informal lending networks, or from the recruiter or employer themselves, are administered with unfavorable repayment schedules that essentially bind workers to their employment. This, in turn, increases worker vulnerability to employment-related exploitation and abuse, as workers are less able to report workplace or employment violations due to their debt-repayment obligations. This is especially the case with migrant workers whose immigration status is linked to their employment through single-employer work permits. The Private Employment Agencies Convention, 1997 (C181) explicitly prohibits the charging of any fees to workers, and a similar provision is included in the EU Directive on Temporary Agency Work.

3. *Respect for freedom of movement.* Recruitment intermediaries should ensure that migrant workers are not required to provide a monetary deposit or other collateral as a condition of employment and are not subject to the destruction, confiscation or withholding of identity documents, wages or other personal belongings. Identified as an indicator of forced labor, document retention limits the free mobility of workers, including their ability to leave abusive working relationships. Although sometimes justified as retention for "safekeeping," the confiscation of passports by agents or employers is illegal, as the said document is considered to be the property of the issuing government. The right to freedom of movement is established in different international instruments, including the

Approaches in Promoting Ethical Recruitment and Fair Migration

Universal Declaration of Human Rights and the International Covenant on Civil and Political Rights.

4. *Respect for the right of freedom of association and collective bargaining.* Freedom of association and collective bargaining is well rooted in international labor-rights instruments, including the ILO Declaration on Fundamental Principles and Rights at Work. In order to help ensure that foreign workers are guaranteed the same labor rights as nationals, recruitment intermediaries should not interfere with migrant workers' rights to worker representation.

5. *Respect for decent work and accommodations.* Recruitment intermediaries should take appropriate measures to ensure that migrant workers enjoy safe and decent work. In addition, when they provide accommodation to migrant workers, they should make sure that these are safe, clean and hygienic. The right of migrant workers to safe and hygienic conditions has been compiled in the Dhaka Principles for Migration with Dignity.

6. *Respect for transparency of terms and conditions of employment.* Recruitment intermediaries should ensure that, prior to deployment, migrant workers are provided with written contracts in a language each worker understands, detailing the terms and conditions of employment including but not limited to the nature of the work to be undertaken, rates of pay and pay arrangements, working hours, vacation and other leave, and all other lawful deductions from pay and benefits of employment in accordance with national law. Additionally, the contract should not be substituted for one of less-favorable conditions upon deployment. The newly adopted Forced Labour (Supplementary Measures) Recommendation, 2014 (R203) specifically states that "the relevant information on the terms and conditions of employment should be specified in an appropriate, verifiable and easily understandable manner, and preferably through written contracts in accordance with national laws, regulations or collective agreements."

7. *Respect for equal treatment and non-discrimination.* The principle of non-discrimination and equal treatment is recognized in various international human-rights instruments, such as the International Covenant on Economic, Social and Cultural Rights, and several ILO conventions, including the Discrimination (Employment and Occupation) Convention, 1958 (C111) and the Equal Remuneration Convention, 1951 (C100). Consistent with these instruments, recruitment intermediaries should treat migrant workers without discrimination on the basis of race, color, sex, religion, political opinion, national extraction, social origin, sexual orientation, age, disability or any other form of unlawful and unethical discrimination covered by national law and practice.

8. *Respect for confidentiality and data protection.* Respect for personal data is a principle enshrined in most national legal frameworks and referenced in the Private Employment Agencies Convention, 1997 (C181). Therefore, ethical recruitment intermediaries should not record, in files or registers, personal data that are not required for judging the aptitude of migrant workers for jobs for which they are being or could be considered, or that are required to facilitate their deployment. Additionally, recruiters must ensure that all personal data that they collect, receive, use, transfer or store is treated as strictly confidential and shall not be communicated to any third party without the prior written approval of the worker.

9. *Respect for access to remedy.* Access to effective remedies is one of the three pillars of the United Nations' "Protect, Respect and Remedy" Framework for Business and Human

Rights. Still, access to state-based mechanisms are particularly challenging for migrant workers due to language and cultural differences as well as immigration status. Ethical recruitment intermediaries should ensure that migrant workers have effective access to remedy, as provided by law, and to effective operational-level grievance mechanisms in relation to their recruitment activities without fear of recrimination, reprisal or dismissal.

Current international efforts in promoting ethical recruitment

ILO conventions and instruments have been adopted to guide governments in regulating recruitment intermediaries. The most important are the above-mentioned Private Employment Agencies Convention, 1997 (C181) (specific to the private recruitment and employment industry) and Forced Labour Convention, 1930 (C029), with its protocol and recommendation. Additionally, the Domestic Workers Convention, 2011 (C189) specifically addresses the recruitment and employment of domestic workers, requiring signatories to ensure that domestic workers are covered by minimum wage statutes, have fair terms of employment, are given transparent written contracts, and have access to remedy. Finally, the ILO has also recently launched the Fair Recruitment Initiative, which aims at preventing human trafficking, protecting the rights of workers – including migrant workers – from abusive and fraudulent practices during the recruitment and placement process.

Within the European context, the EU Directive on Temporary Agency Work applies to temporary employment agencies and guarantees a minimum level of protection to temporary workers, such as prohibiting the charging of recruitment fees to workers. Additionally, the Council of Europe's European Convention on the Legal Status of Migrant Workers provides minimum standards on labor and human rights for migrant workers, such as a guarantee of equal treatment with nationals, support for the principles of non-discrimination and freedom of association, and the provision of access to redress mechanisms.

Finally, in the South Asian regional context, the Association of Southeast Asian Nations (ASEAN) adopted the Declaration on the Protection and Promotion of the Rights of Migrant Workers, which calls on origin and destination countries to promote the fundamental rights of migrant workers and their families already residing in the destination country. This includes obligations for countries of origin to regulate recruitment practices and eliminate unethical practices, as well as calling on countries of destination to facilitate access to effective remedies for migrant workers.

National good practices on ethical recruitment regulation

The United Kingdom of Great Britain and Northern Ireland

Responding to abuses in the fresh-produce supply chain (agriculture, horticulture, shellfish gathering and food processing and packaging industries), the Gangmasters Licensing Authority (GLA) was created to protect workers in these industries from exploitation by regulating

Approaches in Promoting Ethical Recruitment and Fair Migration

businesses that provide recruitment and employment services. The Authority's licensing scheme ensures that these labor providers are compliant with employment standards. Registered companies are audited against GLA licensing standards, which cover elements such as fee-charging, health and safety, pay, accommodation, transport and training. Non-compliance can result in licence revocation and the public naming of revoked licensees on an openly published list. While this initiative has been applauded for its rigorous approach, which has resulted in improved working conditions for vulnerable workers in these sectors, the limitations of its mandate have raised concerns that recruitment intermediaries operating in other affected sectors, including hospitality and construction, remain under-regulated.

Canada

In the Canadian context, the regulation of recruitment intermediaries falls under provincial, rather than federal, jurisdiction. As a result of allegations of recruitment-related abuses of migrant workers, several provinces have enacted legislation to regulate the activities of intermediaries involved in overseas recruitment. Manitoba's Worker Recruitment and Protection Act of 2008 addresses the vulnerabilities of migrant workers by licensing recruitment intermediaries and requiring employers of foreign workers to be registered by provincial authorities. Licensees are required to pay a CAD 10,000 bond and are forbidden from charging fees to job seekers. Employers are required to pay any related recruitment fees and are held liable for the actions of the recruitment intermediaries they engage with.

The Philippines

As a major country of origin for workers, the Philippines has taken an institutional approach toward protecting its citizens who seek overseas employment, including through the regulation of recruitment intermediaries. The Migrant Workers and Overseas Filipino Act of 1995 grants a mandate to the Philippine Overseas Employment Administration (POEA) to license and regulate private recruitment and employment agents by, for example, prescribing the types of fees that recruitment intermediaries can charge to job seekers and limiting these fees to a maximum of one month's salary. Agents must submit to inspections as part of the registration process and during their licensure. Non-compliance may result in sanction or the denial of an initial or renewal licence.

Industry-driven and civil society initiatives to promote ethical recruitment practices

Industry groups representing private employment and recruitment agencies have made efforts to promote the integrity of their members. Representing 49 national federations and eight large staffing companies, the International Confederation of Private Employment Agencies (Ciett) has a code of conduct that prohibits fee-charging to job seekers and requires respect for laws and transparency in the terms of employment. Taking a regional approach, the

Alliance of Asian Associations of Overseas Employment Service Providers adopted a Commitment to Action in Pursuit of Ethical Recruitment and a Joint Statement in Pursuit of Ethical Recruitment to bolster its members' support for ethical recruitment practices.

Civil society organizations have also created nonbinding tools and guidelines to support the promotion of ethical recruitment in the context of safe and fair migration. The Institute for Human Rights and Business launched the Dhaka Principles for Migration with Dignity in 2012, which are based upon international human and labor rights standards and draw on the U.N. Guiding Principles on Business and Human Rights. The Dhaka Principles call for no fees to be charged to migrant workers, clear and transparent contracts, no retention of identity documents or passports, and access to remedy for violations. Similarly, Verité and ManpowerGroup (a not-for-profit organization and a multinational employment agency, respectively), jointly released a strategic document in 2012 (An Ethical Framework for Cross-Border Labor Recruitment) that outlines the main issues and risks of engaging with unethical recruitment intermediaries and provides mitigation strategies designed for employers. Additionally, Verité has pioneered an online Fair Hiring Toolkit that offers open-source tools and guidance for governments, multinational brands, suppliers and auditors to support the ethical recruitment and hiring of migrant workers.

Limitations of current approaches

Despite these efforts to regulate and reform recruitment practices, there remain regulatory and enforcement gaps throughout the world. Regarding regulation, the primary weakness relates to the absence of any comprehensive legal frameworks in many countries. When existing, these regulations often apply only to certain recruitment intermediaries and do not extend throughout the labor supply chain to the subagent or informal intermediaries. Furthermore, there are enforcement gaps due in part to insufficient resourcing, but also due to the extraterritorial nature of recruitment activities that span multiple jurisdictions. In the absence of bilateral or multilateral agreements, the ability to enforce regulations across countries of origin and destination is impeded. Additionally, many regulatory enforcement mechanisms are complaint-driven rather than reliant on regular inspections. While this can be a way to balance the administrative burden of inspection and avoid "over-regulation," investigations are consequently triggered by the complaints of migrant workers who are often not empowered to seek remedy for multiple reasons, including language or literacy limitations as well as fear of deportation of and/or retribution against themselves or their family members.

Concerning industry-driven and civil society efforts, although they provide very useful guidance for private-sector entities in self-regulation, the inherent absence of enforcement in nonbinding tools constitutes an important limitation. Critics have also cited the weakness of self-regulatory monitoring systems due to flawed practices, such as "checklist" mentalities, pre-announced audits and poor or nonexistent access to remedy.

In this context, it is difficult to differentiate bona fide intermediaries from mala fide ones. This is especially the case for small and medium-sized end-user employers with limited human-resources expertise to identify transparent and accountable counterparts transnationally.

Approaches in Promoting Ethical Recruitment and Fair Migration

Furthermore, while the negative outcomes endemic to unethical recruitment practices are more acute in certain countries or regions than others, due to the cross-border nature of international labor recruitment, the issue remains a global problem.

IRIS: an innovative approach

The International Organization for Migration (IOM), together with the International Organisation of Employers (IOE) and a coalition of stakeholders committed to ethical recruitment, is developing a certification system known as the International Recruitment Integrity System (IRIS). IRIS aims to fulfill three objectives: 1) promote the work of recruitment intermediaries who are committed to a business model based on fair recruitment practices; 2) enable employers and recruitment intermediaries to recognize like-minded partners who share their commitment to fair recruitment and labor practices, as well as mitigate their risk of labor exploitation in their global operations; and 3) complement and support government, private-sector and civil society efforts to regulate recruitment intermediaries and foster international coherence of ethical recruitment practices consistent with the U.N. "Protect, Respect and Remedy" Framework for Business and Human Rights.

The overarching goal of the International Recruitment Integrity System (IRIS) is to bring transformative change to areas of the recruitment industry pertaining to cross-border recruitment, particularly where the business model is largely based on excessive fee-charging and exploitation of migrant workers. It will do so through the creation of a level playing field that promotes good practice and encourages a labor market free from exploitation and labor abuses.

The IRIS certification process is anchored by a code of conduct and an operational protocol, both of which are firmly rooted in internationally recognized human rights and labor standards, including relevant U.N. and ILO instruments. The code of conduct establishes benchmarks for fair and ethical labor recruitment, while the operational protocol provides certifiable performance indicators for recruitment intermediaries. IRIS is being developed and piloted in several phases, which will ultimately lead to its independence as a self-governing entity. IRIS is also being closely coordinated with the ILO's Fair Recruitment Initiative.

By supporting ethical practice and mitigating risks of labor exploitation linked to abusive practices that have been employed by part of the recruitment industry, IRIS will benefit migrant workers and lower the costs of migration. Furthermore, by bridging regulatory enforcement gaps, IRIS will help governments better regulate transborder recruitment activities and protect labor-migration programs. Finally, companies committed to ethical recruitment and fair labor principles will be better equipped to reduce reputational and legal risks related to unethical recruitment practices.

Challenges for the development and the implementation of IRIS

IRIS will first be tested in a pilot phase in specific labor-migration corridors involving committed governments, initially focusing on jurisdictions that have existing regulatory frameworks.

These pilots will involve private-sector counterparts from identified sectors, including ones that involve higher- and lower-skilled occupations as well as ones that are multinationals and small and medium-sized enterprises. The goal is to test the IRIS certification system and its monitoring and compliance mechanism to ensure that they uphold the principles of ethical recruitment entrenched in the IRIS code of conduct with measurable integrity gains. IRIS will need to balance operational efficiency while maintaining the integrity of a robust certification system.

How will IRIS succeed in promoting ethical recruitment?

The majority of approaches to promoting ethical recruitment practice have focused on exposing bad actors within the recruitment industry or on punitive action, as is the case with most national regulatory frameworks. However, these methods give no visibility to those doing a good job. Ideally, IRIS will focus on creating a community of best practice by acknowledging industry leaders that follow an ethical recruitment business model. Also, by highlighting these good examples, IRIS will create aspirational goals for other recruitment intermediaries to follow.

On a different note, companies' interest in the promotion of ethical recruitment and transparency in the recruitment industry has been fueled by several pieces of influential legislation on supply-chain transparency. In the United States, two pieces of legislation have been adopted to address companies' obligations to ensure the absence of human trafficking and forced labor in their supply chains. The California Transparency in Supply Chains Act of 2010 imposes obligations on companies to disclose their efforts to eradicate slavery and human trafficking within their global supply chains. Executive Order 13627 (strengthening Protections Against Trafficking in Persons in Federal Contracts) of 2012 addresses unethical recruitment practices in public procurement by prohibiting federal contractors from charging fees to job seekers or confiscating identity documents. IRIS will enable companies to demonstrate adherence to these regulatory efforts by identifying reliable intermediaries committed to ethical recruitment.

As a certification process, how will IRIS find the right balance between integrity and administrative burden?

The legitimacy of any certification system rests mainly on the credibility of its operational procedures, including the eligibility criteria for membership and compliance measures that ensure adherence to these criteria. Certification schemes have been criticized for their lack of capacity to assess companies' performance in the long term. On the one hand, ongoing performance assessments can create financial and administrative burdens. In today's proliferation of certification schemes of various modalities covering a range of issues, companies are increasingly being asked to comply with auditing obligations. In addition, most of the current certification schemes based on an auditing system are not adapted to the needs of small and medium-sized enterprises and can impose heavy burdens on companies with fewer resources.

Approaches in Promoting Ethical Recruitment and Fair Migration

On the other hand, concerns have also been raised about the methodologies used. For example, auditing based on short, pre-announced visits or solely on desk review have proved to be insufficient to assess companies' performance in the protection of workers' human and labor rights, and they have failed to expose major labor violations in supply chains. Often, consulting companies offering auditing services to review companies' performance on social-sustainability indicators lack the capacity to assess the complexities of human trafficking and forced labor.

IRIS will need to explore a balance between robust certification with strict monitoring requirements and a system that is accessible to smaller actors and tailored to the variety of recruitment intermediaries. A system built on company reporting and a thorough examination of practices, as well as complemented by continuous feedback from workers, should be explored. Embedding alternative information sources on companies' performance into the certification and monitoring processes should also be examined to build a mechanism that is able to rely less on traditional auditing schemes and more on alternative monitoring mechanisms. These should be based on dialogue with workers and their representatives as well as with other players, such as labor attachés of countries of origin and civil society organizations.

In this regard, trade unions and worker advocacy groups can play an important role by assisting migrant workers in exercising their legal rights and seeking redress when necessary. These groups can bolster IRIS by acting as the "eyes and ears on the ground" of the system to ensure compliance with the certification process. In particular, collaboration with NGOs can help facilitate ongoing communication with migrant communities.

How will IRIS foster international cooperation between origin and destination countries?

While IRIS's primary objective is to enable businesses to better identify recruitment intermediaries that are committed to ethical recruitment, IRIS also seeks to complement government regulatory efforts in addressing the lack of coherence among national instruments as well as the absence of an international framework. The nature of international recruitment processes is steeped in extraterritorial challenges. The difficulty in establishing serial liability of corporations, both in terms of their supply chains and the multinational nature of their operations, has been the object of extensive debate in recent years. As examined earlier, even when countries have enacted national legislation to regulate the activities of recruitment intermediaries, a lack of international cooperation between countries of origin and destination can hinder efforts to effectively enforce the law.

In its initial pilot phase, IRIS will harmonize efforts from countries of origin and destination that have existing regulatory frameworks, with companies that demonstrate solid commitment to ethical recruitment principles. In creating a level playing field that rewards good actors in the recruitment industry, IRIS seeks to consolidate support for fair practice and an ethical recruitment business model that is predicated on the protection of labor rights and a marked reduction in exploitation and abuse within the recruitment industry.

References

Colombo Process. Achievements 2014. www.colomboprocess.org/About_the_Colombo_Process_Achievements-5a-4.html.

Colombo Process. Objectives 2014. www.colomboprocess.org/About_the_Colombo_Process_Objectives-5a-3.html.

AAAOESP (Alliance of Asian Associations of Overseas Employment Service Providers). "Commitment to Action in Pursuit of Ethical Recruitment." IOM Regionale Workshop, Organizing the Association of Employment Agencies in Asia: Moving forward to Action on Ethical Recruitment, 2008.

Agunias, Dovelyn Rannveig. "Guiding the Invisible Hand: Making Migration Intermediaries Work for Development." *UNDP Human Development Research Paper* 2009/22. New York: UNDP, 2009. http://hdr.undp.org/sites/default/files/hdrp_2009_22.pdf.

Agunias, Dovelyn Rannveig. "What We Know about Regulating the Recruitment of Migrant Workers." *Migration Policy Brief*, September 2013. Washington, D.C.: Migration Policy Institute, 2013. www.migrationpolicy.org/research/what-we-know-regulating-recruitment-migrant-workers.

Amnesty International. "False Promises: Exploitation and Forced Labour of Nepalese Migrant Workers." London: Amnesty International, 2011. www.amnesty.org/en/library/asset/ASA31/007/2011/en/b58f0185-455d-425c-bc4f-d6b7fe309524/asa310072011en.pdf.

ASEAN (Association of Southeast Asian Nations). "ASEAN Declaration on the Protection and Promotion of the Rights of Migrant Workers." January 2007. www.asean.org/communities/asean-political-security-community/item/asean-declaration-on-the-protection-and-promotion-of-the-rights-of-migrant-workers-3.

BSR (Business for Social Responsibility). "International Labor Migration: A Responsible Role for Business." Washington, D.C.: BSR, 2008. www.bsr.org/reports/BSR_LaborMigrationRoleforBusiness.pdf.

C029: Forced Labour Convention, June 28, 1930. www.ilo.org/dyn/normlex/en/f?p=1000:12100:0::NO::P12100_ILO_CODE:C029.

C100: Equal Remuneration Convention, June 29, 1951. www.ilo.org/dyn/normlex/en/f?p=NORMLEXPUB:12100:0::NO:12100:P12100_INSTRUMENT_ID:312245:NO.

C105: Abolition of Forced Labour Convention, June 25, 1957. www.ilo.org/dyn/normlex/en/f?p=1000:55:0::NO::P55_TYPE,P55_LANG,P55_DOCUMENT,P55_NODE:CON,en,C105,%2FDocument.

C111: Discrimination (Employment and Occupation) Convention, June 25, 1958. www.ilo.org/dyn/normlex/en/f?p=NORMLEXPUB:12100:0::NO:12100:P12100_INSTRUMENT_ID:312256:NO.

C181: Private Employment Agencies Convention, June 19, 1997. www.ilo.org/dyn/normlex/en/f?p=NORMLEXPUB:55:0:::55:P55_TYPE,P55_LANG,P55_DOCUMENT,P55_NODE:CON,en,C181,/Document.

C189: Domestic Workers Convention, June 16, 2011. www.ilo.org/dyn/normlex/en/f?p=1000:12100:0::NO::P12100_ILO_CODE:C189.

California Transparency in Supply Chains Act of 2010. Cal. Civ. Code § 1714.43 (West 2013).

Ciett (International Confederation of Private Employment Agencies). Code of Conduct. www.ciett.org/index.php?id=6.

Ciett. Membership Overview. www.ciett.org/index.php?id=6.

Ciett. Mission and Objectives. www.ciett.org/index.php?id=35.

Clean Clothes Campaign. "Looking for a Quick Fix: How Weak Social Auditing is Keeping Workers in Sweatshops." Amsterdam: Clean Clothes Campaign, 2005. http://digitalcommons.ilr.cornell.edu/cgi/viewcontent.cgi?article=2077&context=globaldocs.

European Convention on the Legal Status of Migrant Workers, November 24, 1977. http://conventions.coe.int/Treaty/en/Treaties/Html/093.htm.

Exec. Order No. 13627, 3 C.F.R. 13627, September 25, 2012.

EU Council Directive 2008/104/EC, 2008 O.J. (L 327) 9.

Gangmasters Licensing Authority. Mission Statement. July 22, 2013. http://gla.defra.gov.uk/Who-We-Are/Mission-Statement/.

IHRB (Institute for Human Rights and Business). "About the Dhaka Principles." London: IHRB, 2014. www.dhaka-principles.org.

IHRB. "Fees and IDs: Tackling Recruitment Fees and Confiscation of Workers' Passports." London: IHRB, September 2013. www.ihrb.org/pdf/2013-09-06_IHRB_Fees-and-IDs-Report.pdf.

IHRB. "Principles for the Responsible Recruitment and Employment of Migrant Workers." London: IHRB, 2014. www.dhaka-principles.org.

IHRB et al. "The Future of the Gangmasters Licensing Authority and the Employment Agencies Standards Inspectorate: Better regulation for worker protection – Proposal for a common position." London: IHRB, 2011. http://business-humanrights.org/en/uk-gangmasters-licensing-authoritys-remit-should-be-extended-to-more-sectors-in-order-to-improve-labour-standards-enforcement-argues-kate-wareing-of-oxfam#c60285.

ILO (International Labour Organization). 'Towards a Fair Deal for Migrant Workers in the Global Economy." Geneva: ILO Publications, 2004. www.ilo.org/public/english/standards/relm/ilc/ilc92/pdf/rep-vi.pdf.

ILO. "ILO Indicators of Forced Labour." Geneva: ILO Publications, 2012. www.ilo.org/sapfl/Informationresources/Factsheetsandbrochures/WCMS_203832/lang--en/index.htm.

ILRWG (International Labor Recruitment Working Group). "The American Dream Up for Sale: A Blueprint for Ending International Labor Recruitment Abuse." Washington, D.C.: ILRWG, 2013. http://fairlaborrecruitment.files.wordpress.com/2013/01/final-e-version-ilrwg-report.pdf.

Locke, Richard, Qin Fei and Brause Alberto. "Does Monitoring Improve Labor Standards? Lessons from Nike." *Corporate Social Responsibility Initiative Working Paper* No. 24. Boston: Harvard University, 2006. www.hks.harvard.edu/m-rcbg/CSRI/publications/workingpaper_24_locke.pdf.

Migrant Workers and Overseas Filipino Act of 1995, Rep. Act No. 8042, O.G. 4994 (June 7, 1995) (Phil.).

R203: Forced Labour (Supplementary Measures) Recommendation, June 11, 2014. www.ilo.org/dyn/normlex/en/f?p=NORMLEXPUB:12100:0::NO::P12100_INSTRUMENT_ID:3174688.

Swing, William Lacy. "Statement, International Migrants Day – Migration, Development and Global Migration Governance." Geneva: International Organization for Migration, 2013. www.iom.int/cms/en/sites/iom/home/news-and-views/speeches/speech-listing/statement-international-migrants.html.

UN (United Nations General Assembly). Universal Declaration of Human Rights. December 10, 1948. 217 A (III). New York: UN, 1948. http://daccess-dds-ny.un.org/doc/RESOLUTION/GEN/NR0/043/88/IMG/NR004388.pdf?OpenElement.

UN. International Covenant on Civil and Political Rights. December 16, 1966. A/RES/2200 (XXI). www.un.org/documents/instruments/docs_en.asp?year=1969.

UN. International Covenant on Economic, Social and Cultural Rights. December 16, 1966. A/RES/2200 (XXI). New York: UN, 1996. www.un.org/documents/instruments/docs_en.asp?year=1969.

UN. International Convention on the Protection of the Rights of All Migrant Workers and their Families. December 18, 1990. A/RES/45/158. New York: UN, 1990. www.un.org/documents/instruments/docs_en.asp?year=1969.

UN. Convention Against Transnational Organized Crime and the Protocols Thereto, Protocol to Prevent, Suppress, and Punish Trafficking in Persons, Especially Women and Children. A/RES/55/25. Geneva/New York: OHCHR, 2000. www.un.org/documents/instruments/docs_en.asp?year=2000.

UNCTAD (United Nations Conference on Trade and Development). "Fair Trade Requirements." Geneva: UNCTAD, 2014. www.unctad.info/en/Sustainability-Claims-Portal/Discussion-Forum/Fair-Trade/.

UNHRC (United Nations Human Rights Council). Report of the Special Representative of the Secretary-General on the issue of human rights and transnational corporations and other business enterprises, John Ruggie. A/HRC/14/27. Geneva/New York: OHCHR, 2010.

UNHRC. Guiding Principles on Business and Human Rights: Implementing the United Nations "Protect, Respect and Remedy" Framework. A/HRC/17/31. Geneva/New York: OHCHR, 2011. www.ohchr.org/Documents/Publications/GuidingPrinciplesBusinessHR_EN.pdf.

United Nations Entity for Gender Equality and the Empowerment of Women. "Managing Labour Migration in ASEAN: Concerns for Women Migrant Workers." Bangkok: UN Women, 2013. http://imumi.org/attachments/26_1.pdf.

Verité. "Fair Hiring Toolkit." Amherst, MA: Verité, 2011. www.verite.org/helpwanted/toolkit.

Verité. "Help Wanted: Hiring, Human Trafficking, and Modern-Day Slavery in the Global Economy." Amherst, MA: Verité, 2010. www.verite.org/sites/default/files/images/Help_Wanted_2010.pdf.

Worker Recruitment and Protection Act, CCSM, cW197 (Can.).

Development-Oriented Labor Migration Programs and the Role of Non-Governmental Organizations: Examples from the German Centre for International Migration and Development (CIM)

Lotte Nordhus

Development-oriented approach to labor migration

The issue of labor-migration management and regulation is addressed within numerous policy fields with divergent interests and objectives, but perhaps most often within the areas of home affairs and international development. Elaborating and implementing a coherent migration and development policy[7] that creates "triple-win" situations, thus allowing migrants and their families, countries of origin and countries of destination to benefit from labor migration, is a highly challenging task for OECD countries and developing countries alike.

International labor migration to OECD countries is not only structured on the basis of existing legal and political frameworks, but is influenced to a great degree by socioeconomic and cultural factors. The development-oriented regulation of migratory movements calls for a comprehensive and transversal approach that takes into account complex migration decisions and processes, global interconnections created by migrants, and a wide variety of actors in the field of migration, especially non-governmental (migrant) organizations. In this context, the Centre for International Migration and Development (CIM), a joint operation of the Deutsche Gesellschaft für Internationale Zusammenarbeit (GIZ) and the German Federal Employment Agency (BA), has created several tools for fostering the development potential associated with international migration. The Centre's core services involve placing managers and technical experts in positions worldwide and offering advice and support on migration issues. CIM works in partnership with countries of origin and in close cooperation with migrant organizations.

This paper will first examine a CIM pilot project called "Strengthening the Development Potential of the EU Mobility Partnership in Georgia through Targeted Circular Migration and Diaspora Mobilization," which serves as an example of a program seeking the fair regulation

---

7   In the 2013 EU report on policy coherence for development (PCD), migration policy is mentioned as one of five major challenges for PCD. PCD is understood as the avoidance of negative consequences and the use of positive spillovers and potentials for development within poor countries when designing domestic policies and pursuing domestic policy objectives (European Commission 2013: 16).

of migration. The project implements various migration and development tools derived from German development-cooperation institutions. Second, the paper will explore types of involvement and various potential roles played by non-governmental organizations (NGOs) in the field of migration and development, using CIM project experiences as a point of reference.

Fair migration management in EU mobility partnerships: The example of Georgia

The pilot project "Strengthening the Development Potential of the EU Mobility Partnership in Georgia" seeks to implement a comprehensive, development-oriented approach to labor migration with the objective of creating triple-win situations similar to those achieved in several of GIZ's other current health-sector pilot projects (GIZ 2014). In contrast to other triple-win projects, the project with Georgia is embedded within the framework of an EU mobility partnership (MP) that Georgia concluded in 2009 (GAMM 2014).

Despite significant steps by the Georgian government toward the establishment of an effective and sustainable migration policy, support is still needed with regard to providing implementation of the MP with a development orientation. The joint German-Georgian pilot project was initiated with the aim of enabling Georgia to harness the MP's development potential. It provides migration-policy advice for Georgian policymakers and implements a pilot circular-migration program, thereby differing from other programs lacking a specific focus on implementation. Moreover, the project examines ways to use labor migration more effectively for development purposes and will identify good practices worthy of replication elsewhere and will formulate guidelines for other EU mobility partnerships. Running from 2013 to 2016, it is funded by the European Commission through the Thematic Program for Migration and Asylum, with additional financing provided by the German Federal Ministry for Economic Cooperation and Development. It is jointly implemented by CIM, the Secretariat of the State Commission on Migration Issues hosted by the Georgian Public Service Development Agency (PSDA), and the Georgian Small and Medium Enterprises Association (GSMEA). Specific project activities include:

- *The provision of migration-policy advice to relevant government institutions.* A long-term expert from Germany has been placed with the Georgian State Commission on Migration Issues (SCMI). The placement was effected through CIM's "integrated experts" instrument, which recruits and places qualified European experts with local employers according to local demand and provides income supplements to these experts in order to "top up" their local salaries.
- *The design and implementation of a pilot circular-migration scheme.* With the aim of preventing brain drain and putting the triple-win approach into practice, CIM has implemented a pilot-migration program for Georgian professionals migrating to Germany in cooperation with the PSDA. This has included careful labor-market analysis; a needs assessment with regard to occupations, competences and qualifications; and active matching between demand in the German labor market and supply in Georgia. The analysis identified health care and hospitality as promising sectors for the circular migration of professionals moving from Georgia to Germany. Future project activities will focus on the management of all

phases of the migration cycle, from pre-departure training for selected candidates (language, profession-specific skills and intercultural competences) to job-placement services in Germany and ultimately support for the return and reintegration (see below) of up to 40 Georgian migrants (NB: Due to the pilot character of the project, the number of migrant participants is kept small).

- *Mobilization of the Georgian diaspora community for return, employment and entrepreneurship activities.* Under the auspices of the circular-migration program and other schemes, skilled Georgian diaspora-community members in Germany receive CIM support to return to Georgia for employment (receiving advice, job-placement services and salary subsidies through the "returning-experts" instrument) or to start their own businesses (receiving advice, start-up seminars and support in establishing a small or medium-sized enterprise through CIM's "migrants as entrepreneurs" scheme, conducted in cooperation with GSMEA). This project component seeks to promote knowledge transfer and private-sector development through return migration.

All project activities seek to enable a win-win-win situation. In this case, Georgian migrants gain professional and personal experiences in Germany as well as subsequent support in reintegrating into the Georgian economy; the German health and hospitality sectors are provided with skilled workers to help fill labor shortages; and the country of Georgia benefits from the knowledge transferred by returning migrants as well from the help of skilled professionals and migration-policy advice in creating a coherent migration policy. A manual on lessons learned through the program will facilitate the replication of best practices in the context of other EU mobility partnerships.

The "mobilizing diaspora for return" project component demonstrates that diaspora-community members and migrant organizations play an important role with regard to the success of the project in Georgia. Benefits for countries of origin, especially in terms of knowledge transfer, would be difficult to ensure without the mobilization of the diaspora community and the advantages provided by return migration. The crucial role of migrant organizations in creating beneficial migration situations for all parties involved is explored more deeply in the following section.

Roles of non-governmental organizations in fostering migration's development impacts

The field of migration is populated by a diverse collection of NGOs working on local, regional and international levels. An NGO's type (for more on this, see the typology identified by Banulescu-Bogdan 2011: 4), organizational structure and membership affect the role it can play in migration and development. Possible areas of activity may involve:
- Provision of legal or humanitarian services
- Training or capacity-building for migrants and their families
- Cultural and developmental activities in countries of origin
- Advocacy for migrants' rights
- Monitoring and evaluation of government policies

Development-Oriented Labor Migration Programs and the Role of NGOs

- Representation or expression of a collective voice, as provided by umbrella organizations (such as the Migrants' Rights Network or the African Diaspora Platform for Development)
- Policy formulation by working groups (such as the Civil Society Days of the Global Forum on Migration and Development)

Despite wide acknowledgement of the important roles played by NGOs in the migration- and development-policy spheres, and despite efforts to increase dialogue with these groups and include them in policy processes, participation by NGO and migrant organizations in policy development remains at an early stage (Newland 2005; Asquith 2013). Banulescu-Bogdan (2011) formulates several preconditions for the effective participation of NGOs, including the presence of a centralized organizational structure, continuous rather than ad hoc consultations, providing civil society groups with genuine responsibility within the process, and the provision of capacity-building training to civil society groups. Paul Asquith draws our attention to another relevant aspect: When conceptualizing the roles that NGOs and migrant organizations in particular can play, we need to consider "structural inequalities within civil society itself" (Asquith 2013: 11). For example, migrants' points of view and interests might not be reflected in dominant NGO positions on development policies. In order to include migrants in the design of development policy, adequate migrant representation has to be ensured even within civil society organizations. The following sections will present three types of roles that NGOs and specifically migrant organizations can play by citing illustrative project examples in the field of migration and development.

Dialogue and relations with Western Balkan diaspora organizations

Continuous dialogue marked by mutual trust between the government of the country of origin and its diaspora community helps increase diaspora organizations' influence in the area of development. However, this dialogue is often lacking. To address this issue, CIM has organized a series of workshops with relevant state and non-governmental institutions from the Western Balkans with the aim of increasing dialogue with this diaspora community and enhancing its development contributions. The workshop series enables participants to exchange experiences and good practices on issues such as implementing national migration strategies and creating institutions to support migration policy. The fourth regional workshop, which was scheduled to take place in 2014, was facilitated by CIM in cooperation with regional migrant organizations and was intended to specifically address migrant participation in policy processes. The workshop was designed to illustrate the importance of structured and continuous dialogue between governments and their diaspora communities in the development of migration policies. The event was intended to present options for increasing the development impact of remittances and for promoting knowledge transfer through temporary or permanent return.

The workshop series has resulted in the establishment of an informal regional network on migration and development. CIM has been functioning as a matchmaker between governments and diaspora groups, and the workshop results suggest that third-party involvement of this kind is helpful in initiating dialogue between governments and migrant organizations.

Capacity-building on migration and development issues

A further challenge with regard to maximizing the development impact of migration consists in mobilizing diaspora-community knowledge and resources in the form of concrete projects in countries of origin. CIM has supported migrant organizations' development activity by providing training, fostering the construction of networks and co-funding activities. These experiences have shown that close cooperation between these migrant organizations, local partners and other (governmental) development initiatives significantly increases the chances that a diaspora project will be sustainable and beneficial for countries of origin.

The partnership between the Philippines-based NGO Atikha and Philnetz, a Filipino diaspora organization within Germany, illustrates how cooperation of this kind can be used to build capacity and competences, thus enhancing migrants' role as development actors. Atikha provides advice and training to Filipino migrants on financial education and family issues, conducts training for local-government officials and rural banks, and does advocacy work on the national and regional levels. Philnetz is an organization that seeks to mobilize the Filipino diaspora in Germany for developmental projects in the Philippines as well as for cultural activities and advocacy work in Germany. The two organizations have jointly implemented a project called "Mobilizing Resources of Overseas Filipinos in Germany toward Green Economic Development in the Philippines" in close coordination with German development-cooperation institutions active in the Philippines. This project's activities focus on building capacity and competences among Filipino migrants in Germany and includes training for trainers, seminars for migrants on financial literacy and family support, and a forum on development-project options in the Philippines.

The Filipino NGO functions as a bridge-builder between diaspora members and their country of origin by providing information about the Philippines and development-project options. In addition, both Philnetz and Atikha provide education to migrants and actively work to mobilize diaspora-community members for development purposes.

Migrant organizations' involvement in global development processes

Cooperation between migrant-focused NGOs is important not only in the design of development projects, but also in supporting advocacy work and participation in policy processes. Joint agenda-setting and the creation of international networks linking migrant organizations have proved to be important factors in enabling voices to be heard in global processes, such as the U.N. High-level Dialogue on International Migration and Development (HLD) and the state-led, nonbinding Global Forum on Migration and Development (GFMD).

Migrant-focused NGOs in Germany play a limited role in global processes as compared to their peers elsewhere in Europe, particularly in countries such as the United Kingdom and the Netherlands. For this reason, CIM conducted a training session in 2013 with the aim of raising migrant organizations' awareness of global migration- and development-policy processes. This event served as a forum for the discussion of recent trends in migration and development policy as well as of examples and strategies from other European countries. Subsequently,

CIM, in conjunction with the Swiss Agency for Development and Cooperation (SDC) and the International Centre for Migration Policy Development (ICMPD), organized and facilitated the "Diaspora & Development Roundtable: Preparing for the 2013 UN High-Level Dialogue on International Migration and Development" (HLD 2013). This event was held in June 2013 in Eschborn. More than 70 members of the African, Latin American, European, Middle Eastern and Asian diaspora communities residing in Western Europe came together to discuss their role in global development processes (in particular, the post-2015 development framework) and to formulate policy recommendations. A member was chosen by means of a lottery to participate in a civil society hearing prior to the HLD 2013. The roundtable developed a number of recommendations for the HLD 2013, focusing on issues such as the recognition and visibility of the role of diaspora communities as development actors; the promotion of partnership and dialogue between states, intergovernmental bodies and diasporas; the funding of diaspora-community development activities; and the role of migrant women in peace-building and conflict-resolution efforts in their country of origin.

Conclusion

The joint project between CIM and Georgia demonstrates the importance of implementing a comprehensive development-oriented approach to migration in partnership with countries of origin, migrant organizations and diaspora communities. This form of cooperation can help make migration beneficial for all parties involved. The projects that help build relations between origin countries and their diaspora communities, and which help stimulate migrants' participation in global processes, illustrate the need for continuous dialogue between non-governmental and governmental actors. NGO and migrant organizations can perform a variety of roles – from capacity-building to advocacy work and project implementation – in helping migration play a positive developmental role. Enabling local non-migrant NGOs and diaspora-community migrant organizations to join forces is likely to increase the development impact of projects in countries of origin and will help increase migrant NGOs' influence within policy processes.

References

Asquith, Paul. "Diaspora and Development Roundtable on Preparing for the 2013 UN High Level Dialogue on International Migration and Development." Background Paper for the Roundtable held in Eschborn, Germany, in July 2013. Vienna: ICMPD, 2013.

Banulescu-Bogdan, Natalia. *The Role of Civil Society in EU Migration Policy: Perspectives on the European Union's Engagement in its Neighborhood*. Washington, D.C.: Migration Policy Institute, 2011. www.migrationpolicy.org/pubs/EUcivilsociety.pdf.

European Commission. "EU Report on Policy Coherence for Development." *Commission Staff Working Document 456*. Brussels: European Commission, 2013. https://ec.europa.eu/europeaid/sites/devco/files/pcd-report-2013_en.pdf.

GAMM (Global Approach to Migration and Mobility). GAMM Framework. Brussels: European Commission, 2014. http://ec.europa.eu/dgs/home-affairs/what-we-do/policies/international-affairs/global-approach-to-migration/index_en.htm.

GIZ (Deutsche Gesellschaft für Internationale Zusammenarbeit). When Everyone's a Winner. Berlin: GIZ, 2014. www.giz.de/en/workingwithgiz/11666.html.

Newland, Kathleen. "The governance of international migration: mechanisms, processes and institutions." Paper prepared for the Policy Analysis and Research Programme of the Global Commission on International Migration, 2005. Geneva: GCIM, 2005. www.iom.int/jahia/webdav/site/myjahiasite/shared/shared/mainsite/policy_and_research/gcim/tp/TS8b.pdf.

The Fair Management of Migration in OECD Countries and the Role of NGOs

Grace Annan, Onyekachi Wambu

Introduction

This report will discuss the regulation of migration flows and the integration of migrants into OECD destination countries. It will answer the following two questions:
- Are there any programs or initiatives in OECD countries that seek the fair regulation of migration and allow migrants, their families and their countries or societies of origin to benefit?
- What role can NGOs play in helping migrants and their families, as well as countries and societies of origin, to benefit from labor migration to OECD countries (e.g., through knowledge transfer, better mobilization of diaspora communities, etc.)?

The regulation of migrant flows and migrant integration are highly complex issues. Although the concepts of circular migration and "triple-win" migration policy are gaining ground throughout the OECD region, the question of precisely how fairness can be manifested in this context remains subject to considerable debate.

For the first part of this report, the term "fair" will refer to the fulfillment of the "triple-win" definition formulated by Kofi Annan – that is, policies that benefit migrants themselves, destination countries and countries of origin (Annan 2006).

Methodology and limitations

The first part of this report addresses the first question above. It focuses on low- to highly skilled legal workers and on wealthy investors. It examines one country per OECD region – in this case, Portugal (Europe), Canada (the Americas), Australia (Pacific Region) and South Korea (Asia) – as well as an example that encompasses nearly the whole of the European Union's Single Market. These examples have either complied with the concept of "triple-win" migration (Australia, Canada, the European Union's Blue Card scheme, Portugal) or have performed comparatively well with regard to the integration of migrants (South

Korea, Australia, Canada, Portugal). The second part of the report answers the second question cited above. It considers examples from three countries – the United Kingdom, France and Denmark – as well as an example that encompasses the entire European landmass.

Programs and initiatives promoting the fair regulation of migration in the OECD region

Numerous programs and initiatives seek the fair regulation of migration within OECD countries. Yet despite their fairness in theory, some are implemented inefficiently, with at times adverse effects for migrant workers (Australia, Canada).

EU Blue Card

The EU Blue Card is a work and residence permit for highly educated citizens from outside the European Economic Area. It seeks to facilitate access to – and circulation among – 25 EU member states. Approved in 2009, it was finally fully implemented across the signatory region in 2012. Denmark, Ireland and the United Kingdom are not participants in the program.

Key aspects

To be eligible, applicants must fulfill several basic criteria. They must have: 1) a binding job offer or contract with a salary above a minimum threshold; 2) a national long-term visa or valid travel documents and residence permit; 3) proof of health insurance; and 4) proof of higher professional qualifications or proof that they meet legal requirements for regulated professions in the country of destination (EC Directive 2009). After 18 months of residence, Blue Card holders may – subject to national legislation – move to another participant country to take up high-skill jobs there (ibid.). After two years of employment, Blue Card holders gain the same access to high-skilled jobs as that held by the destination country's citizens. On paper, the Blue Card fits the triple-win schema in several ways. First, it benefits the host countries by facilitating access to highly skilled labor in sectors with acute labor shortages. Second, it benefits migrants and their dependents by harmonizing and facilitating access to the bulk of the Single Market and enabling circulation within this region. Moreover, it contains provisions for family reunification and temporary absences from the participating countries (Kroes Advocaten). Third, unlike the U.S. Green Card, the Blue Card places a strong emphasis on the integration of migrants and their dependents. Finally, it also benefits countries of origin by promoting ethical recruitment standards, with the aim of avoiding EU recruitment targeting developing countries with acute levels of brain drain (Africa-EU Partnership, circa 2013). To underscore this commitment, the European Union has conceived the €1.37 billion Euromed Migration program to fund professional and university-based training that meets the needs of countries of origin (Fondation Robert Schuman 2014).

Challenges

The Blue Card has at least two shortcomings. First, it does not replace national programs focusing on highly skilled labor; rather, its application varies from country to country, leaving migrants and their employers subject to considerable red tape (Eisele 2013: 4). Second, the ethical code in the Blue Card Directive is not sufficiently binding. This allows member states to compete with one another and with countries of origin for highly skilled migrants (Fondation Robert Schuman 2014).

Conclusion

The EU Blue Card may be fair with regard to facilitating the entry and integration of highly skilled migrants to the bulk of the Single Market; however, it still has the potential to undermine development in countries of origin.

Portugal

Portugal is one of the European Union's most migrant-friendly countries (MIPEX 2010b). Of its 10.6 million inhabitants, 8.4 percent are immigrants (IOM 2013b). Ranked second out of 31 countries assessed by the Migrant Integration Policy Index (MIPEX), it scored highly with regard to labor-market mobility and family reunion. Moreover, it was ranked first among the countries that have comparatively recently become immigration destinations with regard to migrant education, political participation and anti-discrimination laws (MIPEX 2010b).

Key aspects

Despite the sharp economic downturn of recent years, Portugal has continued to promote migrant integration. In 2012, the government and its social partners signed the Commitment for Growth, Competitiveness and Employment, which aimed at reintegrating unemployed migrant workers into the labor market (EMN 2012: 1). In addition, the 2012 Aliens Act facilitated the transposition of several EU directives into national law, notably the EU Blue Card program and a single application procedure for work and residence permits for third-country nationals (Directive 2011/98/UE) (EMN 2012). Portugal also has a temporary-migration agreement focusing on its diaspora communities and, along with the Netherlands and Italy, Portugal is a participant in the International Organization for Migration's (IOM) Dias de Cabo Verde project, which seeks to build capacities in Cape Verde through knowledge-sharing in selected high-priority areas and in the private sector more generally (EMN 2011: 51; IOM 2013c). Despite the economic downturn, Portugal's government implemented its 2nd National Integration Plan (2010–2013), which sought to streamline the integration of migrants through a number of initiatives, including welcome programs, measures ensuring access to social rights and professional training, and provisions facilitating the creation of new businesses (OECD 2013c: 1).

Challenges

Recent policy has focused on migrants with access to considerable resources rather than on those with skills per se. In 2012, the Portuguese government introduced its Resident Permit for Investment Activities (ARI), also known as the Golden Visa. This is aimed at citizens and companies from outside the European Union or Schengen areas that are willing to invest at least €1 million, purchase property worth at least €500,000 or create at least 10 jobs (EMN 2012: 2; Ferreira, Gonçalves and Caldas 2013). In addition, the government has reduced the number of long-term and student visas issued to non-EU migrants (OECD 2013c: 1).

Conclusion

On the one hand, the government is pushing ahead with the integration of migrants and the promotion of capacity-building in their countries of origin. The Blue Card program, the 2nd National Integration Plan and the cooperation agreement with Cape Verde provide clear examples of this strategy. However, the government is also indirectly facilitating discrimination between migrants on the basis of their skills and wealth.

South Korea

South Korea is a recent country of immigration. It changed from being a net emigration country to a net immigration country only in 2005 (OECD 2013d: 1). Currently, 2.5 percent of its 49.3 million inhabitants are immigrants (IOM 2013d). Around 47,000 of all migrant workers in South Korea are highly skilled; around 547,000 – or nearly 50 percent – are low-skilled workers, mostly recruited through the Employment Permit System (EPS), which focuses on temporary rather than long-term migration (OECD 2013d: 1).

Key aspects

In terms of migrant integration, South Korea has performed exceptionally within the category of countries that have only recently become immigration destinations (MIPEX 2010c). Receiving 60 out of 100 points on the Migration Integration Policy Index, its integration polices are deemed "slightly favorable"; in particular, it has made significant progress with regard to labor-market support, access to education for migrant children, migrants' voting rights and support for immigrant associations (ibid.). Legally resident migrant workers can access jobs in the private as well as public sector, and – as in Canada – are granted the same rights as Koreans, at least in theory (ibid.). Furthermore, South Korea changed its EPS system in 2011 to foster points-based employment permits (OECD 2013d: 1). The government also increased the number of support centers for foreign workers from seven to 27 in 2011 (ibid.). To attract highly skilled labor, the government enables eligible resident migrants to advance to a more comprehensive residence status; this includes permits for their families (F-2 status) and access to permanent residency permits (ibid.).

Challenges

Significant shortcomings remain with regard to the implementation of immigration policies, ranging from family reunification to intercultural education, political participation by foreigners, naturalization and the support of migrant associations (MIPEX 2010c). According to Amnesty International, the EPS can be easily exploited to deny migrants the right to form trade unions (Wickramasekara 2011: 53–54, 79).

Conclusion

South Korea may be comparatively strong among recent immigration destinations with regard to the formulation and implementation of immigration policies. Yet it still lags considerably behind the more traditional destination countries with regard to the application of fair immigration policies, particularly in terms of labor policies affecting low-skilled workers.

Canada

Canada is one of the world's prime destination countries. Out of its 35.2 million inhabitants, nearly 21 percent are immigrants (IOM 2013b). The country is ranked third out of 31 countries on the Migration Integration Policy Index with regard to immigrant integration (MIPEX 2010a).

Key aspects

Canada has one of the world's strongest anti-discrimination and equality laws, a highly attractive system for migrant workers and their families, very accommodating measures for migrant students, and an ambitious program to foster the recognition of foreign qualifications across Canada (MIPEX 2010a). Canada also fosters triple-win migration policies; for instance, in 2012, the International Organization for Migration (IOM) in Canada launched the Guyanese Diaspora Project in conjunction with the Guyanese Ministry of Foreign Affairs (IOM 2012). The Seasonal Agricultural Workers' Program (SAWP), which counts Canada, Mexico and the Caribbean Commonwealth countries as members, allows Canadian farmers to hire around 20,000 migrant workers per year for up to eight months (Wickramasekara 2011: 54). It is often cited as a model of best practice, as it facilitates the migration of low-skilled labor, induces a high rate of voluntary return after employment, and is sustainable (ibid.).

Challenges

The SAWP has a number of unintended side effects that disadvantage migrant workers. The United Food and Commercial Workers Canada trade union described SAWP as "Canada's shameful dirty secret"; it filed lawsuits against provincial authorities for the exclusion of migrant workers from the provisions of the Occupational Health and Safety Act, despite their contribution of CAD 11 million every year in the form of unemployment insurance premiums (Wickramasekara 2011: 54). Furthermore, migrants under the SAWP program cannot apply for family reunification or for permanent residence even after years of circular migration (ibid.).

Conclusion

Although Canada is at the forefront of immigrant integration and places great emphasis on fair migration policies, it still falls short in a number of areas. Although they may be unintentional side effects of well-meant policies, these shortcomings raise questions about the overall fairness of Canadian immigration policies, notably with regard to lower-skilled workers and their countries of origin.

Australia

Australia is one of the top three OECD countries in terms of population born abroad (nearly 28%; IOM 2013a), net migration inflow, the number of foreign students in tertiary education, and the number of people (such as backpackers) who combine work with touristic activities (Pryke 2013). Australia's immigration system is based on a points system and facilitates the migration of workers from nearby countries (Landgrave 2013). Unlike the immigration policies of some Nordic European countries that enable immigration on humanitarian grounds, Australia's selective immigration policy targets young, skilled individuals in particular (Keeley 2013).

Key aspects

The government has reduced the number of skilled-migration visa categories from 27 to 11 (OECD 2013a). The economic upturn in Australia has attracted a large number of New Zealanders; as part of the Trans-Tasman Mutual Recognition Agreement between Australia and

New Zealand, over 44,000 New Zealanders entered Australia in the 2011–2012 period, or almost 1 percent of New Zealand's population (ibid.).

Challenges

Several policies make migrant entry and integration somewhat difficult. First, Australia obliges sponsors to prove that they can provide private health care for elderly family members should they wish to be reunited (Landgrave 2013). Second, the introduction of the Significant Investor program in November 2012 may have fostered the expansion of a discriminatory, multi-tier immigration process. Unlike family reunification, the scheme is not subject to upper age limits for migrants (AGDIBP 2014). Finally, both Australia's low-skill-oriented Seasonal Workers' Program and its predecessor, the Pacific Seasonal Worker Pilot Scheme (2008–2011), have had low levels of participation by target migrants (Doyle and Howes 2013a). The Pilot Scheme suffered as a result of competition from backpackers and illegal immigrants, insufficient promotion of the scheme, comparatively high labor costs and significant red tape (ibid.). The Seasonal Workers' Program, too, is suffering from low participation rates; launched in 2012 and expanded from the horticultural sector to the aquaculture, cane, cotton and accommodation industries, only 16 of the 1,550 available permits for 2013–2016 in the latter four areas had been taken up by July 2013 (Doyle and Howes 2013b).

Conclusion

Australia's immigration policies attract a large number of temporary workers. Yet various categories occasionally interfere with each another, which has particularly hampered the success of policies aimed at lower-skilled legal migrants from the Pacific region.

The role of NGOs in facilitating triple-win outcomes for migrants and their families

The last 10 years have seen a growing number of small-scale and pilot initiatives focusing on diaspora communities and development projects. The key features of these initiatives have been to encourage skills transfers and sharing through volunteer work, and to support diaspora- and migrant-led development projects in Africa across a range of thematic areas. Although it is possible to judge the immediate impact of many of these initiatives, it is too soon to assess their scalability and long-term sustainability.

The Africa-Europe Platform

The Africa-Europe Platform (AEP) is a European-wide network of African diaspora organizations with the goal of engaging migrants and other parties with an interest in development.

Its creation has been facilitated by the European Commission in cooperation with the Swiss Agency for Development and Cooperation (SDC), the Dutch Ministry of Foreign Affairs (MFA) and the German Gesellschaft für Internationale Zusammenarbeit (GIZ). The platform is intended to foster contributions to African development by established African diaspora or migrant organizations based in the 28 European Union states, as well as Norway and Switzerland. Phase one of the project has been driven by five partners: the African Diaspora Policy Centre (ADPC) in the Netherlands, the Forum des Organisations de Solidarité Internationale issues des Migrations (FORIM) in France, the Coordination Générale des Migrants pour le Développement (CGMD) in Belgium, the African Foundation for Development (AF-FORD) in the United Kingdom, and the Vienna-based International Centre for Migration Policy Development (ICMPD).

Key aspects

The platform's aims are: 1) to strengthen migrant and diaspora contributions to development; 2) to improve the coordination and sharing of migration and development best practices; 3) to build capacities within migrant and diaspora communities, enabling them to take part in platform activities and implement development projects; and 4) to strengthen channels of communication and knowledge exchange between diaspora organizations and partners in Africa. Phase one of the platform involved the creation of a map of migrant and diaspora organizations in the European Union, as well as the production of e-learning and training materials on alliance-building and advocacy, policy briefs and best-practice toolkits. Three expert meetings were held, and the five partners made initial visits to five African pilot countries (Morocco, Senegal, Cameroon, Ethiopia and Angola).

Challenges and conclusions

Phase two of the project was slated to begin in the summer of 2014. It will aim to strengthen and consolidate the platform, while expanding its co-development potential by building on the initial pilot-country visits. It is therefore premature at this stage to assess the diaspora-community or development impacts.

United Kingdom

The U.K. government has conducted a number of pilot initiatives managed by NGOs and foundations. The most high-profile of these to date have been the Diaspora Volunteering Alliance (DVA) and the Common Ground Initiative (CGI). The DVA was based on a GBP 3 million fund provided by the Department for International Development (DFID), as well as additional resources from the Big Lottery Fund. Active between 2008 and 2013, its goal was to support the members of U.K.-based diaspora communities and migrant organizations in providing volunteer capacity-building services in their countries of heritage. The grant was managed by the United Kingdom's leading international volunteer agency, Voluntary Service Overseas (VSO). The separate Common Ground Initiative was also supported by the DFID, with GBP 20 million provided in the initiative's first phase (2012–2014) for the support of development work in Africa carried out by diaspora organizations and small charities (defined as those with an annual budgets of less than GBP 1 million). The DFID's GBP 20 million was matched by another GBP 20 million from major charity Comic Relief, which also managed the CGI program.

Key aspects

Under the DVA program, 14 partners and a total of 631 individual volunteers participated in structured volunteer programs (eight African, six Asian) in 12 countries (Nigeria, Tanzania, Zimbabwe, Malawi, Kenya, Ghana, Sierra Leone, India, Pakistan, Sri Lanka, Nepal, Bangladesh). The volunteers supported all eight Millennium Development Goals (MDGs), working with health, education, HIV/AIDs, secure-livelihood, governance and disability-focused projects. Over 16,000 people were directly affected, with a further 5,000 receiving indirect benefits (DVA 2013). The CGI, by contrast, focused on funding projects that fell under Comic Relief's thematic areas of support (women's and girls' development issues, people affected by HIV, slum dwellers, children and young people at risk, improved health for children and women, and access to education). In addition to these program areas, the CGI introduced funding in the new area of enterprise and employment. Beyond the project funding for African projects, the CGI also implemented a number of other features focused on diaspora communities in the United Kingdom. These included support for building community members' capacity to engage in advocacy; peer learning; organizational development grants; a diaspora leadership program; and the production of improved research and data on the issue of diasporas and development. So far, the program has engaged with more than 6,000 diaspora individuals and organizations involved in international development.

Challenges and conclusions

The on-the-ground volunteer aspect of the DVA program in Africa and Asia received the DFID's highest possible rating in terms of development impact, and the capacity-building element was positively evaluated by an independent evaluation team (Malfait, Cottrell and Wells 2013). Nevertheless, the DFID discontinued funding for the program around the time that it established funding for the CGI. Questions had been raised about the cost and sustainability of the project. The African Foundation for Development (AFFORD) participated in the volunteer aspect of the project and estimated the cost of each volunteer (flights, accommodation, ground transportation, food and other expenses) at between GBP 2,500 and GBP 3,000, depending on the time of year. However, AFFORD's own medium-term evaluation of the

DVA's impact also indicated that a reference to the initial costs for the two to three weeks of volunteering was not the most effective way of measuring value or impact, as the missions successfully catalyzed other outputs and outcomes. In the case of the AFFORD missions, the program led directly to improvements in more than 800 businesses supported in Ghana and Sierra Leone; prompted the long-term return of 14 skilled diaspora-community professionals to their countries of heritage; increased diaspora investment in local African businesses; enabled the training of 30 local business-support coaches in Sierra Leone; led to the establishment of a business-development support agency in Sierra Leone; created jobs and expanded investment following the establishment of an AFFORD Business Centre; and led to the creation of Business Bomba, a national business-plan competition that has now provided capacity-building and over $200,000 in aggregate investment to Sierra Leone SMEs. Thus, in AFFORD's estimation, the intervention's medium- to long-term outputs and outcomes appeared cost-effective even given the relatively high short-term costs of the volunteering. With reference to the CGI, an evaluation of the program's first phase was underway as of the time of writing (with an expected publication date of August 2014). DFID has committed an additional GBP 12 million for a second phase (through 2019), which will again be matched by funds (GBP 8 million) from Comic Relief. The outputs for phase two will be shaped by the results of the evaluation.

Denmark

Launched in 2012 and funded through 2015, the Danish Refugee Council's (DRC) Diaspora Program (DP), supported by the Danish International Development Agency (Danida), aims to encourage diaspora communities to shift their social and financial remittances toward development-focused, relief and rehabilitation projects. It also seeks to strengthen the role of diaspora communities as development agents, gathering and sharing evidence of this activity in order to inform and shape humanitarian programs and responses. The DP is focused on the Somali and Afghan diaspora communities, each of which has a significant presence in Denmark.

Key aspects

DP has two main features. First, the program administers a fund that supports development projects conducted by Somali and Afghan diaspora organizations in their countries of origin. Second, the program collects data and accumulates evidence with regard to the link between diaspora communities and development. As a part of these tasks, it also provides training and capacity-building for organizations and offers support in the design and management of projects. The diaspora communities are given direct input through two elected advisory boards, consisting of seven Afghans and seven Somalis, though an executive committee oversees the program and has the final say on funding applications.

Challenges and conclusions

The election process and involvement of the diaspora-community members on the DP advisory board has deepened democratic participation within the Afghan and Somali communities in Denmark, increasing social cohesion and integration. Furthermore, the program has encouraged consultation and feedback, as the participation of local groups in the country of heritage is necessary, and evidence from these local partners is needed to prove that projects will not undermine other local efforts or build structures parallel to those that already exist. As a means of further increasing the sense of ownership, a minimum of 15 percent of the project's budget must be provided by the diaspora organization and the local partner, although this can take the form of in-kind contributions. Projects that are partisan, discriminate against elements of a local community or cause conflict are not eligible for support. Discussions on the potential expansion of the program to other diaspora communities within Denmark are underway.

France

The Programme d'Appui aux projets des Organisations de Solidarité Internationale issues de l'Immigration (PRA/OSIM) is a coaching and funding program targeted at local development projects managed by France's Forum of Solidarity Organizations for International Migrant Issues (Forum des Organisations de Solidarité Internationale issues des Migrations, FORIM), an NGO. FORIM is a national platform that brings together about 700 diaspora and migrant networks, federations and other groups from Africa, the Caribbean, Eastern Europe, Asia and the Pacific region. Eligible countries are those that qualify for support from the OECD's Development Assistance Committee (DAC), with the exception of Comoros, Mali and Senegal, which already receive specific French co-development funds. The PRA/OSIM program is currently supported by the French Ministry of Foreign Affairs (its sponsoring authority has changed over the years). Grants under PRA/OSIM are limited to €15,000, 70 percent of which must be spent on local development projects.

Key aspects

The key goals of PRA/OSIM are to encourage migrants and diaspora communities to make more significant contributions to the development of their countries of origin; to strengthen civil society participation and partnership between the Global North and South; to strengthen citizenship and participatory democracy; and to integrate migrant-development programs more effectively. The number of requests for PRA/OSIM funding ranged between 23 and 221 per year between 2003 and 2013 (Pluricité 2013: 77). Over the course of that period, the program sponsored more than 200 projects in 23 countries worth more than €3 million in total (FORIM 2013a). The projects focused on socioeconomic issues ranging from agricultural development to sports; the top five funding areas between 2003 and 2013 were health (19.2%), education (18.5%), agricultural and rural development (18%), water (14.4%) and economic development (11%). The majority of PRA/OSIM projects in this period were carried out in Africa; the top five countries in terms of projects implemented were Morocco (26), the Democratic Republic of Congo (23), Benin (16), Guinea-Bissau (15) and Cameroon (13) (FORIM 2013b). However, according to Pluricité, an organization that published an evaluation of the PRA/OSIM, assessing the overall effectiveness of projects implemented between 2003 and 2013 was a challenge (Pluricité 2013: 77).

Challenges and conclusions

Although Pluricité's evaluation of PRA/OSIM was in general very positive, it did highlight several shortcomings within the program. A number of participants criticized the progressive shift by both FORIM and OSIM toward the PRA/OSIM program, to the detriment of collaboration with other domestic and international partners (Pluricité 2013: 78). Moreover, the evaluators cited a potential conflict of interest in cases where the funding and project management came from one and the same source (ibid.). The evaluators additionally called for a more effective structure regarding the tendering of projects and their size (FORIM 2013b: 82). OSIM members called for a greater volume of approved funds, longer funding periods and an increased presence of so-called opérateurs d'appui (OPAP) – representatives of PRA/OSIM who provide advice on and receive funding applications – outside Paris (Pluricité 2013: 7, 79).

Conclusion

The regulation of migration flows and subsequent integration of migrants into destination-country societies are hampered by discrepancies between the formulation and implementation of the underlying immigration policies. As the examples cited in this report demonstrate, a number of theoretically migrant-friendly measures in fact require improved implementation to become fully compliant with the "triple-win" concept.

Throughout the OECD region, countries – whether affected particularly strongly by economic downturn (Portugal) or new to the group of immigration-destination countries (South Korea) – are trying to balance the costs of integrating migrants and their dependents with the benefits these newcomers bring. The majority of EU member states have introduced the Blue Card, which facilitates entry and integration for highly skilled migrants throughout most of the Single Market. Portugal is increasingly mixing migrant-integration policies and support for countries of origin with the facilitation of significant foreign direct investment. South Korea has made critical advances on paper, but significant room remains for improvement with regard to integration, particularly in the case of low-skilled migrants. Despite its overall highly migrant-friendly policies, Canada still requires significant changes to otherwise successful policies, such as the SAWP, in order to comply with the triple-win concept in practice. Similarly, Australia's immigration programs remain biased toward benefits for the host country, as policies affecting the elderly and low-income earners as well as the examples of temporary permits for Pacific migrant workers show.

NGOs play a significant role in helping immigrants and their countries of origin benefit from labor migration. Innovative measures include the Africa-Europe Platform, whose second phase late in 2014 is slated to deepen engagement with stakeholders and consolidate a platform for diaspora-community activity. The United Kingdom's Diaspora Volunteering Alliance (DVA), managed by the Voluntary Service Overseas NGO, as well as the Comic Relief-managed Common Ground Initiative (CGI), are two significant measures facilitating diaspora-community development activities within countries of heritage. However, despite positive evaluations, the U.K. Department for International Development discontinued funding for the DVA. As of the time of writing, the CGI was undergoing an evaluation that would shape its GBP 20 million second phase (GBP 12 from DFID and GBP 8 from Comic Relief). The Danish Refugee Council's Diaspora Program is encouraging Somali and Afghan migrants to support development programs that benefit a wider range of people than their immediate families in their countries of heritage; the program may be expanded to include other diaspora groups in Denmark. The French government-backed PRA/OSIM program is promoting development projects and knowledge transfer across Africa, the Caribbean, Eastern Europe, Asia and the Pacific region; the €2 million fund is managed by FORIM, an umbrella NGO that brings together 700 diaspora and migrant networks.

References

Africa-EU Partnership. Mobility and Circular Migration. www.africa-eu-partnership.org/areas-cooperation/migration-mobility-and-employment/mobility-and-circular-migration.

AFFORD Business Centre. Homepage. www.affordbusinesscentre.org.

AGDIBP (Australian Government Department of Immigration and Border Protection). "Is there a points test or an age requirement for the Significant Investor visa?" Canberra: AGDIBP, 2014. www.immi.gov.au/FAQs/Pages/Is-there-a-points-test-or-an-age-requirement-for-the-Significant-Investor-visa.aspx.

Annan, Kofi. "How We Envy the World Cup." UN speech held on June 30, 2006. www.un.org/sport2005/newsroom/worldcup.html.

Comic Relief/Common Ground Initiative. Homepage. www.gov.uk/international-development-funding/common-ground-initiative-cgi.

Danish Refugee Council. Diaspora Programme. http://drc.dk/relief-work/diaspora-programme/.

Doyle, Jesse, and Stephen Howes. "The official evaluation of the Pacific Seasonal Worker Pilot Scheme: an opportunity missed." Development Policy Blog, May 24, 2013a. http://devpolicy.org/the-official-evaluation-of-the-pacific-seasonal-worker-pilot-scheme-20130524-2/.

Doyle, Jesse, and Stephen Howes. "Few takers in new trial sectors for Australia's Seasonal Worker Program." Development Policy Blog, June 28, 2013b. http://devpolicy.org/few-takers-in-new-trial-sectors-for-seasonal-worker-program-20130628.

DVA (Diaspora Volunteering Alliance). Homepage. www.diasporavolunteeringalliance.org.

DVA. Diaspora Volunteering Program Statistics. 2013.

EC Directive. Entry and residence of highly qualified workers (EU Blue Card). 2009/50/EC of May 25, 2009. http://europa.eu/legislation_summaries/internal_market/living_and_working_in_the_internal_market/l14573_en.htm.

Eisele, Katharina. "Why Come Here if I Can Go There? Assessing the 'Attractiveness' of the EU's Blue Card Directive for 'Highly Qualified' Immigrants." *Justice and Home Affairs, Liberty and Security in Europe Papers*. Brussels: Centre for European Policy Studies, 2013.

EMN (European Migration Network). "Temporary and Circular Migration: Empirical Evidence, Current Policy Practice and Future Options in EU Member States." Brussels: EMN, 2011. http://ec.europa.eu/dgs/home-affairs/what-we-do/networks/european_migration_network/reports/docs/emn-studies/circular-migration/0a_emn_synthesis_report_temporary__circular_migration_final_sept_2011_en.pdf.

EMN. Country Factsheet: Portugal 2012. http://ec.europa.eu/dgs/home-affairs/what-we-do/networks/european_migration_network/reports/docs/country-factsheets/portugal-emn-ountry-facthseet_en.pdf.

Ferreira, Rogério M. Fernandes, Mónica Respício Gonçalves and Catarina Caldas. "Portugal: The New Portuguese Golden Visas." Mondaq, October 14, 2013. www.mondaq.com/x/268912/work+visas/The+New+Portuguese+Golden+Visas.

Fondation Robert Schuman. "A Review of Post-Lampedusa: What Type of EU Migratory Cooperation with Third Countries?" Brussels: FRS, 2014. www.robert-schuman.eu/en/european-issues/0301-a-review-of-post-lampedusa-what-type-of-eu-migratory-cooperation-with-third-countries.

FORIM (Forum des Organisations de Solidarité Internationale issues des Migrations). *Seminaire National "10 An du Pra/OSIM" 2003–2008*. Paris: FORIM, 2013a. www.forim.net/sites/default/files/SYNTHESE_206%20projets%20Copy.pdf.

FORIM. Évaluation du programme d'appui aux projets des organisations de solidarité internationale issues de l'immigration (PRA/OSIM) 2003–2012. Rapport final. June 2013b. www.forim.net/sites/default/files/Rapport_Final_Evaluation_PRA%20OSIM.pdf.

IOM (International Organization for Migration). "Guyanese Diaspora Project Launched in Canada." December 7, 2012. www.iom.int/cms/en/sites/iom/home/news-and-views/press-briefing-notes/pbn-2012/pbn-listing/guyanese-diaspora-project-launch.html.

IOM. Australia Facts and Figures. 2013a. www.iom.int/cms/en/sites/iom/home/where-we-work/asia-and-the-pacific/australia.html.

IOM. Canada Facts and Figures. 2013b. www.iom.int/cms/en/sites/iom/home/where-we-work/americas/central-and-north-america-and-th/canada.html.

IOM. Portugal Facts and Figures. 2013c. www.iom.int/cms/en/sites/iom/home/where-we-work/europa/european-economic-area/portugal.html.

IOM. South Korea Facts and Figures. 2013d. www.iom.int/cms/en/sites/iom/home/where-we-work/asia-and-the-pacific/republic-of-korea.html.

Keeley, Brian. "The impact of immigrants – it's not what you think." *OECD Insights,* June 13, 2013. http://oecdinsights.org/2013/06/13/the-impact-of-immigrants-its-not-what-you-think/.

Kroes Advocaten. "EU Blue Card." www.kroesadvocaten.nl/eu-blue-card.

References

Landgrave, Michelangelo. "Immigration Reform 2013: 6 Ideas We Should Steal From Australia." Policy.Mic, October 18, 2013. www.policymic.com/articles/68821/immigration-reform-2013-6-ideas-we-should-steal-from-australia.

Malfait, Richard, Sophie Cottrell and Gillian Wells. Independent Review of the Diaspora Volunteering Capacity Building Program (April 2008 – March 2013), VSO, 2013. SEEDA/Remitskills, www.afford-uk.org/index.php/enterprise-and-employment.

MIPEX (Migrant Integration Policy Index). Country Report – Canada. 2010a. www.mipex.eu/canada.

MIPEX. Country Report – Portugal. 2010b. www.mipex.eu/portugal.

MIPEX. Country Report – South Korea. 2010c. www.mipex.eu/south-korea.

OECD (Organisation for Economic Co-operation and Development). International Migration Outlook 2013 – Australia Factsheet. Paris: OECD, 2013a. www.oecd.org/els/mig/AUSTRALIA.pdf.

OECD. International Migration Outlook 2013 – Canada Factsheet. Paris: OECD, 2013b. www.oecd.org/els/mig/CANADA.pdf.

OECD. International Migration Outlook 2013 – Portugal Factsheet. Paris: OECD, 2013c. www.oecd.org/els/mig/PORTUGAL.pdf.

OECD. International Migration Outlook 2013 – Korea Factsheet. Paris: OECD, 2013d. www.oecd.org/els/mig/KOREA.pdf.

Pluricité. Évaluation du Program d'Appui aux Projets des Organisations de Solidarité Internationale issues de l'Immigration (PRA/OSIM), 2003–2012. Paris: Pluricité, 2013.

Pryke, Jonathan. "Australia, a migration giant." Development Policy Blog, September 12, 2013. http://devpolicy.org/australia-a-migration-giant-20130912/.

VSO (Voluntary Service Overseas). "Diaspora Partnerships." www.vso.org.uk/about/working-in-partnership/diaspora-volunteering/diaspora-partnerships.

Wickramasekara, Piyasiri. "Circular Migration: a Triple Win or a Dead End?" *Global Union Research Network Discussion Paper No. 15*. Geneva: Global Migration Policy Associates, 2011.

IV. The Way Forward: Fostering Fairness in Migration Policy

Global Skill Partnerships: A Proposal for Technical Training in a Mobile World

Michael A. Clemens

The migration of skilled labor is often seen as unfair, benefiting rich countries at the expense of poor ones. A common reaction is to call for limits on the migration of skilled workers. But there is an alternative: Change the terms on which migration among the highly trained occurs so that the countries involved agree to terms that are mutually beneficial.

What would such an agreement look like? This note describes one of many ways that migration of skilled labor could be structured to benefit everyone involved. I call this model a global skill partnership (GSP).

A global skill partnership is an agreement between two entities in different countries. One partner trains people in a country from which some trainees later depart as migrants. For instance, this might be a nursing school in a developing country. The other partner benefits from migrants' acquired skills in a second country that serves as a destination country for migrants. This might be a developed-country hospital that employs migrant nurses, for example. The partners agree beforehand how the beneficiaries of migrants' skills in the destination country will help create skills within the origin country – both for individuals who later become migrants *and* those who have no intention of migrating. The two partners make this agreement before the migrants acquire these skills.

This note explains why a GSP can be mutually beneficial, even with limited return migration; it describes the economic gaps that give a GSP its power to create value; and it discusses some of the key features that might be included in a functioning GSP. For the sake of concreteness, the note discusses a hypothetical country pair (Moldova and Germany) and skilled occupation (nursing). However, partnerships of this kind could be formed by almost any pair of developing and developed countries involved in skilled migration, and in a wide variety of technical fields.

A GSP can benefit everyone involved

A global skill partnership creates value for the country migrants come from, for the country migrants go to and for migrants themselves. A simple example will demonstrate how this can take place, though the following represents just one of many ways to structure a GSP.

Global Skill Partnerships: A Proposal for Technical Training in a Mobile World

Suppose that the partners are a nursing school in Moldova and a hospital in Germany. The German hospital agrees to pay for the training of three nurses in Moldova for each one that it would like to hire in Germany. For one of the three nurses trained, the German hospital facilitates employment-based migration to Germany, providing assistance such as language training and visa sponsorship. The German hospital furthermore assists the Moldovan nursing school in adjusting the program to German regulatory requirements and employer needs, including curriculum standardization.

Both countries involved, as well as all trainees whether intending to migrate or not, are better off with this agreement than without it, as indicated below:

- *The origin country:* Moldova ends up with more nurses than it started with, a stronger nursing school with expanded capacity and EU-harmonized standards, and an inflow of training funds instead of an outflow.
- *The destination country:* Germany gets nurses to fill its labor shortages; German employers and the public save significant amounts of money on training expenses, as training in Germany is far more expensive than in Moldova; patients and employers get nurses with the technical and tacit skills that they want because the German hospital was involved in training its immigrant employees; and Germany acts as a good global citizen by using its labor needs to create more nurses abroad rather than depleting the origin country's supply.
- *Migrants and non-migrants:* Young Moldovans can receive subsidized high-quality training even if they wish to stay in Moldova, in addition to excellent professional opportunities abroad if they do not; they need not be tied to a specific employer or country by onerous obligations; and they need not invest their own capital in training, thus enabling students from any background to participate in the program.

Crucially, Moldova receives the above-noted benefits even if every migrant trainee remains in Germany and sends nothing home in the form of remittances. That said, it is likely that a number of people who train for work abroad *would* ultimately come back, becoming return or "circular" migrants. Moreover, many migrants, both permanent and temporary, would interact with Moldova in a variety of ways over time. This might include sending money home or providing ideas to those who have remained behind. But the benefits of a GSP to Moldova do not *depend* upon return migration or remittances. Return migration or remittances would represent additional benefits above and beyond the benefits listed above.

A GSP's power stems from two large arbitrage opportunities

Why would a German employer want to help support the training of *non*-migrants? The power of a global skill partnership comes from two very large differences in prices that exist between numerous pairs of countries. A GSP turns these price differences into arbitrage opportunities – chances to create value for everyone involved, without any party suffering a net loss.

The wage gap: The first opportunity lies in the fact that that nurses' wages differ massively between countries. It is common for nurses' wages in destination countries to be more than 10 times higher than wages in migrants' home countries. In Moldova, for example, a nurse typically earns less than €250 per month (Cruc et al. 2009; BNSRM 2014). In Germany, a foreign-trained nurse can start at €2,500 per month and earn substantially more thereafter.

The training-cost gap: The second opportunity is associated with the fact that the cost of training a nurse likewise varies massively between countries. In many migrant-destination countries, it costs vastly more to train a nurse than would be the case in a country of origin. For example, in Moldova, the state pays a cumulative total of about €2,500 to train one nurse over the course of three years (WHO 2014). In Germany, three years of nurse training – the cost of which is typically shared between employers and the state – cumulatively cost at least €65,000 (Clemens 2015).

The training-cost gap makes the GSP beneficial even when the deal involves the subsidization of training for non-migrants. Suppose that training a nurse in Moldova to perform at EU standards requires an additional premium of €1,500 per nurse, for a total of €4,000 per individual. Even if the German employer must support the training of three nurses in Moldova for each one it hires, the total cost for all three (roughly €12,000) still enables tremendous savings compared to the cost of training a *single* nurse in Germany (at least €53,000 *more*).

Figure 1: Two arbitrage opportunities at the heart of a global skill partnership

These gaps, illustrated in Figure 1, help explain why skilled migration is often seen as inherently inequitable. If skilled migration happens without a structured agreement, such as a GSP, the wage gap (on the left) produces a gain typically captured by migrants, while the training-cost gap (on the right) produces a savings typically captured by employers in the destination country. Without an up-front partnership, little benefit accrues to the country of origin unless migrants are subject to return obligations or repayment sanctions.

A GSP can be seen as a way to share the benefits of migration more equitably. Skilled migration creates tremendous value by exploiting both of these arbitrage opportunities simultaneously. A GSP ensures that some of that created value accrues to the origin country, giving it a stake in the agreement. Origin countries need such a stake in order for it to be worth their while to cooperate, and skilled migration works much better for everyone involved when it takes place under cooperative rather than adversarial conditions. This cooperation can mani-

Global Skill Partnerships: A Proposal for Technical Training in a Mobile World

fest itself as ethical recruitment practices among destination countries, the transfer of technology to origin countries and the reduction of restrictions on migrants.

A GSP is by far preferable to its alternatives in some settings

There are many alternatives to partnership agreements, such as a GSP, as well as alternative means of rendering the migration of skilled labor better or at least less bad for migrant-origin countries. But the realistic alternatives have major drawbacks that can make a GSP more attractive by comparison.

One alternative is to try to limit the extent or duration of migration, for instance, by blocking the international recruitment of skilled workers or by obliging skilled migrants to return home. Each of these methods has significant limitations, however. An origin country's efforts to block migration could run afoul of human-rights treaties (such as the United Nations Universal Declaration of Human Rights) that specifically ban limits on emigration, including for skilled workers. And even if the policy respected skilled migrants' rights, forcing them to stay or return home after migrating is often of limited effectiveness in building long-term stocks of human capital in developing countries. Even if *half* of all emigrant African physicians were somehow obliged to return to their home countries, just 6 percent of Africa's physician shortage would be mitigated, according to OECD estimates (OECD 2007). Limiting migration does little to address the real and growing shortages of skilled labor in developed countries, giving them limited incentives to cooperate in agreements to address the shortcomings of unstructured migration.

Another alternative is for countries of origin to demand cash payments from countries of destination in exchange for skilled migrants. These "compensation payments" are frequently recommended, but the model contains numerous drawbacks. Many skilled migrants depart after providing years of service in their home countries, and it is not clear how to factor in the value of that service when estimating the proper compensation. It is also unclear whether transferring the cost of an emigrant's training into the origin country's treasury will result in the training of a new worker. Aid is partially fungible, and some of the compensation payment is likely to finance unrelated spending. Finally, destination countries' priorities for development assistance may not match origin countries' fiscal priorities. For example, if Germany has €50,000 in assistance funds earmarked for the promotion of health in Tanzania, it is unclear whether it should spend that money as compensation for the training cost of one emigrant physician or use it to purchase anti-malaria bed nets for more than 3,000 Tanzanian households. Tanzania made the political decision to provide free education to the physician, but this might not reflect the political priorities underlying German assistance.

What these alternative approaches have in common is that they define the two countries as competitors in a zero-sum contest for control of a fixed-quantity resource – skilled workers – with little regard for the incentives provided to or the real interests of migrant professionals or destination-country societies. Taking a different path would enable countries to collaborate in accepting and planning for the reality of skilled migration in a mobile world that faces global skill shortages as well as in leveraging the opportunities that migration creates.

Practical concerns and design features

Nothing exactly like a GSP exists today, but many initiatives around the world exhibit key features of this model. For example, the German government is currently working with employers to recruit nurses around the world, from Serbia to Vietnam, to fill shortages in Germany. This shows that elements such as proper language training and employer cooperation are possible in the nursing sector. Virsagi Management, a Singaporean firm, trains skilled construction workers in South Asia prior to their migration to Singapore for work. This is paid for by Singaporean employers, who would otherwise have to pay much more to train potential employees in Singapore. Arrangements of this kind show that pre-migration training financed by destination-country employers has ample precedent (Clemens 2015; Clemens, Graham and Howes 2015).

These experiences suggest design features critical to the success of a GSP. Employers would need to be involved in customizing training in the origin country to their needs as well as in ensuring quality control – an up-front investment. The partnership would require a contingency plan for those who complete training with the intention to migrate but ultimately fail to do so, a group whose numbers are likely to be limited. It would also require a plan for portability between employers to avoid the problems that can arise when trainees are tied inextricably to a single employer, as there are sure to be cases in which trainees migrate but ultimately go to work for a different employer than the one involved in the partnership. Employers that financed training should be compensated in such cases; however, this compensation should not be an onerous obligation for the trainee in question, given the low cost of training in the origin country relative to earnings within the destination country. Finally, the program would require careful planning in order to avoid tensions between the two "tracks" of trainees – those who intend to work abroad and those who intend to stay at home. In every developing country, there are numerous young people interested in a professional career strictly within their home country, and it would be critical to identify and clearly communicate with such individuals in order to find appropriate trainees for the home-country service track. If these trainees were to choose to emigrate outside the auspices of the partnership, they would have a more difficult time than their peers. Experience shows that skilled migration without language training, placement assistance and skill-accreditation mechanisms can face great obstacles. To bolster the integrity of the two tracks, the destination-country health ministry could consider policies such as accrediting only those trainees who had originally opted to work toward emigration.

More broadly, the partnership would require the implementation of many features necessary for agreements on skilled migration of any kind. For instance, it would require governmental collaboration to ensure that migrants' skills are recognized within the destination country. It would require consultation with destination-country labor organizations to ensure that native workers understand which shortages are being filled and why. And it would require working across ministries in the destination country, perhaps through an institutionalized interministerial working group. A nursing GSP, for example, would be difficult without the collaboration of the health ministry, the employment or labor ministry, and the ministry responsible for immigration (often the interior ministry or immigration ministry) to ensure that trainee-migrants can speedily acquire both accreditation and work permits.

Global Skill Partnerships: A Proposal for Technical Training in a Mobile World

GSPs in the health field, in particular, would face a unique challenge in countering the widely held but mistaken idea that the World Health Organization (WHO) has banned any recruitment of health professionals in countries where health staffing is below a certain threshold. No such ban exists. The WHO has established a threshold of health-worker staffing levels below which recruitment deserves careful scrutiny. However, the researchers who calculated this threshold describe it as "a suggestive guideline, not a definitive benchmark," and the WHO agrees that quantitative thresholds "are not a substitute for specific country assessments" (Angenendt, Clemens and Merda 2014). GSPs are designed to link the international recruitment of health professionals with the creation of new professionals within the origin country. Properly designed, partnerships such as GSPs violate neither the letter nor the spirit of the WHO Global Code of Practice on the International Recruitment of Health Personnel. On the contrary, they are designed to use the power of migration to reduce human-capital shortages within origin and destination countries alike, addressing the WHO's legitimate core concerns about the unstructured migration of health workers.

Planning for a mobile world

Many features of GSPs could be adapted to individual circumstances. For example, if licensing regulations in the destination country required graduation from a local training institution, trainees could *complete* their training at that destination-country institution after starting their training abroad. Even shifting some portion of migrants' training to the origin country, accompanied by technical and financial support for that training, would tangibly benefit the origin country by strengthening its training institutions and adding to its human-capital base. The model can accommodate many modifications. The core requirement is that skilled migration occur within an agreed and mutually beneficial structure that does not oblige workers to live in any particular place against their will.

Global skill partnerships exemplify a particular approach to managing skilled migration that stands in contrast to others we might choose. To be sure, it is possible to treat skilled workers as if they were a fixed quantity to be pushed from one country to another as governments unilaterally determine, with one country's gain necessarily another's loss. We can treat skilled migrants themselves as selfish and disloyal, imposing punitive sanctions on them and denigrating their actions as a "drain" on their compatriots. This approach results in policy recommendations that include recruitment bans and compensation sanctions.

But there is another choice. We can explicitly recognize the tremendous benefits and opportunities generated by enterprising migrants alongside the global need for their skills. We can work collaboratively across borders to structure migration so that those benefits are more equitably shared, turning migration into an engine of human-capital creation. This fundamentally different approach will require new institutions and new ways of interacting across borders. But a mobile world demands such institutions, and global skill partnerships represent one promising way forward.

References

Angenendt, Steffen, Michael Clemens and Meiko Merda. "The WHO Global Code of Practice: A Useful Guide for Recruiting Health Care Professionals? Lessons from Germany and Beyond." *SWP Comments* 2014/C 22, May 2014. Berlin: Stiftung Wissenschaft und Politik, 2014. www.swp-berlin.org/en/publications/swp-comments-en/swp-aktuelle-details/article/who_verhaltenskodex.html.

BNSRM (Biroul Național de Statistică al Republicii Moldova). *Cîştigul salarial mediu lunar pe activităţi economice, 2014*. Chişinău, Moldova: BNSRM, 2014. http://statbank.statistica.md/pxweb/Dialog/view.asp?ma=SAL0150&ti=Castigul+salarial+mediu+dupa+Activitati+econ omice%2C+Ani%2C+Sector+si+Luni&path=../quicktables/RO/03%20SAL/SAL01/serii% 20lunare/&lang=1.

Clemens, Michael A. "Global Skill Partnerships: a Proposal for Technical Training in a Mobile World." *IZA Journal of Labor Policy* 2015 (forthcoming).

Clemens, Michael A., Colum Graham and Stephen Howes. "Skill Development and Regional Mobility: Lessons from the Australia-Pacific Technical College." *Journal of Development Studies,* 2015 (forthcoming).

Cruc, Olesea, Onorica Banciu, Iurie Brinişter, Maria Vremiş, Viorica Craievschi-Toartă and Alexandru Sinchetru. *Study on Social Protection and Social Inclusion in Moldova*. Chişinău, Moldova: Institute for Development and Social Initiatives "Viitorul" (prepared for the European Commission, Directorate-General for Employment, Social Affairs and Equal Opportunities), 2009. http://ec.europa.eu/social/BlobServlet?docId=4348&langId=en.

OECD (Organization for Economic Co-operation and Development). *International Migration Outlook: SOPEMI 2007 Edition*. Paris: OECD Publishing, 2007. www.oecd-ilibrary.org/con tent/book/migr_outlook-2007-en.

WHO (World Health Organization). "The Costs of Training Health Professionals in the Republic of Moldova." *Republic of Moldova Health Policy Paper Series No. 12*. Copenhagen: WHO Regional Office for Europe, 2014. www.euro.who.int/__data/assets/pdf_file/0016/251170/The-costs-of-training-health-professionals-in-the-Republic-of-Moldova-Eng.pdf.

Fairness and Development in the Global Governance of Migration

Gregory A. Maniatis

More people than ever are seeking safety and a better life through migration. Yet the legal options for doing so are far too limited to meet the existing demand. This imbalance empowers unethical smugglers, recruiters and employers, leading to rampant pathologies; for instance, 40,000 people have died in transit since 2000 (Brian and Laczko 2014), while migrants lose up to 35 percent of their wages to middlemen and an average of 8 percent in remittance-transfer fees (World Bank 2014). The burden falls especially heavily on the 35 million migrants under the age of 20 (UNICEF 2013). Even when migration takes place within the framework of bilateral agreements, the terms of such programs often neglect migrants' basic rights. The international refugee protection system, meanwhile, is grossly insufficient.

The potential of multilateral cooperation to protect democracy, the rule of law and migrant rights

The failure of states to ensure that as much migration as possible occurs in a safe, legal and morally responsible way harms not only individuals, but also the common good. It undermines trust in government, justice and the rule of law; exacerbates inequality at the national and global levels; hinders migration policies that help the broader economy; and abets a pestilent nationalism that turns societies against ethnic and religious minorities. All these dangers are present in developed countries that have long had substantial migrant populations; they are perhaps even more acute in the developing world, where nearly half of all migrants go today, and where many states lack effective institutions to manage diverse societies and migration.

Such challenges related to migration will not all be solved in one place. They remain primarily the domain of states, which fiercely guard their sovereign right to determine who crosses their borders and on what terms. Despite this, migration policymaking in most governments is an underfunded backwater, taking a backseat to economic, security and social concerns. The rise of anti-migrant populism, meanwhile, has led to ever-more reactive and myopic behavior by politicians.

Fairness and Development in the Global Governance of Migration

It is equally clear, however, that governments acting unilaterally cannot address many of these problems. They are not, on their own, able to crack down on the criminal syndicates that have made human smuggling the world's largest illicit trade, generating more revenue than even drugs or arms. In the absence of cooperation, governments cannot create conditions in which labor-market supply and demand is brought into equilibrium. Many transnational networks of exploitative employers and recruiters remain out of their reach.

Multilateral and regional cooperation can help fill these voids. Until recently, migration debates at the United Nations were acrimonious and polarized. Most developed countries adamantly opposed multilateral debate, let alone action, on migration. Many countries of origin, meanwhile, fought fiercely to bring migration into the U.N.'s normative embrace. The result was deadlock and polarization. The onset of the global financial crisis and the subsequent rise of anti-migrant populism should have made progress at the multilateral level even more elusive.

Counter-intuitively, perhaps, while the political toxicity of migration has impeded domestic policy advances, it has by contrast accelerated progress at other levels of governance. Multilateral institutions, local governments and the judiciary have been stepping into the policy gap and playing an increasingly important role in regulating migration and facilitating immigrant integration during the past decade.

At the global level, state engagement has intensified. One indication of this is membership in the International Organization for Migration, which has leapt from 91 to 157 states since 2001. The international community's signal institutional achievement was the 2006 creation of the Global Forum on Migration and Development (GFMD), which has become the principal forum in which governments regularly gather to discuss migration issues, analyze policy and foster cooperative efforts. The GFMD has played a crucial agenda-setting role, as well – for instance, in advancing the inclusion of migration in the Post-2015 U.N. Development Agenda. It also has brought civil society organizations firmly into the international policy conversation.

There have been other notable advances at the multilateral level, too. The Domestic Workers Convention, adopted in 2011, has now secured 16 ratifications (ILO 2013) – including several major European countries that had previously been averse to signing any migration-related treaties. Remittance fees paid by migrants have dropped by 6 percent on average since the turn of the century, translating into an additional $30 billion reaching some of the world's poorest families every year. The number of state programs designed to engage with diaspora communities has skyrocketed. Migration, meanwhile, is today poised to become part of the Post-2015 U.N. Development Agenda, an important step in repositioning migration as a positive force among key stakeholders. Moreover, a group of countries led by the United States – which has long been averse to multilateral engagement on migration – is pursuing an initiative to provide systematic protection to migrants in countries in crisis.

The coming years are likely to see gradual institutional progress at the multilateral level – the deepening of international cooperation through the GFMD, more frequent high-level dialogue at the United Nations, the closer integration of the International Organization for Migration into the U.N. system, or even the creation of a new, technically oriented body focused on facilitating inter-state agreements on migration. All this will contribute to sounder policymaking, as better data and policy analysis reach ever-larger communities of bureaucrats and other stakeholders.

This deeper, broader and shared understanding of migration should increase the likelihood of common efforts aimed at addressing many of the challenges posed by migration – especially those that involve targeting bad actors, such as smugglers, traffickers and rapacious recruiters – as well as particularly egregious state actions, such as the detention of migrant children. It should abet more effective joint efforts to reduce the costs of migration (such as remittance fees) and to stimulate innovation in the field (with programs such as migration insurance, for instance). It will also be crucial in preventing the spread of bad ideas and negative trends, such as the increasingly stingy posture of developed countries with regard to providing protection to asylum seekers and others in need.

More ambitious goals – such as a viable new convention on migration or the decriminalization of migration offenses – are likely to be stalled, although specialized treaties on specific aspects of migration (e.g., recruitment) might well see some progress. It is likely to be left to national and international courts, however, to render decisions on crucial questions, such as whether the refugee convention can be expanded to include new categories of forced migrants.

Such progress would be modest and insufficient. The problems related to migration are likely to grow in the coming decade, not diminish, especially given the anti-migrant sentiment currently prevailing in many countries and the vast demographic imbalances between the developed and developing worlds.

Awareness of how policymaking can positively influence the course and outcomes of migration is at its very early stages, roughly equivalent to where the environmental movement was in the early 1980s. In order for the movement to grow, those who believe migrants deserve greater policy attention and public compassion will need to ensure that migration is understood by the public not as an isolated subject, but as one that is linked to far broader social concerns, such as inequality and nationalism.

A decade of modest progress in international cooperation

At the turn of the century, migration was largely a dead letter at the multilateral level. Despite the enormous potential for policy to amplify migration's benefits and mute its dangers, there was little international cooperation specifically targeted at achieving such gains. This was symbolized by the Convention on the Protection of the Rights of All Migrant Workers. Adopted in 1990, it was (and remains) the least-ratified of all the major human-rights conventions. The terrorist attacks in the United States, London and Madrid early in the millennium further chilled the West's willingness to bring migration into the multilateral realm.

Nonetheless, U.N. Secretary-General Kofi Annan was drawn to the issue and sought to energize U.N.-level engagement. He asked Assistant Secretary-General Michael Doyle to lead an internal review of possible courses of actions. The resulting 2003 report offered an incisive analysis of how international cooperation could improve migration outcomes, but it was never made public. The politics around the issue were too volatile, constraining Annan's ability to act. Instead, he looked to the Global Commission on International Migration, a blue-ribbon group of politicians and experts, to give guidance. Their report, which offered an overall view of migration, was released in autumn 2005 to little institutional effect. (It is also worth noting in this context that migration was not included in the Millennium Development Goals.)

By this time, migration-related debates in U.N. bodies, such as the Commission for Population and Development, were characterized by polarized rhetoric that at best offered an abstract vision of a rights-based migration system, but more typically descended into political invective that split along North/South or origin-country/destination-country lines. Dueling dogmas and taboos blocked the path to serious discussion, and the fundamentalist guardians of orthodoxies prevailed. It was far safer and easier to indulge in rhetoric than to do the hard work of building a common understanding on migration, which would involve compromise and cooperation.

With migration set to be the focus of a U.N. General Assembly (GA) debate in autumn 2006, Annan appointed Peter Sutherland to serve as his special representative on migration. Sutherland was tasked by Annan with ensuring that the GA's High-Level Dialogue (HLD) on International Migration and Development – scheduled for September 2006 and marking the first time in history that the General Assembly would debate migration – did not further divide countries. Sutherland, one of Europe's most respected statesmen and the main architect of the World Trade Organization, believed that the only way to achieve this was to set an ambitious goal. To this end, he proposed the creation of the Global Forum on Migration and Development.

The GFMD proposal struck a delicate balance. It was designed to bridge the two main sides within the United Nations – those states that wanted to keep migration out of the multilateral arena, and those that wanted it to be brought into the U.N.'s normative embrace. (This divide, though not as acutely expressed, remains alive today.) The Forum would be led by member states, not international institutions, but would be tied to the United Nations through the figures of the secretary-general and his special representative. This structure recognized that the main locus for action on migration would remain national capitals. Its structural placement outside the U.N. proper also allayed concerns that the migration debate might be calcified by bureaucracy or, more menacingly, that the United Nations would wield decision-making power on the issue.

In its design, the Forum recognized that migration had been politicized before it had been analyzed. As such, the organization was conceived as a space to allow policymakers to meet regularly, to develop a common understanding on the issues raised by migration, to analyze policies and practices, to define mutual interests and to foster cooperation. The underlying assumption was that better-organized migration could lead to better outcomes – for migrants, for the communities that received them and for the families left behind. By the end of the HLD in 2006, with the critical support of a handful of states (Belgium and Sweden, above all), the Forum had been willed into existence by Annan and Sutherland.

The inaugural GFMD was held in Brussels in June 2007. In the seven years since, the Forum has become the main (though underpowered) engine of international cooperation on migration. On average, about 150 states, together with hundreds of civil society representatives and experts, gather each year to carefully examine the evidence and deliberate on practical solutions to problems – from how to reduce the costs of remittances and recruitment to how to protect migrant rights, engage diaspora communities effectively and match the labor needs of countries of origin and destination. The Forum's work is done by groups of government policymakers who meet throughout the year to prepare the week-long main event, assisted by international organizations and experts. It also has succeeded in bringing civil society productively into the debate.

Importantly, the Forum has thrived *despite* the toxic domestic politics of migration in many states. Its advent, just before the onset of the global financial crisis and the subsequent rise of anti-migrant populism in many countries, was not fortuitous. Yet domestic deadlock on migration has created an even greater need for international action. By staying out of the political limelight and focusing on generating solutions to practical problems, the GFMD has become a pole of attraction for policymakers rather than the third rail of their careers. Even delicate issues such as illegal migration and migrant rights, too sensitive to be included in the early days of the Forum, are now routine topics of conversation there. The growing demand for practical policy solutions is also reflected in the fast-rising membership of the IOM.

The GFMD will meet for the eighth time in 2015 in Istanbul, and its near future is secure – Bangladesh will be host in 2016, followed by Morocco in 2017. (A third High-Level Dialogue will likely take place in 2019.) The GFMD will continue to build bridges among key communities that were once at odds with each other – North and South (if that distinction matters any longer), states and civil society, sending and receiving countries, the private and the public sectors. By fostering mutual understanding grounded in sound evidence, the Forum will continue to set priorities.

But the GFMD is hardly the only indicator of progress in the past decade. There are many others of note, including the following positive signs:

Recognition of migration as a force for development: The GFMD represents the pinnacle of the current multilateral recognition that migrants are a powerful force for development. But the recasting of migration in this way has had a much broader and deeper impact, as policymakers around the world are now incorporating migration into their economic and poverty-reduction strategies. This is in part financial: Annual global remittances by migrants total nearly $600 billion, with over $400 billion sent to developing countries – triple the amount of official development assistance (World Bank 2014); moreover, migrants' annual savings are of a similar magnitude and represent one of the largest potential sources of financing for development. But perhaps most critically of all, the reframing of migrants as positive actors in this way has the potential to soften public skepticism toward migration. The incorporation of migration into the Post-2015 U.N. Development Agenda (through a plank still under negotiation as of this writing) would underscore this shift. Many development agencies and stakeholders have long considered emigration as an indicator that their development efforts had failed; it has taken intense advocacy to start persuading them that migration is a force that can abet development when the right policies are in place.

Adoption of the Domestic Workers Convention: Adopted in 2011 and already ratified by 16 countries, the convention (C189) is a sign of growing understanding of migrants' true vulnerability, as about half of the world's domestic workers are migrants. Arguably, the treaty succeeded because it framed migration in a broader context, placing migrants in a category of workers widely recognized as needing greater protection. It also is notable that several EU states have ratified C189, even though no EU country has ratified the 1990 migrant workers convention.

Fairness and Development in the Global Governance of Migration

Reduction of remittance costs: In the most practical terms, the greatest success has been in the reduction of money-transfer costs, from an average of almost 15 percent of the total transferred at the turn of the century to around 8 percent today. This has been achieved by a combination of awareness-raising, advocacy, technological innovation, new market actors and regulations – forces that must continue to be harnessed in order to drive the costs down toward zero.

Growth of policymaking capacity: While still grossly inadequate, policymakers' attention to migration has grown, as measured, for instance, by the proliferation of bilateral agreements, regional consultative processes and free-movement regimes within regional economic communities. The IOM's staff has increased exponentially, from 1,000 individuals at the turn of the millennium to almost 10 times that today. At the United Nations, the creation of the Global Migration Group has improved coordination among international organizations responsible for migration. And the decision in December 2014 by the U.N. General Assembly to convene regular High-Level Dialogues on Migration and Development ensures that the issue now has a permanent place at the pinnacle of multilateral co-operation.

Intensified engagement with diaspora communities: The intensity of engagement by states with their diaspora communities has grown vastly over the past decade, in large part due to recognition of the enormous contributions migrants can make to economic, social and political progress – assuming the right policies are put in place. Nearly a hundred countries now have departments or ministries dedicated to reaching out to emigrants with the aim of increasing revenues (diaspora bonds, investment, philanthropy); drawing on diaspora skills by encouraging circular migration, networks and virtual return; tying their countries into the global economy; and strengthening cultural and social ties.

All of this marks progress. But, while notable, these achievements pale in comparison to the lost opportunities and problems that have resulted over the past decade through failures of policy and an all-too-frequent lack of cooperation. The thousands of migrant deaths every year in the Mediterranean, the Gulf of Aden and the South Pacific are just one symptom of this.

A generational agenda for progress on international cooperation

In folklore, a bullet cast from silver is often the only weapon that can slay a werewolf, a witch or other monsters. It is a commonplace among migration experts and policymakers to say that there is "no silver bullet" for migration (in fact, a Google search of "silver bullet" and "migrants" turns up over 2 million hits).

This tired cliché underscores an inherent defeatism among migration stakeholders and even among passionate advocates of migrant rights, and it is indicative of an ambient perception that migration is mostly a problem. This sense, of course, has been amplified in recent years by the rise of anti-migrant populists and has taken firmer root in homogenous societies in which citizenship has long been defined by blood rather than by civic participation. But it is abetted as well, and more perniciously, by self-styled liberals who also want to be seen as muscular defenders of national sovereignty.

Ideally, migration stakeholders could exit this defensive crouch and advocate a more positive vision – one in which a public debate grounded in facts, rather than myths, helps set more reasonable terms for immigration and immigrant integration. Migration will always generate challenges and tensions, since it involves change – in the lives of individuals, for communities and in the social calculus. But with the right policies in place, migration can be much more beneficial and less divisive than it is today.

In the coming years, however, at least in most of the world, migration policies are likely to be made against a backdrop of fear. Nonetheless, there is a deep and meaningful agenda for action around which the international community – or at least coalitions of willing countries and other stakeholders (especially civil society and the private sector) – can and should rally.

The goals we need to pursue are not ones that pit states against other states or the interests of migrants against the interests of citizens. In the main, they are policies that squeeze out bad actors – rapacious recruiters, venal smugglers, unscrupulous employers – and return their ill-gotten gains to migrants and to states. None of these aims necessarily imply that states must increase migration flows; while many might well want to do so, these are changes that increase the quality of the migration experience for all legitimate stakeholders involved in the process.

Among the goals for international cooperation could be the following (these echo goals articulated by Peter Sutherland, the U.N. Special Representative for International Migration):

- *Reduce remittance costs to zero:* In the era of mobile banking, remittance fees should be near zero. Cutting them to 3 percent – a goal likely to be articulated in the Post-2015 Development Agenda – will deliver an additional $25 billion annually to families in the developing world. A combination of (de)regulation and private initiative can achieve this by 2025.
- *Lower recruitment costs:* Fees paid by workers to middlemen, both legitimate and illicit, can consume over a third of wages. Already, private-sector pioneers are trying to bring these figures down through the promotion of ethical recruitment practices. Government regulation and international cooperation will be indispensable in this regard, and a specialized treaty may even be necessary. If successful, this will leave an additional tens of billions of dollars in the hands of migrants every year.
- *Ensure that migrants keep their earned social security benefits:* Only 20 to 25 percent of international migrants are able to take their pension rights with them when they return to their country of origin. Some countries do an excellent job of protecting this right, such as Morocco, Algeria and Turkey, which have signed agreements to ensure that the majority of their registered migrants abroad (89% in the case of Morocco) are covered by bilateral pension-portability agreements (Newland and Plaza 2013). This should become the global standard.
- *Recognize migrant skills:* Too many migrants work in jobs that do not utilize their full skills. Deficits in the cross-border recognition of skills and certifications deprives migrants of opportunities and are detrimental for development in countries of origin and destination.
- *End the detention of migrant children:* A meaningful reform agenda must also include non-financial goals, and the most morally urgent one involves banning the detention of migrant children – tens of thousands of whom are put behind bars every year, including hundreds in solitary confinement, merely for civil violations.

Fairness and Development in the Global Governance of Migration

- *Increase protections for the most vulnerable migrants:* Beyond the plight of children, the international community's efforts should be focused on the most vulnerable migrants – those dying in transit or those most heavily exposed to human-rights abuses. Small efforts in this respect are underway, such as the "migrants in countries in crisis initiative" mentioned earlier. But solutions also will have to be found for more intractable problems, such as the thousands of migrants who perish in the Mediterranean, the Gulf of Aden and other troubled waters. One area of focus for reformers must be establishing safer access to asylum and expanding resettlement capacities.
- *Invest in innovations such as migration insurance:* Technological and other innovations are likely to transform how people move and live across borders in coming years. One idea offering particular potential is insurance for migrants, provided either collaboratively by governments, employers or other stakeholders. By offering a safety net for social benefits and lost wages that does not directly draw on the public purse, migration insurance can protect the rights of migrants while also taking some of the sting out of the political debate in destination countries.
- *Institutionalize diaspora engagement:* While the number of governments with policies and institutions designed to engage their diaspora communities has soared in the past decade, the knowledge and tools facilitating this task have not yet been concentrated and institutionalized. This shortcoming could be addressed by the creation of regional or global diaspora development banks.

This list could be much longer. Advancing this agenda would constitute critical incremental progress that could materially improve the lives of hundreds of millions of people; communities in destination countries also stand to gain enormously by the righting of policy and quelling of political tensions. Of course, it is easier to write all this than to achieve it.

The level at which this cooperation unfolds should and will vary from issue to issue. In some instances, new conventions might even be envisioned, taking inspiration from the Domestic Workers Convention that now has been ratified by 16 countries. Institutional changes will also be needed; among those debated are creating far greater capacity to address migration in regional forums, such as the Association of Southeast Asian Nations (ASEAN) and Mercosur, for instance, and bringing the IOM closer to the United Nations.

The harder battles – such as decriminalizing civil migration violations and redesigning the international refugee-protection system so that it is more generous and suited to the needs of the 21st century – will take longer. Equally difficult will be progress at the national level in much of the world, where advances are impeded both by widespread misinformation and by the normal human fear of change.

The fundamental prerequisite for such deeper change is for migration to become part of a broader narrative of how the 21st century is evolving so that migrants are seen as more than individuals simply needing protection and special support, and so that migration policymaking becomes a mainstream issue, not a backwater. This will involve the injection of several themes into the public debate, most obviously by relentlessly highlighting how migrants and migration contribute to our communities and to development; by showing that migration is a natural response to inequality, and that a smart policy approach to it can reduce inequality not only between countries, but also within them; and by stressing that the degree of generosity we show in our response to migrants is a bellwether of our own moral standing.

To achieve all this, believers in positive change on migration will have to reach out to advocates dealing with the other broad challenges of our century, such as labor unions fighting low wages, civil society groups battling discrimination and those seeking to mitigate climate change. Doing so is, in effect, the mirror image of what has created the perception that migrants are a problem: Immigration was placed in broader frames of security/terrorism, the loss of sovereignty due to globalization and growing middle-class economic insecurity, thus allowing opponents to scapegoat migrants.

In some places, this cross-fertilization of movements is starting to happen. But it is an effort that will take grit and resolve over a generation or more.

References

Brian, Tara, and Frank Laczko (eds.). *Fatal Journeys. Tracking Lives Lost during Migration*. Geneva: International Organization for Migration, 2014. http://publications.iom.int/bookstore/free/FatalJourneys_CountingtheUncounted.pdf.

ILO (International Labour Organization). *Ratifications of C189 – Domestic Workers Convention, 2011 (No. 189)*. September 5, 2013. www.ilo.org/dyn/normlex/en/f?p=NORMLEXPUB:11300:0::NO::P11300_INSTRUMENT_ID:2551460.

Newland, Kathleen, and Sonia Plaza. *What We Know About Diasporas and Economic Development*. Washington, D.C.: Migration Policy Institute, 2013. www.migrationpolicy.org/research/what-we-know-about-diasporas-and-economic-development.

World Bank. Migration, Remittances and Diaspora. 2014. http://go.worldbank.org/0IK1E5K7U0.

UNICEF (The United Nations Children's Fund). *International Migration, Children and Adolescents. Population Dynamics*. October 2013. www.globalmigrationgroup.org/sites/default/files/uploads/gmg-topics/mig-data/Brief-Children-Adolescents-Population-Dynamics-Oct-2013.pdf.

Policy Recommendations for Fair Migration Governance

Najim Azahaf, Ulrich Kober, Matthias M. Mayer

Migration and globalization represent two sides of the same coin. As the nature of communications grow increasingly interconnected and higher standards of education foster economic development, the likelihood of migration increases. People leave their homelands – voluntarily, partially voluntarily or of necessity – in search of new opportunities for themselves and their families. For migrants, this can represent a positive development, as migration often brings social advancement and improved living standards. For destination countries, migration can precipitate a variety of positive developments in numerous ways: migrants rejuvenate aging populations, contribute to public finances and promote innovation, while their well-integrated offspring can provide social returns and enrich societies by contributing to cultural diversity. There are positive developments for their countries of origin, too, which benefit from remittances sent back by migrants as well as the transfer of knowledge and investments and the development of new business relationships.

If self-determined mobility can offer these sorts of opportunities to migrants, their destination countries and their countries of origin, it must be seen as a positive and should be encouraged. This lies primarily within the purview of the individual countries that place the greatest value on structuring migration within their national responsibilities. However, international cooperation has an increasingly important part to play here. By enabling self-determined migration within its borders, the European Union (EU) has become a model for mobility.

While a unified international migration policy remains a pipe dream, there has been a boost in international discourse on fair migration, particularly when it comes to the links between migration and development policies. The goal here must be to create the right balance between supply and demand within fair framework conditions at the national, European and global levels while avoiding excessive regulation to structure migration in such a way that – like the social market economy – it functions to the benefit of all involved.

Policy Recommendations for Fair Migration Governance

Trends and drivers in international migration and their impact

The demographic shift is increasing international competition for skilled labor

According to calculations issued by the United Nations (U.N.), by 2050, Africa's working age population will increase by 910 million, with Asia seeing an increase of 517 million over the same period. Political crises and economic hardship, on the one hand, economic advances and improved standards of education, on the other – they all increase the likelihood that people in developing countries will wish to emigrate. As a result, we will see increased migration pressure on OECD countries, particularly from Africa.

At the same time, most OECD countries are undergoing a dramatic demographic shift. With falling birthrates, the (working-age) population of these countries will shrink over the coming decades and societies will become older. By 2050, Europe's working-age population will decline by 96 million. Germany, for example, can expect a fall in the potential labor force of 40 percent, from around 45 million to 27 million, without migration. Other countries can expect similar scenarios. As a result, international competition for labor will increase.

In the mid-term, we will also see countries that have traditionally experienced high levels of emigration – as well as so-called emerging countries, such as China – recruiting staff from other countries at an ever increasing rate. Aging societies will require not only highly skilled professionals, but also less-skilled and even unskilled workers. The nature of global demographic developments is such that this will require more than simply headhunting workers from abroad: Future efforts to a secure a sustainable workforce will see a greater focus on investment in origin countries and on training the global workforce.

How international mobility patterns – and their perceived benefits – are changing

Migratory movements have changed in recent decades, giving rise to new geographic patterns of migration. Along with the "south-north" trend of migration from developing countries to industrialized countries which has dominated to date, increasing mobility between developing countries – and between developing and emerging countries – has seen an increase in "south-south" migration. Patterns of migratory duration are also changing: Temporary migration and recurring, or circular, migration is on the increase.

It is not just the form and scale of migration that presents development cooperation with new challenges; recent years have also seen a shift in how the benefits of migration are perceived. Where the migration of labor forces from developing countries was once seen almost entirely as a net loss to the labor force in the country of origin, this view has since been expanded to consider the opportunities migration brings to such countries. In particular, there has been increasing focus on the benefits associated with remittances from migrants and the role of diasporas in development policies, as well as on the emigrant communities at large that actively support their countries of origin.

Regional conflicts are increasing the flow of refugees

Political crises and civil wars in the Middle East and Africa, as well as in Eastern Europe, have forced many to flee in search of a better future. Most refugees seek sanctuary in neighboring countries where asylum systems are often ill-equipped to cope with the overwhelming flow of refugees. And increasing numbers of refugees are coming to Europe. In Germany, for instance, the number of asylum applications more than doubled between 2011 and 2013 to reach 127,000.

With ongoing conflicts, we can expect to see increased movements of refugees, many of whom will be unable to return to their homelands any time soon. The international community is therefore confronted with the challenge of not just offering temporary protection for refugees, but also integrating them into society – which also provides opportunities for the labor market.

Fair migration underpinned by the "triple win" principle: Ideal and reality

Self-determined migration, that is, migration that is based on an individual's independent, opportunity-oriented decisions, offers opportunities to migrants, their countries of origin and their destination countries. But migration can also entail risk. Under certain conditions, foreign recruitment can diminish development opportunities in countries of origin, leading to a reduction in the skilled labor base ("brain drain"). This is felt in such areas as the health sector, with doctors and nursing staff leaving the homelands where they are sorely needed. Migrants are often treated unfairly in destination countries, are unable to work at the level for which they are qualified ("brain waste"), or can even fall victim to exploitation at the hands of people smugglers and corrupt employers.

Finally, migration can have a negative effect on destination countries – in the form of wage dumping, for instance. Efforts aimed at developing the potential of the domestic workforce may also diminish. If migrants are not sufficiently integrated into the labor market and into society, destination countries are subject to an increased risk of social tension. Populist movements exploit these integration deficits with the aim of marginalizing migrants. This weakens the fabric of liberal democracy and its emphasis on human dignity.

The standard for fair and effective migration management is the achievement of threefold gains. Migration is sustainable only when it considers the interests of all concerned: migrants, the populations of origin countries and the populations of destination countries.

There has been increasing support for this "triple-win" concept since the mid-2000s, particularly from such bodies as the U.N.'s Global Commission for Migration. In real terms, however, current migration structures rarely embody the threefold advantage for all concerned. Within destination countries, there are tensions and trade-offs between stakeholders: Certain immigration policies might serve the interests of employers but conflict with the interests of domestic employees. To date, no country can point to a model for managing migration that truly embodies the triple-win concept.

But when it comes to managing migration, fairness is more than an ethical imperative; it can also generate locational advantages in the global competition for talent. Fair processes of

Policy Recommendations for Fair Migration Governance

migration and integration make destination countries attractive to skilled workers. Far from being mutually exclusive, justice and efficacy are, in fact, mutually dependent factors when it comes to managing migration.

Making migration fair and effective – a 10-point agenda

On the one hand, migration policy touches upon the very core of national sovereignty and, with regard to future decisions regulating immigration, will remain principally a matter of national policy. On the other hand, migration is a transnational phenomenon and, by its very nature, cannot be addressed exclusively by national policy. Therefore, fairness in migration cannot be achieved by countries working on their own. Indeed, it is reliant on consistent cross-border cooperation.

In order to manage global migration and integration policies in a way that is both fair and effective, the various national, bilateral and multilateral levels of governance must be taken into consideration, and pragmatic objectives and corridors of action developed:

- At the national level, a coherent policy must be developed with the participation of central stakeholders from business and society (recommendations 1 and 2), immigration regulations must be optimized and the entire migration cycle structured fairly (recommendations 3 and 4). In the face of the current global refugee crisis, the interface between managed labor migration and the intake of refugees must be recalibrated (recommendation 5). Finally, the issue of immigration must be broached in the public arena to ensure the buy-in of the general population (recommendation 6).
- At the bilateral level, cooperation between destination countries and countries of origin must be organized in a fair and effective manner (recommendation 7). Qualification partnerships represent one particularly fruitful approach here (recommendation 8).
- At the multilateral level, the European Union (recommendation 9) and the international community (recommendation 10) must press ahead with cooperation on migration issues.

1. Developing coherent policies on the basis of national immigration strategies and institutional reforms

Effective migration management is contingent on the kind of coherent policy (the "whole of government" approach) seen in the Swedish model. This requires a unified national immigration strategy that is subject to approval by the legislature. A common strategy only becomes workable when it is effectively secured by inter-ministerial coordination between the relevant departments. Here, it is particularly important to consider development-policy issues as well as the interrelation of migration through both legal and illegal channels.

Where possible, the central competencies for migration and integration should be brought together in one powerful ministry. This ministry would have primary responsibility for implementing immigration strategy and coordinating with other departments, as well as with national and international partners.

2. Incorporating central stakeholders from business and society

Migration processes are complex and affect numerous actors in business and society. Developing sound solutions in migration policy requires a multistakeholder approach in which state actors work together with non-state actors. Hearings and consultation processes can help secure the consistent involvement of employers, unions as well as civil society representatives. This cooperation is not just beneficial for strategic measures, but in the operational structuring of immigration policy, as well.

Parastatal and commercial recruitment agencies can play an important part in managing migration. Working within the framework of bilateral agreements, for instance, they often have the necessary structures and capacities for tailored recruitment and preparation of migrants in their countries of origin. International standards oriented toward fairness can be anchored in a certification system for recruitment agencies. Here, it is important to note that a fair immigration system that is responsive to demand entails (initial investment) costs. The question of which actors (migrants, private sector, public sector) are responsible for these costs, and to what extent, should be clarified in policy debates.

3. Optimizing immigration management for workers

International experience shows that hybrid systems that incorporate a supply-and-demand approach to migration management are particularly expedient. It would therefore be prudent to further promote such systems. This reflects the fact that there are inherent weaknesses in systems that are solely focused on either the labor market or on realization of potential. If management is purely aligned to conditions in the labor market at a given point in time, problems can emerge when that market changes or undergoes a crisis, which may see labor migrants with limited qualifications losing their positions. Where management is purely oriented toward potential, there is a danger that immigration will not meet the needs of the labor market, and that integration of immigrants will become more difficult.

However, immigration management can only do so much. Migration flows cannot be turned on and off like a tap. Where the demand for labor is concerned, the most important factor is transparent and scientifically credible prognoses on demographic developments and migration streams.

4. Making the entire migration cycle fair for migrants

To realize the full potential of self-determined mobility for migrants, receiving countries and countries of origin, the entire migration cycle must be accompanied and structured by appropriate services and regulations.

a) *Integration measures that begin in the country of origin*
   Selected services relating to integration within destination countries should, in line with the Canadian model, be available even before migrants leave their countries of origin in the

form of Internet seminars, for instance, or facilities on the ground. These services could incorporate language courses; information on the working culture, housing market and educational facilities in the destination country; as well as job opportunities for family members.

b) *Securing recognition for foreign qualifications and enabling prior checks before the decision to emigrate*

There is an urgent need for legal frameworks that allow for the recognition of foreign professional qualifications. Germany's legislation on recognition can be cited as a model here. This type of initiative must be continually monitored in the light of experience and improved where necessary. Where professional qualifications are unrecognized or only partially recognized, a path toward qualification must be laid out, and affordable retraining opportunities identified.

c) *Making it easier to acquire permanent residency or citizenship*

Long-term immigration should be the norm, and even finite residency permits should come with generous conditions. A targeted approach would incorporate residence permits that could be extended according to clear criteria; where feasible, permanent residency permits should then be granted as early as possible. It is essential that the pathway to citizenship be made easier and faster. Dual citizenship must be an option. Well-integrated migrants should be eligible for naturalization after three years.

d) *Incorporating diasporas in fair migration structures*

Improved connections between diasporas and their countries of origin can promote knowledge transfers and, consequently, development. A critical mass of immigrants with the same or similar backgrounds makes it easier for migrants of the groups in question. Countries of origin should be supported through the establishment of appropriate networks and databases. An active exchange between relevant communities and countries of origin can also make a potential return easier, which benefits the country of origin. Innovative financial instruments, such as diaspora bonds, represent another means of incorporating the diaspora in development efforts.

e) *Enabling return or onward migration*

Immigration laws of nation states should support individual mobility decisions by granting immigrant workers and their families extensive long-term residency and working rights early on, which would remain in force in the event of return or onward migration. This includes the right to take any accrued social-welfare entitlements – and to avoid double taxation. The unrestricted option to return in the event of temporary departures is also important. This can increase migrants' interest in permanently or temporarily returning to their homelands, where they can contribute to economic and social development.

5. Making it easier for refugees to enter the labor market

Humanitarian migration has a different logic than economic migration, as the intake and fair treatment of refugees is mandated by international conventions. Thus refugees with no foreseeable hope of return must be granted access to the labor market as soon as possible. One practical step toward achieving this goal would be for the potential and qualifications of individual refugees to be documented at the point of intake. Later, they must be offered the option of moving from refugee status to the pathways laid out for labor migrants. Pilot projects for promoting integration of refugees in education and the labor market that are already up and running – in Germany, for example – should be evaluated and, where necessary, improved as well as certainly furthered and scaled up.

6. Gaining public support for immigration with fairness and transparency

Fairness in migration structures is in no small part reliant on the agreement and support of the general population. Fairness in dealing with the established domestic population is a precondition for societal acceptance of immigration and for fostering an environment of openness and welcome. It is important to avoid wage dumping and the displacement of domestic labor forces by aligning immigration opportunities with the needs of the labor market and by evaluating employment conditions. Moreover, politicians, the social sector and civil society must work together to increase employment rates for the domestic population. Immigration alone will not meet the challenges of demographic transformation; rather, it must be integrated into an agreed overall strategy. The interaction between immigration and qualification measures for the domestic population must be subject to empirical enquiry, the results of which should inform policies governing immigration, education and employment.

Discussions on migration should not be left up to the elite alone. It is vital that the opportunities and risks that accompany immigration be made transparent to the public. In traditional destination countries, such as Canada, there is a broad-based consensus among the population that immigration is of benefit to the country. However, in other countries, the issue of immigration is often subject to entrenched skepticism. Consequently, the most important task when it comes to the emotionally charged debate around foreigners is to work from facts, invalidating potential concerns while counteracting populist tendencies.

7. Strengthening bilateral agreements by careful selection of partner countries

Agreements between destination countries and countries of origin represent an opportune means of creating fair framework conditions for migration. As long as negotiations are informed by a spirit of partnership, this form of coordination can generate a triple-win effect for all concerned. Some destination countries, such as Germany, have followed this path: With the cooperation of social partners and civil society, they have come to bilateral immigration agreements affecting professionals in certain industries that are subject to labor shortages: the nursing sector, in particular, but also engineering.

To ensure fair recruiting within the framework of a bilateral agreement, it is essential that partner countries be chosen with care on the basis of transparent criteria that are sensitive to development needs. Such touchstones are likely to include demographic and economic factors, the government's stance on labor migration, workable and transparent administration, the compatibility of the education system as well the ties between countries of origin and destination

Policy Recommendations for Fair Migration Governance

countries that have evolved over time. These bilateral agreements should be constantly monitored in regular governmental consultation in the framework of development cooperation efforts, taking into account the national development strategies of the partner countries. Using this evaluation, successful cooperation measures should be expanded and, where necessary, scaled up.

Countries of origin can also leverage their capacity to structure a migration process that is both profitable and just, as seen in the example of the Philippines and its measures for preparing and protecting migrants. Drawing on a country of origin's development strategy, destination countries should work from and support development cooperation work. Here, it makes sense for countries of origin to focus on developing training and educational systems and labor markets. But capacities for governmental migration management and support of migrants are also important. The targeted support of personnel offered by the Philippines' emigration system makes it unique throughout the world, and it should serve as a model.

8. Promoting global skill partnerships

The global competition for talent will increase in the coming decades. For aging societies throughout the OECD, it is therefore not enough to simply recruit skilled professionals from other countries. In the long term, there will be greater emphasis on the development of new human capital. The triple-win approach in structuring migration through global skill partnerships holds strong potential in this regard. In the nursing sector, for example, actors in destination countries experiencing personnel shortages can work with actors in countries of origin to offer qualification measures to potential emigrants as well as those interested in working in their homelands. Such partnerships would represent a channel for investing in the development of skilled professionals – for the benefit of destination countries, now able to recruit personnel with precisely tailored profiles, but also for the country of origin, which can now gain personnel for its own labor market. No less important is the benefit to those seeking new opportunities through temporary or permanent migration.

However, global skill partnerships can only be successful in the long term when the costs are fairly balanced between business, the public sector and migrants. Both destination countries and countries of origin should participate in new initiatives for global skill partnerships that could be launched through bilateral agreements with the support of national stakeholders from the business sector as well as international actors, such as the World Bank.

9. Expanding migration cooperation at the European level and EU mobility partnerships with third countries

The free movement of individuals within the EU is one of the greatest achievements of European integration and a source of prosperity and European cohesion. No EU member state can ignore European agreements and guidelines when formulating migration policy.

The European Union is working toward greater cooperation with third countries. Mobility partnerships represent a central instrument in this effort. They form a vital framework for concrete cooperation between signatory states. To date, mobility partnerships have been agreed upon with Armenia, Azerbaijan, Cape Verde, Georgia, Jordan, Moldavia, Morocco and Tunisia. Here, however, the emphasis has been on restrictive mechanisms aimed at stemming irregular migration by preventing document forgery, boosting border security and repatriating migrants.

There is great untapped potential in these mobility partnerships. They could offer direct support to migrants with concrete employment prospects in the EU, prepare outward-bound migrants with language and professional training, regulate the transferability of social-welfare entitlements, support economic and social reintegration in the event of return, and make it easier to send remittance payments. Mobility partnerships should be further developed in this direction and scaled up by increasing the circle of participating member states and partner countries.

The EU has launched a range of guidelines for the legal entry and residency of particular groups of migrants. One stand-out example is the Blue Card, which allows highly qualified professionals to take up employment in EU member states. Around 15,000 Blue Cards were granted in 2013, around 14,000 of them in Germany alone. However, when you compare this rate with the situation in Canada, which welcomes 250,000 qualified immigrants per year, it soon becomes apparent that Europe is trailing behind in the global competition for talent. EU member states should strengthen their bid for qualified immigrants from third countries. At the same time, legal migration channels within Europe should be opened up to medium-skilled and unskilled migrants. This would provide realistic migration opportunities to individuals seeking to escape economic uncertainty. It would also reduce the likelihood of their falling into irregular migration channels or residency conditions, or of being exploited by human traffickers and dubious employers.

10. Expanding multilateral cooperation in global migration structures

It is also important that international efforts to support fair migration management be advanced beyond the European framework.

A global migration policy with internationally applicable standards of fair migration is still in an embryonic stage. But in the wake of the U.N.'s Global Commission on International Migration in the mid-2000s, significant progress has been made in international cooperation in migration management, particularly in the links between migration and development. Representatives of over 150 countries now meet every year to discuss these issues at the Global Forum on Migration and Development (GFMD), where they provide advice and impetus for anchoring fairness – as well as the interests of countries of origin – in the international community's political guidelines.

While there is no immediate prospect of a global agreement on fair migration to compare with the 1992 Framework Convention on Climate Change agreed to in Rio de Janeiro, it is an objective worth pursuing. Until then, aspects of fair, multilateral migration management must be further developed in a pragmatic manner through the appropriate forums. Negotiations on the successor goals to the Millennium Development Goals (post-2015 process) offer an appropriate framework in which to anchor greater linkage of migration and development as well as efforts aimed at reducing the costs involved in remittances and the recruitment of labor migrants. No less important is the question of how migration is financed; this must be resolved and costs fairly allotted among the affected parties. In particular, destination countries that have profited from migration should work toward improving global frameworks for migration.

Major actors in international cooperation include such bodies as the World Health Organization (WHO), with its Global Code of Practice on the International Recruitment of Health Personnel; the International Labour Organization (ILO), with its commitment to greater protection of labor migrants; and the International Organization for Migration (IOM), with its initiative on an integrated recruitment system. The World Bank has both improved knowledge management (e.g., the KNOMAD program, or Global Knowledge Partnership on Migration and Development) and put it to profitable use (e.g., the Centre for Mediterranean Integration's International Labor Mobility (ILM) Program). Underlying data that is both robust and internationally comparable is vital for international migration management. Current data deficiencies mean that there is an acute need for action in this area.

Conclusion: A social market economy for migration contributes to global prosperity

Self-determined mobility has the potential to provide benefits not just to individual migrants, but also to destination countries and countries of origin. For this to happen, hurdles faced by immigrants must be removed, and fair conditions created. From a regulatory-policy perspective, it is easier to implement such framework conditions on the model of the social market economy in the national rather than the international context.

Politicians at the national and international levels must come up with a new agenda on fair migration management that allows migrants to realize their full potential, and that improves the development opportunities of both countries of origin and destination countries. It is important that those working at various levels of government expand their perspective beyond the interests of destination countries to also encompass the interests of migrants and their countries of origin. With this perspective begins a new era in migration policy characterized by greater international cooperation in the fair management of migration, an inevitable by-product of globalization.

The focus here is on the individual and his or her self-determined mobility decisions. Under fair conditions, self-determined mobility represents an opportunity for personal, national and global development. Destination countries can use these opportunities to further open up to migrants and to secure national prosperity in the long term through active management of migration and integration policy in the spirit of a "social market economy for migration." There are global limits to the extent to which migration can be steered or controlled. The goal should be to create a multilateral order with workable regulations and institutions for the fair structuring of migration.

Social market economies aim to achieve "prosperity for all." Global governance for fair migration that is informed by this model can make a significant contribution to global prosperity.

The Authors

Najim Azahaf

Najim Azahaf has been a Project Manager at the Bertelsmann Stiftung since 2009. Before assuming his current position with the "A Fair Deal on Talent – Fostering Just Migration Governance" project in the Integration and Education program, he completed the Stiftung's two-year Young Professionals program and followed this by working for the Sustainable Governance Indicators (SGI) project. Prior to receiving his Executive Master in Public Administration from the Hertie School of Governance in Berlin, Najim Azahaf was Assistant to the Director of the Institute for Development and Peace. He has also worked with the Deutsche Gesellschaft für Technische Zusammenarbeit (GTZ) GmbH in Eschborn and Nairobi as well as with InWEnt GmbH.

Nilim Baruah

Nilim Baruah has worked on migration issues since 1998 and in the development field for even longer. Before assuming in 2011 his current responsibilities as Senior Migration Specialist at the ILO Regional Office for Asia and the Pacific in Bangkok, he was the Chief Technical Advisor of ILO technical cooperation labor migration projects in Southeast Asia and Eastern Europe/Central Asia. From 2002 to 2007, he headed the International Organization for Migration's (IOM) Labour Migration Division in Geneva. He has extensive experience concerning labor migration issues and governance and has published several works on labor migration and remittances. He is co-author of the OSCE-IOM-ILO Handbook on Establishing Effective Labour Migration Policies (2006), which has been published in several languages. Prior to the IOM, Mr. Baruah worked with OXFAM as the Country Representative in Yerevan and Regional Representative in Bhubaneshwar. He studied Development Studies at Carleton University, Ottawa, where he obtained an MA in International Affairs.

The Authors

Jad Chaaban
Jad Chaaban is an Associate Professor of Economics at the American University of Beirut. He is also currently the Team Leader and Lead Author of the upcoming UNDP Arab Human Development Report 2015. Mr. Chaaban's research interests focus on development economics and industrial organization and include public economics of health, education and labor policies, environmental economics and population studies. Mr. Chaaban has served as an economic policy advisor to various Lebanese ministries and public agencies. He is also President and founding member of the Lebanese Economic Association (since 2007) and contributes regularly to economic policy analyses of various international agencies. Mr. Chaaban holds a BA in Economics from the American University of Beirut, an MBA from the European School of Management (2000), a master's in Agricultural, Environmental and Natural Resources Economics (2001) and a PhD in Economics (2004) from the Toulouse School of Economics in France.

Michael A. Clemens
Michael A. Clemens is a senior fellow at the Center for Global Development, where he leads the Migration and Development Initiative and serves as a research manager. His research focuses on the effects of international migration on people from and in developing countries, and on rigorous impact evaluation for aid projects. He is a research fellow at IZA, the Institute for the Study of Labor in Bonn, Germany, and an affiliate of the Financial Access Initiative at New York University. Mr. Clemens completed his PhD in Economics at Harvard University, specializing in economic development, public finance and economic history. His past writings have focused on the effects of foreign aid, determinants of capital flows and the effects of tariff policy in the 19th century, and the historical determinants of school system expansion. Mr. Clemens has served as an Affiliated Associate Professor of Public Policy at Georgetown University, a visiting scholar at New York University and a consultant for the World Bank, Bain & Co., the Environmental Defense Fund and the United Nations Development Program. He has lived and worked in Colombia, Brazil and Turkey. In 2013, his research was awarded the Royal Economic Society Prize.

Jonathan Crush
Jonathan Crush holds a Research Chair in Global Migration and Development at the Balsillie School of International Affairs in Waterloo, Canada, and is Honorary Professor at the University of Cape Town. He directs the Southern African Migration Programme (SAMP) (www.queensu.ca/samp) and the African Food Security Urban Network (AFSUN) (www.afsun.org). He has published extensively on migration and development issues in Africa including, most recently, *Zimbabwe's Exodus: Crisis, Migration, Survival* (Ottawa: IDRC, 2010).

The Authors

Aart De Geus

Aart De Geus has been Chairman and Chief Executive Officer of the Bertelsmann Stiftung (Gütersloh, Germany) since August 2012. He has been a member of the Bertelsmann Stiftung's Executive Board since September 2011, overseeing projects on Europe, employment and globalization. Prior to joining the Stiftung, Mr. De Geus served as Deputy Secretary General of the Organisation for Economic Co-operation and Development (OECD) in Paris. From 2002 to 2007, Aart De Geus was Minister of Social Affairs and Employment in the Netherlands.

Jörg Dräger

Jörg Dräger is Member of the Executive Board of the Bertelsmann Stiftung (Gütersloh, Germany), Managing Director of the CHE Center for Higher Education (Gütersloh, Germany) and Adjunct Professor for Public Management at the Hertie School of Governance in Berlin. From 2001 to 2008, Jörg Dräger served both as Hamburg's Minister of Science and Research and Minister of Health and Consumer Protection.

Jean-Pierre Garson

Jean-Pierre Garson, currently Senior Lecturer at Sciences-Po, Paris School of International Affairs, is an economist and former Head of the International Migration Division at the Directorate for Employment, Labour and Social Affairs of the OECD. From 1989 to 2011, Mr. Garson was responsible for the annual OECD flagship publication, International Migration Outlook, in addition to other publications on migration and development issues. Since 2008, he has also been responsible at the OECD for issues associated with employment and social policies in non-member OECD economies.

Andreas Heimer

Andreas Heimer is Vice Director of Prognos AG, where he also serves as Head of Strategy and Program Development. At Prognos, he has been involved in a variety of projects and served as a consultant in areas ranging from labor market and qualification issues, family and social policy, and the cultivation of civic engagement. Mr. Heimer led the research conducted for the Reinhard Mohn Prize 2015.

The Authors

Kate Hooper
Kate Hooper is a Research Assistant with the Migration Policy Institute's International Program, where her research areas include labor migration, diaspora engagement and immigrant integration. She holds an MA with honors from the University of Chicago's Committee on International Relations and a BA in history from the University of Oxford. She also holds a certificate in International Political Economy from the London School of Economics.

Paweł Kaczmarczyk
Paweł Kaczmarczyk is Deputy Director of the Centre of Migration Research at the University of Warsaw and Assistant Professor at the Faculty of Economic Sciences, University of Warsaw. He is a fellow at IZA, the Institute for the Study of Labor in Bonn, Germany, and at TFMI, the Transcontinental Forum on Migration and Integration. Mr. Kaczmarczyk also serves as a SOPEMI correspondent for Poland at the OECD. From 2008 to 2011, he was a member of the Board of Strategic Advisors to the Prime Minister of Poland, which was responsible for issues related to demographic change, migration and the Polish labor market. His research focuses on the drivers and consequences of labor migration, highly skilled mobility, the methodology of migration research, labor economics, population economics, demography, international economics and migration policy.

Ulrich Kober
Ulrich Kober is Director of the Integration and Education program at the Bertelsmann Stiftung, which explores issues addressing immigration, social inclusion and education. Prior to joining the Stiftung in 2000, Mr. Kober, who holds degrees in Theology and Sociology (London School of Economics and Political Science), worked with church organizations in formal and informal education as well as with independent organizations on youth support initiatives both in Germany and abroad, including in South America.

Guna Sankar Ramasamy Kone
Guna Sankar Ramasamy Kone is a Policy Analyst with the OECD International Migration Division in Paris. At the OECD, Mr. Kone works on a range of labor migration policy issues and the 2014 International Migration Outlook publication and its country reviews. Before joining the OECD, he worked at the New Zealand Ministry of Business, Innovation and Employment as Research Manager for Migration. Mr. Kone has more than 15 years' experience working in research, evaluation and management in the New Zealand public sector, including the Ministry of Social Development. He has also worked in areas addressing welfare assistance, active-labor-market policies, settlement, integration and migration dynamics. Mr. Kone holds an MA in Public Policy and a PhD in Political Science. He has extensive applied knowledge of how policy design, service delivery and research utilization interact.

The Authors

Georges Lemaître
Georges Lemaître is an international migration analyst, recently retired from the OECD. Before becoming involved in the analysis of international migration phenomena and policies, he carried out labor market analysis for the OECD's Employment Outlook and headed the social statistics area when the PISA assessments were developed and launched. His work in international migration has covered the harmonization of immigration statistics, the analysis of immigrant integration and integration policies, and the management of migration in OECD countries. He is currently a consultant based in the Paris area.

Martina Lubyova
Martina Lubyova is Director of the Institute for Forecasting of the Slovak Academy of Sciences and Lecturer in Social Statistics and Sampling Surveys at the University of Economics in Bratislava. Ms. Lubyova holds a PhD in Economics from the State University of New York and the Centre for Economic Research and Graduate Education of Charles University in Prague. She also holds a PhD in Statistics from the University of Economics in Bratislava, a Doctor of Law and MSc in Biophysics from Comenius University in Bratislava. Prior to taking up her current position, she served as Director of the International Labour Organization's Sub-regional Office for Eastern Europe and Central Asia in Moscow, as Employment Specialist at the ILO Office in Moscow, and as Employment Development Specialist with the ILO Multidisciplinary Team for South Asia in New Delhi. Other international posts include stays at the University of Toyama (Intellectual Exchange Fellow of the Japan Foundation), the Tinbergen Institute in Amsterdam, the OECD (Directorate for Education, Employment, Labour and Social Affairs) in Paris, and the Czech Academy of Sciences and Charles University in Prague. Ms. Lubyova has published on issues addressing labor economics, education, international migration, social affairs and forecasting. She has been a member of the OECD Expert Group on Migration (formerly SOPEMI) since 1995, and she has served on the editorial boards of several academic journals.

Manjula M. Luthria
Manjula M. Luthria leads the International Labor Mobility Program within the framework of the World Bank's Social Protection and Labor Global Practice. This program, based at the Center for Mediterranean Integration in Marseille, France, focuses on providing analytical and technical advice, as well as practical support, to facilitate the liberalization of global labor markets.

Gregory A. Maniatis
Gregory A. Maniatis has served since 2006 as Senior Advisor to Peter Sutherland, the U.N. Special Representative for Migration. He is also Senior European Policy Fellow at the Migration Policy Institute in Washington, D.C. In addition, he is a writer whose reportage and commentary have been featured in the The Washington Post, the International Herald Tribune, The Wall Street

The Authors

Journal, New York magazine, The Washington Monthly, PBS Television and other media outlets. Earlier in his career, Mr. Maniatis was founder and publisher of Odyssey magazine, an English-language bimonthly that is the leading international magazine about Greece and Greeks around the world, with more than 60,000 readers in 35 countries. Mr. Maniatis is a graduate of Princeton University's Woodrow Wilson School of Public and International Affairs, and a recipient of a certificate from the Institut d'Etudes Politiques in Paris. He is a Member of the Council on Foreign Relations.

Matthias M. Mayer

Matthias M. Mayer is a Project Manager with the Integration and Education program at the Bertelsmann Stiftung and a member of the Reinhard Mohn Prize 2015 team. Before joining the Stiftung, he served as both a Research Assistant at Germany's Federal Office for Migration and Refugees in Nuremberg and an Office Manager of the High-Level Consensus Group on Skilled Labor Demand and Immigration for the Expert Council of German Foundations on Integration and Migration (SVR) in Berlin. He received his PhD in European Studies from the London School of Economics and Political Science in 2011.

Jean-Baptiste Meyer

Jean-Baptiste Meyer is Senior Researcher at the Institute of Research for Development and professor at various universities in Europe and Africa. He has directed research and higher education programs at the National University of Colombia, the University of Cape Town, the Latin American Faculty of Social Sciences in Buenos Aires and, more recently, at universities in North Africa. His publications include *El nuevo nomadismo cientifico: la perspectiva latinoamericana* (ESAP 1998), *Scientific Diasporas* (IRD editions 2003), *La société des savoirs: trompe l'oeil ou perspectives* (Harmattan 2006), *A Sociology of Diaspora Knowledge Networks* (2011) and *Diaspora: the New Frontier ... and How to Reach it* (IRD/UDELAR 2015). Mr. Meyer also serves as Coordinator of the CIDESAL European Research and Development project, which targets the creation of diaspora incubators and the development of new methods and instruments for global mobility understanding and management. More information on this project can be viewed on YouTube at the following links:
FR: www.youtube.com/watch?v=EIwcY5HlQ_E
ES: www.youtube.com/watch?v=sYMX9lxSaF0
EN: www.youtube.com/watch?v=S81zTfn4dRk

Claudia Münch

Claudia Münch is Project Director for Strategy and Program Developmentat at Prognos AG. Ms. Münch works on labor market, education and immigration issues. Together with Andrease Heimer, she led the research conducted for the Reinhard Mohn Prize 2015.

The Authors

Lotte Nordhus

Lotte Nordhus works at the Centre for International Migration and Development (CIM), a joint operation of the Deutsche Gesellschaft für Internationale Zusammenarbeit (GIZ) GmbH and the German Federal Employment Agency. She advises the German Federal Ministry for Economic Cooperation and Development (BMZ) on migration and development. Her work focuses primarily on remittance issues. Prior to joining CIM, she worked for NGOs in Mexico and Germany. She holds a BA in European Ethnology from the University of Freiburg and an MA in Sociology with a focus on Migration Studies from the University of Amsterdam.

Bernd Parusel

Bernd Parusel works as a migration expert for the Swedish national contact point of the European Migration Network (EMN) at the Swedish Migration Board in Norrköping. He also serves as a research officer for the Swedish Migration Studies Delegation (DELMI) in Stockholm, an independent committee on migration studies that was launched by the Swedish government in 2013. Before taking up his current functions, Bernd Parusel was a researcher at the Federal Office for Migration and Refugees in Nuremberg and a lecturer at the University of Erlangen-Nürnberg in Germany. Mr. Parusel studied Political Science at the Freie Universität Berlin and holds a doctorate in Modern History from the Institute for Migration and Intercultural Studies (IMIS) of Osnabrück University. His research interests include international migration patterns, migration and asylum policy in Sweden and the European Union, and Europeanization processes.

Khushwant Singh

Khushwant Singh studied Ethnology, Social Anthropology and Educational Sciences in Heidelberg and London with a focus on migration, intercultural issues and religion. He now works in the field of international cooperation for the Deutsche Gesellschaft für Internationale Zusammenarbeit (GIZ). From 2012 to 2015, he was a member of the team responsible for the Make it in Germany initiative, which is implemented by the German Federal Ministry for Economic Affairs and Energy. Currently, Mr. Singh is a GIZ advisor on values, religion and development for the Federal Ministry for Economic Cooperation and Development. He is Chairman of the Council of Religions in Frankfurt. He publishes articles on Sikh religion and migration, is involved in voluntary youth work and is the producer of the international documentary film "Musafer – Sikhi is Travelling."

The Authors

Madeleine Sumption
Madeleine Sumption is Director of the Migration Observatory at the University of Oxford. The Migration Observatory provides impartial, independent, authoritative, evidence-based analysis of data on migration and migrants in the U.K. used to inform media, public and policy debates and to generate high-quality research on international migration and public policy issues. Ms. Sumption's research interests include labor migration, the economic impacts of migration policies, and immigrant integration. She has also done comparative research on government policies addressing immigrant investors, illegal employment, immigration in trade agreements and the recognition of foreign qualifications. Before joining the Observatory, Ms. Sumption was Director of Research for the International Program at the Migration Policy Institute in Washington, D.C.

Espen Thorud
Espen Thorud is Senior Advisor at the Norwegian Ministry of Children, Equality and Social Inclusion, Department of Integration. He has been involved in designing migration, refugee, integration and minority policies in various positions, departments and ministries in Norway since 1986. Over the years, he has represented Norway at a wide range of international meetings and forums. He has represented Norway since 2004 in the OECD's Expert Group on International Migration. As part of this position, he is in charge of the annual report from Norway to the OECD on immigration and immigrants.

Triadafilos Triadafilopoulos
Triadafilos Triadafilopoulos is Associate Professor of Political Science at the University of Toronto. Triadafilopoulos received his PhD in Political Science at the New School for Social Research and is a former Social Sciences and Humanities Research Council of Canada (SSHRC) Postdoctoral Fellow. He also held a two-year visiting research fellowship at the Institute for Social Sciences at the Humboldt University in Berlin through the German Academic Exchange Service (DAAD). Mr. Triadafilopoulos was a Visiting Professor at the Hertie School of Governance in Berlin in 2012 and a Visiting Fellow at the Institute for German Studies at the University of Birmingham in 2013. He is the author of *Becoming Multicultural: Immigration and the Politics of Membership in Canada and Germany* (University of British Columbia Press 2012), short-listed for the Canadian Political Science Association's 2013 Donald Smiley Prize for the best book in Canadian politics and 2014 Comparative Politics Prize. He is the editor of *Wanted and Welcome? Policies for Highly Skilled Immigrants in Comparative Perspective* (Springer 2013) and co-editor (with Kristin Good and Luc Turgeon) of *Segmented Cities? How Urban Contexts Shape Ethnic and Nationalist Politics* (University of British Columbia Press 2014). Mr. Triadafilopoulos' current research examines the extension of public funding for Islamic religious education in Canada and Germany. He is also interested in how center-right conservative parties in Europe and North America are adapting to more culturally diverse electorates.

The Authors

Florian Trauner

Florian Trauner is Deputy Director of the Institute for European Integration Research at the University of Vienna and Visiting Professor at the College of Europe in Warsaw (Natolin Campus). His research interests concern the field of European integration, in particular dynamics of EU decision-making, EU justice and home affairs, fundamental rights and rule of law promotion, and EU-Western Balkans relations. His articles have appeared in international, peer-reviewed journals, such as the *Journal for European Public Policy, West European Politics* and the *European Journal of Migration and Law,* and with renowned publishing houses, including Oxford University Press. Recent publications include "Policy Change in the Area of Freedom, Security and Justice: How EU Institutions Matter" (Routledge 2015, with Ariadna Ripoll Servent). Florian Trauner also acted as advisor and external expert for the Foreign Affairs Committee of the European Parliament, the International Centre for Migration Policy Development and the Macedonian government.

Clara Pascual de Vargas

Clara Pascual de Vargas is currently working as a consultant for the Labour Migration and Human Development (LHD) division of the International Organization for Migration (IOM), based in Geneva, where she provides technical expertise on issues related to ethical labor recruitment and labor exploitation in global supply chains. Prior to joining IOM, Ms. de Vargas has worked in counter-trafficking. With six years' experience, she helped develop tools to help businesses tackle human trafficking and forced labor in their operations and supply chains. She was also a founding member of the first specialized service for trafficked persons in Geneva.

Onyekachi Wambu

Onyekachi Wambu is Director of the African Foundation for Development (AFFORD), a U.K.-based charity with a mission to expand and enhance the contributions Africans in the diaspora make to Africa's development. AFFORD is a pioneer and innovator in the field of policy and practice of migration and development. AFFORD's advocacy work contributed to U.K. and international recognition of the role of the diaspora in African and international development, and in the subsequent initiation of new policies, programs, funds and schemes. Educated at the University of Essex and Sewlyn College, Cambridge, Mr. Wambu worked previously as a print and broadcast journalist, with a stint as a senior producer and documentary director at the BBC. He has written extensively on Africa and its diaspora. His publications include *Empire Windrush – 50 Years of Writing About Black Britain* (Phoenix 1999) and *Under the Tree of Talking – Leadership for Change in Africa* (British Council 2007).

The Authors

Casey Alexander Weston

Casey Alexander Weston is a Migration Specialist with the International Labor Mobility Program. He has focused on the analysis and evaluation of migration policies in the Gulf Coordination Council Countries, as well as the design and replication of urban policies aimed at fostering migrant inclusion in labor and housing markets.

Lara White

Lara White is a Senior Labour Migration Specialist for the Labour Migration and Human Development division of the International Organization for Migration (IOM), based in Geneva, where she provides technical and policy guidance related to temporary and permanent labor migration. She also acts as the division's primary liaison with the private sector and other governmental, intergovernmental or civil society stakeholders on issues related to labor supply chain transparency and the promotion of ethical labor recruitment. Prior to this, Lara had worked for the Government of Canada, bringing with her extensive experience in policy development and implementation of labor market programs administered by Economic and Social Development Canada. Most recently, she was manager of the operations unit of the Temporary Foreign Worker Program, charged with the national implementation of federal legislation, regulations and policies governing the program. Prior to this, she was the senior policy analyst for the Seasonal Agricultural Worker Program, a bilateral managed migration program designed to provide Canadian agricultural employers with temporary foreign workers. Additionally, she has worked in several divisions of Canada's employment insurance program as a policy analyst, adjudicator and training development officer.

The RMP team would like to thank Liudmyla Teslenko for her support and help in the publication of this book.